PATH TO
COLLECTIVE MADNESS

A STUDY IN SOCIAL ORDER AND POLITICAL PATHOLOGY

DIPAK K. GUPTA

PRAEGER

Westport, Connecticut
London

Library of Congress Cataloging-in-Publication Data

Gupta, Dipak K.
    Path to collective madness : a study in social order and political pathology /
Dipak K. Gupta.
        p.   cm.
    Includes bibliographical references and index.
    ISBN 0–275–97220–8 (alk. paper)—ISBN 0–275–97221–6 (pbk. : alk. paper)
    1. Group identity.   2. Identity (Psychology)   3. Collective behavior   4. Social
conflict.   I. Title.
    HM753.G86   2001
    302.4—dc21   00–064955

British Library Cataloguing in Publication Data is available.

Library of Congress Catalog Card Number: 00–064955
ISBN: 0–275–97220–8
        0–275–97221–6 (pbk.)

First published in 2001

Praeger Publishers, 88 Post Road West, Westport, CT 06881
An imprint of Greenwood Publishing Group, Inc.
www.praeger.com

Printed in the United States of America

The paper used in this book complies with the
Permanent Paper Standard issued by the National
Information Standards Organization (Z39.48–1984).

10 9 8 7 6 5 4 3 2 1

To Shalini and Rohan,
with the hope that they and their generation
will find the right balance

"Who is a Saint?" "Who is a Sinner?"
Who can really tell?
In men they reside side by side—
in men, heaven and hell.

—Free translation of a famous Bengali poem

CONTENTS

Preface   ix

Acknowledgments   xiii

Part I.   Setting the Stage   1

1.   "The Children Did Not Cry": The Face of Collective
     Madness   3

2.   At the Great Divide of Identity: Individual and Collective   19

3.   The Confusions of a Singular Worldview   49

Part II.   Path to Collective Madness   69

4.   *Homo Collectivus*: The Social Man   71

5.   The Slippery Slope: From Identity to Madness   103

6.   Madness or Not: The Ends of the Spectrum   149

Part III. In Search of Policy   205

7.   Where There's a Will . . . : Can Anything Be Done?   207

8.   Collective Madness: Looking into the Future   229

Bibliography   247

Index   273

PREFACE

I still see the little boy in my mind, his cherubic face framed by glowing hair against the setting sun on a brilliant late summer day at the Belgrade airport. As I boarded the plane, I could still spot him among the throng, sitting on his dad's shoulder and waving his tiny hand. By this time, his tears had melted into a radiant smile reflecting the sky behind the father and son. That would be the last time I would see Daniel. In 1976, I spent six months in Belgrade as a post-doctoral fellow at the Institute for International Politics and Economics. During my stay as a paying guest in his family's home, Daniel and I became friends. Our friendship was greatly aided by my knowledge of Serbo-Croatian, which was a perfect match for the verbal eloquence of a four-year-old. In many ways, Daniel was unique, and yet he was not. His father was a Serb, and his mother a Croat. But such minute differences in the dialect of the language, religion, and collective history were of little concern to the boy. As my airplane took off, I cast a last wistful glance at "Beograd"—the white city—nestled on the bank of the Danube, never even imagining that within a very short time, it would turn purple in fratricidal rage.

Then, some seventeen years later, when the television pictures started streaming in from the hapless nation, I looked at the faces of the young men to find any trace of resemblance to my young friend. By now about to enter the gates of adulthood, he was in the prime cohort of those who would be among the first victims of collective madness. I saw his face among the soldiers, kissing the bombshells before lobbing them into the homes of their erstwhile neigh-bors. And I saw his face among those emaciated bodies—the walking skeletons—with a wan smile, across the barbed wire fence of a concentration camp. To me, both faces belonged to the victims; one of collective rage and the other of the consequent cruelty.

I was puzzled. During my stay, I traveled extensively, frequently trying my newly acquired language skills on the unsuspecting Yugoslavs. Yet I missed it completely. In 1976, I came back with memories of a typical country. Sure, there were disparaging comments about the "others," and certainly I heard a good number of jokes—the same stories recycled over and over throughout the world—at the expense of rival groups. I learned to tell the difference between the Serbs and Croats by listening to the number of victims attributed to the Chetnics and Ustashe—the two hypernationalistic gangs that existed during World War II—as each group was prone to exaggerate the other's atrocities. I also heard derogatory remarks about the Muslims and the Jews. But, being from India and having lived in the United States, those hate-talks often seemed remarkably tame in comparison. Sipping my thick, dark coffee in the sidewalk cafés of Belgrade, Skopie, and Sarajevo, watching the parade of happy, smiling faces, young, old, and everything in between, I could never have imagined the fate of that beautiful country. I now wonder if many in Yugoslavia had realized that the cancerous cells of hatred were about to metastasize and that the nation had only a few years to live. I was puzzled at the speed with which the entire country fell apart in small fragments, the way a fine crystal glass would shatter all over the floor. However, to me it was not a distant land with unknown faces. To me the agony of Yugoslavia was real and personal.

This book is an outcome of my sad bewilderment at our ability to make enemies of our fellow human beings. In the process of explaining the path to collective madness, I have ventured into many areas, often partitioned by pedagogic purity. In this book, I attempt to tell a coherent story by culling insights from the various disciplines of social sciences and psychology.

THE AUDIENCE

This book is written primarily for the general public. In many appearances on radio and television programs and lectures to community groups, I have found an incredible desire to learn more about our collective pathological behavior. However, in the social sciences we often manage to obfuscate the obvious. I have made every attempt to make my discussion accessible and relevant to a general audience. If someone gets tired of reading about the theoretical aspects of the subject, there will be little harm in starting the book at Chapter 4.

PLAN OF THE BOOK

This book is divided into three nearly equal parts. Part I sets the stage for discussion of what I call collective madness. I define collective madness as a psychological state where people submerge their individual identities and assume a group identity; they choose actions that will benefit the group even to the detriment of their individual selves. I argue that, through our evolutionary process, we are born with a duality of identities. While all collective actions require the presence of a collective identity, what I call collective madness is a special case of collective identity gone berserk. The first chapter provides snapshot examples of incidents of collective madness from all over the world. These examples present a vivid description of what I mean by the term "collective madness." The second chapter places the discussion in a philosophical context, where the history of our intellectual evolution is seen as a constant struggle between the identities of the self and of the collective. This conflict pits the aspirations of an individual against the comfort of a collective womb. When a society moves to the extreme ends of the identity spectrum, revolutions start; people in societies based on individualism look for a cause greater than their personal selves, while for those in theocratic or communistic nations, the comfort of the collective quickly turns claustrophobic.

In the final analysis, this book is about collective action. Through advances in microeconomics, we understand the motivations of actions where the primary objective is the welfare of the self. However, in Chapter 3 I demonstrate that tools of microeconomic analyses are inadequate for a fuller understanding of our collective yearning. The assumption of self-utility maximization gets us bogged down in the inescapable quagmire of the so-called free-rider problem. A number of social scientists have attempted to circumvent the paradox by providing partial solutions. However, I argue that we have little to gain by holding on to a contrived definition of human rationality as an article of faith, particularly when it comes to some forms of collective action.

In Part II, I offer an alternative theory for analyzing collective action and then, based on this expanded behavioral assumption, examine the path through which a society descends into the depths of collective madness. Chapter 4 introduces my hypothesis of individual rationale for participation in a collective action. I posit that, at the core, an individual's perception of personal well-being is hopelessly intertwined with that of one's group. An individual's decision to choose between short-term self-utility and the utility of the group is predicated upon the opportunity, cost of time, and the strength of the individual's collective identity. I argue that a person's collective identity is not something inherent, but is shaped and strengthened by the effectiveness of a political entrepreneur. Political entrepreneurs, like their counterparts in the business world, frame the past and present of a group's history into an overarching mythology consisting of "good" and "bad," "heroes" and "villains." If this framing of identity resonates with an individual, a potential activist is born. However, in the final analysis, an individual's choice is determined by three basic motivations: greed (selfish interest), fear (cost), and ideology (group preference). I therefore argue that people join collective movements from a variety of motivations. Developing this idea further, Chapter 5 identifies three groups of participants in collective actions. Those who are motivated

primarily by goals of the collective I call the *true believers*. Those who are motivated mainly by their own narrow self-interest are the *mercenaries*. And those
whose primary motivation is fear (cost of nonparticipation) are the *captive participants*. On the other side of the fence, those who choose not to participate
are also classified into three groups. The *easy riders* do not take part because of
the cost (fear); the *collaborators* work for the other side for greed; and the
conscientious objectors risk their lives for ideology. With the help of my basic behavioral hypothesis and the resulting classifications of participants and
nonparticipants, the rest of Chapter 5 traces how political entrepreneurs, by
exploiting dynamic environmental conditions, mobilize people by influencing
their followers' preference structures. Chapter 6 studies three cases: in two
cases (Rwanda and Jonestown) political entrepreneurs, through clever use of
time-honored tactics, bring about collective madness. Most books and articles
that offer hypotheses regarding people's participation in acts of collective rebellion concentrate on cases where mass violence has taken place. Rarely do
they offer an explanation of the absence of a revolution. However, in the third
case study, I demonstrate how the United States—despite the persisting social
and economic gaps between blacks and whites—has successfully averted a violent rebellion by its black population in recent years.

Part III considers ways to avert the outbreak of collective insanity. Chapter
7 discusses long-term and short-term (strategic) actions to prevent outbreaks
of collective madness. The long-term strategy involves instituting a liberal democracy with a guarantee of procedural justice, free flow of information, and
free discourse. Only the citizens of the country can adopt the true antidotes to
collective madness. In contrast, short-term measures can be taken by the international community, varying from diplomatic initiatives to the use of multinational peacekeeping forces. Also, private initiatives from various NGOs
(nongovernmental organizations) can also play an important role in stopping
the spread of ethnic and sectarian violence. The final chapter looks to the future and finds the continuing existence of two conflicting forces. On the one
hand, it finds that the spread of a global market promotes the individual over
the collective, which may prevent outrages such as those described at the beginning of the book. Yet, at the same time, without a collective cause an individual is often lost. Besides, the spread of a global market is leaving huge gaps
in its development. Together, these factors prepare the ground for further outbreaks of collective madness, particularly in the vast reaches of Africa, Asia, and
Latin America. Unfortunately, when they erupt in their fratricidal fury, the
Western world, without a looming image of an overarching enemy in the
post–Cold War era, may not be able to respond to the cries of the victims of
collective madness.

ACKNOWLEDGMENTS

A number of friends and colleagues have freely given their comments. Their intellectual contributions have added enormously to the value of this work. Among them, I must mention Alex Schmid, Berto Jongman, Lawrence Baron, Marco Walshok, Samarendra N. Das, Edmund Acosta, and Eunice Farris. I am grateful to a number of my able students. Among them, my gratitude is the deepest for Orna Sara Kvashny, Rebecca McCarty, Joana Odencrantz, and Paul Wilkins. Sara constantly supplied me with relevant literature; Rebecca, Joana, and Paul read the entire manuscript and made extremely helpful comments. They added significantly to the quality of the book. However, for the completion of this project I am most grateful to Professor Timur Kuran and Christopher Clague. Without their encouragement, this book might not have been completed.

Finally, I also thank the Fred J. Hansen Foundation and San Diego State University's Graduate Division for their generous help in the research phase of my book.

PART I

SETTING THE STAGE

CHAPTER 1

"THE CHILDREN DID NOT CRY": THE FACE OF COLLECTIVE MADNESS

> You are an apostle of evil.
>
> —U.S. District Judge Kevin Duffy to the
> Trade Center bomber Ramzi Yousef[1]

THE AFFLICTION: A FEW SNAPSHOTS

In the lush, green undulating hills of the tiny East African village of Nayatovu, just north of Kigali, Rwanda, where the last of the morning mist desperately clings to the red serpentine dirt road, Juliana Mukankwaya wore a vacant look as she explained why she, herself a mother of six, along with a number of other women from her village, rounded up two children of her Tutsi neighbor and bludgeoned them to death. Juliana thought she was doing the little boy and girl, whom she had known since their birth, a favor, since they were sure to face a much harder life under the civil war that was raging all around them; their father had been hacked to pieces in front of their eyes, and their mother was dragged away to be raped and then killed. "The children did not cry, because they knew us," the stoic woman added. "They just made big eyes. We killed too many to count."[2] A London-based human rights group, Africa Watch, reported women's participation in the butchering of over half a million people in three months—from cabinet ministers and regional administrators to professionals, housewives, teachers, nurses, and even nuns. According to an Associated Press report, several nuns implicated in the massacre called Tutsis "dirt" and supplied gasoline to burn some alive, including the immediate families of fellow Tutsi nuns.[3]

The child's muffled sob that filled the somber sky of former Bosnia must have asked the question, "Why?" Around 1993, many horrific stories of brutality and violence filtered out of the tormented East European nation. However, perhaps nothing shocked the world like the story of a seven-year-old girl who was publicly raped by her father to demonstrate his loathing for the rival ethnic group to which the little girl's mother belonged.[4] Since our simian days, groups of men (and women) have fought each other. In those battles, just like all the primates of today, men of one group have killed those of the others. Soldiers have engaged in rape and torture from time immemorial. Yet what happened in modern Yugoslavia appalled even the most hard-boiled chroniclers of the politics of pain. Perhaps for the first time in recorded history, rape and torture were used as deliberate policies of the various warring factions. They were used to crush the emotional backbone of the people of the rival groups. They were undertaken with extreme premeditation so that neighbors could never live next to one another in harmony and trust. These are the tools of ethnic cleansing. As the federation of Yugoslavia was disintegrating, most of the former republics experienced some form of atrocities. But what happened in Bosnia, where the mix of various ethnic and religious groups was the deepest, defied description. The human rights tribunal at The Hague has documented many tales of horror. Despicable in their brutality as well as their pervasiveness during nearly three years of madness, these atrocities, sadly, were not the work of a small number of isolated zealots. They were perpetrated by ordinary men and women, no different than most of us.

In his instant bestseller and, at once, highly controversial book, *Hitler's Willing Executioners,* Daniel Goldhagen narrates in nauseating detail the participation of ordinary Germans—not just the SS, the Nazi zealots, or the state operatives, but ordinary people—in the mass killings of the Jews.[5] In his book, the picture of an attractive young German woman, Vera Wolhauf, the wife of a captain in the German military police, tanned and athletic, prancing and smiling seductively on fresh snow in a skin-tight outfit on a bright winter day—stares at the reader in stark contrast to all others showing either the victims of the Holocaust or the stern-eyed, jack-booted SS men.[6] This charming housewife, looking no different from other young women of her time and ours, symbolizes Goldhagen's willing executioners. In the summer of 1942, Vera, already pregnant, joined her husband in Poland as his battalion was in charge of "pacifying" the Polish countryside. On August 25, she attended a mass killing at Miedzyrzec. As Goldhagen narrates:

The roundup, the driving of the Jews from their homes to the market square, was perhaps the most brutal and licentious of all those that Police Battalion 101 conducted. The men left hundreds of dead Jews strewn about the streets. The scene at the market square was also among the most gruesome. Some of the notable features included the Germans forcing the Jews to squat for hours in the burning sun so that many fainted, and shooting any Jew who did nothing more than stand up. The market square became littered with the dead. Such shootings naturally included many children, who found it particularly difficult to remain immobile in such discomfort for hours on end. The Hiwis and some of the Germans in the Miedzyrzec's German *Gendarmerie* also used the occasion to satisfy their lust for cruelty. They entertained themselves by flogging Jews with whips. Not only was Frau Wolhauf a party to all of this, but so were the wives of some of the locally stationed Germans, as well as a group of German Red Cross nurses. . . . This is how the pregnant Frau Wolhauf spent her honeymoon.[7]

The presence of a pregnant hausfrau, walking around the market square in civilian clothes observing and participating in mass murder with apparent glee, disturbed many men of Police Battalion 101.[8] Goldhagen, in his book, brings indictment, not against the Nazis and the Gestapo, but against the entire German nation. Without getting involved with the controversy surrounding the blanket accusation of culpability of the entire nation, it is safe to say that a significant portion of the greater German society, including all other German-speaking people of the neighboring lands, became involved one way or another. For instance, historians have documented that even the Catholic Church became an all-too-willing partner of Hitler's atrocities.[9] "We have always unselfishly worked for the people without regard to gratitude or ingratitude," a German priest wrote, not without a great deal of pride. "We shall also do our best in this [sorting out people of Jewish descent] service to the people."[10] In fact, this was no extraordinary priest. He was simply one of many within the Church who took part in the Holocaust; he was among only a handful who bothered to record their sentiments.

The diminutive man, reaching slightly above five feet, looked puzzled. The grave-looking judges of the military court, the military police towering over him, the unblinking television cameras trained on him, the intimidating surroundings made him look even less significant. Yet the charges brought against him were extremely serious; a landmark case, the first of its kind where a nation had decided to try one of the members of its armed forces with a war still raging. This was Second Lt. William L. Calley, Jr., the platoon leader under whose command a search and destroy mission massacred a village full of Vietnamese people, men, women, and children.

The account of the crime was gruesome. On March 16, 1968, the day after an emotional funeral of a sergeant killed by a booby trap, the men of Charlie Company were given an order to root out the Forty-Eighth Viet Cong Battalion from their base in the nearby area of My Lai village. But the men of Charlie Company found no trace of Viet Cong soldiers in the village of My Lai. During the day when able-bodied men were out working, the village was filled with only old men, women, and children. What happened next shook the world. According to eyewitness testimony, the squad began to set fire to the hamlet.[11] As nineteen-year-old Nguyen Thi Ngoc Tuyet would later recount: "A baby was trying to open her slain mother's blouse to nurse. A soldier shot the infant while it was struggling with the blouse, and then slashed it with his bayonet."[12]

Others told of a mother being raped after her children were killed, and a thirteen-year-old girl was killed after being raped. Nguyuen Khoa, a peasant, reported that the GIs tore the clothes off his wife as she was drenched in the blood of her six-year-old son. The soldiers let her live.[13]

"The red train differs from other long-distance trains in that those who have embarked on it do not know whether or not they will disembark," explains a sardonic Aleksandr Solzhenitsyn with appropriate sarcasm in his Nobel Prize–winning book, *The Gulag Archipelago*.

When they unloaded a trainload from Leningrad prisons (1942) in Solikamsk, the entire embankment was covered with corpses, and only a few got there alive. In the winters of 1944–1945 and 1945–1946 in the village of Zheleznodorozheny (Knyazh-Pogost), as in all the main rail junctions in the North, the prisoner trains from liberated territories (the Baltic states, Poland, Germany) arrived with one or two carloads of corpses tacked on behind. That meant that en route they had carefully taken the corpses out of the cars that contained the living passengers and put them in the dead cars. But not always. There were many occasions when they found out who was still alive and who was dead only when they opened up the car after arriving at the Sukhobezodnaya (Unzhlag) Station. Those who didn't come out were dead.[14]

The frail woman greeted her visitors warily with yellow cakes and sunflower seeds, oranges and hard candies, smoking tea, and an American cigarette bought on the black markets of Beijing.[15] But Mrs. Yang shook trying to remember her days during the Cultural Revolution. How could she bury her *qi* (anger), she wondered aloud. As a young girl in Changsha, she was married to a son of a wealthy landlord. Her husband fought the Japanese in the Chinese Nationalist army, while she was captured and raped by the invaders. After the war, her husband, then an important person in the new regime, brought her to Beijing to a life of comfort. Quickly came Xiao Hua, a little girl, to the proud parents. But soon the Communists took power. Because her husband had surrendered early, the Yangs were treated relatively well. Although he was not allowed to work, Mrs. Yang managed the indignities of having to clean up in a government restaurant.

But a storm cloud loomed on the horizon. On May 16, 1966, Chairman Mao launched the Cultural Revolution. The old man was under no illusions. As Mrs. Yang went off to the Neighborhood Committee to listen to stories of the proletarian victory over their "class enemies," her husband stayed home to listen to the news on a transistor radio. He was white-faced when she returned home. "It's all over," the terrified frail old man told his wife. That night he fell ill with fever and died. "He was lucky, of course," Mrs. Yang said with a sigh.

Before long, she and her daughter Xiao Hua, then a sixteen-year-old middle-school student, were bouncing to and fro in the endless series of "criticism meetings," making lengthy self-accusations, expunging their collective sins against the working people, accumulated over generations of "bourgeois existence." While the mother somehow managed to survive the meetings, the young girl did not. Filled with intense hatred toward her former Nationalist mother, she passed her nights tossing and turning in her bed, crying out in her dreams, even denouncing her mother in her sleep. One night, Mrs. Yang suddenly woke to the stillness of the room. Xiao Hua's bed was empty, the quilt neatly folded, papers from last night's "confessions" strewn about the floor. On her desk was an empty bottle of liquid pesticide. The older woman spent the night searching the riverbank, calling out her name. None of her neighbors would help a "class enemy." The next day, Xiao's body was found, washed up against a factory sewage pipe. Perhaps no one but her mother shed a single tear for the unworthy girl.

The emerald green forest engulfed and isolated the Americans in far-away Guyana. Tim Carter, a former Catholic priest and then a follower of Reverend Jim Jones, approached Gloria, his wife, also a former Catholic. On an otherwise unremarkable steamy summer day in the Southern Hemisphere, she was kneeling in the mud next to the lifeless body of their fifteen-month-old son, Malcolm. The child, healthy, normal and playful like any other child his age a few minutes ago, had been injected with a lethal dose of poison. Sitting by his side, Gloria pressed a cup filled with a strawberry-flavored drink laced with painkillers, tranquilizers, and cyanide against her lips and drank without hesitation. The camp physician, Dr. Laurence Schacht, with the help of two of his head nurses, had concocted the potion for mass suicide. Next to Gloria in various states of impending death were three of her young nieces. Tim sat down and hugged Gloria as her body went into convulsions. "I love you," he whispered in the ear of his dying wife, and then, in a fit of panic, took off for the jungle outside the campground. Tim Carter survived the day of collective madness to tell the tale of the final moments in Jonestown, a mini country that Jim Jones had founded in an isolated corner of the world. On that November day in 1978, nearly a thousand people lost their lives. Most committed suicide; the infants and a few rebellious ones were killed. The group had many old men and women, but nearly one-third of Jonestown's population was under sixteen. Even Jim Jones' pet monkey got a bullet through its head.[16]

The involvement of "ordinary white folks" in the murder of blacks was large by any measure in the United States, particularly in the South. Threatened by growing participation by the blacks in the open job market, whites took to intimidating them by lynchings, which often became spectacles of sadism. Between 1882 and 1927, about 3,500 African Americans were lynched by vigilante groups. Lane and Turner describe three situations:

In 1899, at Palermo, Georgia, excursion trains brought thousands on a Sunday afternoon to see a black man burned alive, but only his ears, toes and fingers were cut off and passed to the crowd, his eyes gouged, his tongue torn out, and his flesh cut in strips with knives; afterward, his heart was cut out and slices of it were sold as souvenirs. In May 1911, a black, charged with murder, was taken to the local opera house in Livermore, Kentucky, and tied on stage to a stake. Tickets were sold, and orchestra seats entitled men to empty their revolvers into the victim. Gallery seats gave them one shot apiece. In 1918 there was a five-day orgy of killing in Georgia, in which eight blacks died, one pregnant woman was slowly roasted alive, and the baby cut out and trampled. The charges on which such atrocities were based ranged from murder and rape to such offenses against the racial system as striking or talking back to the whites, testifying against them, making boastful remarks, or using offensive language.[17]

THE THIN LINE OF SANITY

From the killing fields of Cambodia, the Holocaust, and the massacres of the indigenous population in Latin America to the turn-of-the-century vigilantism in the United States, human history is full of such appalling stories. These are stories of collective madness—of human minds going over the precipice of what we normally uphold as "humanity." We wonder when we think that, as the little girl in Bosnia was being subjected to the incredible act of degradation, or when the Rwandan children were being clubbed to death by their trusted neighbors, there was perhaps not a single voice raised in protest from among the gathered crowd. We wonder, are these people members of the same species of human beings as the "normal" us, who love our families and go about our everyday lives? Or are they from a separate gene pool?

I call the phenomenon *collective madness,* a singularly unscholarly term, imprecise and ill-defined. Yet, in some intangible away, the term captures the essence of the afflicted society's mind-set. Scholars and politicians have used the term genocide, or even Holocaust, all too frequently. *The New Webster's Dictionary* defines genocide as a "deliberate mass murder of a race, people, or a minority group." Similarly, the word Holocaust is derived from Greek *holokausten,* a compound of *holos,* "whole," and *kustos,* "burned."[18] In all of these terms, rooted deeply in the experience of Nazi Germany, the notion of a helpless group of victims is strongly imbedded. Collective madness, in contrast, describes a wider spectrum of dysfunctional social behavior.

In many parts of the world mired in fratricidal frenzy, there is no one single group of victims and another group of perpetrators of crimes against humanity. In the frenzy of a civil war, we kill each other. The television pictures of the combatants on all sides in the former Yugoslavia, kissing their rocket shells before aiming for the homes of their erstwhile neighbors and friends, speak volumes of this condition. It is this pathological behavior, where fathers can publicly rape their daughters, otherwise sane women can club their neighbors' children to death, mothers can coolly administer poison to their sons and daughters in the name of God, and nuns and Red Cross nurses can participate in mass killings and torture, that confounds us. It is collective madness that allows a pregnant wife to spend her honeymoon gleefully participating in the killing of total strangers.

These acts of unspeakable savagery in collective madness are not the actions of a single individual's passion or anger against another individual. These acts, unlike ordinary street crimes, are also not done entirely for profit. Nor are these acts reflective of a small bunch of crazed persons, a band of psychopaths. They are different. This is a situation of mass insanity, perhaps close to the primordial feeding frenzy of sharks. These are situations when a group of people working for a shared ideology know of no boundaries to achieve their shared goals—legality, civility, or even the most basic humanity. In times like these, we kill other human beings, not because they have done something personally to offend us, but because their very existence as members of a particular group poses an affront to us. We form bonds in our shared hatred with those similar to us, and spare nothing to inflict pain and punishment on the odious others. Collective madness, a blood fever gripping a group of people, can take many forms. It can cause a mob attack, ethnic cleansing, crimes of obedience like the My Lai massacre during the Vietnam War, participation in the Holocaust, or Stalinist purges. What defines collective madness is the total merging of individual identities into a collective one. It is as if everyone in the group possesses one mind, one goal, and one all-consuming desire to strike a blow at the enemy.

The other aspect of collective madness is that its presence is not apparent to those who are afflicted by it. Talk to a Serbian patriot, a Neo-Nazi, or a religious fanatic. They will justify their actions and their hatred by recounting a thousand years of injustice. They will tell you about the imminent threat of the rival groups—the way "those people" exploit "our" goodness and generosity, the way "they" are casting their covetous eyes upon our nation, our freedom, and our women; the way "they" smell bad and the way they breed like rabbits to one day relegate "us" to the status of a minority. Those who heed the calls of the collective will tell you that it should be self-evident to every reasonable person that "we" stand for honor and justice. The activists will insist that God is on "our" side.

Although I call the affliction collective madness, I must confess that the name is a complete misnomer if it implies that those who take part in actions of hyper-identity with a group are "insane." The term collective madness refers only the ambient condition prevailing in the society at a particular time. In fact, most studies of political killings indicate that the participants show few signs of mental disorder.[19] Indeed, compared to "ordinary criminals," or those who are not motivated by any collective cause, the political murderer is significantly more "rational" and socially adjusted than the nonpolitical murderer. For instance, in Ulster, a city often in the grip of extreme emotions, a psychological study of the two kinds of murderers found that while 58% of the nonpolitical killers could be classified as mentally ill, only 8% of the political killers could be classified as such. Even in family history there is a significant difference. While 9% of nonpolitical murderers had a family history of personality disorder, only 2% of political offenders had such a family history.[20] Another study found no evidence of psychological disorder in the behavior of the urban terrorists.[21]

Collective actions of the vanquished groups are vilified by the victorious. We can be certain that the atrocities detailed by Goldhagen would have been glorified in history if the Germans had won the war, and maybe later the victorious Germans would have come around to confronting their atrocities. Historian Raul Hilberg points out that different societies confront their own holocausts at different times, but always belatedly.[22] It was only in 1995 that the French president, Jacques Chirac, publicly apologized for French officials' role in the deportation of France's Jews. Around the same time, the Japanese prime minister offered a flaccid apology to the thousands of Korean "comfort women" who were forcibly abducted during World War II and were enslaved in brothels for the Japanese soldiers. Over 500 years after the worst crimes of the Spanish Inquisition were committed, in November 1998, Pope John Paul II decided to reevaluate the role of the Catholic Church.[23]

Submersion of individual identities into a group identity does not necessarily lead to genocide or a violent civil war. In many cases, a strong group identity can lead to extreme dedication to a common cause. For instance, Mother Teresa and her followers immersed their individual identities into the larger identity of the Catholic Church. Their selfless work in the hellish slums of Calcutta is a prime example of the benign face of collective identity.

The line between sanity and insanity is often a thin one. In the middle of the nineteenth century, the British, along with their French and Turkish allies, were locked in a fierce battle with the Russians in the Crimean region. Near the town of Balaklava, the Russian forces surrounded a valley where a small brigade of lightly armed British cavalry was encamped. Although outnumbered and vastly outgunned, the British cavalry attacked a heavily fortified Russian position, knowing full well the futility of the charge. The order to charge was given because of the stupidity and personal rivalry of two high-ranking British officers. But the order was carried out as a symbol of unwavering loyalty to the military code of conduct. Nearly 250 of the 673 men in the "Light Brigade" were either killed or seriously wounded. Yet this fools' errand was immortalized by poet Alfred Lord Tennyson to inspire generations of British children "not to reason why . . . but to do and die" for the Crown, the nation, and military honor. His poem was a glorification of mass suicide for blind obedience, an intellectual monument built upon an episode of collective madness.

At this point, I should mention that although collective identity encompasses the notions of "us" and "them," it is not necessary for a group to have a deep sense of both. For instance, there are members of religious orders, from the Amish to the Hare Krishna movement, who may submerge their individual identities into the collective, which consists primarily of the notion of "us." For them, the notion of an "enemy" is not important.

COLLECTIVE MADNESS AND ORGANIZED ANARCHY

What I call collective madness is an extreme case of a group of people's collective identity gone wild. It is a condition where individual identities are submerged into a larger collective. However, I argue that such behavior falls only at the end of a spectrum spanning the extremes of individualism and collectivism. Just as the lines of demarcation between love and obsession, art and pornography, are often opaque, the point at which our zeal to do good for our group crosses the boundary of patriotism and altruism to collective madness is not very well understood. Therefore, in this book, I seek an explanation of collective actions of all sorts, of which what I call collective madness falls only at the very end of the entire range.

On the other side of collective madness, which binds individuals with a commonality of purpose and hatred toward a shared enemy, is the world of unfettered individualism. We know of no society built on individualism alone, because the very idea of a society presumes the existence of some sort of collectivism; where everyone pursues self-utility without any regard to others, there can be no society. However, there are differences between societies in terms of the relative emphasis they place on individualism. The nations based on the values of individualism provide a long list of inalienable rights, offering protection from tyranny, but mention few of the duties of citizenship. In contrast, collective societies specify duties to the nation, state, religion, or state ideology without mentioning the rights of the individual. This fundamental difference permeates the very core of societies and is reflected in the everyday discourse of common citizens. I offer an example.

I often think of the Iraqi father who was interviewed on television at the outset of the Gulf War. The old man squinted at the blazing sun; his stoic weather-beaten face belied an immense pride. In the midst of approving nods of the gathered elders, he told the American reporter that he had five sons, three of which he had lost during the war with Iran. He would gladly sacrifice the remaining two to the Great Satan in the event of an invasion. In stark contrast, the U.S. father of a slain GI in Somalia was visibly angry—angry at the inexperienced president and those in the Pentagon who had sent his son into harm's way on such an "ill-planned" mission. The television camera quickly moved on from the face of the angry father to the bereaved family and friends of the young man whose lifeless body had been dragged through the dusty streets of Mogadishu by the ragtag forces of the local warlord. The nation quickly learned the name of the fallen soldier. Tears were shed even by those who never knew him.

Is there a fundamental difference between the two fathers and the two societies? What about "national pride," or making the ultimate sacrifice for the collective good? After all, Tennyson's Light Brigade willingly faced certain death with the knowledge that the command to charge an entrenched enemy position was given in error. How can we explain this difference in perception? Does the explanation lie in differences in culture or history, or is there such a thing as a national mind-set that can be taken for granted as offering an explanation?

Obviously, the U.S. father represents a culture constructed on the firm ground of individualism. In the social science literature, a free market democracy is often called a world of organized anarchy. A logical extension of Adam Smith's description of the "invisible hand" that sets market prices, labor wages, and corporate profits without any outside interference, organized anarchy recognizes the supremacy of individual rights and voluntary exchange with minimal management by a democratically elected government. In the free market democracies of Europe, North America, and parts of Asia, people generally pursue their individual aspirations, often oblivious of collective goals and responsibilities. The primary concern of the citizens of these societies is the benefit of the self. In these countries, other than paying taxes and adhering to the law, sacrifices for the collective welfare are strictly voluntary. In an aptly descriptive book, Benjamin Barber calls this the McWorld.[24] This is the world of unbridled individualism—the golden arches of McDonald's, CNN, MTV, and the Internet. This is the world where the calls of the collective are rarely heeded. This is the world that worships the prophets of personal achievement, from Bill Gates to Michael Jordan. In this world, insanity is personal and is not shared. It is a world that spills over national boundaries. Just as there are pockets of extreme tradition-bound communities with ideals of the collective in the Western nations, there are groups in most traditional societies which are Western in their outlook. On the one hand, the Amish people in the United States, for instance, reject the idea of extreme individualism. On the other hand, the elite of most so-called Third World nations shape their external behavior by the ideals of the cult of the individual, shedding their traditions and seeking bonds with those in the Western world.

As the world entered the last decade of the twentieth century, optimism was in the air in the West. It was pervasive, seeming to have permeated every area of Western political and economic life. The West finally did slay the monster of collective ideology, communism. We woke up with the pounding noise of the newly freed people demolishing the wall that had separated communist Europe from the rest of the continent. The euphoric Germans destroyed the most telling symbol of the Cold War, the Berlin Wall, brick by brick, exactly the same way the French revolutionaries demolished the Bastille. People all over the world dreamt of yet another New World Order, where the world—free of the Cold War, free of the fear of mutual annihilation—held out the possibility of peace, economic prosperity, and even the end of history.[25] We witnessed the momentous point in history when, in South Africa, the last bastion of institutionalized racism collapsed and Nelson Mandela was sworn in as the head of its multiracial government. Democracy seemed to be flourishing all over Latin America. The emerging nations of Southeast Asia, once known for their perennial poverty, held out bright prospects for economic prosperity. Even in the broad area of human rights abuses by the nations, there seemed to be a significant improvement. All over the world, the politics of pain appeared to be on the wane. An exalted Charles Humana, in the preface of his much celebrated 1993 book on human rights, stated:

The swiftness with which this major transformation has taken place, the number of people who are now free to choose their governments, and, in the case of Europe and excepting Yugoslavia, the avoidance of bloody revolution, must be considered one of the most uplifting achievements of our social evolution. The compiler has therefore been fortunate that the succeeding updates of his work have coincided with such an era.[26]

Those heady days of optimism, like the desert blooms after a rain shower, were short-lived. In fact, within a year of the publication of Humana's book, its main conclusions were repudiated.[27] In 1994, when President Bill Clinton, while visiting the site of the Berlin Wall, delivered a speech on the theme "Berlin is now free," he sounded awfully trite and out of date. Although only five years had passed since the fall of the wall, the young president's rousing speech did not bring back the image of his hero, President Kennedy. Rude reality had taken the air out of his balloon.

Looking at the world, we found little to cheer about. According to one estimate, since World War II, more than 160 million people have lost their lives, victims of many forms of collective madness.[28] This is more than half the population of the United States. In 1992, the United Nations High Commissioner on Refugees estimated that there were in excess of 40 million people uprooted from their own homes and living as refugees in foreign countries. If the trend continued, this number, the High Commissioner estimated, would explode to an unimaginable 100 million by the end of the twentieth century.[29]

In this book, I have tried to explain this complex human motivation by bringing together insights from various disciplines that make it their business to study human behavior. Toward the end of the nineteenth century, the gods of academia destroyed the Tower of Babel and created various branches of social science. So the social scientists go about talking only to those with a common language, squarely ignoring the rest. When we look into the various disciplines of political science, sociology, economics, anthropology, and psychology, we find a great deal of understanding and deep insights. But they reside in overlapping fragments, in isolation from the others. I have attempted to bring them together here to form a more coherent story. As a part of this story, I would like to raise two interrelated questions. First, does the world, gone insane by collective madness, have anything to learn from the multicultural experience in the United States? And second, does the United States need to be fearful of a similar destiny? This book asks the inevitable question, Can we do anything about caging the beast, or are we destined to suffer the ravages of collective madness? After all, if the motivation to participate in collective actions does not change, our capabilities for inflicting harm are increasing rapidly. I propose that we look the monster squarely in the face and understand the true character of collective madness in its complexity and its ambiguity.

ME, US, THEM, AND YOU

Given the path of human evolution, from group-bound primates to the modern me-centric yuppies, it is just as natural for us to try to maximize our own individual utility as it is to want to do good for our own groups. Human history reflects the inner tension of this dual motivation—a schizophrenic tug-of-war between the individual and the collective. While the basis of liberal democracy is "me"—the individual—the fundamental building block of any collective action is "collective identity" or one's identification with a group. The interesting aspect about groups is that they are formed from any number of sources: nationalism, ethnicity, race, religion, language, or even gender and sexual orientation. How close one feels to the group determines how much time, energy, and money one invests. This is the "us" aspect of collective identity. When we feel akin to a group, we often surpass our own individual limits. Our collective society and even corporations spend a great deal of effort in harnessing the power of the collective. The development of group dynamics and organizational development, where workers are motivated as a group, is a testament to the importance of group motivation. Nations try to create this group-person in military boot camps, where the individuality of the recruits is systematically pruned away—in looks, in action, and, if possible, in thought as well—to create a "uniform" person.[30] The rugged individualist Henry David Thoreau colorfully described the process of losing one's individuality:

Visit the Navy Yard, and behold a marine, such a man as an American government can make, or such as it can make a man with its black arts—a mere shadow and reminiscence of humanity, a man laid out alive and standing, and already, as one may say, buried under arms with funeral accompaniment. . . . The mass of men serve the State thus, not as men mainly, but as machines, with their bodies.[31]

We may cry for the soul of the Marine with Thoreau, but the effort to create a mass-person is seen everywhere in our individual-based society. Coaches in organized sports engage in similar exercises. In fact, a civil society cannot survive on the backs of individuals alone; for its preservation and propagation, it needs the collective "us." Any time we need a public good that is going to benefit people regardless of contribution, we need the strength of collective identity. It is this desire to do good for our community that overwhelms our selfish inhibitions. People vote for a candidate according to their ideology, often to the detriment of their own interest. They take time off from family, job, and recreation to become activists. We often make sizable donations in complete anonymity. Despite the public's low opinion of politicians, the men and women of the U.S. Congress do frequently vote their conscience rather than crudely pursuing the votes of their constituents or special interest contributions.[32]

The force of the collective is awesome. We scale mountains, cross seemingly impassable deserts, sacrifice everything in our possession, including the lives of our dearest ones, for a cause. We achieve the seemingly impossible when driven by the rationality of the group. So it is hardly surprising that we would want to harness its power. Group feeling provided the fervor that allowed Islam to conquer vast tracts of Asia, Europe, and Africa. This is the stuff that allowed impoverished Germany to achieve an unprecedented rate of economic growth under Hitler's rabid nationalism. Nationalism propelled a defeated Japan to become the world's second largest economic power with an astonishing speed. Corporations all over the world try to harness its power by forming workers' groups like quality circles in the production line.

Yet the other side of the often-benevolent "us" is the malevolent "them." We are mythmaking animals. In our history, culture, philosophy, and folklore, we not only glorify our collective, but also, at the same time, vilify somebody else as the "other." This entrenched feeling of "them," which is constantly being reinforced through the process of life experience and conscious or unconscious policies of governments, political elites, and cultural icons, leads the way to collective madness. In the process, we forget individuals and view them merely as representative of the loathsome other. Being threatened—which lies at the root of any perception of "them"—we deny the humanity of those we consider to be our enemies. Similar to the papal decree with regard to Native Americans, we actually need to assure ourselves that these individuals do possess souls.[33] If we don't, from that point, the slide toward genocide or racial violence is a matter of course. When we behave as a group toward any other group, we force them to share our perception, and they, in turn, view us the same way we see them. The cycle of violence begins. Being threatened, disparate communities suddenly unify in their common hatred; vigilante groups are formed, villagers stream out of their homes with whatever weapons they can find, chanting "Slay the monster." If the threats are immediate and short-lived, the collective identity also becomes ephemeral. For instance, communities hearing that a convicted rapist is to be paroled among them, or that a boarding house for the mentally ill is to be opened in their neighborhood, or that an airport is to be built in the vicinity, suddenly rise up with a ready list of enemies. The community feels united, and everyone agrees with everyone else, creating a warm, fuzzy feeling of fraternal joy which quickly disappears like the early morning fog as the threat dissipates. However, for a long, sustained community action, such as a war of attrition, or a protracted struggle, the community needs a stronger and more resilient collective identity.

But if it is part of our instinctive nature to create the enemy in our own image, then where does it stop? History tells us that the cycle is often broken, past enemies become friends and neighbors, swords are beaten into plowshares. There are many countries around the world where past enemies have become friends and peaceful neighbors. By our psychological process, this happens when we recognize the individual "you," someone different from me—or even the collective "us"—but someone who is an individual human being nevertheless. Only then is the cycle of violence broken. This book is written to shed light on the complex interaction between "Me," "Us," "Them," and "You." I underscore the point that human actions are reflective of these four perceptions and, in the end, form a confusing continuum from the civilized to the savage, from beauty to the hideous beast.

This book is about understanding our collective behavior. As individuals we excel or fail in our personal lives. We love, hate, go to work, raise families; some of us commit crimes and acts of passion. These are all acts of the individual. On the other hand, as a part of a collective, we build nations, establish frameworks for law and order, maintain organized societies; also as a collective we engage in social conflict and political and sectarian violence and bring about destruction on an unimaginable scale. Today, the world's population is more prosperous, better educated, more closely linked to the wider community of the outside world, and less ridden with diseases than ever before. At the same time, killings and torture seem to have reached a new height with every new ethnic conflict. As television cameras take us face to face with the beast, we see the face of collective madness. We are repelled by the horror, often not realizing that it resides deep in our psyche along with desires for peace, harmony, justice, and all other sentiments of lofty ideals. We can, of course, reach the solution of the ostrich; we can set aside the ugly as acts of irrational madmen and insulate ourselves with the comfortable thought that, after all, we could never behave like that. Unfortunately, even our immediate history tells us that we can and do behave like savages. The question then becomes, will we turn into the beast once again? Or, once turned into a beast, can we find our humanity once again?

As social animals, it is impossible for us to live alone in complete isolation from everyone else. Our need for social association is fundamental to our essence as human beings. On the one hand, human civilization is capable of creating art, literature, and science, all that is graceful, noble, and even divine. On the other hand, we do not seem to be able to eliminate this darkest side of our character. In our hearts they reside side by side, often in total confusion; the wish to lead a peaceful and harmonious life intertwines with the instinct to become vengeful marauders. In the labyrinth of human motivation, nobles change into savages, saints into sinners, patriots into scoundrels.

In popular discourse, psychological terms like paranoia, schizophrenia, delusion, or deprivation are frequently used to describe collective actions of violence, mass destruction, and mayhem. However, these terms are profoundly individual, applicable to the psyche of a single man or woman, one at a time. But what I describe is singularly distinct; as individuals, people do not share the same dream; they are not tormented by the same demons in their nightmares. This is the case with *collective madness*. In this process, we are afflicted by the same malady of the mind, sharing the same hope, chased by the same beast. The key to the understanding of individual madness lies in the biology, genetics, or chemistry of the brain. The clues for understanding collective madness lie deep beneath the dynamic folds of the society as they affect individuals.

Surprisingly, the path to collective madness is remarkable in its sameness. When we study the sequence of events that transforms a relatively peaceful society into one that gets embroiled in sectarian violence, what frightens us the most is the similarity of the symptoms. In this book, having demonstrated the process through which a society turns insane with communal rage, I ask the question, Is it inevitable that we must self-destruct? Is there nothing we can do to prevent ourselves from being dragged by the Pied Pipers of hate to a communal suicide?

NOTES

1. *San Diego Union Tribune,* January 9, 1998, A2.
2. Fritz (1994).
3. See McDowell (1995: A12).
4. The story appears in Schmid (1993). This story was also reported during a workshop on "The Crime of Torture: Causes, Consequences, Cures," 11th International Congress on Criminology, Budapest, Hungary (August 22–27, 1993). Dr. Åke Björn, M.D., of the Swedish Medical Center for Refugees, indirectly confirmed the story through the following e-mail message to the author: "I have from a clinical point of view closely followed many refugees and survivors from concentration camps in Bosnia and I have no reason to doubt the authenticity of your particular story. As an example of collective pathological behaviour during 1992 to 1995 in Bosnia & Herzegovina it bears similarities to many, many other stories which I could confirm" (November 13, 1996).
5. See Goldhagen (1996: 241–4).
6. Ibid., 243.
7. Ibid., 241–42.
8. I should point out, however, as Goldhagen remarks, that the policemen's disapproval was not directed at their actions of the day but at the fact that a German woman, who should be protected from the uglier side of life, would be so involved with it. "Their objections bespeak no shame at what they were doing, no desire to conceal from others their contribution to mass annihilation and torture, but rather a sense of chivalry and propriety that Frau Wolhauf's presence violated, particularly since this ghetto clearing was, even by their standards, unusually brutal and gruesome" (243).
9. See Lewy (1964); also see Gutteridge (1976).
10. Goldhagen (1996: 110–11).
11. See Goldstein, Marshall, and Schwartz (1976: 133).
12. See Kelman and Hamilton (1989: 4).
13. See Hersh (1970: 72).
14. See Solzhenitsyn (1973: 573).
15. See Heng and Shapiro (1986: 105–7).
16. Nugent (1979).
17. See Lane and Turner (1983: 15–16).
18. Funk (1978: p. 273).
19. See M. Taylor (1988).
20. See Lyons and Harbinson (1986: 193–98).

21. See K. Haskin (1980). However, it is interesting to note that while aggregate studies of the political prisoners and terrorists show few signs of psychological abnormalities, clinical psychological studies of the presidential assassins in the United States, in contrast, have shown deep narcissistic personality disorder. For instance, Rothstein (1975: 282) studied a number of high profile assassins, such as John Wilkes Booth (President Abraham Lincoln's assassin in 1865), Leon Czolgosz (the killer of President William McKinley in 1901), Dr. Carl Austin Weiss (who murdered Sen. Huey P. Long in 1935), Lee Harvey Oswald (the killer of President Kennedy in 1963), and Sirhan ibn Bishar Sirhan (killer of Robert F. Kennedy in 1968), suffering from narcissistic personality disorder. For an excellent definition of the disorder, see Akhtar and Thompson (1982).

22. See Hilberg (1992).

23. See Hughes (1998: A26).

24. See Barber (1995).

25. See Fukuyama (1992).

26. See Humana (1992).

27. See Gupta, Jongman, and Schmid (1994).

28. See Rummel (1994). Also see Harff and Gurr (1989); Kuper (1984); Wallimann and Dobkowski (1987); Stohl and Lopez (1986).

29. *United Nations High Commissioner on Refugees* (1992).

30. For an excellent description of how the individuality of cadets is broken down, see Ricks (1997).

31. See Thoreau (1968: 414–15).

32. See Kalt and Zupan (1984).

33. Pope Paul III, in the 1537 Bull (Sublimis Deus), proclaimed that American Indians were rational beings with souls, whose lives and property should be protected. Thanks to Thomas Davies.

CHAPTER 2

AT THE GREAT DIVIDE OF IDENTITY: INDIVIDUAL AND COLLECTIVE

To the Baule [a West African tribe] a crocodile holding a big fish in its mouth is a sacred symbol. A Baule legend tells of a war with the Ashanti. The Ashanti had chased the Baule to a deep river. There was no bridge, so the Baule asked the crocodiles to help them across. The crocodiles agreed, but in return they demanded the most precious thing the Baule people had. Tearfully the queen gave them her only son. Then the crocodiles lined up side by side in the water, and the Baule walked across their backs to safety.

—Margaret Musgrove[1]

I do not mean to exclude altogether the Idea of Patriotism. I know it exists, and I know it has done much in the Present Contest. But I will venture to assert, that a great and lasting War can never be supported on this principle alone. It must be aided by a prospect of Interest or some reward. For a time, it may, of itself push Men to Action; to bear much, to encounter difficulties; but it will not endure unassisted by Interest.

—George Washington[2]

THE GREAT DIVIDE

The naked apes, destined for undisputed dominance over their environment, looked remarkably undistinguished standing in the savanna. The pathetic lot did not have the physical strength, agility, or even the basic tools of nature to survive attacks from their predators. Like the other primates and many other creatures around them, the early humans survived by forming groups. The primal colonies of the hominids were very much like those of the chimpanzees—without a definite familial line, everyone copulating with everyone else. However, as *Homo sapiens* staked their claims to humanity, the realization of the self emerged slowly from the penumbra of the collective; with social evolution, the overwhelming need to form groups for the protection of the individual made room for the looming interest of the self.

In this chapter, I paint with the broadest possible brush the ongoing conflict and the resulting confusion between the two essential identities that make up the human psyche. I will attempt to demonstrate that the needs of the collective have always been in constant struggle with the aspirations of the individual. Through centuries of intellectual revolts against the collective, the individual has taken the center stage in the current Western social philosophy. In contrast, religious fundamentalism, communism, and hyper-nationalism, all of which place the collective above the individual, have thrived in non-Western thinking.[3] However, the fall of communism in Eastern Europe and the spread of the global marketplace have created hopes for the ultimate victory of the individual.

Yet, the news of the death of collectivism remains exaggerated. Unbridled individualism cannot solve most of the social problems that require collective action. The limitations of individualism keep on bringing back the ideologies of the collective, often through violent revolutions. On the other side, the suppression of individualism within collective societies causes counterrevolutions. Like most things in life—analogous to Goldilocks' finding a bowl of porridge not too hot and not too cold—we seek balance in a political system where the rights of individuals are recognized without losing a vision of a collective society.

Before proceeding further, however, I would like to attempt to define the terms *individualism* and *collectivism*. Unfortunately, despite their wide use, there is no one acceptable definition for the two terms. Therefore, I will define individualism as a social philosophy which places its primary emphasis upon protecting the rights of the individual, and collectivism as a philosophy that aims at furthering the goals of the collective by prescribing the duties of the individual members. I should also point out that these ideal types are not restricted by any political boundaries, nor do they have a single dimension. Thus, a nation can espouse one set of philosophies but may contain within it subnational groups that adhere to a different set of values. For instance, the United States may be regarded as a nation based upon the unquestioned adherence to individual rights. Yet, until the passage of the civil rights laws, many African Americans were denied their fundamental rights. Also, it is possible to have groups or nations with many conflicting dimensions of the ideological poles. Thus, in Sweden, the rights of individuals are protected. Yet they have created a much more socialistic state.

IN THE WOMB OF THE COLLECTIVE

Writing in the seventeenth century, English social philosopher Thomas Hobbes was in the middle of the bloodiest civil war his country had ever seen.

The forces of Oliver Cromwell were challenging the power of the ruling monarch of England. In the midst of this political chaos, many of the old values that governed the society were falling by the wayside like the lopped off head of Charles I. The lofty ideals of Puritanism and republican democracy were clashing with the tradition of the king's divine right to rule his people. In these confusing times when good and evil, nobility and savagery, blended into a uniform gray, Hobbes held a rather dismal view of human motivations. He saw human beings as basically selfish. Hobbes theorized that the only way this wayward ape could be brought under control was by the fear of retribution from an even more powerful force—the mythical monster Leviathan, symbolizing the power of the organized government. Hobbes imagined life in the state of nature as solitary and anarchic—"poor, nasty, brutish and short" with "warre of every man against every man." Hobbes argued that since every man was endowed with almost equal amounts of *will* (desire to dominate others and acquire goods) and *prudence* (the capacity to learn from experience), when there was no power to *overawe* these almost equal beings, there had to be a state of chaos. To Hobbes, the only escape from this horrible fate was the coercive power of a benevolent king.

However, the Hobbesian faith in absolute monarchy ran headlong into the republican aspirations of Jean-Jacques Rousseau. In contrast to the more methodical analysis of Hobbes, the romantic writings of Rousseau painted an idealized picture of the state of nature, where men did not experience envy or engage in violence. A blissful harmony prevailed until "unnatural" institutions such as monogamous marriages and private property were introduced and, consequently, the paradise was lost.

Recent advances in anthropology and the biological sciences, however, indicate that both Hobbes and Rousseau were only partially right.[4] Hobbes was wrong because primitive man could not have survived a solitary life under the baleful condition of "warre of all against all," since a defenseless human being leading a solitary life would soon be dead. The molecular evidence indicates that human beings are extremely closely related to the chimpanzees. In fact, by the DNA measure, the genetic distance between us and the chimpanzees is only about 1.6%, a veritable whisker among the species of the animal world. It is less than the difference between a chimp and a gorilla (2.3%), or between such closely related North American bird species as red-eyed vireos and white-eyed vireos (2.9%).[5] Therefore, in many ways, chimpanzee social structure provides us with a view of our evolutionary past. Jane Goodall was the first to observe the wild chimpanzees at close quarters. She opened her observation post in the Gombe National Forest in Tanzania in the early 1960s. At first her studies revealed the picture of a generally congenial beast living in harmony within its group.[6] Goodall's observations generally supported Rousseau's vision of the idyllic state of nature, which became spoiled only when selfish desires surfaced through monogamous sexual relationships and individual claims to property; the recognition of the self ultimately separated the new species from its group-bound ancestors.

Rousseau's enduring view of the noble savage was further reinforced by the work of luminaries in the field of sociobiology, such as Konrad Lorenz, who claimed in his much celebrated book, *On Aggression,* that animals' aggressive behavior is tempered by their natural inhibitions against murder. After all, killing another human with bare hands is arduous and messy. But the stability of human group relationships was upset with the invention of weapons.

Alas, upon closer examination, the vision of the paradise turned out to be largely a mirage. Goodall in her later studies noted unusual violence within the groups of wild chimps.[7] Frans de Waal, a Dutch primatologist, observed one of the largest captive groups of chimps in the Arnhem Zoo in the Netherlands. In a most interesting case, de Waal observed that in a group with three nearly equal sized males, the two lesser males conspired and formed an alliance to overthrow the dominant (alpha) male through violent clashes. As a result of this vicious uprising, a second male would become the alpha male of the group. Soon the deposed male would form an alliance with the other disempowered male to plot to depose him. No matter who became the dominant male, before long the other two would form a rival group of conspirators. Ultimately, the daisy chain of power struggle among the three males came to an end when the oldest alpha male was brutally attacked by the other two and killed.[8] In a later study, Richard Wrangham and Dale Peterson also witnessed an actual genocidal attack by one group to simply annihilate its rival group of chimpanzees.[9] So much for the paradise in Rousseau's state of nature!

Savagery and nobility, selfishness and generosity, cruelty and kindness—the basic emotions of the two sides must have been imprinted in us from our evolutionary past. In that distant mirror we see the reflection of the two faces of our dual identities, as an individual as well as a member of a larger collective. They are opposite yet at once intertwined, distinct yet superimposed. Both are necessary and yet, in the extreme, they are detrimental to our survival. The history of human civilization is the story of a dialectical tension between the individual and the collective. From the dawn of civilization, we have suffered from this duality of our being, a kind of schizophrenia, which still haunts us. This duality has been reflected in the intellectual development of our art, history, philosophy, and every aspect of sociology, political science, and economics. Its roots were germane in the conflict between the democratic Athens, where the rights of the individual (male) citizens were recognized as the very mark of their social existence, and the authoritarian Sparta, where individual beings were meshed into a collective lump. This conflict transcended their physical struggle, becoming a contest for hearts and minds for generations to come.

The intricate history of human civilization, all over the world, weaves rich tales of self-sacrifice for satisfying the needs of a common good where the duty to the gods, the nation, and the family forms a common identity. Thus, in the book of Genesis, when the god of the Israelites commands Abraham, without the slightest hesitation he raises his hand to slay his eight-year-old son Isaac. Of course, it was only a test of Abraham's true devotion. At the last moment God stays his hand and orders Abraham to slaughter a ram instead.

The creation of a collective personality was further aided by constant chanting of mythologies, passed on orally from one generation to the next. We are compulsive mythmaking animals. In mythology, we find solace in the knowledge that there are superheroes to rescue us in our hour of need, if only we make ourselves truly worthy of their compassion. Our need to "fit in," to belong to a larger entity, is inherent. In mythology, we are comforted to know that we belong to a group, a clan, a nation. Although heroes come with a thousand faces, mythologist Joseph Campbell points out that they have one thing in common: through their trials and tribulations, the heroes learn about something beyond their personal experience which they share with the awestruck reader.[10] Thus, in the Hindu *Ramayana,* the hero, Rama, abdicates his rightful place on the throne and accepts a fourteen-year-long (nearly a lifetime, considering the life expectancy in antiquity) exile in the forest to fulfill his father's ill-advised promise to Rama's stepmother. While traveling through the forest, his wife Sita is abducted by the evil Ravana, the demon king of the island nation of Lanka. With the help of an army of fanciful creatures, Rama crosses the ocean and, after a long battle, slays Ravana. Rama rescues his wife and returns in triumph to his kingdom in Ayodhya. However, there is suspicion in the kingdom about the fidelity of his wife during her captivity. Even though Rama is convinced of Sita's innocence, which she proclaims through repeated denials and trials by fire, others are not. The kingdom is rife with gossip. Rama acknowledges the duty of a "just king"; as a popular king, he understands the value of political symbolism. Rising above his personal feelings, he banishes his wife back to the dangers of the forest. Thus Rama, through his personal tragedies, like Gilgamesh, Odysseus, Abraham, Moses, and other heroes across time, space, and culture, passes the test of faith and shows his commitment to a larger cause. Similar stories form the staple of ancient tales, from folklore to religious mythologies, memorized and chanted in endless repetition, dramatized and reenacted over and over through eons of social evolution. All of these stories carry the same moral line: Submit your individual desires, aspirations, and interests to the gods of the collective.

However, there is one important problem with following the call of the collective: Who speaks for the good of everybody? Wishes of the taciturn gods need to be interpreted. Therefore, the need to accept of the divine right of the monarch, or the infallibility of the pope, or at least the authority of the head of the family remains paramount in a collective society.[11] In plural societies, devoid of an overarching authority figure, it is impossible to define collective welfare. Research in the economics of social choice, firmly encased in the forbidding logic of mathematics, comes to the conclusion that it is impossible to pick any single course of action for the entire society as the "will of the people."[12] Unless some extremely restrictive assumptions are made about people's preferences, it literally takes the pronouncement of a dictator to define collective will.[13]

But the legitimacy of someone else's authority has to be inculcated in the minds of the people. They have to be taught, often at the cost of extreme punishment for the slightest transgression. If the fear of social ostracism and excommunication does not work, the dread of eternal damnation must be used to instill hesitation in the heart of the worshiper of the self. If all else fails, the heretics and blasphemers may have to be burned alive in the town square to set an example for all other prospective rebels.

INDIVIDUAL: THE DELIVERANCE

In the history of human civilization, the acceptance of the primacy of the individual is of recent origin, and its acceptance is certainly not uniform across cultures. In fact, the notion of the supremacy of the individual is an unqualified modern European invention. People in medieval Europe were less concerned about their individuality, which took a back seat to the greater concern for the church, the crown, and the tribe. A man's identity was indistinguishable from his collective persona. Thus, a man would be known by his familial line, his religious affiliation, or his allegiance to a king. Medieval social values demanded total conformity in deeds and words and even in secret thoughts to the collective will as expressed by the state and the official church.[14] This submersion of the individual into the collective was reflected amply in art, literature, and in the general attitude toward life. Painters or sculptors seldom showed any interest in depicting the true likeness of their subjects. Religious paintings were iconic. For an early medieval Christian to describe an icon of Mary as "lifelike" would have been quite different from a Renaissance viewer of Leonardo da Vinci's *Madonna of the Rocks* or Raphael's *Cowpar Madonna* to say so.[15]

In medieval literature, individual love for one another was not the most popular theme; rather, virtuous love for God or the crown was glorified. Even the savvy Elizabethan audience might not have considered *Romeo and Juliet* as a love story. Instead, it was often viewed as the folly of two impudent youths who did not go by the accepted laws of their families and, consequently, brought misery and death upon themselves and shame upon their kinfolk.[16] We can only imagine the overwhelming dominance of the collective—the family, tribe, crown, and church—in the medieval mind when we realize that even as late as the eighteenth century, the notion of marriage for love was considered to be an absurdity. Reflecting the traditional views of the day, Jonathan Swift in 1723 called romantic love "a ridiculous passion which hath no being but in plays and romances."[17]

In medieval Europe, the process of indoctrination in the defense of the collective and submission to the will of authority started early in life. In 1732, Susanna, the mother of John Wesley, the founder of the Wesleyan movement, ran a rectory for adopted children at Espworth. She explains her secret for a peaceful home thus: "When turned a year old, and some before, [the children] were taught to fear the rod and cry softly, by which means, they escaped the abundance of correction they might otherwise have had, and that most odious noise of the crying children was rarely heard in the house." The reason children were drilled into strict submission parental authority was always made clear in contemporary books on child rearing. The object was to "conquer their will and bring them to an obedient temper." For whenever a child is being punished, "it must be conquered." Thus, in 1783, in his *Sermon on the Education of Children,* John Wesley instructs parents: "Break the will of your child, to bring his will into subjection to yours, that it may be afterwards subject to the will of God."[18]

Coerced by parents, threatened by the Church, sanctioned by the king—the medieval mind-set was thus shaped. Historian Lawrence Stone points out that the strict adherence to the collective turned medieval men into compulsive perfectionists with an overwhelming desire to conform to authority and an unyielding sense of self-righteousness.[19]

The dawn of the age of reason, however, brought the individual out of the shadow of the collective. The seeds of revolution were planted around the middle of the thirteenth century in Cologne, Germany, by St. Thomas Aquinas. The pugnacious priest proclaimed man's emancipation from "original sin" and acknowledged his ability to choose right from wrong independent of a preordained divine direction. The recognition of the possibility of a choice of destiny set those who could grasp its implications apart from the heroes of the ancient epics and mythologies, who were forever being inexorably swept away by their fate. The revolution for the individual, however, started in earnest nearly 200 years later when another German sounded the first note of the trumpet that would ultimately crumble the walls of the citadel of the collective. Not a priest, but a printer, Johannes Gutenberg and his wooden printing press brought the realm of God closer to the domain of the mortals; now anyone could develop a personal relationship with God without an intermediary. The age of questioning the authority of the spokesman for the collective god had started.

The revolt of the individual started at the intellectual level of the priests, academics, scientists, and philosophers in Europe. However, the emergent era of questioning also found its roots in the discoverers of new lands and new ideas. "The world we now view from the literate West," writes Daniel Boorstin, "the vistas of time, the land and the seas, the heavenly bodies and our own bodies, the plants and animals, history and human societies past and present—had to be opened for us by countless Columbuses. In the deep recesses of the past, they remain anonymous. As we come closer to the present they emerge into the light of history, a cast of characters as varied as human nature. Discoveries become episodes of biography, unpredictable as the new worlds the discoverers opened to us."[20] But the history of social evolution does not take place in neat chronological order. Like the shingled roof, where one square is overlaid onto another in a seemingly seamless quilt, history evolves. Therefore, my chronicle will sometimes be chaotic and will often leapfrog, but I hope to present a coherent story in the process.

The glorious path that delivered individualism went through Bacon, Descartes, Spinoza, Locke, Hume, Kant, and Schopenhauer; an intellectual challenge was thrown to the entrenched power, resting on the pillars of theology and unquestioned faith. Unfettered for the first time, the emergent philosophy demanded that all knowledge in consequence must begin with the individual mind and self. With egregious hubris, the individual proclaimed its very existence through reason: *Cogito, ergo sum* (I think, therefore I am). Descartes' three words were destined to shape how modern humans would perceive themselves for ages to come.

The challenge to the collective did not remain confined for long within the upper crust of society or the insular world of the forbidding philosophers. The need for empirical verification flooded all branches of the natural sciences, thereby severely truncating the power of mythologies of the collective. However, if Gutenberg sounded the trumpet that cracked walls, over 300 years later Charles Darwin delivered the decisive blow which forever weakened the pillars of the temple of the collective. The notion of an evolution from insignificant amoebae to a rational human being shook the core of our fundamental belief system, leaving little room for the world to go back to the days of authoritative proclamations.

Today, in our discourses, we take the values of individualism for granted. French philosopher of science Michel Foucault calls it the "positive consciousness" of knowledge. He defines it as "a level that eludes the consciousness of the scientists and yet is part of scientific discourse."[21] Foucault places the origin of the values of individualism around the sixteenth century. He claims that these values, which have been part of our positive consciousness, are no older than a mere 200 years.[22]

The pent-up fury resulting from the hithertofore denial of the self found its champion in the utilitarian philosophy of John Stuart Mill, Auguste Comte, and Jeremy Bentham and in the nascent study of economics by Adam Smith. In their philosophy, they not only portrayed man as a rational actor, but also proceeded to define the very essence of rationality as the pursuit of one's self-interest. This assumption was later aided by the Social Darwinism of Herbert Spencer and the behavioral inquiry of Emile Durkheim. Durkheim, through his statistical analysis, demonstrated that even the most emotional act of committing suicide could be accounted for by external conditions. Therefore, if suicide is not a rational act, it certainly is a reasoned one. This line of argument was later taken to the extreme in neoclassical economics, where the pursuit of self-interest was taken as the very definition of human rationality.[23]

A true revolution in social thinking, however, had started in 1776 with the publication of Adam Smith's *The Wealth of Nations.* Smith sought the maximization of the wealth of nations in unbridled self-interest; if everyone pursues their own interests, happiness, and desires, then the entire society benefits from the enlarged sum of total products resulting from the relentless work of its individual members. To Adam Smith, there was something inherently "natural" about the market process of demand and supply. Using black mourning cloth as an example, he explained that when there is a temporary shortage of a particular article, its price rises in the short run and the prices of competing goods are reduced. However, attracted by the possibility of added profits, this increase in prices brings new suppliers into the market, which, in turn, reduces the price of black cloth in the long run to its "natural level." Thus, only the current prices and temporary price manipulations are the province of market demand and supply. Given time, the prices of each commodity bought and sold in the market (including labor) will converge, reaching its "true value." This assertion leads to some of the most enduring presumptions of the individualist society and serves as the source of the most powerful and perpetual parables of capitalism.

In the market, individual actors get their just deserts through the inherent merit of their own devices. If they succeed, it is because they are the most deserving of the lot; if they fail, it is also because their failures are warranted by a lack of talent in producing goods that the market demands. The apparent congruity between the market process and the Darwinian assertion of "natural selection" fascinated many in the nineteenth century. This fascination culminated in the writings of Herbert Spencer and his theory of Social Darwinism. If in nature only the fittest survive, then isn't evolution synonymous with progress?

On the flip side, drawing from the Darwinian theory of evolution, the philosophy of the individual holds that most social misery results from unwise interference in the "natural" forces of market clearance by some external force, namely, the state. The rapidly changing European world in the early nineteenth century, hungry to replace the obstructionist Church, found its salvation in the pursuit of self-interest. In the late nineteenth and early twentieth centuries, the challenge of the collective came not so much from the Church but from Karl Marx and his followers. Like the Church, Marxism held out promises for the future. The followers of Marx were comforted to know the eventual destiny of the society, and that it would be a just society.

Facing the growing challenge from ideologies of the collective, the apostles of individualism struck back. The first decade the twentieth century established a firm link among individualism, capitalism, and economic prosperity. In 1904, Max Weber published *The Protestant Ethic and the Spirit of Capitalism*. It was a rapidly changing world. Revenues from the colonies along with swift changes in technology were completely overhauling the European power structure. The old feudal ties were being replaced by a new group of elite, the entrepreneurs. There was a wholesale change afoot; old tradition, culture, and morality were being rendered meaningless by the juggernaut of the changing times. At this time, Weber argued that Protestant merchants in Northern Europe fostered a changed outlook toward the material world. The new mode of production was solidly based on the individual rationality of the Protestant work ethic. It no longer looked to the Catholic Church for moral guidance. Instead, each individual looked inside and found reasons to work hard, pursue self-interest, and thereby bring prosperity to the land. No more was asceticism held to be morally superior to acquisitiveness. To Weber, the Protestant elite had finally been able to throw away their hairshirts and self-flagellating denial of material pleasure. In their pursuit of material well-being they had finally set free the individual from the womb of the collective.[24]

The turn-of-the century economist Joseph Schumpeter further expanded the role of the individual in changing the course of the economy. In his famous book *The Theory of Economic Development* (1912), he introduced the role of an "entrepreneur" or an "innovator."[25] Schumpeter argued that society ascends from one level of economic development to the next not simply because brilliant scientists invent new tools in their insulated laboratories, but because of the works of innovators, people like Henry Ford and Bill Gates. These entrepreneurs translate esoteric knowledge into commercially viable products and change the course of economic development·

The central position of the individual in the Western intellectual tradition was further made secure by Sigmund Freud. Unlike the followers of the ideology of the collective, Freud did not look for explanations of people's aberrant behavior in the seduction of the Devil or the huge contradictions between the economic classes. For him the cause lay buried deep inside our psyche. As individuals, each of us tries to grapple with the dialectical tension between love and death, Eros and destruction, floating between conscious and unconscious, tossed around among the id, ego, and superego. From this complex psychological framework, we relate to the society at large. The relationship among sex, culture, and society is interactive; only in our inner conflict do we find our place within the folds of the society, uphold its traditions and values, or rebel against it as individuals. In his later life Freud brought his insights from clinical psychology to bear to explain the workings of society. In *Civilization and Its Discontents,* he finally and definitively declares men's proclivity to rebel against society to be instinctive and outside the purview of human rationality. "I take the standpoint that the tendency to aggression," Freud asserted unequivocally, "is an innate, independent, instinctual disposition in a man."[26] As a logical consequence of this point of view, Freud had to confess to having "no consolation to offer" in curbing violence in society. However, the inescapable conclusion of Freudian psychology, which so influenced the evolution of Western social philosophy, was that every single individual was responsible for his or her actions. Without an overall explanation, from the perspective of the most noted psychologist acts of collective madness are not distinguishable from other deranged deeds of individual psychosis.

As the philosophy of individualism was getting permanently rooted in the Western mind, there was, however, one important problem facing the nascent discipline of individualism. It is obvious that the market is biased toward the rich and the powerful. While Weber could trace the path to prosperity through the Protestant work ethic, it left an important question of ethics hanging in the balance. Although new modes of production brought unprecedented prosperity, especially to Protestant Europe and America, there were gaping holes in the blanket of comfort. Between 1800 and the birth of the welfare state in the 1930s, literature revealed the other face of the laissez-faire society. The dreadful misery of Dickensian England was matched by the feudal Russia of Dostoyevsky. In the New World, portrayals of the wretched underclass by O. Henry, Upton Sinclair, and John Steinbeck speak volumes about living conditions under a free-for-all economy. Therefore, for a complete social philosophy, it was important for the proponents of the free market to develop a coherent perspective on social and economic inequality.

While parts of Catholic doctrine were definitely egalitarian (e.g., "It is easier for a camel to pass through the eye of a needle than for a rich man to go to heaven") or placed strong emphasis on charity, the neoclassical economics of market forces had nothing to say about social justice. The ethical question of a highly skewed distribution of income and wealth was a nagging one. On the one hand, it is easy to argue that without government interference market processes will find their own equilibrium. On the other hand, it is not so easy to justify the equilibrium if it creates widespread poverty with only pockets of affluence. All through the second half of the nineteenth century John Stuart Mill's *Principles of Political Economy* was widely regarded as the economists' bible. Mill, Bentham, Comte, and other *Utilitarian* philosophers argued that a society must not only obtain the maximum level of economic prosperity, it must also want to maximize the arithmetical sum of "utility" of all its citizens. The inescapable implication of this postulation is that if there is an additional dollar to be distributed in the economy, the society will benefit more if it goes to a poor person, since his utility out of that dollar is likely to be higher than that of the wealthy. This may actually mean compromising the principle of unhindered competition, a most dangerous proposition for proponents of the free market. In fact, Mill admitted that "laissez-faire should be the general practice; every departure from it, unless required by some greater good, is a *certain evil.*"[27]

This academic contradiction was eventually overcome in 1909 with the publication of Vilfredo Pareto's *Manuel d'économie politique,* which economic historian Mark Blaug calls the "most famous untranslated [into English] book in the history of economics."[28] Pareto, countering the growing intellectual threat from Marxism, argued that it is impossible to make an interpersonal comparison of utility, therefore, such an attempt must be off-limits; we can be categorically certain that a society's overall welfare position has improved when at least one person's economic condition improves without anyone else having to sacrifice his personal well-being. Pareto's theory, therefore, disregards all redistribution of income and wealth regardless of the original state of the income gap between rich and poor. This extremely conservative position allowed mainstream economists to close their eyes to the question of relative distribution of income, one of the most critical issues of social instability. Instead, Pareto's hypothesis leads to the conclusion that a society can reach its objective of achieving the optimum level of allocation of resources when it can provide a condition of perfect competition, unspoiled by private monopolies or undue government interference. Armed with Pareto's theory of ethics, Western economics could proclaim the supremacy of the individual over any collective value judgment regarding the level of distribution of income and wealth.

This important development allowed at least the academics a good night's sleep, knowing that all a society must strive for is free competition. The moral superiority of free market competition was such that the true believers argued that in a competitive market, there can be no racism, sexism, or any other kind of systematic discrimination! Thus the conservative Milton Friedman claims: "A businessman or an entrepreneur who expresses preferences in his business activities that are not related to productive efficiency is in effect imposing higher costs on himself than other individuals who do not have such preferences. Hence, in a *free market* they will tend to drive him out."[29] Note that Friedman's arguments of a discrimination-free marketplace relate only to "free" or "perfect" market conditions. In economics, this ideal condition is known as "perfect competition." At this state, all participants in the market are small and there are numerous buyers and sellers of every kind of commodity. There is no monopoly; no one individual can change the course of the market. Under such conditions, whatever one gets is his "just" remuneration, since if someone asks for more than he is worth, he will soon be unemployed. On the other hand, if an employer pays a worker less than what he truly deserves, then soon there will be better offers for him to change jobs, reflecting his true value.

The most wonderful aspect of this line of reasoning is that a society can completely ignore its current state of inequality, what we broadly call social injustice. In its best interpretation, it is forward looking, in the sense that it says, "Let us strive to level the playing field and give everyone an equal chance to prosper." In its worst interpretation, it preserves status quo and, under the guise of promoting equal opportunity, closes its eyes to the growing concentration of income in fewer and fewer hands.

The unquestioned market process places the individual in the exalted center of the social universe. It is the individual who determines what is best for his own self and makes decisions accordingly. Given the supremacy of individual choice, capitalism propagates the myth that "you can be whatever you want to be." In its essence, it promotes the possibility of achieving one's dreams without much regard to the actual probability. At its core, the theology of the individual is unrealistic in its optimism. With regard to an individual, it promotes the delusion of equal opportunity. And for the society, it peddles the hope of eventual development with time. The mythology of individualism, spun around the kernel of optimism, becomes its biggest selling point. For each member of the society, it holds out the promise of individual achievement. For nations struggling with the problems of poverty and lack of economic development, it pledges an eventual place in the sun, following the well-trodden path of other nations at the top.[30] In the process, it completely ignores the barriers of institutional rigidities, monopoly power, and widely held prejudices. As an analogy, we can think of the free market system as pouring water on an uneven surface. As long as the barriers are porous (or there is perfect social mobility and equality of opportunity in the true sense of the term) there will be equality in the level of water. However, if the barriers are solid, the water level will never be the same.

Rapid changes in social philosophy have occurred at times of calamitous events such as wars, revolution, or natural disasters or during swift changes in technology. For example, the two world wars assaulted deeply held beliefs in society with unprecedented power. From the bombed-out rubble of civilization emerged the nihilistic philosophy of existentialism. Rejecting tradition, faith, or even a firm conviction, one of the main proponents of existentialism, Jean-Paul Sartre, put the sheer existence of a human being firmly before his essence.[31] The uncertainty of the Vietnam War and the possibility of global annihilation through thermonuclear exchange between the superpowers further nurtured the fruits of existentialism. Fed by cynicism and mistrust of authority, devoid of any overarching moral absolutes, the West became awash with anti-establishment movements, which saw no end of individualism. The absence of a universally accepted moral standard—outside the bounds of what is strictly legal—often produced an "everything goes" hedonistic culture pushed to the extreme.[32]

ROMANCING THE COLLECTIVE

Although the rise of individualism was almost entirely European innovation, the call of the collective remained strong in most other parts of the world. The irrepressible desire to question authority started the revolution of the West. Today the term "Western" is synonymous with a number of propositions. On the positive side, to be Western means to recognize the rights of the individual, to question authority, and to accept nothing without empirical proof. On the negative side, the term implies self-absorption, denial of tradition and faith, and pushing the limits of vulgarity and self-indulgence. In its highest form, individualism promotes democracy based upon the inalienable rights of the individual; in its worst, it is an excuse for rapacious exploitation and disregard for the overall welfare of mankind, the environment, and any higher aspirations beyond the narrowest definition of the self.

With time Western civilization claimed the primacy of motivations based on the individual, yet the need for the collective remained strong. The psychological need to belong remains strong even among the staunchest individualists. If unbridled individualism holds out the dreams of self-elevation, the ideology of the collective offers comfort through belonging to a group.

As the West veered onto the path of individualism, most of the world remained within the comforting yoke of the collective. Much of the non-Western world sought its destiny within ideologies that emphasized duty of individual members of the society at the expense of individual rights. Thus, in many parts of the Islamic world, a man can be arrested for not praying during the assigned time and a woman can be humiliated for uncovering her face. The Catholic countries would prohibit divorce. At least in Jerusalem, the Jewish state attempts to maintain strict Sabbath laws. In Communist China, the mere act of protesting against a government policy can be regarded as a crime against the nation. In Japan, children may be taught the value of buying Japanese products even when they are significantly more expensive than imported items. Collectivism remained alive and thriving in the form of religious fundamentalism, hyper-nationalism, and communism.

As Adam Smith and the Utilitarians in the British Isles were busy promoting the individual, the voice of the collective resurfaced and found its expression across the Channel in the writings of Jean-Jacques Rousseau. Rousseau romanticized the collective. In a confusing time, where the moral values of common men and women were being tested as they had never been before, he preached about the comforting voice of the people, which he called "general will" (*volonté générale*). In Rousseau's mind, the general will presented a unique fact about a community. To him, it has a universal collective good which is not the same thing as the sum total of private interest of the individual members. Like a living organism, the "general will" has its own life, fulfills its own promises, and suffers its own fate. But at the same time, Rousseau was a product of the age of reason, which placed individual rights above the needs of the collective. So it was only natural that, like so many of his intellectual descendants, he would be quite confused about reconciling the two. The more he tried to show that the rights of the individual emanate from the predominance of the collective, the deeper he went into a conceptual quagmire.[33] However, that confusion did not deter those who, like the messengers of God, had claimed to have a direct link with "the people." Wars have been fought, ultimate sacrifices have been made, and genocides have been committed by the followers of those who could speak for the general will of the people.

The goals of the collective were further advanced by the work of Friedrich Nietzsche. Like most intellectuals of his time, Nietzsche was fascinated by the evolutionary theories of Darwin. He argued that morality and even theology needed to be reconstructed in terms of evolutionary theory. However, while Spencer found the rise of the individual in social evolution, Nietzsche wanted to control and shape it. For him, democracy—where each adult is counted equally—was a vast anthill of individuals. Instead, he proposed a willful Superman, the natural leader, who would rise above the common to become the guiding light, a godlike Zarathustra. So for Nietzsche, people are destined to either be "great" or "servant of the great." The super race of greats can rule over the vast tide of humanity, creating its own morality, choosing its own destiny. It is easy to see how the Nazis—preoccupied with the notion of racial superiority—would reformulate Nietzsche's philosophy to suit their political purpose. It is also not difficult to imagine how, given the state of the defeated and demoralized Germany after World War I, the Nazis were able to sell this odd concoction based on mythology and sheer wishful thinking to the German people. Opting to submerge their individual souls in the collective, many Germans quickly became Hitler's willing executioners and full participants to collective madness.

The pursuit of the ideology of the collective took another sharp turn. Among the nineteenth-century philosophers nobody comes as close to promoting the cause of the collective as Karl Marx. Marx not only glorified collective action but also found in it society's ultimate destiny. In the history of human civilization, he saw the tension between two opposing groups. During the period of feudalism, the dialectical forces that propel society along its evolutionary path came from the conflicting interests of the feudal lords and their subjects. The rise of capitalism changed the faces of the adversaries; in a society no longer based on old traditions and theology, the primary conflict was now between the capitalists (the bourgeoisie) and the hapless workers (the proletariat). Although in this struggle the workers faced incredible odds against the organized and powerful capitalists, the workers finally overcame their keepers. They would inevitably earn victory in the battle because capitalist society carries within itself the seeds of self-destruction. To Marx, these seeds were planted by the blind self-interest of the capitalists, the very engine that yanked capitalism out of the womb of feudalism. Their relentless greed and insatiable desire to accumulate wealth guide the economy to the path of eventual destruction through a falling rate of profit. The free market technology always displaces labor with machines that produce goods and services with an incredible and ever-enlarging voracity. As a result, the overmechanized production lines produce more than the market can absorb. The over supply of commodities relative to their demand causes market prices to tumble. The fall of market prices prompts businesses to lay off workers as a cost-cutting move, which in turn further depresses prices. This cycle of layoffs and reduction in prices and profits continues as the economy gets sucked into the whirlpool of a great depression.

The cause of proletarian revolution is further aided by the displaced workers, who become keenly aware of their separation from the means of production. This separation, Marx argued, causes the psychology of alienation among the proletariat. Together, economic depression and active rebellion fueled by a pervasive feeling of alienation ultimately destroy capitalism. The destruction of capitalism ushers in the new age of socialism, which replaces the capitalistic democracies with a "dictatorship of the proletariat."

The problem with the notion of "dictatorship of the proletariat" is not with dictatorship, which the Soviets and their protégés in Eastern Europe, China, Southeast Asia, and Cuba readily supplied. The problem was with "the proletariat." Even if we get past the conundrum of the definition of who is a proletarian (a great deal of highly destructive energy went into the effort of defining the term in the post-revolutionary communist countries and in China, during the Cultural Revolution) the question remains, Who speaks for them? Rousseau was lost in trying to find the individual in the midst of general will, and the communists were no closer to the answer.[34] Therefore, quickly and predictably, the dictatorship of the proletariat became the dictatorship of a small group of mostly men in the Communist Party. As long as history allowed, the Soviet Union remained viable. When it fell apart, it simply imploded and, like the demolition of a large, abandoned building, collapsed into a heap of tangled rubble. Francis Fukuyama saw in the demise the end of history, where for the last time the dragon of the collective had been slain. The history of human civilization, the story of conflict between the individual and the collective, was now over. The individual had won, decisively and forever.[35]

But news about the death of the collective proved to be somewhat exaggerated. Just when we were ready to blow the final whistle, indicating that the game was over, there was a discordant note. The ebullient world, rejoicing around the incredible sights of breaking down the Berlin Wall, looked up to find itself awash with other causes of the collective: religious fundamentalism and ethnic hostility.

Religion is a true cause of the collective. Born into a religion or caste, you are born into a geography and a history from which there is no escape. For some, this bondage is confining; for others, it is a source of comfort. Religion has often found coexistence with individualism difficult. The citadel of religious belief is founded upon the pillars of faith.[36] Religious faith is based on deductive logic. It starts with a premise the validity of which cannot be questioned. Thus, if one accepts the books of religion as the words of God, then the resulting conclusions cannot be considered illogical. On the other hand, if one turns the logical process upside down and accepts only that which can be empirically proven as truth, it quickly takes us away from fundamentalist religious dogma. The epistemological evolution of Descartes, Spinoza, and, ultimately, Kant turned away from dogma by pursuing reason. Later, Karl Popper, the philosopher of science, proclaimed the test of nonfalsifiability of hypotheses. For a hypothesis to be considered scientific—whether it is in the realm of the social or natural sciences—it must be "falsifiable," that is, capable of being proven incorrect with the help of empirical observation. For instance, most of the laws of physics are observable. Even the fundamental hypotheses of relativity and quantum mechanics can be tested with data, albeit indirectly. In the social sciences, hypotheses regarding human behavior can be proved or disproved with revealed behavior. But matters of religious dogma (or, for that matter, Marx's labor theory of value) cannot be empirically verified.[37]

Mutual suspicion and hostility have been the hallmark of the two opposite world views. Reflecting the biases of enlightenment, sociologist Edward Shils suggests: "Religious knowledge . . . has been regarded as the very epitome of all that reason refuses. Prejudice, dogmatism, superstition, taboos against rational thought, and plain error have been regarded as the marks of religious belief. . . . The rationalistic rejection of religious knowledge has given the word belief a bad name."[38] The idea of individual-centered secular humanism, which permeates every aspect of our current intellectual life, like oxygen in the air that we breathe, without our being conscious of it, did not triumph without considerable opposition from many groups, including the church. If the society is based on the individual, what then becomes of sacrifice in the name of God and country? In mythology, the deviants are banished from paradise or turned into a pillar of salt. Even entire cities with all the residents are obliterated for disobeying the word of God. In allegory, it is the voice of the collective gods that is addressed to the entire congregation; it is Satan who lures away the hapless individuals. Throughout history theology has clashed with those who placed individuals over the collective. The eighteenth-century church threatened excommunication to the believers of "Hobbesian blasphemy." The primacy of the individual horrified a contemporary observer, who, with understandable passion, claimed that "where [Hobbesian] principles prevail, adieu honour and honesty and fidelity and loyalty; all must give place to self-interest."[39]

Today the same sentiment echoes in the sermons of the preachers of fundamentalism. The creed of individualism is now synonymous with the West. Its strict separation of the church from the state and its recognition of reason over faith threaten religious fundamentalists to the core. From the fiery ministers of the Protestant faith to the mullahs of the Middle East, from the strident rabbis of radical Judaism to the self-appointed champions of fundamentalist Hinduism, the message is the same: "We must resist the vile influences of the West." As the West defined reason in terms of empirical verification, it turned away from the biggest question of mankind, its fundamental relationship with its soul.

The West is seen as decadent and self-absorbed, where the inalienable rights of the individual are protected as the most sacred covenant, without a single word about the corresponding duties. In the political world of state-mandated religion, the list of duties is clear. From the sacred texts, each aspect of human action is strongly prescribed or strictly proscribed, from birth to death, from procreation to religious observance.[40]

The problem with a theocratic society, however, is typical of any collective society: Who speaks for the will of the gods? We can all look for guidance to the Koran, the Bhagavad Gita (the Hindu book of religion), or the Bible. But life today is a lot more complicated than it was when these books were written. For instance, in order to determine public policy with regard to the latest telecommunication system or biotechnology in strict adherence to the broad teachings of these ancient books, religious laws have to be stretched and reinterpreted. As long as people accept the interpretation of God's will by the ayatollahs, the minor mullahs, the priests, or the self-proclaimed spokesmen of God, the society remains viable. When they are questioned, the society simply collapses. In sum, the fundamental problem of individual-based societies is that, without an overall premise of social welfare, they cannot address questions of social injustice. In contrast, the problem of collective societies is that while they find no dearth of spokespersons who would interpret the "truth" according to God, the Prophet, or the grand philosopher, with time others inevitably start questioning their authority to do so.

The third tributary of the ideology of the collective is made up of those professing nationalism. After millions of deaths in warfare between and within nations, standing at the end of the most violent millennium, where carnage of unprecedented proportions has been carried on in the name of nation and nationalism, it is indeed difficult to realize that the very concept of nationalism is but a nineteenth-century Western European invention. In popular parlance the word *nation* crops up everywhere with its infinite attempt to define everything: living entities, symbols, or even concepts. We take pride in national heroes, name national animals and plants, measure national income. Yet after 200 years of continuous use and abuse, the concept of nationhood is still largely undefinable. Thus, we can only echo what nearly a century ago Walter Bagehot—like U.S. Supreme Court Justice Potter Stewart, who could not define pornography without seeing it first[41]—observed, "We know what [a nation] is when you do not ask us, but we cannot very quickly explain or define it."[42] Tracing the intricate history of nations and nation building, E. J. Hobsbawm could simply point to the confusion regarding why certain groups of people become "nations" and others do not.[43]

In fact, everything about the nation is mixed with irony. Karl Marx viewed the entire notion of nations and nationalism with suspicion, arguing that the concept was invented by capitalist society to mask the fundamental contradiction of the battle between the "haves" and the "have-nots." When his disciples took power in the Soviet Union, the communist ideologues did everything to obliterate national identities within their own country and to scoff at national aspirations of countries within its hegemonic sphere. Yet, it was left up to Joseph Stalin to come up with one of the most succinct working definitions of *nation*. In his *Marxism and the National Colonial Question* (originally published in 1912) he defined a nation as "a historically evolved, stable community of language, territory, economic life and psychological make-up manifested in a community of culture."[44]

Yet we can take each one of those criteria that Stalin suggested and show that none of them individually or collectively makes or unmakes a nation.[45] Common language did not create one single nation in Spanish America or keep the United States and Canada united with Great Britain. On the other hand, India, with its seventeen national languages, can still claim to be a state.

The lack of a common territory did not deter the Zionist activists from claiming their nationhood in Israel. Common economic interest has not yet bound Western Europe into a common nationhood. In terms of defining a community of culture, it is impossible to determine where one ends and another one begins. Historically, there was no Italy or Germany before their unification. India, if it existed as a nation, did so only in the scattered lyrics of its literary texts before British colonial rule. The situation in Africa is even more confusing, where nations were built according to the convenience of the European colonialists. The absurdity of nation building in Africa is perhaps best exemplified when we consider that Cameroon, one of the West African hodgepodge nations got its name from its Portuguese colonialists. Finding a large quantity of small crayfish that looked like shrimp (*camaroes* in Portuguese) in the Wouri River, they named the country after this culinary delight—certainly not an inspiring tale for forging unity in a nation comprising diverse tribal identities, at least three religions (Christianity, Islam, and animism) and many distinct language groups.

Nationalism has been thought of both as the product of right-wing and left-wing, progressive and conservative movements; one which aspires to unshackle the chains of oppression and, at the same time, wants to engage in ethnic cleansing and commit genocide. The liberal face of nationalism is one that is given by the Jacobins, inspired by the uplifting words of Rousseau, one which found expression in the writings of Giuseppe Mazzini, and John Stuart Mill and achieved a moral high ground through the participation of Mahatma Gandhi. The other face of nationalism is the domain of the genocidal maniacs and the war criminals. The corresponding need to subjugate others and rob them of their basic humanity soils the lofty ideals of national identity and the desire to work for the common good. Despite the two opposite views, in the post–Cold War world, nationalism has been the prime catalyst that has torn the world apart.[46]

SINGULAR WORLDVIEW: THE CONFUSION

Living in the West, we can readily recognize the indomitable spirit of the individual. It is the motivation of the collective that often confounds us. We understand that an individual is going to be motivated primarily by self-interest. However, what about those loftier goals of self-sacrifice for the collective?

The singular worldview based on either the collective or the individual has inevitably led to confusion among its main proponents. This confusion has been amply reflected in philosophical developments as well as material policies of the states espousing the rival ideologies. The collective philosophies have attempted to uplift the human soul but have failed miserably to accommodate the spirit; in contrast, the individualistic societies nurtured the individual spirit but could not find a way of expressing the needs of the society, except during times of war.

The dialectical tension between the individual and the collective has led to confusion and glaring contradictions. Both sides of the debate have tried to portray their philosophical worldview as a universal solution. However, in the process both sides have become mired in conceptual confusion; each side has attempted to come out of it through promising far more than it can possibly deliver.

The framers of the United States Constitution could not escape this ambivalence. On the one hand, there was the need for self-sacrifice for the nascent nation; on the other hand, there was the constant danger of collective tyranny and political corruption in the name of the state. In their quandary, the revolutionary leaders stressed the need for individual sacrifice during the War of Independence, emphasizing commitment to the public good. Nevertheless, despite the dire needs of the collective, questions about the rights of the individual kept surfacing. During the war, General George Washington voiced his skepticism about the long-term viability of patriotism as an ideology. The articulation of self-interest, a small stream during the American Revolutionary War, turned into a torrent after independence. When the framers sat down to write the Constitution, the political leadership had fundamentally changed its rhetoric, now stressing the need to protect the individual. For them, the basis of the newly formed government was not going to be the citizens' obligation to the collective. Instead, the new nation would be founded on the firm ground of individual self-interest. Eventually, the U.S. Constitution, through its first ten amendments, collectively known as the Bill of Rights, became long on individual rights, but failed to point out the corresponding duties of its citizens. As a result, much of the Supreme Court's effort is directed at resolving the conflict between the fundamental rights of the individual and the requirements of society. Perhaps that is why the nation stood up and listened with such startled interest when in his inaugural address President Kennedy told his countrymen not to ask what their country could do for them, but what they could do for their country. A line that would have been part of everyday political rhetoric in most countries around the world struck the nation as something novel and became enshrined in its political lexicon.

. . . IN WOMEN, SAVAGES, AND CHILDREN

Perhaps nothing shocks the Western world as much as the sight of a mob. In the Western mind, the mob and the collective society become one, which stands in stark contrast to the order of societies based on the ideology of the individual. The picture of the murderous mob painted by the Bard in *Julius Caesar* is compelling. Incited by the clever oratory by Mark Antony, the crowd, which was celebrating the demise of a dictator moments ago, is thirsty for blood, the blood of their enemies—those conspirators who had taken the life of their suddenly beloved Caesar. His death has to be avenged. In the process, they stumble upon an unfortunate poet bearing the same name as one of the conspirators. On a crowd gone insane, the voice of reason makes no impact; in one of the most violent scenes in Shakespearean drama, hapless Cinna the poet is torn from limb limb by the bloodthirsty mob.

The sight of a mob has fascinated people throughout the ages. Scripture describes the scene eloquently, and master painters have shown savage crowds watching as Jesus is being dragged to his death. Their jeering, cruel faces—resembling a pack of wild hyenas more than human beings—evoke unfathomable revulsion. The ancient Greek philosopher Plato saw in the Athenian *demos*—the crowd—an ignorant and irrational bunch, too eager to be used as weapons by some unscrupulous demagogue. How can a young man resist the plaudits of the mob, asked Plato,

[w]hen they crowd into the seats in the assembly, or law courts or theater, or get together in camp or any other popular meeting places and, with a great deal of noise and a great lack of moderation, shout and clap their approval or disapproval of whatever is proposed or done, till the rocks and the whole place re-echo, and re-double the noise of their boos and applause. Can a young man be unmoved by all this? He gets carried away and soon finds himself behaving like the crowd and becoming one of them.[47]

Among the ancient scholars, Aristotle devoted the most effort to studying rebellion. Aristotle pointed out that it was the jealousy of the dispossessed that starts a revolution. On the other hand, the middle class, which gets a little taste of the good life and, therefore, keeps its hopes of joining the privileged alive, turns out to be the pillar of stable societies.[48]

The Roman historian Livy, while analyzing the causes for Rome's downfall, puts a large part of the blame on the enemy within—the Roman mob and its agitators. Livy argues that Rome could have achieved much more and that the republic would have lasted much longer had it devoted its attention to the internal enemies instead.

The destruction of the Roman Empire ushered in the Middle Ages. The huge transcontinental empire fragmented into small principalities surrounded by rural areas. This diffusion of political power robbed medieval people of a definite symbol of political power to be destroyed. The medieval principalities built no Bastille to galvanize the populace, offered no czars to be shot. In medieval Europe, what came the closest to providing a symbol of political power was the Vatican. With the universal Church laying down rules of conduct which governed medieval lives from taxes to marriage, property settlements to moral obligations, the popes often served as ready targets of popular uprising.[49] The greatest threat of crowd violence in the Middle Ages, however, came from the millenarians, who, incited by religious zealots drawing from the Book of Revelation (as is still done now among fundamentalists like Jim Jones and David Koresh), prophesied a bloody war with the anti-Christ, usually the pope. Although kings and princes were often spared by the rebellious crowd, the nobility was acutely aware of the need to keep the masses under tight control. Sir Thomas More draws the picture of a perfect society in a true tongue-in-cheek manner in his famous book *The Best State of a Commonwealth and the New Island of Utopia* (1516) and contributed the term "utopia" (a Greek derivative meaning "nowhere") to the English language. Written in Latin (the elitist More never intended his book to be read by the common lot), *Utopia* is written as a dialogue between More and Raphael Hythlodeus (whose surname is a Greek word meaning "learned in nonsense"), a diplomat from the mysterious island Utopia. Hythlodeus tells More that Utopia is a planner's dream. All the public decisions are based on "rational functionality." For example, unlike in More's England, there is no death penalty for stealing. This is because a man who knows that he has nothing to lose if he is caught committing a petty theft will not hesitate to kill his captors.[50] Instead, the thieves in Utopia are sold into slavery, where they can increase the wealth of the nation. Lest they run away, their hair is cropped above their partially chopped-off ears. The slaves are put to death only if they are seen talking to other slaves, a reasonable measure, once again, to prevent slave rebellion. Realizing where the true danger lurks, the Utopians reserve the death penalty for rebellion by slaves, for the second offense of adultery, and for discussing politics outside the Senate.[51]

Machiavelli was a more astute observer of social behavior than the religiously motivated More. Machiavelli found sound political reason to establish a rule of law, which gave the masses a stake in their own governance. In medieval times, war was the business of every prince; if he did not take the initiative, he was likely to lose his advantage by having to fight his opponents at their chosen time and place. However, fighting a war is an expensive proposition. Fighting forces could be assembled from the allies of the prince, by recruiting a mercenary force, or by creating his own militia with the willing help of his subjects. Machiavelli advised his prince to choose the third option. He reasoned that the allies would fight for their own self-interest and, therefore, would likely be most unreliable when their interests would come in conflict. Having a mercenary force was extremely expensive and required taxing one's subjects to the point of economic ruin. Further, a strong and disloyal mercenary force increases the risk of a military coup. Therefore, Machiavelli wanted the prince to safeguard the rights of his subjects so that when the moment came to bear arms, they would do so willingly to preserve their lives and liberty.

The sight of a murderous mob during the French Revolution left an indelible mark on the hearts and minds of intellectuals in Europe. After all, the Paris riots of 1789 turned into something much bigger—the French Revolution. The stories—some true, some highly exaggerated—of rampant looting and destruction of the most civilized city on earth shook up Europe.

Fear of the mob played a large role in the writing of *The Federalist Papers* across the Atlantic. In the nascent United States, the authors stressed the need for a strong government to counter the threat of rising demands from the masses.

The cause of the rebel was not served well in the aristocratic circles of haughty academics and the literati by the rise of Karl Marx and his followers.

The rise of the Paris Commune and the accompanying riots instilled a tremendous fear among those holding the reins of power. To the beleaguered upper crust of society, it was a serious problem of securing the gate, a constant vigil to protect the citadel from the hungry crowd laying siege to the civilized order of the privileged. As the essentially decentralized medieval political order changed into the nineteenth-century nation-states in Europe, the metamorphosis provided the crowd with ready targets of derision, the center of political power. So it is hardly surprising that nineteenth-century theorists were apt to compare the crowd of their own day to the barbarian armies that sacked Rome. In their stereotype of the barbarian mind, they saw the same predominance of emotion over reason, hostility toward expressions of civility, and unquestioned obedience to the leader. Extending this logic of mistrusting the wisdom of the crowd, John Stuart Mill argued in 1861 that democracy was impossible in multiethnic societies, especially in those where the population was subdivided into divergent linguistic groups.[52]

French social thinker Gustave Le Bon, a physician by training, watched with extreme fascination mixed with revulsion the rebellious mob going through the streets of Paris, destroying everything that he cherished as a civilized man. "How could rational men do such a thing?" he asked. In the ultimate analysis, the answer to his rhetorical question turned out to be that, when in a group, men don't act rationally or even like *men*. Le Bon repeatedly compared the impulsiveness, "incapacity to reason, absence of judgment, and exaggeration of the sentiments" that characterize a crowd to the tendencies found in "inferior forms of evolution—in women, savages and children, for instance."[53] Le Bon observed three qualities in a crowd: suggestibility, impulsiveness, and changeability.

Amazingly, Le Bon's book, first published in 1877, is still being brought out in new editions, with the introduction written by yet another erudite scholar of the day. Its runaway success is explained by the fact that Le Bon really created a bogeyman, a monster. Like the great ape King Kong or the great white shark of the movie *Jaws*, this was the "crowd man." Le Bon ensured that we fully understood the vicious, bloodthirsty nature of this malevolent beast by repeatedly using capital letters to emphasize his points. We feel fascinated by Le Bon's analysis; we are repulsed by the beastly crowd-man, and yet are drawn to it from our primordial fear of being seduced by its uninhibited glee of acting upon our hidden passions. Looking at Le Bon's monster, we see the darker side of our character; we are afraid to see our own faces in the mirror. We hear the frightful din of breaking glass shattering in the still Kristallnacht, looting, burning, creating mayhem, feeling a rush of the stuff that makes our hearts beat faster, shamefully and at the same time with a wild pleasure, being a part of that group. In sum, we fail to trust our own sanity. Therefore, even after a century, Le Bon's monster, like Mary Shelley's *Frankenstein*, remains popular.

Sigmund Freud was much impressed with the astute observations of Le Bon. In his later life, Freud became interested in extending his individual-based psychological theories to society in the aggregate. Unlike another famous Hegelian, Karl Marx, Freud did not see the evolution of society as the outcome of a dialectical conflict between economic classes; instead, his dialectics involved conflicts between love and death, Eros and destruction. To him, people in society relate to one another through libidinal ties.[54] Freud criticized Marx and his followers for assuming, like Rousseau, that humans are instinctively good. He also found no reason to believe that aggression at the social level would disappear once private property is abolished. Freud generally agreed that aggressive behavior is linked to a feeling of frustration or provocation by external forces. However, above all to him, aggression is instinctive; it is buried deep inside the subconscious as a secret "death wish," which, in turn, is related to suppressed sexuality. Therefore, Freud reasoned that, while aspects of economic privation are important factors for generating social conflict, they are not the strongest; aggression resulting from sexuality will prevail even in a classless society. Freudian men are, therefore, driven by the instinctive force of a secret death wish and are bound to everyone else in the crowd by a feeling of subconsciously repressed sexuality.

At this point, Freud disagreed with Le Bon. Le Bon's crowd man, like the Roman citizens of *Julius Caesar,* is simply an irrational human being, living at the very edge of his emotions. But Freud saw order even in this disorder, a reason in their madness—the arousal that one feels in being part of a crowd is real. It is similar to intense sexual arousal, linked directly from an individual participant to the leader of the crowd, on one hand, and the hated enemy figure, on the other. The lowly followers are attached to their leader, who serves as their surrogate father. In contrast, they relate to the authority figure against whom they are taking up violent action as a part of their Oedipal complex. Like the mythical Greek king Oedipus, men of our species feel a primal jealousy toward their father for having sex with their mother. This suppressed jealousy takes its most violent form in patricide; a revolutionary sees in the authority figure his own father, whom he tries to slay in his own subliminal drive. In contrast, a female revolutionary acts upon her subconscious jealousy because she lacks the dangling appendage between her legs, what Freud called "penis envy."[55]

Psychologists often tell us that we frequently do things in a group that we would never do on our own. Therefore, Le Bon's arguments assume that nobody is able to resist his impulses in a crowd. However, the problem with such a blanket assertion about human behavior is that if the seduction of a group were that compelling, everyone would eventually join one marauding group or another. Violence would never end.

THE WAR OF THE WORLDS: INDIVIDUAL VS. COLLECTIVE

There are two worlds, one based on the unquestioned primacy of individual rights, and the other based on the premise of a collective good and the corresponding unquestioned authority of a few to articulate those goods for the rest of the society. As they collide and confront, repel and resist, they also are drawn to one another in an inseparable embrace. For too long, the two combatants have eyed each other with suspicion. The daily news amply reflects this contradiction. While Western Europe, prompted by new technology, expands trade, and while a commonality of worldview attempts to forge an integrated political entity, subnational aspirations rise in many parts of the world, including even Western nations such as Canada, Belgium, and Spain. In the former Soviet Empire, like the Russian doll, as one nation breaks away, new demands for separation arise from groups within it.

The leaders of all shades of collective ideology have articulated their fears with the help of the most vivid imageries. Listen to the sermons of the Ayatollah Khomeini, the speeches of the leaders of the Cultural Revolution in China, or even the proponents of hyper-nationalism. In all of these speeches and writings, the champions of collectivism denigrate the heretical cult of the individual. To the defenders of God, individualism is vile, egotistical, and immoral. To the communists, it is exploitative, rapacious, and predatory. And to the hyper-nationalists, it is bent on destroying the glorious tradition and values of the nation, tribe, or clan.

In *Jihad v. McWorld*, Benjamin Barber argues that in today's world, individualism pushed to the limits is epitomized as the McWorld, which is locked in an eternal fight with the forces of jihad. Colorfully, Barber paints the rival scenarios:

The first scenario . . . holds out the grim prospect of a retribalization of large swaths of humankind by war and bloodshed: a threatened balkanization of nation-states in which culture is pitted against culture, people against people, tribe against tribe, a Jihad in the name of a hundred narrowly conceived faiths against every kind of interdependence, every kind of artificial social cooperation and mutuality: against technology, against pop culture, and against integrated markets; against modernity itself as well as the future in which modernity issues. The second paints that future in shimmering pastels, a busy portrait of onrushing economic, technological, and ecological forces that demand integration and uniformity and that mesmerize peoples everywhere with fast music, fast computers, and fast food—MTV, Macintosh, and McDonald's—pressing nations into one global theme park, one McWorld tied together by communications, information, entertainment, and commerce. Caught between Babel and Disneyland, the planet is falling precipitously apart and coming reluctantly together at the very same moment.[56]

Mutual fear has guided publication of many acclaimed books and articles on both sides of the divide. Periodically, super-nationalistic books peddling fear of the West become instant bestsellers in Japan and China. Likewise, using a much simpler paradigm of cultural fault lines based on Christianity on one hand, Islam and other Eastern religions on the other, Harvard political scientist Samuel Huntington argues for an inevitable clash of civilizations.[57] He sees the difference between Christianity and other religious views, whether in Japan and Singapore or in the non–Judeo-Christian Middle East, as being so great that, as Rudyard Kipling prophesied, East and West shall never meet.

In this scenario, both are hostile and both are fearful of the other. In the West, the fear of the "collective bogey-man" has inspired innumerable novels, notably in science fiction, where we project our current anxiety into the future. Aldous Huxley saw a brave new world where the rights of individuals did not matter to the collective society. Similarly, George Orwell in *1984* drew a bleak picture of a collective society. Motion picture director Stanley Kubrick in *A Clockwork Orange* made us shudder at the prospect of the triumph of the collective over the individual. Perhaps the most quintessential of American television series, *Star Trek* often introduced us to this alarming prospect. This theme runs through a number of episodes (the Klingons as a group are, after all, a lot more controlled than those belonging to the United Federation of Planets).[58] However, it is particularly obvious in one episode, where Captain James T. Kirk and his crew battle the sinister forces of Landrew, which reduce individuals into a collective "body." As Kirk destroys the machine that kept the inhabitants of this planet under Landrew's spell, individualism sprouts everywhere like spring flowers; we are told with a great deal of satisfaction that incidents of individual quarrels and fist fights are being reported all over the place. With that comforting piece of news, we feel relieved as the starship *Enterprise* sails off into unknown space for yet another encounter with yet another sinister alien force, presumably yet another one of the collective.

NOTES

1. Musgrove (1977: 1).
2. Quoted in Mansbridge (1990: 7).
3. Of course, both communism and nationalism were European inventions. However, in the post–World War context, they are in the domain of non-Western social philosophy.
4. See Hayek (1988).
5. See Diamond (1992: 23).
6. The primate groups, however, do not live in idyllic conditions of peace and harmony. For example, Jane Goodall and de Waal report many "human" vices, including infanticide, cannibalism, and murder, among the chimpanzee groups. See Goodall (1986, 1990). Also see de Waal (1982); Keeley (1996); Diamond (1992); Alcock (1984).
7. See Goodall (1991).
8. de Waal (1986: 237–51).
9. See Wrangham and Peterson (1996).
10. See Campbell (1968).
11. In an old Sanskrit saying recited over and over to many school children in Northern India, they were told that "your father is the creed, the heaven, the ultimate

of all devotion. The pleasing of the father puts a smile on all the gods in heaven." In another often repeated hymn, the children were told that "mother and motherland are more glorious than heaven."

12. See Sen (1984).

13. See Arrow (1963).

14. See Stone (1973: 229).

15. See Belting (1994).

16. *The Tragedy of Romeo and Juliet* has been interpreted and reinterpreted over the years. Such interpretations range from the lovers' star-crossed fate, to the Freudian view of the young lovers' subconscious death-wish, to love conquers hate, to the neo-orthodox Elizabethan dangers of passion. The story of Romeo and Juliet was already an old one when Shakespeare decided to dramatize it for the Elizabethan stage. There were at least a half dozen versions of the story circulating in Italy, France, and England. However, the earlier versions lack "the sense of mutual dedication and individual purpose that inspires Romeo and Juliet" (Cole 1970: 5).

17. Quoted in Stone (1978: 467).

18. Ibid.

19. Ibid., 468.

20. See Boorstin (1983: xv).

21. Foucault (1970: xi).

22. Ibid., xxiii.

23. For a discussion of economic rationality, see Becker (1976b); also see Muth (1961).

24. The apparent link between wealth and the natural selection of the "fittest" in the marketplace did not escape notice and, as part of social Darwinism, continued to influence many writers. For instance, Milton Friedman (1953) argued the complementarity of Darwin's theory of evolution and the market process. Friedman argues that market competition represents a Darwinian process that produces exactly the same results that would follow if all consumers maximized their utility and all business firms maximized their profits. For an excellent analysis, see Blaug (1980: 180).

25. See Schumpeter (1961).

26. Freud (1930: 102).

27. Quoted in Blaug (1968: 221). Emphasis added.

28. Blaug (1968: 589).

29. See Milton Friedman (1962). Emphasis added.

30. For a discussion of the inherent message of optimism of neoclassical development economic literature, see Yotopoulos and Nugent (1976: 9).

31. Sartre (1948: 13) proclaimed "Existence before essence."

32. Like a cranky curmudgeon, Allan Bloom laments the situation thus: "The family['s] spiritual void has left the field open to rock music, and they cannot possibly forbid their children to listen to it. It is everywhere; all children listen to it; forbidding would simply cause them to lose their children's affection. . . . If he has early sex, that won't get in the way of his having stable relationships later. His drug use will certainly stop at pot" (1987: 76).

33. For a brilliant discussion, see Sabine (1969).

34. The question of who speaks for the society has engaged much of the debate in the area of welfare economics. Through the celebrated work of Kenneth Arrow

(1963) and Sen (1984) we have learned the impossibility of defining the true choice of the society, unless one makes some extraordinary set of restrictive (and highly unrealistic) assumptions.

35. See Fukuyama (1992).

36. Max Weber, however, found within the Protestant belief structure the seeds of individualism.

37. Since the labor theory of value is the stepping stone of Marxist dogma, some critics have contended that it is a fetter to the overall Marxist theory. See, for example, Ian Steedman (1977).

38. See Shils (1981: 94).

39. John Bramhall, *The Catching of Leviathan* (1658), quoted in Mansbridge (1990b: 306).

40. For a brilliant discussion of life inside Khomeini's Iran, see V. S. Naipaul (1981). Also see his later assessment (1997).

41. Potter Stewart, "I know [pornography] when I see it." *Jacobellis v. Ohio,* 378 U.S. 184, 197 (1964).

42. Walter Bagehot, *Physics and Politics* (1887), quoted in Hobsbawm (1990: ii).

43. Hobsbawm (1990).

44. See Stalin (1975: 12).

45. In fact, by the indicators of a monolingual, mono-religious, mono-ethnic "nation state" standard, only Iceland may qualify for a full nation status. See Ra'anam (1990).

46. See Pfaff (1993).

47. Plato (1963: 492).

48. Aristotle noted: "In every state the people are divided into three kinds: the very rich, the very poor, and thirdly, those who are between them. Since, then, it is universally acknowledged that the mean is best, it is evident that . . . a middle state is to be preferred; for that state is most likely to submit to reason" (*Politics,* iv.11). Aristotle further added a grave word of warning: "But it is clear that the state where middle rank predominates is the best, for it alone is free from seditious movements. Where such a state is large, there are fewer seditions and insurrections to disturb the peace; and for this reason extensive states are more peaceful internally, as the middle ranks are numerous. In small states it is easy to pass the two extremes, so as to have scarcely any middle ranks remaining; but all are either very poor or very rich."

49. The fragmentation of the political states diverted the focus of popular wrath of the medieval crowd from the king to the Church with its center and the symbolic seat of power in the Vatican. In an excellent exposition of the history of crowd psychology, McClelland pointed out:

Popular revolts were bound to peter out in societies in which rule was so diffused that there was no centre of sovereignty which could be assaulted, even symbolically. Medieval kingdoms had no Bastilles. The only thing that looked like a centre was monarchy, and the only chance a leader of popular revolt had of succeeding was to pretend to be a forgotten and sleeping king suddenly awakened. (1989: 64)

50. It is interesting to note the similarity of arguments used by the critics of the current "three strikes and you are out" policy of crime control some 500 years after More.

51. See Ridely (1983).

52. See Mill (1861).

53. Le Bon (1960: 15).

54. Freud observed:

We see that [culture] endeavors to bind the members of the community to one another by libidinal ties as well, that it makes use of every means and favours every avenue by which powerful identification can be created among them, and that it exacts a heavy toll of aim-inhibited libido in order to strengthen communities by bonds of friendship between members. Restrictions upon sexual life are unavoidable if this object is to be attained. (1929: 80–81)

55. See Wolfenstein (1967).

56. Barber (1995: 4).

57. I posit that Huntington's arguments are based on the shallowest understanding of religion as a unifying force in history. Throughout history, religion alone has never provided common ground for disparate people to get together either to form a nation or to establish a new world order. The worldwide spread of Islam soon broke up into hundreds of factions and subfactions. Crusaders left a dubious mark on history as to their true purpose and their ultimate contribution to the Christian world. Religion as the sole rallying point made little sense in the medieval period; it makes even less sense today. See Huntington (1996).

58. This is also true of George Lucas' Star Wars series. The members of the Empire are all faceless robotic characters, while the opposition is fiercely individualistic.

CHAPTER 3

THE CONFUSIONS OF A SINGULAR WORLDVIEW

Rationality *requires* inaction.

—James Buchanan[1]

[P]eople who 'really care' about an issue can . . . overcome all difficulties.

—Jack Nagel[2]

First we will kill all the subversives; then we will their collaborators; then their sympathizers; then the indifferent, and finally the timid.

—A former governor of Buenos Aires[3]

THE PUZZLE

"The fire of Waco was burning inside the man." Recalling the 1993 siege of a fundamentalist Christian enclave in Texas by agents of the U.S. government that ended in the fiery death of seventy-four people—men, women and children, Timothy McVeigh's lawyer attempted feebly to explain his client's part in the 1995 Oklahoma City bombing, the largest act of terrorism on the U.S. soil.[4] McVeigh bombed the Murrah Federal Building in Oklahoma City because he was upset about the U.S. Government's role in Waco. In his futile bid to save McVeigh from a certain death sentence, his attorney tried to put a human face on him. "Do not demonize this man, he can be your son," his court appointed defense team pleaded with the jury and, in fact, the entire nation, to soften the image of the convicted bomber and spare him from the ultimate punishment.

Yet, to the nation, at one level, it was easier to understand another home-grown terrorist, the so-called Unabomber, the mentally unstable Theodore Kaczynski. The motivations of the hermit, environmental zealot, and former Berkeley mathematics professor were comfortably "irrational." We recognized him as such. His apparent mental depravity provided a ready answer to the curious nation. But Tim McVeigh, the quintessential "boy next door"? In his relaxed moments, videotapes of which were shown over and over on television during his trial, he could have been the young man who brought home his date a bit too late for her parents' comfort. His quick yet shy smile on a boyish face certainly did not make him look like a monster. But, as the jury saw him when the government witnesses spoke about Waco, his relaxed mood disappeared quickly. McVeigh clutched the railing hard, turning his knuckles white; his eyes narrowed, facial muscles tight, the jury saw the face of a killer who acted with extreme premeditation and with no regard for the lives of innocent people, young, old, men, women, black, white, government employees, and innocent bystanders. In his face, there was no trace of compassion for the relatives of the victims, no remorse for the wanton devastation brought about by his act against his own people. Yet, ironically, these were the same people, the same nation, the same government for whom only a few years earlier he was ready to lay down his own life. A decorated Gulf War veteran, known for his valor—kind, considerate, and dedicated to his friends and comrades—Timothy McVeigh instantly became an enigma to a bewildered nation. After the trial, the jury was reassembled for a press conference. A reporter asked, if they could address one question to Tim McVeigh, what would it be? The former jurors, after hearing weeks of testimony and observing Timothy McVeigh at close proximity in a confined courtroom, without hesitation and in unison, replied, "Why?"

Repugnant as it was, McVeigh's act is fundamentally different from those committed by other mass murderers, from Jack the Ripper to Theodore Bundy. While these mass or serial killers kill out of personal rage, for sexual gratification, or for profit (if it is done during a robbery), collective activists all over the world—from left, right, and center—kill in the name of a cause. If we want to understand their motivation, we must understand the call of the collective.

In the previous chapter, I traced the path of our intellectual evolution, which pitted the motivations of individuals against those of the collective. However, these philosophical questions relate to the overall perspective of the society. In this chapter, I look at individual motivations. Drawing upon the actions of the likes of Timothy McVeigh, I seek the answer to the jurors' question in the labyrinth of microeconomic theory. In this chapter I demonstrate the inadequacy of traditional economic reasoning, based squarely on the assumption of self-utility, in understanding people's collective motivations. Since microeconomic arguments form the basis of much of political science and sociology under the rubric of "public choice theory," it is important to show why we need to expand our behavioral assumptions. Toward this goal, I first discuss the problem known in the literature as the "social dilemma," then attempt to demonstrate that under the assumption of the self-utility maximizing *Homo economicus,* there is no getting around the dilemma without altering the basic behavioral assumption.

SOCIAL DILEMMA: OLSON'S PARADOX

Among social scientists only economists attempt to model human behavior by using a universal behavioral precept. For them, a human being is a perennial short-term utility maximizer.[5] Evolved over 200 years of intellectual development, the self-utility maximizing creature known as *Homo economicus,* economic man, assumes the central position in economic analyses. Economic historian Mark Blaug attributes the first articulation of economic man to John Mill Senior's famous 1836 essay, "On the Definition of Political Economy."[6] In his article, Mill states: "What is now commonly understood by the term 'Political Economy' . . . makes entire abstraction of every other human passion or motive; except those which may be regarded as perpetually antagonizing principles to the desire of wealth, namely, aversion to labour, and the desire of the present enjoyment of costly indulgences."[7] The behavioral assumption of economic man was originally developed to analyze market behavior.[8] Early economists were preoccupied understanding supply and demand of physical commodities. In contrast, when people engage in political activities, they aim at getting "public goods," many of which are not bought and sold in the market. However, the success of the economic paradigm in analyzing and predicting short-term market behavior encouraged others to enlarge its domain. Therefore, the question of participation in the attainment of public goods remained outside the purview of the discipline until recently.

By definition, a public good has two characteristics. First, public goods are for joint consumption. In other words, if I am consuming (or deriving utility from) a public good, its consumption by an additional person would not diminish my utility from it. Thus, the birth of a baby does not reduce my sense of security from foreign invasion; it costs no more to defend a country of 1 million people than to defend a country of 999,999. Second, it is impossible to exclude individuals from the enjoyment of a public good. For instance, if our national defense force is successful in averting an attack from abroad, everybody in the country benefits; there is no way we could exclude any single inhabitant of the country from the benefits of a secure land.

Standard neoclassical economics has no problem in laying down rules for private goods, based on the assumption of self-interest. It is the allocation of public goods that creates problems. Being totally self-motivated, pure economic man is a one-dimensional creature who is not inspired by the good of the collective. Yet, as we look around, we can readily see that our lives are surrounded by public goods that have been attained by placing the interests of the group above those of individuals. Within a family parents frequently forgo the desire for immediate personal consumption, saving money for their children's education (a public good from the perspective of the family). But how do we decide to get these public goods? How do utterly selfish individuals get together to provide many of these goods that we take for granted? In fact, that is the biggest unanswered theoretical question in economics: *How are public goods provided?*

Most economists would readily agree that such a truncated behavioral assumption compresses a complex multidimensional being into the straitjacket of a unidimensional character. However, success in predicting short-run market behavior based on this cryptic assumption has given *Homo economicus,* the veritable caricature of a market-driven, soulless man, a permanent place in the discipline of mainstream economics. In fact, maximization of self-utility is regarded as the "fundamental assumption"—the starting point—of all economic analysis. Despite its obvious shortcomings, so successful has this reductionist assumption of human nature been that it is used widely in the sister disciplines of political science and sociology under the rubric of "public choice."[9]

The use of a self-utility maximizing being as the model in the discipline of political science, however, poses some rather intractable conceptual problems. Political science is preoccupied with collective action. After all, if we follow the history of the word *politics* far enough, we will discover its beginning in the Greek word *polites,* or "citizens." And *polites* is derived from *polis,* "city."[10] Since cities were nation-states in ancient Greece, today's English words "politics" and "political" are inextricably intertwined with the collective bodies of human society. Yet adherence to the assumption of *Homo economicus* creates a stumbling block for understanding the motives which may prompt a rational human being to take part in actions for the greater good of the collective at the expense of his own.

Economist Mancur Olson first demonstrated the logical lapses of a model of human behavior based on self-utility alone.[11] In his much-celebrated book, *The Logic of Collective Action,* Olson points out that, if collective actions are undertaken by the participants to obtain a public good, then it is irrational for anyone to participate in a collective movement.[12] This is because a public good, by definition, benefits everyone in a group but costs only those who decide to participate. In simple terms, if you can get the benefits without paying for them, then why pay?

Consider the following example. Suppose it is in the interest of every member of a group to get rid of a tyrant who is ruling the nation with an iron fist. If the citizens succeed in getting rid of him, each one of them will enjoy the fruits of freedom. Yet, as each individual citizen ponders his or her options, the picture is abundantly clear. If the tyrant is removed, everybody in the nation benefits. However, the costs of attempts to remove him (the possibility of loss of income, social privileges, physical security, liberty, even life) fall primarily on those who dare to challenge the despot. Thus, in this scheme, the choice between participation and nonparticipation can be expressed as follows:

Revolutionary = Benefit (freedom) + costs (physical punishment, social and economic loss)

Free rider = Benefit (freedom)

Judging from this angle, every "rational" individual would rather be a free rider and wait for the others to volunteer to fight for everyone else's freedom. The dilemma of participation gets deeper as the size of the group increases. In a small group, it is conceivable that the probability of achieving a particular public good may increase with the participation of each additional member, but in a large group the impact of one additional member's participation is nearly zero. Also, in a small group other members keep an eye on those who fail to comply and can bring social pressure to bear on them. In contrast, in a large group where there is no one to detect defection and each member realizes the insignificance of his or her own contribution, prospective participants will tend not to join. Thus, in a society of "perfectly rational" individuals, no public good will ever be produced. In fact, it is difficult to imagine how a group of *Homo economicus* would even form a society.

Drawing on the problems of free-ridership, Gordon Tullock, one of the pioneers of the "public choice" school of political economy, posed what he called the "paradox of revolution."[13] Tullock states that those who claim to take part in a revolutionary movement out of purely altruistic concerns are either irrational or have ulterior motives of personal gain.[14] Hence, the explanation of "rational choice" theory of an individual's participation in a collective movement is based either on logical incoherence or on plain political hypocrisy. Therefore, by not accepting the inspiration of the collective, in the "public choice" analysis there is no difference between the motivations of a common criminal and a political activist.

This line of argument leads us to conclude that Henry Longfellow's adulation of Paul Revere was either misplaced or misunderstood, for Revere was riding through the New England towns in the cool April night warning the townsfolk of an impending British attack not out of any sense of "patriotism." He must have either anticipated some personal gain (perhaps a higher sale of his silver and copperplated engravings, or at least the adoration of his fellow colonists), or he was getting some irrational pleasure from his nocturnal activities. Similarly, we would presume that when a young Tamil woman tied belts of explosives around her body, shook hands with the ex–prime minister of India Rajiv Gandhi, and then coolly pulled the string of the detonator, she was merely trying to maximize her self-interest. And when the *kamikaze* pilots of the Imperial Japanese Air Force in their last act of patriotism crashed their planes onto the invading ships, they were either insane (acting upon irrational sentiment) or were revealing their idiosyncratic taste.

Collective actions, however, do not have to be as dramatic as the act of a suicide bomber. They are part and parcel of everyday life. As social beings, we solve problems of Olson's dilemma in almost every instance of our conscious and unconscious decision-making processes. Collective actions—from raising a family to participation in revolutionary acts—are part of our daily lives.

The solution to the free rider problem can take many forms. For instance, the elderly may opt to pay higher taxes for better public schools even when they no longer have school-age children or grandchildren[15]; we may dutifully take the trouble of locking our car door knowing full well that we are insured against theft[16]; workers in large organizations do an honest day's work without shirking their responsibilities even when their chance of getting caught is minimal[17]; people keep commitments even when offered a chance to renege[18]; common folks, such as the Minutemen during the American Revolution or in any other war of patriotism or ideology, participate at the risk of great physical injury and even death.[19]

We take part in collective actions, overcoming Olson's paradox, also known as the "social dilemma," without much trouble. The question, however, remains how to explain it within the only paradigm of human behavior that is available to the social scientists. Confronting this logical dilemma, we can either (a) dismiss participation in collective actions as acts of emotion (or "taste") which fall outside of rational calculation, or (b) seek partial solutions to the conceptual quagmire.

DISREGARDING THE DILEMMA

The narrow definition of human rationality has caused social scientists on both sides of the conceptual divide to circumvent the dilemma. Thus, in his early work, political scientist Ted Gurr advanced the theory of relative deprivation, which implies that people rebel when they don't get what they believe to be their legitimate due.[20] In sociology, Neil Smelser argued that social imbalances, such as discrepancies in status, income, and so on, cause turmoil.[21] Similarly, scholars such as Skocpol, who analyzed the causes of revolution,[22] or Arendt, who explored the minds of genocidal killers such as Eichmann, have done so without paying any attention to this theoretical conundrum.[23] Some have argued that it is the mobilization of potential participants that creates a "bandwagon effect" to draw more people into a collective action.[24] In sociology, one dominant group of theoreticians argues that in order to mount a social movement, the most critical ingredient is the garnering of resources; like any organization, a movement requires trained personnel, means of communication and transportation, and so on.[25] Movements that are able to amass the necessary resources are successful.[26] Following these lines of arguments, an impressive amount of scholarly effort was directed toward developing statistical models correlating rebellions with various indicators of deprivation, social imbalances, and acquiring of resources.[27]

However, there is one huge conceptual problem on this side of the argument also. Although these larger macro theories ignore the problem of individual participation, they imply another kind of inevitability: when there is widespread relative deprivation or deep imbalances in the structure of a society, there will always be a rebellion. Yet, history tells us that many endure even the most extreme cases of social injustice without rising up in rebellion.

Therefore, the practitioners of collective action—the Marxist revolutionary writers, such as Lenin, Trotsky, Mao, and Castro—have implicitly recognized the free-rider problem. On the one hand, Marx professed the inevitability of social evolution toward communism, yet, at the same time, he recognized the need to organize the oppressed class into a revolutionary force; the proletarians were exhorted by his famous phrase in his *Manifesto*, "You have nothing but your chains to lose." This contradiction played out in later debate among the Marxists between those who wanted to organize labor and peasants into an army of revolution and those who believed that such efforts are pointless in view of the inevitable destiny of social evolution.[28]

Therefore, in sum, *the problem with theories based on economic definitions of rationality is that they cannot explain why people actually take part in a collective action. In contrast, social theories which disregard the dilemma cannot explain why people often do not rebel.*[29]

THE PARTIAL SOLUTIONS

Political economist Mark Lichbach has argued in his massive work *The Rebel's Dilemma* that Olson's paradox can be partially addressed through what he calls *market, community, contract,* and *hierarchy*.[30] The market solution refers to the changing of a potential participant's perception of the benefits and costs of joining a collective action. The community solution is based on developing *Gemeinschaft*, a common belief system. The contract solution depends upon *Gesellschaft*, the portrayal of an enemy image, where neighbors keep an eye on neighbors for possible defection. And hierarchy solutions are predicated upon the formation of organizational hierarchy for an organized collective action.[31] Lichbach contends that market and community solutions take place in a largely unplanned way, while contract and hierarchy solutions require conscious planning.

Before delving deeper into the market solutions to Olson's paradox, we should further refine the decision scheme open to each individual member in considering whether to join a collective action. In the above discussion, I presented the scheme in a deterministic world of costs and benefits. However, in life neither the benefits nor the costs are certain. Few would join a collective action without even a seed of doubt about its prospects for success. Similarly, facing the option to join, few would know beforehand the exact probability of getting apprehended or the extent of the costs, which can vary from a relatively minor loss of time to the ultimate—the loss of life and liberty. Hence, following the rules of decision making under uncertain conditions, the scheme takes the following shape[32]:

Expected benefit = probability of success × the actual benefit

Expected cost = probability of incurring cost × the actual cost

The above scheme points to four components of the decision-making rule: benefits, costs, and their respective probabilities. Lichbach claims that a market solution to Olson's dilemma is reached when for an individual actor one or more components of the above decision scheme is altered either by the actions of the leadership or as the result of a change in an objective condition in the society. In such cases, an individual overcomes the dictates of economic rationality and joins the forces of collective rebellion.

There is, however, a big problem with finding a market solution to Olson's paradox. Microeconomic analyses can produce brilliant results when we consider a trade-off between two private goods, such as apples and oranges. They also provide invaluable insight into allocation of resources between present and future consumption. However, when the choice is between participation in a collective action or the pursuit of private utility there is hardly a simple solution.[33]

Take, for example, the case of increased benefits. If the price of apples goes down, we would tend to demand more of them. When the size of the prize goes up in a state lottery, people line up to buy tickets. However, when it comes to collective actions, such assumptions may not work, for two primary reasons. First, most outcomes (benefits) of collective action happen in the long run, yet the costs have to be paid immediately. Any "rational" actor engaged in the present value analysis of the net benefit of participation will soon find out the "irrationality" of participation in most collective movements.

The second problem stems from the fact that the exact nature of the benefits of collective action is often difficult to define. For instance, if I am involved in a collective action aimed at closing down an adult entertainment facility in my neighborhood, will I put forward more effort if offered work on a national morality campaign? Not necessarily. Former House Speaker Tip O'Neill made the phrase "all politics is local" part of the American political lexicon. This gem of wisdom from a seasoned politician underscores the basic fact of Olson's paradox: The larger the group size, the greater the temptation to ride free and to wait for others to do our bidding.

Even if the group size remains the same and the desired outcome gets more attractive, will people be more willing to participate? For instance, suppose I am part of in a national action committee trying to change a particular public policy supported by the president. Instead, I am offered the opportunity to participate in an effort to impeach him or to topple the entire administration. With everything else remaining the same, will we necessarily jump at the prospect? Since, unlike a private good, we may not be able to readily define what exactly is a "greater benefit" in the context of a public good, the answer is not going to be as obvious as choosing an apple over an orange.

In any case, the problem remains that the argument of increased benefits fails to overcome the social dilemma if the benefit gets distributed universally in the group and the costs fall only on the participants. If the paradox is not solved by increasing the amount of benefit, then how about the case when the increase in benefit is restricted to only those who participate? That is, if the revolution comes, these are the people who are going to be the "first among equals" for the spoils of war. Would not the prospect of a larger personal reward overcome the obstacles of the social dilemma? Sociologist Sidney Tarrow has attempted to show that selected benefits may prompt some to participate in collective action.[34] Unfortunately, the answer still remains an unequivocal "no." If we accept the proposition of differential individual benefit based on participation, the outcome no longer remains a pure public good, since *by definition* public good precludes restricted benefits to a selected group of individuals within a larger amalgam of beneficiaries.

If not benefit, how about considering a change in cost? Standard neoclassical economics argues that an increase in cost would reduce people's appetite for extralegal activities.[35] On the other hand, presumably a lowering of cost will induce many more fence sitters to join in the fray. Before examining this argument closely, let us define "costs" of participation in a collective action.

The costs of participation have two components, which we can alternately call *market* and *nonmarket* or *economic* and *noneconomic* costs. Market costs involve the loss of time and the consequent forgone income (the opportunity cost), while physical punishments (from beatings and imprisonment to death) imposed by the regime or the opposition group are classified as nonmarket costs of participation.

The case of opportunity cost is relatively clear-cut. Look at any picture coming from an area plagued by mass violence. You will see an overwhelming proportion of young unattached males among the participants. In most urban guerrilla groups, from the Shining Path in Peru to the Naxalites in India and the Basque nationalists in Spain or the various rebel forces in Africa, it is the youth who carry the torch of rebellion. The reason for this overwhelming participation rests with their low opportunity costs. Yet to enter the job market and often assured of free room and board from their families, young men and, in lesser numbers, women, fill the ranks of the revolutionaries.[36] Although the predominance of male faces is clearly evident in all collective movements, young women also take part in such activities in large numbers. Since women often did not take on formal employment, they had the time to join protest movements; women have historically been active in almost every collective movement. They joined in the French[37] and the Russian Revolutions in large numbers.[38] Women overwhelmingly supported the Gandhian anti-colonial movement in India.[39] Mothers of lost children in many parts of Latin America have carried on long-drawn-out protests.[40] Although some scholars have pointed out that women are often constrained by the demands of their reproductive activities and their domestic duties,[41] all over the world young women join terrorist organizations in significant numbers.[42] Just as low opportunity costs may prompt the young to take part in collective movements, high market costs of participation can prevent other groups from joining rebel forces. These are typically the peasants and the poorest of the poor—the *lumpenproletariat*. The peasants are difficult to recruit into the causes of revolution because they face extremely high opportunity costs of time. If they miss the planting season, they may have to starve for the rest of the year.[43] In his political rhetoric, Ho Chi Minh claimed that: "one becomes revolutionary because one is oppressed. The more oppressed one is, the more unshakably resolved one is to carry out the revolution."[44] Yet at the same time, like Mao and Lenin, Ho was careful to point out that before peasants take part in a collective movement, they must first be carefully indoctrinated.[45]

The nonmarket or the physical side of cost is what a government or an opposing party imposes on the dissidents. Naturally, the extent (the probability of getting caught) and severity of punishment vary from nation to nation. Thus, in a totalitarian nation, such as in today's China, the dissidents risk a far greater chance of being apprehended than in a less coercive society such as India. Also, once apprehended, punishment is likely to be heavier in Communist China than in democratic India.

However, the real puzzle is to formulate a rule as to how people are likely to alter their behavior in the face of an increased level of coercion. Economic theory predicts that as costs increase, an individual's desire to participate decreases correspondingly.[46] If the price of beef goes up, we consume less beef. Yet, the link between participation and punishment is anything but clear.[47] For instance, alongside the argument of fear as deterrence, we can also argue that to resist force with counterforce is part and parcel of human nature. Therefore, as repression rises, so does the urge to apply counterforce. According to this line of reasoning, an increase in the costs of participation would lead to more, rather than fewer, dissident activities.[48] For instance, the tactics of open repression used in 1963 by Sheriff Eugene "Bull" Connor of Birmingham only helped solidify the opposition among the civil rights activists. Facing these two opposing views, even empirical studies fail to provide a definitive resolution. Some argue that when a regime applies coercive force, dissident activities go up in democratic regimes; in nondemocratic nations, they also go up, but after a threshold of high protest and high repression, antigovernment movements are squashed into silence.[49] Others have hypothesized that although coercion reduces the level of rebellion, it is only a short-run solution. In the long run, past repression helps escalate dissent.[50] Yet others argue that coercion causes rebel groups to change their tactics; in response to the government's tactics, dissident groups switch between violent and nonviolent forms of protest.[51]

It is reasonable to assume that a change in the perceived probability of success would encourage a prospective participant to take part in a collective action.[52] Thus, if I am convinced that a successful revolution is at hand, I may be more willing to jump on the bandwagon. Even in this case, the simple logic of economic rationality may not hold water for collective action. However, let us first discuss how the percived probability of success can change. Then I will demonstrate why an increase in the probability of success may not draw more participants into a collective movement.

Probability of success of a collective movement can increase for one or more reasons. The political leadership can take certain strategic actions that may cause the potential participants to perceive an increased probability of success. These actions would include nonviolent actions, such as a work slowdown,[53] to acts of violent terrorism.[54] In fact, all of these political actions are designed to communicate with a certain audience. Through political actions, a dissident organization sends messages about its strength or its moral or ideological stance to potential participants, the enemy camp, or its benefactors.

Individual inertia in joining a collective action can be successfully overcome by blocking all sources of information but those coming from the group's leader. All enforcers of the collective will—from Mao and the Ayatollah Khomeini to Jim Jones—have created a basic asymmetry of information between leaders and followers.[55] The dissident organization attempts to maintain this asymmetry of information by making the cost of getting information favorable to the group cheap and/or by making the cost of receiving contrary information expensive. The former is accomplished through ample propaganda, while the latter is imposed through punishment. Anyone visiting a country based on collective values is immediately struck by the pervasiveness of propaganda, from billboards to state-controlled newspapers and radio and television broadcasts extolling the virtues of the group's worldview. At the same time, one of the most treasonous offenses for the populace of such nations can be reading magazines and newspapers not published by the state-controlled presses, or receiving foreign radio and television broadcasts. These acts of defiance are accorded the severest punishments in collective countries from North Korea to Saudi Arabia. All of these acts are designed to keep followers convinced of the overwhelming power of the group leaders and the consequent probability of attaining the promised goals.

However, an increase in the probability of winning may not be sufficient in prompting a prospective participant to join the forces of rebellion. Unfortunately, as the probability of success increases, Olson's paradox once again rears its ugly head. With the goals increasingly at hand, a "rational" human being is apt to argue for less participation, since no one wants to be the last casualty of the war. If every potential participant made decisions according to the precept of economic rationality, no war would ever be won, no revolution would be complete, no collective good would be attained.[56]

REALITY AT RISK: A THEORIST'S CONUNDRUM

Lichbach argues that the rebel's dilemma can be solved through market solutions of lowering costs or by altering the probabilities of costs and benefits.

This may be true in the "real world," but, unfortunately, in the conceptual world, where many of Lichbach's arguments reside, he chases his own shadow. On the one hand, as he correctly points out, "The Rebel's Dilemma . . . holds. If the benefits, however massive, accrue to a dissident, regardless of his or her actions, why pay *any* costs?"[57] He is absolutely correct: Why pay *any* cost when you can get away with paying nothing? However, only a few pages later, he squarely contradicts himself by saying, "The *Lower Costs* solutions to the Rebel's Dilemma prove to be particularly insightful."[58] Read side by side, the two statements amply reveal their contradiction.

The truth of the matter is that *the dilemma rests squarely with the academics who pose this contrived riddle based on a truncated assumption of human behavior. If we accept the behavioral assumption of Homo economicus, then there is no conceptual solution to the social dilemma whatsoever, total or partial.* In contrast, to a living, breathing activist in collective actions of every sort, it is not an insoluble problem. Elinor Ostrom says it best in the opening statement of her presidential address to the 1997 American Political Science Association meeting:

> Let me start with a provocative statement. You would not be reading this article if it were not for some [of] our ancestors learning how to undertake collective action to solve social dilemmas. Successive generations have added to the stock of everyday knowledge about how to instill productive norms of behavior in their children and to craft rules to support collective action that produces public goods and avoids 'tragedies of commons.' What our ancestors and contemporaries have learned about engaging in collective action for mutual defense, child rearing, and survival is not, however, understood or explained by the extant theory of collective action.[59]

FINDING FAULT WITH *HOMO ECONOMICUS*

Criticisms of the assumption of self-interest as the lone human motivator are as old as the assumption itself. Apart from the problem of lack of realism and the conceptual free-rider problem, this restrictive assumption has important shortcomings far beyond its inability to explain collective action.

The most glaring problem with this assumption is that it fails us both in prescription and in prediction. Thus, if we assume that all acts of law breaking are similar in motivation, then the only policy prescription that is open to us is stiffening the penalty. In economic literature on crime, the most common assumption is that if the cost of engaging in criminal acts goes up, like all other commodities, its demand will necessarily go down.[60] However, as I have discussed, the link between dissident action and costs of participation is not a simple one.[61] The models based on the assumption of self-utility maximization can only prescribe the imposition of ever-harsher punishments that increase the cost of participation in dissident activities. These dangerous prescriptions are not only erroneous, but also dangerous, particularly when there is so much abuse of human rights all over the world, directed primarily at political activists.

Further, the problem with analyzing our social behavior within a narrow definition of motivation is that, ultimately, we need to seek solutions outside of the model; the comparatively static analysis of microeconomics takes a detailed look at trees but misses the forest. Microeconomics offers an excellent explanation of the world as it is, taken as a snapshot, but cannot explain the bigger picture of social evolution. As a solution to this problem, economist Joseph Schumpeter pointed out the role of the entrepreneur in the process of economic evolution. John Maynard Keynes later demonstrated the inability of market forces to determine a stable course for the economy. The entire thesis of Keynesian economics was based on "market failure." In his prescription for curing the economic ills of recession, inflation, or poverty, Keynes pointed out that the solution does not rest within the market process. Instead, external agents like the government, the Federal Reserve, and (of late) the International Monetary Fund or the World Bank have taken active leadership in putting the economy on an even keel.[62] Similarly, many of what Lichbach identifies as "market" solutions in fact originate outside of the market. In *community*, we need to assume the role of a "common knowledge," in *contract*, an ever-vigilant social organization, and in *hierarchy*, a political entrepreneur. Once we make the assumption of self-utility maximization, we can only analyze each case as a distinct phenomenon. What it does not offer is a coherent theoretical perspective from which these actions can be explained.

Second, the problem with models based on self-interest is that they offer very few predictive capabilities.[63] There is a good deal of distinction between explanation and prediction. A tide table predicts the ebb and flow of the ocean but does not explain why it happens. The Darwinian theory explains evolution but can only weakly predict its course. Newtonian physics both explains and predicts, albeit within a limited set of parameters. It is not necessary that a great theory have predictive capabilities.[64] However, when the very logical structure of a theory precludes prediction of an important area of human interaction, such as collective action, we must address its shortcomings, much the same way quantum mechanics changed Newtonian physics.

SOLACE IN SELF-INTEREST

The adherents of the self-interest assumption have dealt with these problems in several ways. Some have argued that the models based on economic rationality have been "incorrectly confused with a general theory of human behavior."[65] Therefore, don't expect these models to provide answers for every kind of human behavior. In other words, we should be happy with a partial explanation of human behavior, even when the "anomalous" behavior forms the core of our social interaction. The rest, we are assured, can be relegated to the realm of irrationality or arationality.

To some others, this truncated assumption of human behavior is a reflection of practicality. In a complex world, the monolithic explanation provides the anchor for an ever drifting ship. We cloud our explanation by bringing in other factors. Hence, they have argued that in the final analysis, models based on self-interest are in fact superior to those based on psychology and biology. Thus, Becker states that "our assumption of stable preferences (based on self-utility alone) was intended not as a philosophical or methodological 'law,' but as a productive way to analyze and explain behavior. We are impressed by how little has been achieved by the many discussions in economics, sociology, history, and other fields that postulate almost arbitrary variations in preferences and values when confronted by puzzling behavior."[66] However, even if we do not question the futility of a multidisciplinary approach, I do wonder about characterizing much of our collective behavior as "puzzling." To be sure, Becker in his many-faceted work concentrates solely on issues of private participation, where an individual considers only his *private benefits* and *costs.* Where one must act upon one's perception of group utility (e.g., "independence from colonial rule will benefit everyone in the nation") Becker shows little interest in extending his analyses. Therefore, it should not surprise us to note that while he has impressive publications on marriage and crime, he says absolutely nothing about participating in a revolution.

The economists and their intellectual progeny, the public choice economists, have found solace in their assumption of self-interest in another curious fact. Lichbach points out that although most people and groups have serious grievances, "at least ninety five percent of the time, in at least ninety five percent of the places," they do not rebel.[67] Therefore, if we to explain both action and inaction, the self-interest–based theory does work very well at least 95% of the time. This is an extraordinary claim coming from someone attempting to explore the root causes of mass revolt. It is analogous to a geologist finding comfort in the fact that his theory is right (at least 95% of the time, no less) in explaining terrestrial stability, or someone interested in weather patterns taking pride in developing a model which predicts calm weather but fails to predict a tornado.

The final argument for continuing the assumption of self-interest is that to do otherwise would lead to a tautological explanation, that is, the claim that theories of the real world have to offer a partial explanation. The *reality* is too complex to fit into any theory. Therefore, any theory that offers to explain everything becomes a "vague and unfalsifiable sponge."[68] To me, this is the most confounding of all the arguments. It is indeed true that a theory must follow Karl Popper's dictum of falsifiability.[69] That is, to be scientific, a theory must offer hypotheses which will allow empirical testing to prove or disprove it. Metaphysical queries such as the existence of God or soul are therefore not scientific, since we cannot collect verifiable empirical data to prove our hypothesis. The problem of using this criterion in the social sciences is that if we use self-interest in the narrow sense, it becomes falsifiable and is readily falsified by our everyday experience of myriad acts of self-sacrifice. On the other hand, if we broaden the concept of self-interest to include even the most egregious feats of self-sacrifice as reflections of maximization of self-utility (since they may accord the actor immense respect in history, may assure him a place in heaven, or may help him preserve his gene pool), such a definition becomes tautological, and hence patently unfalsifiable.

In any case, the strongest argument for holding on to an inadequate theory for the explanation of collective action is that there is no alternative. No established theory is discarded or significantly altered without another one replacing it. With no other alternative in sight, Ostrom could assert, "While incorrectly confused with a general theory of human behavior, complete rationality models will continue to be used productively by social scientists, including the author."[70] Therefore, with considerable justification, Lichbach found solace in the assumption of self-interest: "I therefore find assumptions about rational dissidents to be neither always true nor always good, merely almost always useful."[71]

In the following chapter, I offer an alternative that can explain collective action by expanding the basic behavioral hypothesis of economic man. In it, I argue that the motivation for participating in a collective action must come from the social psychology of an actor's formation of collective identity.

THE ONE-DIMENSIONAL ACTOR: THE WOES OF AN INCOMPLETE BEING

While the theorists split hairs over the question of individual rationality, social experiments are being done all over the world. Two conflicting theories are continuously being put to the test by the political leadership in the individualistic West and in the collective East. Societies based on values of the two extremes compete for the hearts and minds of others in the rest of the world.

Yet, creatures of two identities, human beings feel incomplete when put in the straitjacket of a single motivation. The collective societies aim at creating collective beings by obliterating all traces of individualism. But the indomitable spirit of the individual inevitably rebels; counterrevolutions begin. At the opposite end of the spectrum, devoid of a collective purpose and feeling spiritually alone, people seek a collective meaning. In its benevolent form, this search leads people to join charitable and cultural organizations, find happiness in community work, and seek solace in religion. But taken to extremes, it leads to racism, hyper-nationalism, religious bigotry, and cultish practices.

The Islamic revolution in Iran promised to bring believers a step closer to paradise on earth. Running the country according to the will of God, the believers were assured of a just society by the ruling clerics. However, writer V. S. Naipaul, revisiting the Islamic Republic of Iran after nearly a decade of revolution, found its tarnished remains.[72] Naipaul found a largely demoralized nation with seeds of deep trouble germinating. A disillusioned former supporter who lost his business to the Islamic cause, a father who lost his sons to a fruitless war with Iraq, and women confined within the restrictive *chador* wonder about the future course of the revolution. The weight of disenchantment is particularly heavy on the young people, who have never known anything but the theocratic rule of the mullahs. Naipaul describes a confused young man who becomes a Nazi, seeking his past with the Aryans.[73] He takes on the dangerous job of picking fights with the *Komiteh,* the Islamic guards, and an angry young woman who sees no future within the strict Islamic society which confines her in the brooding solitude of her room after work.

On the other side of the coin, in a society built around extremes of individualism, many feel lost. The characters of existential novels look on vaguely, longing for and at once rejecting something larger to believe in. In the dismal desolation of suburban society—designed for minimal social interaction, with rows of houses in their monotonic regularity exposing only the garage door for the quickest entry and exit—people often seek a greater meaning in life. Their deep alienation from society manifests itself in self-inflicted wounds of drug abuse, failed marriages, senseless killings, and other forms of socially dysfunctional behavior. In the absence of an overarching standard, many crave spirituality in the moral wasteland of the Western world.

When a society swings to one extreme, a number of people seek solutions at the other extreme. Perhaps that is why history is often seen as strangely circular. Every giant move, either for the individual or for the collective—war, revolution, ethnic cleansing—traverses the same path. Like the links of a giant daisy chain, today's action will be linked to tomorrow's reaction, as yesterday's was to today's.

NOTES

1. Buchanan (1987: 66). Emphasis in original.
2. Nagel (1987: 50).
3. Quoted in Loveman (1998: 477). In her study, Mara Loveman has shown how brave men and women formed human rights organizations in many Latin American countries governed by the worst military dictatorships. This vivid quote from a former governor of Buenos Aires demonstrates the danger facing these individuals.
4. A number of books have been written on the incident in Waco, Texas. For one of the best discussions, see Wright (1995).
5. Self-utility is considered in the short term, because if we consider the long term, we may have to include many more aspects of utility (such as the preservation of children and grandchildren, etc.), which will complicate the fundamental assumption of rationality. Therefore, in this light it is easy to understand Lord Keynes' scornful remark: "In the long-run, we are all dead."
6. See Blaug (1980: 59).
7. See Mill (1967: 321).
8. See Hirschleifer (1985).
9. For an excellent discussion of public choice, see Soltan and Stephen (1996). Also see Mashaw (1997).
10. Funk (1978: 212).
11. See Olson (1965).

12. A *public good* is distinguished from a *private good* by being non-excludable and "non-rivalrous" (Musgrave and Musgrave 1980: 55–58). Non-excludability means that none of the members of the group can be excluded from the benefit of the public good. For example, no one can be excluded from using a highway, breathing clean air, or being protected by the national military force from a foreign invasion. The second characteristic of public good, being non-rivalrous, implies that the good is to be consumed jointly. That is, the utility of a particular public good for an individual will not diminish as a result of another person's use of the same good. Thus, the utility a ship captain's derives from a lighthouse does not decline because another ship is also using the same signals to navigate by.

13. See Tullock (1971).

14. Dennis Mueller (1979: 146) correctly points out, "The economic theory of revolution based on the individual maximizing calculus seems much better suited to explaining coup d'état, where the number of actors is small, the odds calculable, and the stakes seemingly large, than it is at explaining 'grass roots' revolution."

15. See Samuelson (1954: 387–89).

16. In economic literature, this is known as "moral hazard." For an explanation, see, among others, Heimer (1985) and Holstrom (1982).

17. See, for instance, Brehm and Gates (1997). For an earlier discussion, see Alchian and Demsetz (1972).

18. See Williams, Collins, and Lichbach (1997).

19. See Hardin (1968). For similar arguments, see Ekeh (1974); Emerson (1972); and Yamagushi and Cook (1993).

20. See Gurr (1970).

21. See Smelser (1963).

22. See Skocpol (1979).

23. See Arendt (1963).

24. See Tilly (1978).

25. See, for example, Morris and Mueller (1992). Also see Craig Jenkins (1983); Zald and McCarthy (1980).

26. See, for example, McCarthy and Zald (1977). Also see McAdam (1982).

27. See, for example, Hibbs (1973). Also see Venieris and Gupta (1983).

28. For instance, Marx predicted that "when the class struggle nears the decisive hour . . . a small section of the ruling class cuts itself adrift, and joins the revolutionary class" (see Fernbach [1974: 77]). However, Karl Kautski claimed that the birth of such revolutionary consciousness is not automatic and must be raised through "profound scientific knowledge" (see V. I. Lenin [1969: 40]). Although Lenin agreed with Kautski on that point, he warned against the workers getting too involved in the issues of wages, which he called "economism." To Lenin, such a diversion can truly bog down a communist revolutionary movement, as the workers focus on the small issues of wage increases instead of the larger picture of bringing about a total change in the social production relationship (39–45).

29. For a more detailed discussion of this apparent contradiction, see Dipak Gupta (1990: 108–15; 2001a).

30. See Lichbach (1995: 19–21).

31. See A. Rapoport and Borstein (1989).

32. In economic literature, the scheme is known as the expected utility model, where the probability of an actual win is multiplied by the size of the benefits. Thus, if

the reward for a bet on a coin toss is \$2, then the expected benefit is .5 × \$2.00 = \$1.00. See Dipak Gupta (1994: 390).

33. Hirschman (1974: 9) correctly points out that the "preference for participation in public affairs over the 'idiocy' of private life is much more unstable, and subject to much wider fluctuations, than the preference for, say, apples over pears or for present over future consumption."

34. See Tarrow (1994). Dennis Chong (1991) has made similar claims in explaining the civil rights movement. For a detailed response to Tarrow's solution to the social dilemma, see Dipak Gupta (1997).

35. See Becker and Landes (1974).

36. Mason and Krane (1989: 184) show a high degree of correlation between the number of youths in a locality and participation in the death squads. Since high rates of population growth are strongly correlated with higher proportions of young men and women, my cross-national study (Dipak Gupta 1990) found significant correlation between rate of population growth and political protests. Hobsbawm (1981: 31–33) reports that most "social bandits" come from the relatively young in the society.

37. Rudé (1964: 220).

38. See Chamberlin ([1937] 1987: 28).

39. See Juergensmeyer (1984: 17).

40. See Navarro (1989: 257).

41. See Reif (1986: 148).

42. See B. Jenkins (1982: 15).

43. See Popkin (1979) on peasants' natural aversion to risk taking; see Scott (1976) on the opportunity costs of participation in collective action. Also see Coleman (1990).

44. See Ho Chi Minh (1961: 53). Since Marx was keenly aware of the need for indoctrination of the masses to overcome their inhibition toward rebellion ("You have nothing but your chains to lose"), Lichbach (1995: 100) suggests that Marx, in fact, presupposed the problem of the rebel's dilemma. V. I. Lenin, while providing a road map to revolution, states that the revolutionary leadership will not come from the proletariat, but from the bourgeoisie (1969: 40).

45. See Lacouture (1968: 49).

46. The argument goes as follows: As the cost of participation goes up, dissident groups find themselves in a resource crunch, which reduces their capability to engage in dissident activities. For a recent argument along this line, see McAdam, McCarthy, and Zald (1996).

47. See Lichbach (1987).

48. Gurr (1970: 232) states that "the most fundamental human response to the use of force is counter force. Force threatens and angers men, especially if they believe it to be illicit or unjust. Threatened, they try to defend themselves; angered, they want to retaliate."

49. See Gupta, Singh, and Sprague (1993).

50. See Rasler (1996).

51. See Lichbach (1987). For a discussion of the various hypotheses on the relationship between coercion and dissident activities, see W. Moore (1998).

52. See W. Dunn (1994). Also Tarrow (1994: 92) suggests that with more effective means of communication, movements would spread more rapidly.

53. Tarrow (1989: 93), for instance, mentions truck slowdowns at Italian border checkpoints as a successful means of protest.

54. See Schmid and de Graaf (1982).

55. For a detailed discussion, see Lichbach (1995: 86–96).

56. Becker (1996: 1–29), in contrast, offers a slightly different solution to the free-rider problem. He argues that a bandwagon effect starts when an individual joins a collective action and finds that because the others have joined in, his own costs have gone down. This will create a larger demand for participation.

57. Lichbach (1995: 283). Emphasis in original.

58. Ibid., 300. Emphasis in original.

59. See Ostrom (1998: 1). The term "tragedies of the commons" refers to the problem that common-pool resources, such as oceans, lakes, forests, irrigation systems, and grazing lands, can easily be overused or destroyed if property rights to these resources are not well defined (see Hardin 1968).

60. See Becker and Landes (1974).

61. See W. Moore (1998). Also see Gupta, Singh, and Sprague (1993).

62. In the world of commercial advertising, the word "new" is almost inevitably followed by "improved." However, when it comes to the social sciences, such word association remains problematic. Neoclassical economics attempted to improve upon classical economics, the same way Keynesian economics claimed its supremacy over the latter. However, starting in the 1950s, a group of conservative economists set out to destroy Keynesian economics. Through the works of Feldstein (1973), Milton Friedman and Schwartz (1963), Hayek (1988), Lucas and Sargent (1978) etc., the new neoclassical economists thought that they had dealt a mortal blow to Keynesian economics. In fact, Lucas and Sargent flatly claimed, "That the predictions [of Keynesian economics] were wildly inaccurate, and that the doctrine on which they were based was fundamentally flawed, are now simple matters of fact, involving no subtleties in economic theory" (1978: 2). However, through the work of scholars such as Akerlof (1976), Bernanke (1983), and others there has been a resurgence of "new Keynesian economics."

63. As Lichbach (1995: 15) correctly points out, "There is . . . an empirical flaw: CA [Collective Action] theories do not produce a general theoretical statement of the etiology of conflict that one may use to predict protest and rebellion."

64. For an interesting discussion in the context of natural and social sciences, see Kauffman (1995: 23).

65. "While incorrectly confused with a general theory of human behavior, complete rationality models will continue to be used productively by social scientists, including the author" (Ostrom 1998: 9).

66. Gary Becker (1996: 7).

67. See Lichbach (1995: 12).

68. See Lichbach (1997: 95).

69. See Popper (1968).

70. Ostrom (1998: 9).

71. Lichbach (1995: 344).

72. See V. S. Naipaul (1997: 46–49).

73. The word "Iranian" is derived from "Aryan."

PART II

PATH TO COLLECTIVE MADNESS

CHAPTER 4

HOMO COLLECTIVUS:
THE SOCIAL MAN

It is not clear that this is the best way of theorizing about either utopian or religious groups. . . . Where nonrational or irrational behavior is the basis for a lobby, it would perhaps be better to turn to psychology or social psychology than to economics for a relevant theory. The beginnings of such a theory may already exist in the concept of "mass movements."

—Mancur Olson[1]

RECONSTRUCTING THE FUNDAMENTALS

As Timothy McVeigh drove a rented truck filled with explosives, did he think of his personal benefits and costs? Did he think that he was taking his personal revenge on society? Or did he think that he was striking a blow for the white race against what he and others like him believe to be an illegal occupation government, controlled by Jews and other nonwhite usurpers of political power in the United States? If he was prompted by his personal passion, then it was an act of individual rationality. In that case, his act is no different from those of arsonists who set fire for fun, or those of so many disgruntled workers who open fire on their colleagues. On the other hand, if McVeigh really believed that he was doing it for a cause greater than his own, then the question is, Why did he not wait for someone else to volunteer for the job? This simple question goes to the heart of Olson's dilemma; if we believe that McVeigh did it for personal reasons, then there is no free-rider problem. However, if he embarked upon his destructive work for the greater good of those he perceived to be "his people," then by following the logic of self-utility, Tim McVeigh is an irrational person who killed nearly 300 people for fun and perverse excitement.

I would argue that we will go absolutely nowhere trying to understand the motivations of McVeigh and his likes from all over the world—some known, many more unknown, some revered as martyrs, some reviled as monsters—by relying solely on self-interest. Therefore, in this chapter, I propose an expansion of the fundamental assumption of economic rationality by including people's desire to maximize the interest of the group in which they choose to belong.[2]

I submit that unless we recognize that human motivations are the products of dual identities—individual and collective—we will fail to understand human beings as social animals. This chapter develops my own hypothesis for analyzing collective behavior by combining the analytical elegance of economic man with insights drawn from developments in social psychology. Experiments in social psychology—some amusing, some horrifying—amply demonstrate the strength of our desire to associate with others of our species in love and in hate. Perhaps such desires are rooted in our biological evolution. But without a collective motivation, no society would ever have been formed. The problem of incorporating group identity into the fundamental assumption of human behavior is that group identity, particularly in the modern world, can be fickle. In medieval times, an individual was born with indelible identities of clan, tribe, religion, caste, and gender. However, today most of us have a much wider choice. Out of an infinite number of possible identities we embrace only a few. Why and how do we embrace these identities, excluding all else? Or why do we change our group affiliations, based on time, place, and circumstance? I argue that the answer to these questions cannot be found in the sterility of a comparative static analysis of neoclassical economics and instead must be sought in the dynamic interaction between the external environment and an individual's psyche. Changes in economic opportunities allow political entrepreneurs to exploit our deep-rooted hopes, fears, and predilections to develop a collective identity. Based on the depth of our collective identity, we take part in collective actions of all sorts, from mundane to extraordinary, from benevolent to extremely malevolent. Finally, I argue that by expanding the assumption of human rationality we do not engage in tautological reasoning, which can explain every action and thereby explain none. Instead, such extension allows us to have a new set of hypotheses amenable to empirical testing. I end the chapter with my own effort at measuring the strength of collective identity as a motivator for collective action.

Our failure to understand individual aspirations has time and again brought counter-revolutions in collective societies; similarly, the inability to comprehend the strength of collective motivation has left the West to turn to insanity as the only possible explanation for actions taken for the greater good of the group at the expense of the individual. My alternate paradigm integrates the two motivations to develop a more complete being, *Homo collectivus,* a rational human being with two conflicting identities; a creature who, throughout his life, tries to achieve a balance between the two. In the process, sometimes he goes overboard. When he does, at one extreme, he becomes a social recluse; going to the other extreme, he is swept away by the forces of collective madness.

PRIDE AND PREJUDICE: THE NEED TO BELONG AND TO HATE

Forming groups is rooted deep in the human psyche. Post–World War II advancements in social psychology have established our primordial desire to belong to a group, and often to hate those who are perceived to be outside of the group. In many experiments, social psychologists have demonstrated that people form groups almost instinctively. And once a group is formed and the members of the "in" and the "out" groups (or, alternatively, "us" and "them") are identified, the subjects develop ethnocentric pride (favoring members of the "in" group) and prejudice (unfavorable attitudes) toward the "out" group. Nearly four decades ago, Sherif and Hovland conducted a famous experiment.[3] They demonstrated the ease with which two competing groups of boys could develop pride in their group and at the same time learn to look down upon the members of the other group during a period of only three weeks in a summer camp. During the first week, the boys remained within their own group, unaware of the existence of the other group. Toward the end of the first phase, without meeting each other physically, the boys came to know about the existence of the other group. Soon they were found to have developed negative images of the other group. In the second phase of the experiment, the two groups were brought together for a tournament. The experiment had to be terminated to prevent serious injury to the participants. At the end, the two groups (a) showed preference for their own group members, describing themselves as "tough," "brave," and "courageous"; (b) began stereotyping the others with epithets such as "crybaby" and "no-good-cheater"; (c) started to exaggerate the achievements of their own group while minimizing those of the other.

One implication of the economic theories of group formation is that groups are formed because the individual members derive some special benefits from group membership. Second, these theories also imply that, based on the individual interests of the members, these groups compete with others in zero-sum games for limited space and resources.

However, a noted team of researchers, headed by Henri Tajfel at Bristol University in England, gathered experimental evidence that challenged the essential elements of economic theories of group formation. Through a number of elegant psychological studies, they asserted that competition for scarce resources—which is the fundamental assumption of economic theories of group formation—was neither a necessary nor sufficient cause for group formation or "out-group" discrimination. The most powerful implication of their experiments is that the very process of cognition of "in-group" and "out-group" identification can lead to prejudicial attitudes. In other words, we are capable of forming groups in our own minds and of developing aspects of pride and prejudice without even having any "real" basis of group interaction or competition for scarce resources. In some of their experiments Tajfel and his associates told the subjects about imaginary groups. The subjects, of course, did not have direct interaction with the members of the opposing groups, yet, they quickly fell into the trap of developing false pride toward their own and prejudice toward nonexistent groups.[4] Tajfel's experiments inexorably point to the human tendency to seek social identification, regardless of economic gains or competition.

Social psychologists have often been thorns in the sides of those advocating a "rational" self-utility maximizing being.[5] Another aspect of the research by Tajfel and his associates takes direct aim at this mythical *Homo economicus*. In their experiment, they offered the subjects two separate strategies. By following the first strategy, the subjects would maximize the total returns of the "in" and "out" groups. The alternate strategy, however, allowed them to maximize their own "in" group returns relative to those of the "out" group. By following the first strategy, both groups would receive the same amount of return, which is greater than what one group would receive by trying to beat out the other group. For instance, the first strategy would yield $5 for each group, while the second would give $4 to the "in" group and $1 to the "out" group. By the laws of economic utility maximization, a "rational" actor would choose the first strategy since it gives his group the maximum benefit. Yet, in telling testimony to our group behavior, most subjects chose the second strategy.

Therefore, advances in social psychology have shown the fundamental allure of group formation in the human psyche. Given the strength of this proclivity, it is inconceivable that we will be able to understand our social behavior with the help of self-utility alone. Human beings came out of their simian past having formed groups. Chances are, we will continue to form groups until we are no longer in existence. Whether driven by our need for collective survival, need for reciprocal reassurance, selective group benefits of nepotism, or our insatiable need for social identification, formation of groups is as fundamental as (and, in fact, conceptually inseparable from) the maximization of self-utility.

Although these results shed important light on human behavior and motivations, they leave out some important anomalies. The *social identity* theory of Tajfel and his associates shows why and how individuals form groups and then proceed to discriminate against those who are considered to be the outsiders or "them." Yet further research into social identity clearly showed that, in real life, the members of low-status groups (e.g., minorities or economically deprived groups) often favor members of the dominant groups over their own.[6] Thus, a minority group, while evaluating work performance, frequently attributes higher quality to the members of the high-status majority (dominant) group. In fact, the correlation between in-group favoritism and group identification turned out to be much less clear-cut than Tajfel would have expected.

However, the most frightening aspect of our group identity is our proclivity to suspend our own values and judgment in the face of peer pressure or in the presence of an authority figure. In 1974, Stanley Milgram reported the results of an extraordinary series of experiments.[7] The experiments took place at Yale University with male volunteers who responded to newspaper advertisements or mail solicitation. The subjects were between the ages of twenty and fifty and had a wide range of educational backgrounds, occupations, and life experience. When the participants arrived at the laboratory, each was paired off with another fellow participant who was actually part of the experimental team and was trained to play the part of a victim. The men were told that they were taking part in an experiment to study memory and learning, and that one of them was going to be the "teacher" and the other the "learner." In order to complete the charade they were asked to draw slips of paper to determine who was going to play what role. The unsuspecting subjects did not know that the process was rigged and were inevitably chosen as the "teacher." The participants were told that the study was concerned with the effects of punishment on memory retention. Milgram explains the process as focusing on the teacher.[8] After watching the learner being strapped into place, he is taken into the main experimental room and seated before an impressive shock generator. Its main feature is a horizontal line of thirty switches, varying from 15 volts to 450 volts, in 15 volt increments. There are also verbal designations, which range from SLIGHT SHOCK to DANGER—SEVERE SHOCK.[9] The teacher is told that he is to administer the learning test to the man in the other room. When the learner responds correctly, the teacher moves on to the next item; when the other man gives an incorrect answer, the teacher is to give him an electric shock. He is to start at the lowest level (15 volts) and to increase the level each time the man makes an error, going through 30 volts, and so on.

The "learner" was kept in a different room, and an experimenter would stand next to the "teacher." Each time the learner gave an incorrect answer, the teacher was instructed to jolt him with a higher level of electric shock. To standardize the subjects' (the "teachers'") reactions, the responses of the learners were prerecorded. As the level of shock increased, the "teacher" heard the man on the other side of the wall first grunt and then scream in agony, complaining about an existing heart condition. Each time the subject asked about the learner's discomfort, he was told that "although shocks may be painful, there is no permanent tissue damage, so please go on." If the teacher refused to go on, he was given a series of three successively more forceful instructions: "The experiment requires that you continue"; "It is absolutely essential that you continue"; "You have no choice: you *must* go on." If the teacher still refused, the experiment was halted. To the horror of those who have faith in human judgment, two-thirds of the subjects went all the way, administering the highest level of shock with clearly marked switches. They administered the supposedly lethal amount of shock even when they had reason to believe that they were inflicting a tremendous amount of pain and were possibly causing death to a protesting individual. Why did they do it? They did it simply because they were told to do so by an authority figure. As an outside point, Milgram included women as teachers in one of his experiments. Alas, the level of obedience among women was no different than among men, although they seemed to be more conflicted about their task.

This is the process of authorization, where many obey orders, even grossly immoral ones, when they come from an authority figure. Thus, when the word goes out—whether through the taped messages of the Ayatollah Khomeini during the Iranian revolution against the Shah, through instructions of the shadowy, clandestine leadership of the Irish Republican Army, through vague orders down the chain of military command, or through the hate radio messages in Rwanda or Yugoslavia—people take to the streets in murderous rage to take part in acts of violent rebellion. While they follow orders, the participants often do not see themselves as being responsible for the consequences of their actions. In the Nuremberg trials after World War II, as in the case of Lt. William Calley, the primary defense of the accused was that they were simply following orders.

Another interesting aspect of obedience is that the authority does not always have to be the highest political authority. For those engaged in genocide in the Rwandan countryside, or in the towns and villages of the Indian states of Punjab and Bengal during the Hindu-Muslim riots in the 1940s, their implicit or explicit orders could have come from the village elders or even the self-proclaimed leader of a small instantly formed band.[10] For crimes of obedience to take place, orders do not even have to come from a recognized channel of bureaucratic hierarchy. The request implicit in the king's words—"Will someone not rid me of this meddlesome priest"—prompted a band of assassins to behead Thomas à Becket some 800 years ago. In an atmosphere of total control and strong allegiance, even the appearance of an order can provoke acts of gross inhumanity.

Stanley Milgram's experiments had demonstrated the length to which otherwise sane people would go to follow orders, especially when they come down from authority figures. Based on Milgram's work we know that many of us, as individuals, are inclined to obey authority figures and carry out orders to extreme ends. But are there cultures that show greater proclivity in following authority? Are some cultures more authoritarian than others? Are there personality traits that make some people more willing to follow orders than others? Stunned by the wide-ranging participation of Germans in the Holocaust, the American Jewish Committee funded an impressive research project after the war. The extensive report, published in 1950,[11] came to the conclusion that German anti-Semitism developed from a particular personality style called the "authoritarian personality." The authors of the report developed a scale for measuring individuals' authoritarian personality. They argued that authoritarian proclivity is the result of four factors: (1) rigid adherence to conventional values and patterns of behavior, coupled with harsh punishments for slight deviations; (2) an exaggerated need to submit to, and identify with, strong authority figures; (3) a generalized environment of hostility; and (4) a mystical, superstitious frame of mind. This authoritarian personality, according to this report, resulted from early childhood experience with a domineering and strict disciplinarian father and a punitive mother. A child rewarded for strict adherence to rules and orders and not for creativity develops obsessive desires to repeat this behavior when dealing with others who are perceived to be deviants and otherwise outside the norm. Therefore, people of other races, religions, and ideologies, the physically infirm, handicapped, or of "weak" mind, or those with a different lifestyle or sexual orientation are considered to be generally unworthy. The authoritarian personality also exaggerates the importance of "in-group" affiliation, adoring everything about one's own group and denouncing the others.

Although, like many other important studies, *The Authoritarian Personality* has produced a veritable cottage industry of similar studies, it has not escaped criticism.[12] For instance, it does not distinguish between personality traits—developed during child rearing—and social learning. Also, it has been observed that people born of working-class parents tend to be more prejudiced than those born into middle-class families.[13] While it is true that working-class parents, in general, demand stricter adherence to rules and are perhaps more inclined to punish any deviation than their middle-class counterparts, their prejudiced worldview may also be the result of their social environment.[14] Finally, it is also possible that the working class is more prejudiced toward outsiders because they feel much more threatened by possible competition than the middle class, comfortable in the exclusive enclaves protected by their specialized skills. In 1811, the Luddites set out to destroy the textile machines of mass production much the same way that in the late 1970s fishermen off the coast of Louisiana started a campaign of terror and sabotage against Vietnamese fishermen. Without the protection of specialized skills and economic prowess, the working class in every country in the world reacts with prejudice against anything and anyone who threatens their livelihood. As a matter of fact, empirical evidence points to the fact that whenever the middle class feels threatened, the chances of social upheaval go up even more significantly.[15]

Research in social psychology further demonstrates that when people take part in extreme acts of vengeance against a shared enemy, they do so through a complex process of rationalization called *cognitive dissonance*. This is the process which allows otherwise rational individuals to go over the threshold of what we may consider a "normal" response to a threat situation. Psychologists have often wondered about the human mind's ability to rationalize the most heinous acts of irrationality. In our personal lives, we often observe discrepancies between our attitudes and behavior. For instance, someone who has led a promiscuous life and then becomes a convert to religion may become a strident advocate of sexual morality. One who gives up smoking may turn into the most obnoxious enforcer of no-smoking rules. Inspired by the work of psychologist Leon Fetsinger, the theory of cognitive dissonance can often explain this particular anomaly of human behavior.[16]

Fetsinger contends that the anomalous behavior begins when we perceive discrepancies between our deeply held beliefs and some external behavior. This difference creates pressure to reconcile the two divergent aspects of beliefs and perception or attitudes and behavior. When we are hungry or fearful, we take steps to reduce our hunger or our fear. Similarly, dissonance works like any other drive: we try to reduce our levels of internal inconsistencies. In the process, we engage in the grossest kinds of rationalization, often by taking extreme positions.

For instance, from all accounts Timothy McVeigh had distinguished himself as a dedicated soldier during the Gulf War. While other soldiers engaged in recreational activities during their time off, McVeigh kept to himself, studying and preparing for his future assignments. The first shock that the young soldier experienced was when he was rejected for promotion. Deeply disappointed, McVeigh must have tried to reconcile his past devotion to this current antipathy toward the military. But his profoundly held beliefs must have received a rude jolt in 1993, when he saw the federal agents confronting David Koresh and his group in Waco, Texas, which resulted in a fiery end for nearly eighty men, women, and children. McVeigh interpreted this as a deliberate action by the government, controlled by some sinister external force.[17] Reflecting his strong dissonance, at the time of his sentencing, without showing any remorse for his deeds or any emotion for his death sentence, he cryptically quoted U.S. Supreme Court Justice Louis Brandeis by saying, "Our government is the potent, the omnipresent teacher. For good or for ill it teaches the whole people by its example." Perhaps not to jeopardize his chances for an appeal, McVeigh left out other parts of Justice Brandeis' 1928 opinion on the government's use of wiretaps for criminal investigation. What he left out gave a glimpse of how he rationalized the Oklahoma bombing. In his dissenting court opinion, Brandeis went on to say, "If the government becomes a law breaker, it breeds contempt for law; it invites every man to become a law unto himself; it invites anarchy. To declare that the government may commit crimes in order to secure the conviction of a private criminal would bring terrible retribution."[18]

Research in social psychology unequivocally points to our need to form groups with a strong collective identification of in-group and out-group, "us" and "them." Although the link between actual behavior and collective identity is by no means certain, the essential nature of collective or social identity in the human psyche is undeniable. However, the problem with collective identity is that it is not constant, but contextual. Social psychology, in fact, conducts research in static terms, taking a few snapshots over time to determine the linkages between society and individual psychology. The dynamic interaction between the two, by which people's group identity can be manipulated and molded to suit a particular political purpose, is the domain of the social scientists.

IN THE LOVE OF HATE: COMMUNITY AND THE SHARED ENEMY

Collective identity is the product of "us" and "them." The "us" in our conscious choice compels us to feel solidarity with a group, with or without a strong notion of the outside group: "them." This is the generous side of collective identity. Because we feel a sense of oneness with the rest of the group, we can be generous to it, as we are generous to ourselves. When we donate money to or work hard for a worthy cause, we bask in the warm glow of having done the right thing. This is the motivation behind all our altruistic behavior; Florence Nightingale felt solidarity with the wounded soldiers and tended them regardless of the color of their uniforms. Similar feelings have motivated people from all over the world, from the famous to the anonymous, from Mother Teresa to the countless volunteers who give themselves freely to others in the community.

What causes us to be generous? A number of psychological studies on human altruism have found upbringing, religious belief, education, and awareness to be determining factors.[19] The inculcation of the feeling of patriotism is done deliberately all over the world, with poets writing inspiring poems—sometimes to the point of being ludicrous, especially to someone outside the country—and leaders giving stirring speeches often evoking a parental image for the country. As we listen to them, we are moved to defend the honor of the fatherland or motherland; we immediately recognize each and every soul in the nation as a sibling; we are prodded to acts of self-sacrifice for our family. This is the exact same recipe used throughout human history. It inspired the vastly outnumbered Athenians to fight the forces of Darius, the European colonists to raise their national flags in the most remote corners of the earth, the Islamic holy warriors to conquer most of the Old World in the fifteenth century.

It is also interesting to note that the process of the formation of "us" remains clouded in the bewildering mystery of our cognitive process. We can form the feeling of a community where there was none, prompted only by the oratory of a clever demagogue, or even through a popular movie or a novel. For instance, the extreme right-wing nationalists in Russia have recently made support of their brethren in Serbia the litmus test of political allegiance to their cause. The politicians who fail to pass this test or who are deemed too soft in their support of the Serbs are derided as traitors. The most astonishing aspect of this pan-Slavic nationalism is that it never was a particularly potent force in Eastern European politics. Yugoslavia, under Marshal Tito, chose an independent course of action from the Soviet Union and, as a result, faced a blockade by the COMECON countries in the 1950s. Similarly, in British India, nationalism spread to Bengal quickly with the publication of *Anandamath*, a novel by Bankim Chattopaddhay. He contributed the term *Bondematram* ("hail to my motherland"), which served as the war cry for generations of Bengali nationalists.[20] This battle cry was eventually transformed into a Hindu call to arms against the Muslims as the colonial British rulers prepared to leave India.

The darker side of collective identity is the feeling of the "them," the enemy. We are myth-making animals. In our interpretation of history, folklore, and stories handed down from grandparents to grandchildren, we create our enemies. In this process, we create what Carl Jung called archetypes.[21] We vilify the evil ones, removing their individual faces and replacing them with a collective face embodying greed, lust, cruelty, injustice, and all that is repulsive to us. Like the ancient Egyptian jackal-headed god Anubis, these people have the form of a human being but the head of a monster. In the process we can safely deny their humanity. We can even make ourselves believe that these creatures do not feel pain in the same way we do. The racist literature of the adherents of slavery or Jim Crow legislation would have readers believe that African Americans did not feel the same way as they did; GIs in Vietnam told each other that the "Gooks don't bleed," and almost believed it.

TWO FACES OF COLLECTIVE IDENTITY

Collective identity, however, does not have to include both "us" and "them." In fact, a strong collective identity does not necessarily have to be evil. I present my arguments in Figure 4.1, in which I show the strengths of the two factors of collective identity. The vertical axis measures the strength of the "us" factor, while the horizontal axis depicts the intensity of the "them" factor. I argue that when they are both weak, collective actions will fall victim to Olson's social dilemma.

Many groups, particularly some religious orders, thrive on the strength of their group cohesion. For instance, the Amish people have been able to maintain their island of pre-industrial living in the midst of the most industrialized society in the world.[22] The Jews kept their identity against all odds in the far-flung diaspora. Their collective identities are reinforced by the constant reminder of their shared past through the reading of the Scripture, their distinctive clothes, religious practices, and language. Mother Teresa and her small group of Catholic nuns worked in the slums of Calcutta by the strength of their conviction. Such collective actions appear in the upper left-hand corner of the diagram.

Although the strength of the "us" factor can be benign and benevolent, an unquestioned devotion to a cause can be detrimental to the followers. In March 1997, the bodies of 39 men and women, suicide victims, were discovered in a mansion in the exclusive neighborhood of Rancho Santa Fe, near San Diego, California. They were the followers of the Heaven's Gate cult, founded in the 1970s by Marshall Applegate. When the police arrived they found the

Figure 4.1
Collective Actions and Collective Identity

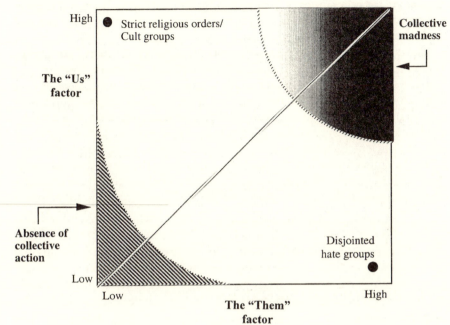

bodies neatly arranged, wearing new black sneakers, black T-shirts, and black sweatpants. Each of them had a $5 bill and five quarters. Most of the men, many as young as eighteen, were surgically castrated. They believed that they were going to join a spaceship hiding behind a comet.

The presence of a shared enemy can also unify a group. Hate groups all over the world are often formed on the basis of communal malevolence toward another group of people. In fact, the presence of a common enemy can unite disparate groups into a unified front, which disappears with the elimination of the perceived threat. For instance, anti-colonial struggles in many countries unified groups with different interests only to witness bloody civil wars after the end of colonial rule. In Figure 4.1, groups where the concept of a shared identity is weak but the identification of a common enemy is strong appears in the lower right-hand corner.

In situations where there is a strong "us," particularly when coupled with a strong "them," conditions become ripe for what I call an episode of collective madness. In Figure 4.1, this situation is represent in the upper right-hand corner.

COLLECTIVE: THE CONTEXTUAL IDENTITY

One of the most significant problems of considering group identity as a part of the fundamental behavioral assumption is that our group identity is fickle.[23]

However, this weakness can also be the source of its analytical strength. Since group identity is not invariant, its inclusion cannot be regarded as leading to a tautological argument. That is, if we were born with our group identities, we could explain away everything and, in the process, explain nothing. If social science makes any claim to be recognized as a "science," its assumptions must pass the test of falsifiability. Since group identity is not imprinted in the genetic map of an individual and is developed through the external world, its existence and its relative strength are amenable to empirical testing. Therefore, we can hypothesize that an individual's group identity and its strength will depend upon a number of "passive" or "environmental" factors, of which perhaps the most important are economic, cultural, religious, and linguistic factors. I call them "passive" because they are part of a slowly changing environment and provide a basis on which people draw boundaries around each other. The divisions along these passive variables are reinforced and shaped into forces of collective action by the catalytic influence of political entrepreneurs.

In every instance of group formation, we define who we are and separate ourselves from the rest. Since these boundaries are based on emotional perception, their strength depends on the development of archetypes of friends and foes, of heroes and villains, and of good and evil. By playing on our hopes and fears, political entrepreneurs develop a collective force of action, drowning out the inertia and hesitancy of those who otherwise would have been fence-sitting free riders.

The economic factors shaping an individual's collective identity would relate to the classical Marxist notion of class consciousness. Whether one divides economic classes according to ownership of the means of production or by income category, it is clear that people tend to react to their own class identity. Any perception of threat brings out those willing to strike a blow to the perceived offenders.

Similarly, people often coalesce around their cultural tradition. As social psychologists have pointed out, we often amplify our minute cultural differences with our next-door neighbors. Our cultural preferences of food, clothing, songs, and color soon assume symbolic significance. For instance, watermelons become vehicles of racial prejudice in the United States, as they are associated with the diets of African Americans. The absurdity of these cultural amplifiers becomes evident to those who do not fall within the cultural groupings, but to those who do, they can verily transmute themselves into vehicles of intolerance and extreme violence.

Religion has been perhaps the greatest force behind generations of collective identity in human history. As the search for higher meaning in life uplifted human spirits and has truly attributed soul to the flesh, religion on the other hand has been the biggest cause of bigotry and intolerance and the source of what I call collective madness. Although great religious teachings do not encourage hate, religion in the hands of political entrepreneurs invites havoc. In a similar manner, languages have been sources of unification and cultural enrichment, yet they have also contributed to the development of the notion of a shared enemy in many parts of the world.

Some of us, I would argue, do not have a strong sense of community but may take part in collective actions based on a sense of a shared enemy. Many isolated hate crimes, acts of vandalism, hooliganism, and even some community actions are based on the notion of an enemy without a sense of a larger cause. In individualistic societies, the "them" can be formed easily and instantly when we feel threatened as a group. Thus, a European football thug looks for his "enemy" among the supporters of the rival team, without adherence to a larger sense of community. Also, the news of the impending release of a serial rapist in its midst instantly galvanizes a community, but its unity disappears quickly when the news turns out to be premature or the felon is denied parole.

ACCOUNTING FOR THE SOCIAL MAN: A THEORETICAL PERSPECTIVE

While economists stress the costs and benefits of the individual, social psychologists emphasize the importance of group identity. This book presents a new hypothesis of human behavior by combining the two great traditions. I argue that if we recognize the dual motivation, then we can understand complex human motivations a bit more clearly. The acceptance of multiple motivations does not rob us of the simplicity of analysis, but, perhaps, brings us closer to the chaos of the real world.[24]

I start with the assumption that in all their efforts, rational human beings attempt to maximize their personal well-being as well as the welfare of the group(s) in which they claim membership.[25] This group can take on an infinite number of forms. Broadly, it can be *ascriptive* (one which requires individuals to be born into it) or *adoptive* (in which membership is voluntarily chosen). Allegiance to one's clan, tribe, ethnicity, nation, language, or religious order can form the core of ascriptive group formation. Although one can marry into another ascriptive group, change one's religion, or learn a different language, for the most part divisions along these lines are determined at birth. In contrast, as adults, we often choose groups to which we wish to belong voluntarily. We become members of groups that promote the cause of a community, such as a civic or cultural organization. Some of us join groups based on political or religious ideologies of all colors and shades. Other than complete recluses or those living on the fringes of society, it is difficult to find people who do not participate in any act of altruism. It is clear that when everyone is a *Homo economicus,* the perfectly self-absorbed economic man, no society would ever be formed, much less function. Similarly, it is conceptually impossible to find a person so dedicated to his cause that he has no concern for his own personal welfare. Without any consideration for one's personal self, it will be impossible to keep body and soul together.

Thus, our daily lives are spent in achieving a balance between the two identities by allocating our available time and resources. For our personal welfare,
we go to work, earn a living, try to get love, affection, power, respect, and rectitude. On the other hand, for our group, we donate our time, energy, money,
and, in extreme cases, make the ultimate sacrifice of life itself.

Where we find the balance between the two is a matter of individual preference.[26] Those of us who are activists or ideologues show deep commitments to collective causes, while the proverbial yuppies remain largely
self-absorbed. Traditional economics considers tastes and preferences as
"given" or outside the realm of explanation. But it is clear that our tastes and
preferences are not things that carry our genetic imprint and, instead, are
shaped by society. We crave objects in fashion, engage in activities promoted by
the larger society, and shun those that are roundly condemned. All of these social trends vary with time. And frequently a charismatic leader shapes them.
Max Weber noted the power of charisma and included it as a source of a
leader's authority.[27] It is the rise of leadership that inspires people to change
their preferences. Privileged white youths in the 1960s responded to the calls
of Dr. Martin Luther King, Jr., and, despite obvious threats to their personal
safety, became freedom riders. They willingly took part in dangerous missions
to organize blacks in the South. The call of Khomeini to sacrifice for Islam was
heeded by hundreds and thousands of Iranian boys barely in their teens. Willingly, they volunteered as Basiji, the paramilitary force composed of the youn-
gest fighters, used for the most dangerous jobs. Wearing red headbands as
symbols of blood sacrifice and keys around their necks to open the closed
doors of heaven, these fighters for God, many not even ready to shave, defused
land mines without proper training. Mohandas Gandhi inspired wealthy, established Indians to give up their jobs with the British Raj and join the freedom
movement. Cult leaders from Jim Jones to David Koresh made their disciples
give up their personal property, sever all ties to immediate family members outside the group, and even take their own lives or the lives of their children. Exhorted by their sectarian leaders, many in Bosnia engaged in fratricide with
astounding alacrity. In order to understand a sudden shift in social preference,
we must understand the role of leadership. Chapter 5 examines its role more
closely.

A person's decision to change the relative importance of the two aspirations
is also a product of the prevailing economic and political conditions. These political and economic environmental conditions determine the "opportunity
costs" of being engaged in activities which produce goods for the individual or
for the collective. By using logical deductions, we can surmise that if the economic opportunity increases relative to the collective opportunities, then people will gravitate toward the former. This situation takes place when the
economy prospers, creating new opportunities and hopes. Under such conditions, unless some well-organized traditional sectors are threatened, people
find the cost of joining political activities too prohibitive. In economic terms, it

is called the opportunity cost of time. High opportunity costs of time prevent people from accepting a tyrant during periods of economic prosperity. Unprecedented economic growth in South Korea kept most happy with the corrupt regime of Park Chung Hee. However, as the rate of economic growth slowed down in the mid-1980s, there were rumblings of protests in the country.[28] Rapid economic growth caused Chileans to accept the repressive rule of General Augusto Pinochet. It is the same reason why revolutions are always fought on the backs of the middle-class youths. Being assured of free room and board and as yet without heavy financial or family responsibilities, from the *intifada* in the West Bank to the Tupak Amarus in Peru, young people all over the world participate in anti-government activities in disproportionate numbers. In contrast, revolutionary recruiters have noted that although the poorest of the poor have "nothing but their chains to lose," they steadfastly remain outside the movement. This is because the urban lumpenproletariat remains too busy eking out a living. Any time away from their daily struggle to survive makes them the most unwilling participants. Similarly, peasants, dependent on the short growing cycle, frequently take the "rational" approach of opting out even when revolutions are waged in their names.[29]

Like economic opportunity costs, a change in political opportunity costs impacts an individual's decision to participate in a collective action. Political opportunity cost refers to the cost imposed by the regime on dissident activities. As the level of coercion increases, people learn to hide their private preferences and put up a public façade.[30] However, if the central government shows signs of political and military weakness, protests rise up all of a sudden like a prairie fire. The weakness of the czarist regime of Nicholas was exposed during the Russian defeat at the hands of Imperial Japan and Germany. The ensuing political chaos paved the way for the Bolsheviks to assume power.[31] The inability of the established government to impose the political will helped Mao in China, Castro in Cuba, and Khomeini in Iran. Even in the United States, wounded by a prolonged and increasingly unpopular war in Vietnam, the 1960s saw a great clustering of political movements. As soon as the war was over, the troops returned home to an economically strong nation, the protest and self-searching era of the liberal sixties and seventies quickly blended into the Reaganomics of the 1980s. The hippies cut their hair and got out of their tattered jeans and into the three-piece suits of the me-centric yuppies.

To summarize, a rational human being maximizes his or her utility by considering three factors:

Maximize net utility = Utility of the self + utility of the group − cost of participation

For want of better terms, we may call them "greed," "ideology," and "fear."

IDEOLOGY AND SELF-INTEREST: WHY MEN REBEL AND WHY THEY DON'T

Professor Gurr called his seminal book *Why Men Rebel*.[32] However, his early work fails to explain why people often choose not to rebel. In this section, I offer a wider and more complex set of reasons for people's action and inaction.

Based on the three factors of motivation, we can distinguish six groups of participants and nonparticipants in collective actions, with the necessary caveat that the distinction of their motivations reflects the *relative* weights they place on the three aspects. The ranks of the participants are made up of *believers, mercenaries,* and *captive participants.* On the other hand, nonparticipants may be classified as *conscientious objectors, collaborators,* and *easy riders.*

In any collective movement, we are likely to find those who are motivated primarily by the "cause" or concern for their group. We may call them the *believers.* The believers are the ones who often initiate a movement or take part in a collective action even at the risk of utmost cost to themselves and their family. These foot soldiers are the ones who often constitute the core of a mass movement.

Surrounding the believers are those who are in the movement for personal gain, loot, glory, career advancement, or other kinds of selfish yearnings. In order to understand or to predict the future course of a conflict, we must understand the motivations of those who have personal stakes in a collective action. We may call these individuals *mercenaries.*

Along with the mercenaries, the ranks of the revolutionaries are often swelled by a group of *captive participants,* who participate out of fear of retribution or peer pressure. Although we may conjecture that relatively few active participants would fall into this category, recounting of history after a defeat finds most claiming to fall in this category.

These are the people who take part in collective actions. But how about those who don't? Thomas Hobbes saw men as savage brutes. Brazen acts of cruelty and depravity experienced all over the conflict-prone world may truly make us believe in such a lowly characterization of human nature. However, higher emotions, such as empathy, compassion, and ideological commitment, are also integral parts of our psychological makeup. Therefore, while we see examples of genocidal murderers and rapists, in our lives and in the pages of history, we frequently encounter others who risk their own lives to save strangers. I call these brave souls the *conscientious objectors* to collective madness. They are the counterparts of the true believers on the other side of the thin line of social insanity.

Then there are the *collaborators.* The collaborators' group interest lies with the revolutionaries, but they do not take part in rebellion and even work against it because they have been co-opted by the regime. These are the renegades, the Benedict Arnolds of the world. History is particularly harsh on them, especially if written from the standpoint of the other side.

Among nonparticipants, the most significant in number are the fence sitters or the easy-riders. I call these groups *easy riders,* since the term "free rider" has been used widely in the context of the self-utility maximizing neoclassical economic paradigm. Typically, these people would have participated had they not feared retribution from the rival group (such as the government in the case of an anti-establishment movement). There are the free riders of revolution. To them, the costs of participation outweigh the perceived benefits. Having too much to lose, they provide their tacit approval to the rebellion. If the calculations change as a result of a dramatic change in the political environment, like the reserve army of a revolution, they stream out of their homes and businesses to join the movement.[33]

For a more concise look, I have presented my classifications of participants and nonparticipants by their primary motivation in Table 4.1. As we can see, ideology moves the believers and the conscientious objectors, greed motivates mercenaries and collaborators, while fear acts as the primary cause behind the compliance of the captive participants and the silence of the easy riders.

At this point, it is important to caution the reader. The purpose of this classification is purely illustrative. Needless to say, it is impossible to peer into anybody's psyche to see whether a participant is a true ideologue or is motivated by greed. We are exceedingly complex beings. None of us understands even our own complex motivations enough to clearly classify them into the three categories.

MANUFACTURING COLLECTIVE IDENTITY

In some ways, the United States offers the epitome of individualism. However, in the middle of the sea of individualism, the needs of the society dictate the creation of islands of values of collectivism. Such sanctuaries are routinely created in all sorts of military and paramilitary groups, from the Boy Scouts to U.S. Marine Corps. These are the organizations that depend in varying degrees on the values of collectivism. In a recent book, Thomas Ricks, a Pentagon reporter fresh from a tour with the U.S. peacekeeping mission in Mogadishu, Somalia, set out to learn the process by which one is made a Marine, the smallest and perhaps the most disciplined branch of the U.S. military services.[34] Over the years, while American culture has become fragmented, in-

Table 4.1
Dominant Motivations and Behavior

Motivation	Participants	Nonparticipants
Ideology (collective identity)	Believers	Conscientious objectors
Greed (self-serving interest)	Mercenaries	Collaborators
Fear (cost)	Captive participants	Easy riders

dividualistic, aimless, and immersed in consumerism, the Marine Corps has stood its ground as a stark anomaly. Ricks studied a group of fresh recruits—mostly from the discards of society, drug addicts, gang members, white supremacists, and children of broken or abusive families—going through the rigors of Parris Island boot camp and coming out as full-fledged members of this proud service. The entire book is a study on how to mesh individual identities into a collective whole. This process of transformation is similar to what other cultish groups would employ to develop a personality of their own making. As for a society, the same set of factors are manipulated by the political leaders to start a collective action, the extreme end of which creates conditions for collective madness.

In *Making the Corps*, Ricks did not change any names, nor did he depend on any secondhand materials. He reported what he actually witnessed. With a few possible exceptions, the recruits are drawn from the wrong side of the ever-widening gap in U.S. society.[35] These were young men who did not attend college and were either from poor or abusive families or had no families. As Ricks points out, "Consciously or not, they don't see much of a place open to them in postindustrial America."[36] To me, this is the first condition for the formation of a collective mind-set. Whether for an individual or for a society, the path to collectivism is often paved by shattered dreams and colored by frustrated expectations. In our failure as individuals, we often seek something beyond our own selves—either someone to blame for our failure or to take pride in our collective achievement.

The second ingredient for manufacturing a collective mind-set is the presence of an authority figure. As in the Milgram experiment, the recruits face the overwhelming figures of the various drill instructors (DIs). The recruits are told in unequivocal terms that, for the duration of their training, the DIs are their gods. They are trained to follow each and every command in their extreme minutiae, without question, willingly and instantly. Even the punishments meted out, either for their own mistakes or for the faults of one of their platoon mates, have to be endured in the same spirit.

What contributes to the creation of a collective mind-set is the overall environment of acceptance of the primacy of the collective over the individual. For the duration of the recruits' stay at Parris Island, they are constantly commanded to discard their own individual identity and, instead, be seen as a member of Platoon 3086 of the U.S. Marine Corps.[37] In a telling passage, Ricks describes the process:

[Sergeant Lewis] withdraws from the recruits the right to use the first person. Their first names also are banished. "From now on you are no longer he, she, it or whatever you was," he says in a clear quiet voice. "You are now 'Recruit-and-your-last-name,' understand?" Coming from a society that elevates the individual, they are now in a world where group is supreme. Using "I" raises suspicions: Why would you care more about yourself than about your unit? You are 3086.[38]

Another important determinant of collectivism is the environment of acceptance of authority over one's own judgment. Arriving at boot camp, a recruit quickly perceives the prevailing culture of the Marine Corps. For instance, they are required to chant "D.I.S.C.I.P.L.I.N.E. Discipline is the instant willing obedience to all orders, respect for authority, self-reliance, and teamwork," over and over, at the top of their voice.[39]

Few collective mind-sets can survive without the definite picture of an adversary. The retention of an overarching "us" requires the presence of a "them." Ricks points out that part of the Marine Corps persona is imbued with a kind of paranoiac view about the outside society, which is viewed with extreme suspicion.[40] To them, the society at large is valueless and rapidly disintegrating. In the midst of the tidal wave of its anything-goes attitude, the Marines offer a shining alternative of a disciplined and purposeful lifestyle.

Collective minds need mythologies which define an individual's place in the otherwise confusing arrangement of life. The heroes and villains determine good and evil, black and white in a gray world of conflicting values and ideals. The recruits are taught the history of the Corps. They are required to memorize tales of the heroes of the past and their sacrifices. Thus, one of the former commandants of the Marine Corps emphasized that history was the glue that helds the Marine Corps together.[41] In a ritualistic display of pride, the young recruits endlessly shout "Honor. Courage. Commitment. Kill, kill."[42] With ample training, minds are formed and warriors are born, ready to lead an assault on any enemy, on command and without hesitation.

The treacherous mind can play tricks on those not fully indoctrinated in the culture of the collective. Therefore, any organization in the business of creating a collective mind-set must make sure that the recruits' brains are not being cluttered with useless information. Hence, boot camp is perfectly designed for information deprivation. For the most part, the recruits are not allowed to ask questions unless spoken to first. Chatting among each other is also actively discouraged. Even their first letter home is a form letter from the commanding officer. The letter cryptically instructs the family not to be alarmed if in his first letter the recruit complains that he has not received any mail from home. Recruits often lose track of time due to the rigorous nature of their training."[43]

Our proclivity for following orders from authority figures is greatly aided by the presence of a hierarchical structure. Besides, the structure provides an organizational capability to shape our minds. The Marine Corps makes sure that the recruits understand the hierarchical structure of the Corps. The recruits are required to learn and recite the entire chain of command, from the first drill instructor to the commander-in-chief, the president of the United States. They read and reread the organizational hierarchy, memorizing it until it is drilled into their brain cells.[44]

The fickle mind of an individual can easily stray from the goals of the collective. Therefore, these goals are reinforced through the rituals of drill. As Ricks points out: "The beginning point of a military society . . . is close order drill. . . .

It is no accident that the sergeants who run boot camp platoons are not called 'military instructors' but 'drill instructors.' Drill—boring, repetitive, and replete with sixty-two basic movements, each containing several subsets of requirements for the location of the rifle, the placement of the hands on the rifle, and the angle of the arms—is the heart of boot camp."[45] As we will see in Chapter 5, even in the larger society, the collective values are reinforced through ritualistic repetitions to inculcate the values of collective identity.

Finally, the adherence of the recruits flows from the expectations of reward for adherence and the costs of noncompliance. The recruits know that by completing boot camp they will fulfill their objective of being inducted into the service. Also, the entire military structure depends on obvious symbolic rewards of putting stripes to stars on soldiers. Unlike in civilian life, where people can be placed on an equal footing without obvious signs of classification, the military depends on such distinctions. This process of instant and recognizable reward for a job well done starts quickly for the recruits. A young man is picked to lead and guide Platoon 3086 as his DI spots him for his intensity and his ability to instantly follow commands.[46]

The other side of reward is, of course, punishment. The training grounds of Parris Island are replete with stories of physical and psychological punishment for even the slightest slipup. Although, in keeping with the times, the Marine Corps has become careful about punishment, Ricks narrates the following story of the costs of noncompliance in the not too distant past:

One night three men who had been censured for ineffectiveness in their assigned tasks were called forward in front of the assembled platoon, ordered to insert their penises into the breeches of their weapons, close the bolt, and run the length of the squad bay singing "The Marine Corps Hymn." This violent ritual ended as the drill instructor left and the three men sank to the floor, penises still clamped into their weapons. [The other recruits] helped them remove the rifles and guided them to their beds. There was considerable bleeding as the men cupped their wounded penises with their hands, curled into balls, and cried.[47]

The deliberate efforts at the training grounds of the U.S. Marine Corps to manufacture of a collective mind-set, which causes an individual to place a higher value on the welfare of the group than on his own, provide us with a road map for the same process in the larger society. Chapter 5 further analyzes this process. Chapter 6 presents two case studies where the processes of creating a collective identity have pushed a nation (Rwanda) and an isolated religious group (Jonestown) to the path of collective madness. Also, as a contrast, I discuss how the lack of such excesses of identity formation has prevented radical confrontation by African Americans as a group with the larger American society.

CAN COLLECTIVE IDENTITY BE MEASURED?

One of the arguments for not enlarging the fundamental behavioral assumption is the fear of engaging in tautology. In this section, I argue that the strength of people's collective identity as an explanatory variable for collective action can be measured.

So far I have presented the case that to form groups is part and parcel of human nature. However, as soon as we form a group, we define who "we" are as a group as opposed to who "they" are as the outsiders. I have also shown how transient these feelings of "us" and "them" can be. How we feel today as a group may change by tomorrow. In fact, in the following chapter, I will attempt to show that collective identity can and is manipulated by clever political operators and group leaders. That is the secret of their success as leaders. While individual identity is invariant and omnipresent, collective identity is malleable. However, the formation of collective identity follows a definite pattern. But before we go into the question of the formation of collective identity, let us look into the question of actually observing and empirically measuring its relative strength.

Since the collective identity of a group is a psychological aspect of human cognition, we can either conjecture its relative strength from the overall social condition at the macro level, or measure it through survey instruments. There are of course no aggregate-level data on collective identity. However, social scientists' zeal for measuring difficult social psychological phenomena cannot be underestimated. In his work, Ted Gurr attempted to estimate what he calls "group cohesion" for a large number of groups around the world.[48] By our definition of collective identity, this group cohesion index comes extremely close to measuring the first half of collective identity, the "us" factor. However, since Gurr makes no attempt to create an index for the intensity of perception of the "out" group, his index only measures half the concept of collective identity.

Although there are no aggregate cross-country data on collective identity, it seems reasonable to assume that the intensity of collective identity within a nation will be greatly influenced by the depth of cleavages within a society. Kelman has pointed out that with increased levels of fragmentation, it is easier for groups to see each other as adversaries.[49] This contributes to the overall level of hostility within a society. By extending Kelman's arguments, researchers have found strong empirical evidence suggesting that in societies where income is concentrated in the hands of a few, and where the literacy rate and the spread of higher education are low, the incidence of ethnic violence is high.[50]

A psychological phenomenon such as the strength of collective identity can be directly measured through personal interviews. In previous research, we examined the reasons why some senior citizens join the American Association of Retired People (AARP).[51] The AARP is perhaps the most influential lobbying group in the United States, ever vigilant in protecting the interests of the senior citizens of the nation. Therefore, belonging to a political action group such as the AARP is also a form of collective action. As a further incentive for joining, the AARP also gives its members a number of discount coupons and a magazine, *Modern Maturity,* which provides information on voter education, health care and quality of life, workers' rights, and retirement. Therefore, like most things in life, it is reasonable to assume that senior citizens have mixed motives for joining the AARP.

For this study, a stratified probability sample of over 600 senior citizens residing in the Youngstown, Ohio, area was interviewed by telephone in 1989. The sample was designed to represent a cross-section of the non-institutionalized elderly community. In this extremely detailed survey, respondents were asked a large number of questions about their physical and emotional health, economic condition, education, and attitudes. They were also asked if they were members of the AARP.

We hypothesized that a person's decision to join the AARP would depend upon four factors: his or her assessment of the personal and collective benefits of becoming a member, the cost of membership, and a set of exogenous factors based on cultural differences or some other aspect of individual "taste." Membership in the AARP entitles people to discount coupons for a wide variety of services (from traveling to health care) and goods for personal use. We assumed that the benefits individuals derived from them would depend upon their relative income and their physical and mental health. Thus, if I do not have any discretionary money, it does not do me any good to have discount coupons for hotel accommodations in vacation retreats. Similarly, if my physical and psychological health are poor, my ability to enjoy those private goods becomes severely restricted. By combining these three factors we arrived at a person's ability to enjoy the private benefits of joining the AARP. We assumed that the greater a person's economic ability and health, the greater is the incentive to join the organization.

The other motivation for joining the AARP is collective: the desire to improve the conditions of senior citizens in the United States. We hypothesized that this desire is directly related to an individual's strength of collective identity. For collective identity, we constructed two separate composite measures of "us" and "them." If an individual pays close attention to the news about senior citizens, gets involved in activities designed specifically for the senior community, and is concerned about the health and welfare of the elderly in general, he or she is assigned a high number for the "us" factor. We measured the "them" aspect of collective identity by asking questions to ascertain whether the respondent views the younger generation in an adversarial context. That is, if an individual feels that the younger generation views the elderly in an unfavorable light and that television and films portray them negatively, then the subject gets a high index for "them."

The cost of joining the AARP is minimal ($5 per year at the time of our survey). Therefore, we assumed that only those senior citizens below the official poverty line would consider this to be a barrier to joining the organization.

Finally, the "taste" factor was measured by asking the subjects about their awareness of and attitudes toward complex issues of public policy and government in general. Those who showed little awareness of social and political issues scored low on the "awareness" variable. Similarly, those who felt that they could never trust the government or that they would not be able to influence public policy received high marks on our "cynicism" scale. Also, for unexplained cultural factors, we introduced demographic variables, such as race, age, and gender.

When we used these four broad factors of individual interest, collective interest, cost of participation, and personal taste in a regression model, we found some extremely interesting results.[52] Our estimation results demonstrated that for the sample population, the strict economic argument of self-interest provides an inadequate explanation of membership in the AARP. When we introduced all four factors, we found that people with a strong collective identity were significantly more inclined to join than those with a weak collective identity. In fact, by using these independent variables we were able to correctly classify over 93% of those who would choose to be members of the AARP. The classification matrix is shown in Figure 4.2.

The cells of the matrix show the number of respondents whom we were able to correctly classify as joiners or non-joiners. Thus, based on our model, we could correctly predict 361 (out of a total of 386 actual members) individuals' decisions to join the AARP. Only 25 members whom we had identified as potential non-members had in fact turned out to be members. Interestingly, while factors of self-interest, collective identity, and cost (poverty level) turned out to be statistically significant, factors of personal taste, other than race (whites are much more likely to join than African Americans), did not.

Our ability to identify those who were most likely to join the collective action stood in contrast with our relatively low predictive capability to identify

Figure 4.2
Classification Matrix

		Predicted		Percent correct
		Non-member	Member	
	Non-member	50	114	30.41%
Observed				
	Member	25	361	93.43%

the non-joiners. Based on the model, we had identified much greater partici-pation. However, 114 individuals whom we thought had every reason to join turned out to be non-joiners. In fact, we were successfully able to recognize less than a third (30.4%) of a total population of 164 non-members. We called this cohort of 114 individuals "true" free riders. This is because those individu-als whom we had successfully identified as non-members had reasons (such as poverty and low collective identity) not to join. Those who should have joined but did not are the ones that puzzled us. Therefore, we specifically looked at the two groups we had successfully identified as non-joiners and "true" free riders. Our statistical analysis of the two groups found that the distinguishing factors were the personal taste factors. Those senior citizens who did not take any interest in the overall political matters and were not aware of the issues fac-ing the elderly in America and those who scored high marks on cynicism chose not to join.

Therefore, our empirical findings point to the fact that collective identity can be measured and that it plays a very important role in people's decisions to join a collective movement. Having established the case for collective identity, let us now examine how political leaders manipulate collective identity.

COLLECTIVE IDENTITY IN CONTEXT

In the rapidly expanding literature on collective action, Mancur Olson's of-ten quoted remark stands out like the Rock of Gibraltar: "Indeed, unless the number of individuals in a group is quite small, or unless there is coercion or some other special device to make individuals act in their common interest, *ra-tional, self-interested individuals will not act to achieve their common group in-terests.*"[53] In other words, if people can get something for nothing, they will not volunteer to pay for it. Since reality clearly shows that they do participate even when there is little to be gained or when they can get the same benefits without putting out the effort, I have argued that the explanation rests with the actor's collective identity. Thus, in contrast to Olson's blanket statement of inactivity by "rational" actors, Tajfel points out that participation in collective movements should be understood on the psychological level as "efforts by large numbers of people, *who define themselves and are defined by others as a group,* to solve collectively a problem they feel they have in common, and which is perceived to arise from their relations with other groups."[54] In social psychology, there are two major strands of theories. In one group, Tajfel and his associates point to the importance of collective identity.[55] The second group takes a wider perspective and stresses the importance of social rewards in an individual's participatory decision.[56] Thus, Bert Klandermans points out that individual participants go through four psychological steps in taking part in a collective movement.[57] They (1) become part of a "mobilization poten-tial." This makes them (2) targets of "mobilization attempts," which (3) moti-vate them to participate, (4) overcoming barriers to participation.

A growing number of studies have attempted to establish the importance of collective identity as a factor in the participatory decision in a social movement.[58] In an empirical work Simon et al. take the middle ground by combining collective identification with social rewards. In this study, through survey analyses the authors look into reasons for the elderly to join the Gray Panther movement and for homosexuals to participate in the gay movement. The authors find three variables to be significantly correlated with participation in the Gray Panther movement. These are (in order of importance), the "reward motive," "identification with the older people's movement," and the "collective motive."[59] The reward motive measures expected personal gains, while the rest are measures of collective identity. However, in the case of the gay movement only two variables turn out to be statistically significant. They are (in order of importance), "identification with [the] gay movement" and the "collective motive." In other words, like Gupta et al., Simon et al. also find actors' collective identities to be the most significant factor in their participatory decision.

During the past four decades, the concept of collective identity has increasingly been the object of inquiry in many academic disciplines. Although the notion of group identity was not unknown in academic circles, its inclusion as an area of serious inquiry appropriately started with the social psychologists. Their experimental research clearly demonstrated the importance of collective identity in the human decision-making calculus.

Thanks to their research, scholars in the disciplines of political science, sociology, and geography are attempting to include social psychology within their parameters. For instance, in their book, Iyenger and McGuire note the expanding domain of social psychology and its strong disciplinary linkage with other branches of the social sciences.[60] However, conspicuous in its absence from this list is economics. Indeed, economics, with its strict methodological tradition, has been slow to embrace social psychology. It is interesting that while many economists and public choice social scientists have criticized the inability of economics to explain collective action, until recently few have attempted to offer any concrete alternative for expanding economic methodology.[61] In fact, expanding multidisciplinary studies have been more or less a one-way street as far as economics is concerned; other related disciplines have accepted economic reasoning within the rubric of "public choice," but economics, other than including a few "noneconomic" variables, has remained steadfast in its methodological purity. Thus, when they have wanted to expand their horizons, economists have followed one of two paths. Most have sought corroboration of their economic arguments in other disciplines. Or they have included a few "noneconomic" variables within their models without significantly modifying the basic assumptions of their discipline. In this book, I offer a way of expanding the behavioral assumptions of economic rationality by borrowing from social psychology without discarding the analytical elegance of economics.

In this chapter, I argue that social psychology has provided a fruitful avenue for expanding economic analysis. Therefore, economics is limited in its refusal to accept psychological rewards of group motivations in an actor's benefit/cost analyses. Similarly, at the same time, social psychology, in its turn, refuses to go beyond the psychological variables and does not take into account nonpsychological "economic" costs of participation. Further, social psychology is typically interested in taking static pictures rather than examining the dynamic interactions within the society. Therefore, I argue that by combining the two rich academic traditions, we may break new ground in our understanding of collective actions.

NOTES

1. Olson (1965: 161–62).
2. In this book, I am arguing for a dual identity. However, the duality of identity in an actor's mind may also be supported by research on the brain's structure. Neuroscientists tell us that our brains have developed through eons of evolutionary process. MacLean (1990) demonstrates that the human brain has a three-level interconnected modular structure. Cory (1999: 2) states, "This structure comprises a self-preservational, maintenance component inherited from the stem reptiles of the Permian and Triassic periods, called the protoreptilian complex, a later modified and evolved mammalian affectional complex, and a most recently modified and elaborated higher cortex." The most primitive part of the brain is called the "protoreptilian complex." This part is used for the most basic bodily functions, such as breathing. The main function of this brain is self-preservation. The second part, or the "paleo-mammalian" brain, governs our instincts and desires to care for our offspring and extended social bonding. The third part of the brain brings a balance between the other two parts through higher level reasoning.
3. See Sherif and Hovland (1961).
4. See, for example, Tajfel (1970, 1978, 1982).
5. Social psychologists Kahneman and Tversky, in a long series of experiments, have demonstrated how we dispense with even the most fundamental precepts of economic rationality when facing uncertain outcomes. See, for instance, Kahneman and Tversky (1984) and Kahneman, Slovic, and Tversky (1982).
6. For a full discussion, see Hinkle and Brown (1990).
7. See Milgram (1974).
8. Ibid., 3.
9. In fact, this designation was written under the switch for 375 volts. The last two switches (435 and 450 volts) were simply marked an ominous XXX.
10. See Gourevitch (1998) for an extraordinary account of group adherence in the Rwandan genocide.
11. See Adorno, Frenkel-Brunswick, Levinson, and Sanford (1950).
12. See, for example, Christie and Jahoda (1954). Also see Kirscht and Dillehay (1967).
13. See Lipset (1960). Also see the later edition (1981).
14. See Sears, Peplau, Freedman, and Taylor (1988: 423).

15. For instance, in my own research, I have found the loss of income share by the middle class to be highly correlated with national political instability. See Dipak Gupta (1990: 238–47).

16. See Fetsinger (1957).

17. See Douglas (1997: A1).

18. Ibid.

19. See Batson (1991). Also see Phelps (1975).

20. See Chatterjee (1998).

21. The concept of "archetypes" constitutes one of the core ideas of Carl Jung and can be found in many of his writings. See, for example, Jung (1959: 3–41).

22. I am particularly grateful to Professor Christopher Clague for this part of my argument.

23. "The preference for participation in public affairs over the 'idiocy' of private life is much more unstable, and subject to much wider fluctuations, than the preference for, say, apples over pears or for present over future consumption" (Hirschman 1974: 9).

24. I have presented my arguments more formally in previous publications. For instance, see Dipak Gupta (1990); Gupta and Singh (1992); Gupta, Hofstetter, and Buss (1997) and Gupta (2001b).

25. The modified model of collective behavior postulates that an individual maximizes utility (U_i) by consuming an optimum amount of the two goods, private and collective, subject to the total available time or endowment (T). Thus, we may formally write:

$$U_i = U(Y_i, P_i) \tag{1}$$

$$\text{subject to } T = T_y + T_p$$

Where: U_i is assumed to be strictly quasi-concave; T_y is the amount of time an individual i decides to devote to the pursuit of economic goods; and T_p is the amount of time spent on the production of public goods.

26. My arguments can be presented with the help of the standard methodological tools of microeconomics. By combining the two motivations, we can posit that an individual's actions are motivated not only by self-interest—as argued by the proponents of public choice—but also from a distinct utility derived from furthering the cause of the group in which he or she claims membership. Within our framework, therefore, a human being is not an unidimensional self-utility maximizer but one who seeks a balance between the conflicting demands of the individual and the collective. We hypothesize that private goods are produced by individual effort, while collective goods are produced either by joint effort or collective movements. This tradeoff can be depicted with the help of the standard tools of microeconomic analysis (Figure A).

In Figure 4.3, the vertical axis measures goods that promote self-interest such as personal income, power, rectitude, etc., accruing to the individual actor as a result of the employment of resources within his/her command. The horizontal axis measures the amount of collective goods (e.g., end of discrimination, gaining of national independence, etc.) the actor can expect to obtain by contributing an additional unit of resources. The indifference curves measure the relative preferences of the two utilities that an actor would attribute to the two utility-producing activities. On the other hand, the budget line measures the resource constraints that an individual would face

Figure A: Private Goods and Collective Goods—Effects of Changes in Political Environment

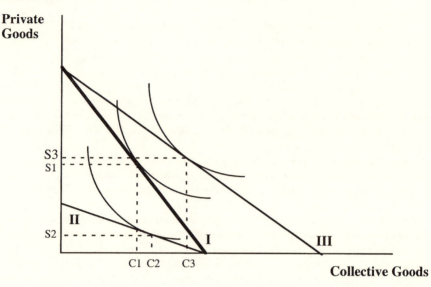

in producing the two utility producing goods. In Figure A, a hypothetical individual attains the point of equilibrium—the ideal mix between the pursuit of self-interest producing goods and collective-utility producing goods—where S1 of the private goods and C1 amount of collective goods are produced.

In strict economic terms, the budget line can be interpreted as how much an individual can expect to produce with the various combinations of the two goods by devoting the total available resources. These resources would include an individual's power, position, and wealth in the community. Therefore, this constraint also measures the "opportunity cost" of time. That is, it shows how much an individual can expect to produce one good by giving up another. However, this budget constraint is not fixed over time and can have shifts based on changed sociopolitical and economic conditions. Specifically, the conditions which may change the slope of this "budget line" can depend on the following factors:

Changes in economic opportunities. If economic opportunities deteriorate and high rates of unemployment plague the nation, the cost of diverting time from the pursuit of economic to collective goods would be relatively small. This situation is depicted in Figure A, where the budget line dips down to (II). As a result, even though the opportunities for producing collective goods do not go up (the government maintains strict law and order), the reduced opportunity cost will produce a higher level of political protests and other forms of collective activities to the changed level of C2. Thus, if the nation experiences an economic decline (such as in Albania and other parts of Eastern Europe), the truncated economic opportunities will tend to fuel people's desire for collective goods. Thus deterioration of economic conditions may bring about collective movements. At this point, it should be noted that in this particular case, I show that a decrease in the opportunity cost of diverting resources to the production of collective goods is creating a greater participation in the collective good. However, in actuality, each individual's decision to allocation of resources between the two goods would be filtered through the relative strengths of *income effect* and *substitution effect*.

In contrast, if economic opportunities improve, an individual will be able to make more goods which create private (self-interest) goods. Therefore, the opportunity cost of resources to divert to the pursuit of collective goods will go up. This will cause an actor to devote more resources to the production of private goods. In order to keep the diagram simple, this changed budget line is not shown. However, by following the same logic, this shift will cause the actor to neglect the pursuit of collective goods, and instead strive harder to achieve private goods. This is typically a situation similar to Chile under Augusto Pinochet, South Korea under Park Chung Hee, and present-day Singapore under Lee Kuan Yew. In these cases, citizens accept lack of individual freedom, corruption, and even gross violations of human rights as they trade those collective goods for personal economic well-being.

Changes in political opportunities. Changes in political opportunities can also cause changes in people's perception of their ability to achieve a proper mix of the two goods. For instance, if the central government becomes weakened from war or some other natural or man-made catastrophe, the lessening of the government's coercive capabilities may cause a bandwagon effect. When the fear of retribution goes down, people feel free to express their disaffection with an established political system. For instance, the virtual explosion of collective movements in the United States during the Vietnam War can be explained with the help of this scenario. Kuran (1991, 1993, 1995a, 1995b, 1997) has ably demonstrated this in a series of books and articles. In Figure A, this changed opportunity causes the budget line (I) to shift to the right to (III). With many expecting to get quick rewards from collective action, protests and rebellions start quickly, often without much prior notice.

Political opportunities can also be determined by the government's attitude toward repressing of views of its political opponents. For instance, if the government decides to crack down on dissidents, it can truly truncate the budget line, thereby causing the prospective participants to openly participate in collective action. This can, as Kuran (1995) has suggested, significantly scale back their involvement and drive a wedge between their public pronouncements and private views. Once again, in order to keep the diagram simple, we have not shown this shift in the budget line in Figure A.

Shift in preference. Another important reason for people's choices of a different mix of private and collective goods is the result of political entrepresneurs' influencing them to cause a shift in individual preferences. Figure B depicts the situation. Since collective identity is not constant and individuals may take on a number of collective identities, it is the political entrepreneurs of all sorts of ideologies who inspire their followers to sacrifice their private goods in favor of collective goods. As can be seen in Figure B, inspiring leadership may cause the indifference factor to shift to the right (II); people place more emphasis on the pursuit of collective goods by becoming political activists of all sorts, from freedom riders to urban guerrillas.

A shift in preference may also take place if the individual members feel a serious threat to their collective identity. A community can feel threatened as a result of some external actions (such as a war), an attack on a recognized symbol (such as flag burning), or the perception of a sudden change in social status hierarchy (immigration issues). In such cases, people may be willing to join the cause of the collective even to

Figure B: Private Goods and Collective Goods—Effects of Leadership

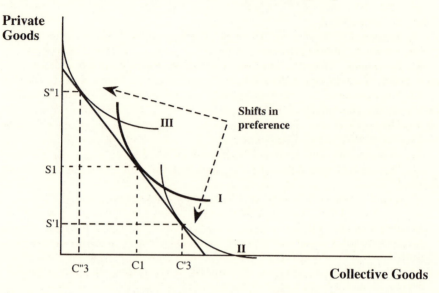

the detriment of their personal safety or at the risk of extreme monetary loss. Throughout history, political entrepreneurs from the Nazis in Germany to the Hutus in Rwanda have manufactured the perceptions of a threat.

27. As sources of bureaucratic authority, Max Weber mentioned the legal structure of a nation, tradition (monarchy), and charisma. For Weber, modern bureaucracy meant an end of traditional and charismatic leadership.

28. See Johnson (1988).

29. See Popkin (1979).

30. See Kuran (1995a).

31. See Trotsky (1932).

32. Gurr (1970).

33. For a discussion of this process, see Kuran (1995a).

34. See Ricks (1997).

35. Although Ricks does not say so, I would conjecture that a good number of the recruits are from families with a military background.

36. Ricks (1997: 30).

37. Ibid., 38.

38. Ibid., 40.

39. Ibid., 71.

40. This sense comes through in many areas of the book. In particular, see ibid., 37–38.

41. Ibid., 66.

42. Ibid., 62.

43. Ibid., 38.

44. Ibid., 66.

45. Ibid., 63.

46. Ibid., 76.

47. Ibid., 90.

48. See Gurr (1993).

49. Kelman (1973).

50. See Dipak Gupta (1990).

51. See Gupta, Hofstetter, and Buss (1997). Also, for a similar approach, see, Simon, Stürmer, Lowey et al. (1998).

52. Since the dependent variable is binary, we used a multinomial logit model for estimating the parameters.

53. Olson (1965: 2).

54. Tajfel (1981: 244). Emphasis mine.

55. Also see Tajfel and Turner (1986); Turner et al. (1987).

56. See, for instance, Ajzen (1991); Ajzen and Fishbein (1980); Fishbein and Ajzen (1975).

57. Klandermans (1997). Also see Klandermans and Oegema (1987).

58. See Kelly (1993); Kelly and Breinlinger (1996); Kawakami and Dion (1993, 1995); B. Simon et al. (1998).

59. Simon et al.'s definition of "reward" should be read as "net reward," for they consider both gains and losses. In estimating the "rewards" for joining a collective movement, the authors considered an expected return model, where the perceived probability of success is multiplied by the expected reward. The rewards included improvement of the actor's own living conditions, social contacts with other older or gay people, and meaningful leisure time activity. They also considered the possibilities of two losses (health risks and loss of time). The identification with older/gay people measures the strength of psychological attachment to the community (similar to the "us" factor in Gupta et al.). Collective motives included goals of the two movements.

60. Iyenger and McGuire (1999: i).

61. For a notable exception, see Ackerlof and Kranton (2000).

CHAPTER 5

THE SLIPPERY SLOPE:
FROM IDENTITY TO MADNESS

Oh Allah, destroy America, for she is ruled by Zionist Jews. . . . Allah will paint the White House black! Clinton is fulfilling his father's will to identify with Israel. The Muslims say to Britain, to France and all the infidel nations that Jerusalem is Arab. We shall not respect anyone else's wishes regarding her. The homes the Jews are building will become Arab property. . . . Allah shall take revenge on behalf of his prophet against the colonialist settlers who are sons of monkeys and pigs.
    —Excerpts from the July 11, 1997 sermon of Palestinian Authority Mufti Ikrama Sabri at the Al Aqsa mosque, Jerusalem[1]

The holy martyr Baruch Goldstein is from now on our intercessor in the Heavens. Goldstein didn't act as an individual: He heard the cry of the Land [of Israel] which is being stolen from us day after day by the Muslims. He acted in order to relieve that cry of the Land.
    —Rabbi Israel Ariel, eulogizing Baruch Goldstein, who opened fire on a group of Muslim Arabs praying in the Patriarch's Cave in Hebron on February 25, 1994[2]

You cockroaches must know that you are made of flesh! We won't let you kill! We will kill you.
    —Warning to the Tutsis on the Hutu-controlled Radio-Télévision Libre des Mille Collines[3]

THE MAKING OF AN ENEMY

Fitting the Image

"In the beginning we create the enemy," writes author Sam Keen. "Before the weapon comes the image. We think others to death and then invent the battle-ax or the ballistic missiles with which to actually kill them. *Propaganda precedes technology.*"[4] Keen is almost correct. We do create the image of an enemy before we proceed to slay it. The concepts of archetypes and collective memory form the core of Carl Jung's explanation of the human psyche. Jung defines "archetype" as follows:

"Archetype" is an explanatory paraphrase of the Platonic ειδοξ. For our purpose this term is apposite and helpful, because it tells us that so far as the collective unconscious contents are concerned we are dealing with archaic or—I would say—primordial types, that is with universal images that have existed since the remotest times. The term "représentations collectives," used by Lévy-Bruhl to denote the symbolic figures in the primitive view of the world, could easily be applied to unconscious contents as well, since it means practically the same thing. Primitive tribal lore is concerned with archetypes that have been modified in a special way. They are no longer contents of the unconscious, but have already been changed into conscious formulae taught according to tradition, generally in the form of esoteric teaching. This last is a typical means of expression for the transmission of collective contents originally derived from the unconscious.[5]

Following Jung, I would argue that all of us have a ready image of the enemy (an "archetype")—complete with its behavioral patterns, habits, and mores—which we superimpose on another group. If we strip away the nonessential parts, then the process enemy making becomes amazingly similar. The way the Jews were presented to the German population by the National Socialist Party, or the Tutsis to the Hutus, or the Bosnian Muslims to the Bosnian Serbs, bear an unmistakable likeness. Even in other forms of group madness, such as in Jonestown or in Waco, the agents of the U.S. government were portrayed as the archenemies, drawing upon all the conscious and unconscious imageries of quintessential evil. The process of enemy creation portrays "us" and "them" in the starkest possible terms.

Of course, I don't mean to imply that the construction of collective identity is always without a firm basis in reality.[6] Freud pointed out that, in search of an enemy, people often base their hostile feelings toward members of another group on some "kernel of truth."[7] This "truth" may be based on historical events of the distant past or on some personal encounter with a particular member of the rival group. For those who are all too willing to fit a group of individuals into the image of the enemy, history often becomes the toolbox from which examples can be picked up at random to suit the purpose. Sabrina Ramet, in analyzing the Balkan mind-set, points out that for zealots history becomes totally telescopic.[8] In the blame game, something that may have happened 2,000 years ago can become just as relevant as an event that took place only yesterday. When the litany of past and present crimes is tabulated, the implied threats of the future become abundantly clear to the receptive ones. And when a source of threat is identified, attempts to eliminate it become the most logical choice.

The process of group formation starts with the creation of a collective identity. In the process we define who we are in relation to each other within the in-group. At the same time, we define the "others," as the enemy. However, it may not be easy to form separate groups from neighbors who have lived next to each other for generations. In such cases, psychiatrist John E. Mack points out that people use "cultural amplifiers."[9] Cultural amplifiers are designed to create mountains out of molehills by magnifying minute differences in culture to an absurd level; after all, in Jonathan Swift's classical political satire, *Gulliver's Travels*, the two groups of Lilliputians were fighting over which end of the boiled egg to crack. Typically, these amplifiers involve ethnic food, color and style of clothes, or variations in dialect. Aspects of "our" food may be portrayed as being as beneficial as mother's milk, while dishes typically consumed by "them" are condemned as unhealthy, sinful, unclean, or simply unappetizing.[10] As an example, in the context of white America, chicken soup can be a life-giving substance, while food consumed by "others"—from kimchi to curry, from falafel to fried chicken and watermelon—takes on more ominous characteristics. In terms of clothing, in deeply divided societies, just as in gang-infested central cities, differences in attire can define a person's collective affiliation. In a state of cultural amplification, even the smallest differences are magnified to the ultimate question, "With so many differences, how could we live next to each other?"

The Political Entrepreneurs

All societies carry in their collective memories tales of heroes and villains, past deeds of right and wrong. Digging deep into this reservoir of hopes and aspirations, despair and nightmares, political entrepreneurs develop their own political platforms. In terms of social psychology, they "frame" an issue. Framing is extremely important in how we view a complex reality. For instance, if a patient is told that he has a 95% chance of survival, then we can get one kind of reaction. However, if he or she is told that there is a 5% chance of death, the reaction is likely to be significantly different. The mastery of political entrepreneurs lies in their ability to frame issues for their audience. Although the importance of framing in our decision-making process has been recognized for a while, perhaps the best example of proof through experimental design can be found in works of Kahneman and Tversky.[11] In their work, they demonstrated that individuals tend to make distinct choices depending on whether the outcomes are framed in terms of gains (e.g., survival) or losses (death). Since their groundbreaking work, the effects of framing have been examined in the diverse fields of cognitive science, communications studies, law, political science, psychology, and economics.[12]

Political entrepreneurs often dredge things up from the past to present a coherent story of historical injustice and exploitation by the opposing group. In their inspirational speeches and sermons, demagogues of all colors, shades, and ideologies use truths, semi-truths, and utter falsehoods in the same breath. In the process, an entire edifice is constructed around a kernel of truth, wherein a coherent chronological account of conspiracy, exploitation, and victimization is told and a pantheon of gods and demons is clearly identified.

By the beginning of the twentieth century, neoclassical economics had gained a great deal of insight in developing models of individual economic behavior. By extending microeconomic analysis, economists could explain the behavior of an individual actor or a firm within the context of a competitive market. Yet, the link between micro and macro remained tenuous at best. Just as a detailed map of the human genome does not get us any closer to the soul, knowledge of how an individual might react to a set of factors defining benefits and costs not led to a complete understanding of overall social dynamics. Comprehension of individual motivation did not provide a satisfactory explanation of overall economic evolution. In 1912, in his famous work, *The Theory of Economic Development,* economist Joseph Schumpeter attempted to fill this void by introducing the concept of agents of change: economic innovators or *entrepreneurs.* In his model, market supply and demand do not determine prices, wages, and interest rates in the long run. Instead, it is the dynamic involvement of innovators such as Henry Ford and Andrew Carnegie, who take the existing technology, elevate it to something new, and, in the process, shape the destiny of the economy. As the entrepreneurs innovate, static analyses of market equilibrium metamorphosize into the inquiry of economic development and social change.

Similar to the central position in the process of economic development accorded to business entrepreneurs by Schumpeter, the rise and fall of political entrepreneurs mark the history of political evolution. These are the political entrepreneurs of all shades, forms, and ideologies, ranging from Hitler to Lenin, Washington, Gandhi, or Khomeini, who take a nation by the root of its collective identity and change the course of history. The political entrepreneur's construction of reality resonates with the people. The multitude sees the world as the leader would paint it for them. They either see their future with high hope or with extreme trepidation through the eyes of their leaders. They cheer with pride at the mention of the names of the heroes of days long gone by; they seethe with anger recalling the crimes of the villains.

Although diverse in time, space, geography, culture, history, and ideology, the political entrepreneurs, especially those who base their message on the ideology of hate, follow some typical patterns. They use a similar set of imageries with familiar analogies from musty old boxes that have been recycled and used throughout history. For instance, the first thing a political entrepreneur does is to clearly define "us" and "them," the "in-group" and the "out-group." With all the tools of cultural amplifiers, the differences between the two are presented in the starkest possible terms. In fact, extending Sam Keen's list, we can develop the following set of overall points of differentiation drawn by political entrepreneurs.[13]

Us	Them
Good	Bad
Indigenous	Outsiders
Victims	Oppressors
Humans	Nonhumans
God is on our side	God is against them

The community of the "in-group" is always portrayed as "good," "brave," and "just." Whether it is the Teutonic race of Hitler's *Mein Kampf*, the Hutus of Radio-Télévision Libre des Mille Collines in Rwanda, or the farmers in Pol Pot's Cambodia, the political leadership constructs political reality for the populace through propaganda.[14]

In his book and in his speeches, Hitler, like all demagogues before and after, clearly identified the community. So powerful has been his identification in the West that even half a century after the fall of the Third Reich, "Aryan" signifies the Nordic physical characteristics of blond and blue-eyed individuals. Yet Aryan was the name of an old Indo-European tribe, originating possibly in the Eurasian plains in the vicinity of Anatolia. The history of the Indo-European people tells that at least two to three millennia ago some migrated westward to Europe, and some eastward to Iran and India.[15] Needless to say, the physical characteristics of the Aryans were figments of the imaginations of Hitler and his contemporaries. Regardless, the image stuck; once the reality was constructed, a true German could be identified. And a "true German" could be distinguished from the interlopers and the invaders, the Jews, the Gypsies, and the Slavs. The complexity of human reasoning is truly astounding. To non-Germans, it has always been a source of amusement to see how, himself the antithesis of the true Teutonic image, Hitler could define purity of racial characteristics. Yet he did just that. The entire Nazi propaganda machine went into full gear trying to establish *Gemeinschaft* and *Gesellschaft*, those belonging to German society and those who did not. Those who did not belong could be eliminated through the "final solution." Nobody should shed a tear for the impostors and social parasites.

In Bosnia, Serbs, Croats, and Muslims all redefined their ethnicity with an alacrity that surprised many. In their zeal, each identified the other as "invaders" and perpetrators of past crimes. The incessant propaganda coming out of each combatant's radio and television stations, newspapers and magazines presented their own claims over the others with utmost contrast. The Ustashe and the Chetnics, two hyper-nationalist gangs who carried out vicious attacks on one another during World War II, came to symbolize the fear and apprehension of the two rival ethnic groups felt toward each other. Those who had already suffered, they were made to feel even more insecure about the possibility that their horrific experience would be repeated. Those who had not were told to beware of their fate, unless they took immediate preemptive moves. Soon, Serbs started calling all Croats "Ustashe"; Croats would describe every Serb as a "Chetnic," and Serbs and Croats would identify Muslims not as fellow Bosnians, but as "Turks" or the descendants of the former occupiers of Serbia, the agents of the former Ottoman Empire. With those epithets, the stage was set for a fierce fratricide.

In Rwanda, in the predictable familiarity of Nazi Germany and Bosnia, the Hutu radio and television started calling the Tutsis "invaders." Ultra-nationalist Jews in Israel deny any legitimate rights of those who lived in the land for the last 2,000 years in favor of those whose children left it millennia ago. Extremist Arabs, in turn, refuse to recognize the right of Jews to live in Palestine. All over the world, regardless of time and culture, sectarian conflicts change history and circumstances, but the rhetoric remains the same. Unfortunately, those infected with the blood disease are hardly able to diagnose their own affliction. Those who are outside look on with incredulity.

If we analyze the three hateful messages at this beginning of the chapter, we can find most of these ideas. Even in these highly cryptic lines, we can see almost all the aspects of the broader message of enemy formation. In all of these the central idea is that either the Zionist Jews, the Arabs, or the Tutsis are "foreigners" to the land; they are evil and are against God; and they are subhuman: pigs, dogs, and cockroaches. In fact, from *Mein Kampf* to the *Turner Diaries,* the messages of hate all over the world are based on these few basic concepts.[16]

Take for instance, Hitler's *Mein Kampf,* which presents one of the most elaborate systems of ideology based on principles of "us" and "them." Like many totalitarian philosophies—such as fascism in Italy or that of the Croix de Feu in France, the Iron Guard in Romania, or the Khmer Rouge in Cambodia—the National Socialist ideology was based on the romantic notion of the bygone days of the simple agrarian life. Borrowing bits and pieces from history, anthropology, and philosophy, Hitler presented a strange concoction of extreme German nationalistic politics. Hitler's world view combined in a strange witches' brew Wagnerian music, the idea of the Superman from the essentially anti-nationalist and anti-German philosophy of Nietzsche, and the evolutionary biology of Charles Darwin.

The National Socialist ideology was based on the notion of the *Volksgemeinschaft*—the folk community—which was going to replace the vile, atomizing industrial society of *Gesellschaft*. The *Volksgemeinschaft* was a total community that regulated every aspect of life of an individual within it. An egalitarian society based on equal rights for its Aryan members was to replace the prevailing society based on economic class and birth. Anyone born in this *Volk* is bound by the identity of a common race. In this new society all men and women would know their place and find meaning in their lives through total dedication to the communal spirit. In return, the new Aryan nation would provide a harmony between themselves and others (the Aryans were going to rule over the non-Aryans) and between the Aryan community and nature. This unity would be based on a mystical nexus among *blut* (blood), *Volk* (the people), and *Boden* (the "German" soil) and on the simple values of Aryan agrarian society. These four essential notions provided symbolic expressions of the Nazi Party: the red color of blood, the black of the soil, and the images of shovel and grain. And, of course, from the Aryan past came the symbol of the swastika.[17]

Hitler proclaimed that the new Germans would build their community through ideals of self-sacrifice, respect for German ideals, and responsibility to the *Volk* to keep it free from contamination from other inferior races. A true Aryan would not approach his duties through intellectual exercise, but would instinctively know what was right. He would "think with his blood." Hitler scolded the Germans for being so simple-minded in their inner goodness that they were oblivious to their obvious superiority. In comparison to the wily, intellectual Jew, Hitler once lovingly called the "Aryan" a "blockhead."[18]

The opposite side of this rabid national identity was the image of the enemy. For this the Jews were perfect matches. Dredging the depths of the prevailing anti-Semitic view of the time, Hitler painted the picture of a Jew in the most menacing manner. In fact, in order to contrast the divine righteousness of the mythical Aryans, he needed an equally vile demonic "other," which he conveniently found in the Jews. Anything that was hideous and heinous, repulsive and repellent was personified in the Jews. Where the Aryans were the builders of beauty and justice, the Jews were the destroyers. Together with the "Judaizers" or the "spiritual Jews"—those sympathetic Germans and other non-Jews—the Jews promoted all the contrary ideas. They did not have the "blood," they were not of the "soil," they were not agrarian, but were the upholders of the twin evils of international finance and international socialism.

This bizarre, hodgepodge philosophy and pseudo-science resonated well with the German people, desperately seeking an escape. The misery of defeat in World War I, along with the economic pain imposed by the Versailles Treaty, provided fertile ground in which the intense collective identity of "us" and "them" could take root. Every misery—real or imaginary, current or of the past—could be conveniently dumped on the shoulders of a shared enemy, the Jews, the Gypsies, and the others outside the *Volksgemeinschaft*.

Mythology, however, knows no boundaries—political, cultural, or temporal. Curiously, the rise of collective identity based on the mythological image of the Aryans has brought pain and misery to yet another part of the world. It is indeed interesting to note how many countries have suffered because political entrepreneurs have manufactured and manipulated such identities. Take, for instance, the case of Sri Lanka, a teardrop-shaped island nation floating in the glistening waters of the Indian Ocean, separated by a narrow channel from India to the north. When it achieved independence from British colonial rule in 1948, experts all over the world gave Sri Lanka the highest odds in the catch-up game with the industrialized West. Its population comprised primarily of two ethnic groups, the Buddhist Sinhalese and the Hindu Tamils, Sri Lanka—then called Ceylon—had the highest literacy rate in the region along with a long tradition of democratic political participation. But, above all, Sri Lanka, unlike its regional neighbors, was at peace. It had a population of manageable size, good infrastructure, and natural resources—including tea and coffee—that could be traded for hard currency. However, despite its tranquillity, trouble was on the horizon.

The name Sri Lanka features most prominently in the ancient Indian mythology of the *Ramayana* (discussed in Chapter 2).[19] In the story, the evil king Ravana's kingdom, Lanka, was an island in the great ocean. As with most mythologies, experts are not sure about the exact location of Lanka, but most would perhaps agree that the epic narrates the story of the Aryan invasion of southern India. It is truly interesting to note that, like the Nazis in Germany, the source of collective identity among the Sinhalese in postcolonial Sri Lanka has been their "Aryan heritage." It is of course true that the Sinhala language is part of the Indo-European language group with ample borrowings from the vocabulary of the rival Dravidian language of Tamil. It is also true that the Indian southern state of Tamilnadu, as its name suggests (the "Tamil land"), is predominantly Tamil. However, what is not certain is how long the vast majority of the Sri Lankan Tamils have been on the island. There is no written record of original settlement. But when two groups collide, the conflict is rarely about documented history.[20]

The problem was that during the period of colonial rule (1796–1948), the Tamils living around the port city of Colombo embraced the English language and Western culture. Also, American missionaries had opened excellent schools in the north of the country where the Tamils are largely concentrated. As a result, the educated Tamils were poised to place themselves in the inner sanctum of power through their entry into the colonial civil service. Therefore, at the time of independence, the minority Tamils exerted a far greater influence over Sri Lankan politics than was warranted by their numerical strength in the nascent democratic nation. The frustration of the non-Westernized Buddhist majority found expression in a 1956 election, when an intensely Sinhalese nationalistic coalition came to power on the platform of making Sinhala the "sole official language of government affairs." The push was on to declare secular Sri Lanka a Buddhist nation. The implication of the government action was clear; it immediately identified the Sinhalese as true sons of the soil and the Tamils as interlopers.[21] Threatened by the possibility of being relegated to second-class citizenship, the Tamils found little use for the democratic system and fought back with force. Soon the nation, previously the envy of the region, descended into an extremely bloody, full-fledged civil war, which is still raging.

This has been the fate of many lands across the world. Political entrepreneurs have successfully been able to channelize frustrations into a coherent force through the clever use of mythology, producing intense collective identity. As a result, in extremist Jewish sermons Arabs are described as the interlopers in Israel, having no right to the land given to the descendants of Abraham and Moses by God. They are characterized with the same negativity present in every culture while describing their enemies and are despised for all their character flaws. The Hindu extremists view the Muslims similarly in India.[22] The Hindus, in turn, are hated by many in Muslim-dominated Bangladesh.[23] The Mohajirs, the Muslims from India, are sources of conflict in Pakistan.[24] The Armenians and the Azerbaijanis view each other with utmost suspicion.[25] The northern Sudanese identify themselves not as Nilotic Africans but with the Arabs.[26] The Catholics and Protestants are at loggerheads in Northern Ireland over who are the "true" Irish.[27] In this grossly incomplete list of antagonists, it is interesting that if we change the names of the righteous and the offender, the blueprint to the land of extreme hate remains—and will continue to remain—invariant.

THE PARTICIPANTS

In Chapter 4 I argued for recognizing three "ideal types" of participants and nonparticipants in any collective movement, based on three primary motivations, ideology (strength of collective identity), greed (selfish interest), and fear (cost). In this section, I extend my line of reasoning to examine these categories with the help of historical examples.

The True Believers

A "true believer" is one whose primary motivation is of the group. These people may suspend their individual judgment and follow the leader in blind obedience. However, we recognize that nobody operates from a single motivation. In fact, no outsider can truly judge another human being's reasons for his or her outward behavior; even we ourselves often do not know our true motivations. Therefore, "know thyself" remains one of life's most profound and, perhaps, unattainable goals. However, biographers have painted pictures of people in many colors. For the sake of argument, we may pick one, not because the particular biographer is entirely correct in the portrayal of a single-minded devotion, but because we can use that picture as the "ideal type" of a person representing a particular category of motivation.

Take, for instance, the case of Maria Katsaris. The child of a Greek Ortho-dox priest and a psychiatrist, Maria was close to her father. Following the old-world Greek heritage, she did not mind her father's strict rules as she grew up; she attended mass at her father's church regularly. At nineteen, she was studying to be a nurse. She had followed her father in anti-war marches. Then, one autumn evening in 1973, Maria went to her first meeting at the Reverend Jim Jones' People's Temple in Ukiah, California. She was quickly converted. John Nugent describes her thus:

Within a few months, Maria Katsaris joined the People's Temple. The next year, she quit studying nursing. . . . She was instantly elevated to Jones's staff—a group of ten women, young and white only, who made up his private harem, which no one dared go near because the penalty was a brutal session with the "board of education" [for a first offense]. . . .

Jones seduced her in all ways possible. . . . She believed him, as she had believed her father—without question. . . . With her, it wasn't a case of being born again, she had just been born.[28]

This is a typical portrait of a true believer. These are the people who are fre-quently allowed in the inner sanctum of the faithful, closest to the center of power. These are the true believers who, like Joseph and Magda Goebbels, would rather kill their children and then commit suicide than surrender.[29] These are the followers of the Heaven's Gate cult, who would willingly castrate themselves and then, when the time came, commit mass suicide. Their unshak-able faith may be rooted in religion or ideology. Their faith may also be the re-sult of anger and extreme anguish, the kind the young Tamil woman who took the life of Rajiv Gandhi in India must have felt when her entire family perished during an Indian military offensive against the Tamil Tigers. Despondent and having little to lose, some of us can become true believers in the fight against a shared enemy, real or simply imagined. However, in order to create true be-lievers, collective ideologies require rituals.

The human mind is fickle. What we need for our own selves, what suits our purpose, or what grabs our immediate attention can keep us occupied. But how do we retain our interest in the collective? For that we need training. To do just that, prehistoric people invented mythology and rituals. Mythologies were handed down orally from one generation to the next. When writing was invented, the sacred texts were written down in copious detail. Nothing was left out. In fact, when the 2,000-year-old texts were discovered in the caves of the Dead Sea, to the amazement of the scholars, little was found to have changed in the Bible throughout two tumultuous millennia.

But it was not enough to simply write down the tales of inspiration, know-ing our own fickle nature. The religious rites required that the pious read them every day with the regularity prescribed by the strictest rituals. Those with photographic memory were amply rewarded with, if nothing else, reverence and awe. Again, to train our irresolute minds, the sacred texts of courage, valor and, above all, sacrifice, were put to music. Ancient people, like their descendants of modern times, learned to repeat over and over again the musical chants, which would penetrate deep inside their brains. It is not very clear what such rituals do to our physical process of cognition or whether changes are made in the basic hardware of the brain, but what is clear is that they reinforce an existing world view with amazing consistency. From the Gregorian chants to the mantras of Hare Krishna, rituals have served this purpose of reinforcement through eons of our social evolutionary process.[30]

The military boot camp, through its mindless rituals, reinforces the identity of the collective. Putting men and women in uniforms is a vivid reminder of collectivity.[31] We sing national anthems all over the world, memorizing their every note, placing hands on our chest in a gesture of extreme love and belonging, paying tribute to our nations wherever we are, in a uniform theme of praise to the greatest country on the face of the earth. The nonmilitaristic civil rights movement incorporated songs such as "We Shall Overcome" with just as much fervor as communists sang the "International" all over the world.[32] With songs, uniforms, and other rituals, individual identity is molded into a firm collective.

The nature of the collective is often not self-evident. Therefore, collective identity among the believers must be raised with the use of symbols. Symbols serve to encapsulate a complex reality in a bite-size morsel. We may not know the history of our nation, or may not have a deep notion of its diversity, but we can visualize the entire country when we witness the fluttering of the flag or sing the national anthem. We raise and lower the national flag with reverence reserved only for religious icons. We sing national anthems in endless repetition at all sorts of ceremonious occasions. As children, we learn to chant the pledge of allegiance. These ritualistic practices take on even greater importance when we join the armed forces. If a group of people is to be prepared to lay down their lives for the collective, we must inculcate the presence of the collective in their minds. With endless rituals, any act of self-sacrifice comes with the ease of trained muscles in a concert pianist or a professional tennis player.

Therefore, a collective movement requires not only leadership and military strategists, but also poets and songwriters. Sometimes leaders turn out to be poets. Thus, the Bosnian Serb leader Radovan Karadzic, an accomplished poet as well as a trained psychiatrist, incited his fellow Serbs through his dark poems, obsessed with threats of extreme violence against an unseen enemy whose identity is readily understood by the intended readers. "A Morning Hand-Grenade" is found in a compilation of his work aptly titled *Crna Bajka* (The Black Fable).

Such exhortations, veiled or explicit, are a staple of almost all collective movements. These are the instruments designed to break down the free-rider problem in all its aspects. Mancur Olson, in *The Logic of Collective Action,* suggested that the problem of the free rider would increase with the size of the group. Looking through the logic of self-utility maximization, it is indeed impossible to see how any large group can overcome this conceptual problem. Yet, these simple and time-tested rituals can reach people far beyond physical boundaries. Adherence to such rituals preserved the Jewish identity through trials and tribulations of all sorts. Such rituals unified the Germans and the Italians. The use of such mythology allowed China to preserve its essential political boundaries for much of its known history.

Therefore, in the ultimate analysis of the process through which a population is mobilized for collective action, what separates the Gandhian movement, with its lofty ideals of nonviolence, and the hate-driven movement of Nazi Germany is their respective messages. What brown shirts and jackboots did for the Storm Troopers, coarse hand-woven white shirts and *dhoti* did for the Indian freedom fighters. Both movements, like all others before and after, made copious use of songs and symbols in their respective interpretations of history.

The Mercenaries: The Seekers of Fun and Profit

It is quite clear that people do not take part in collective movements out of ideological inspiration alone. Most Crusaders did not go to the Holy Land purely out of their commitment to Christianity. Some went for the glory, some for the possible bounties of war, and some seeking adventure. Oskar Schindler did not save his Jewish workers solely out of pure altruism. Therefore, it is undeniable that in any movement we are likely to encounter those whose motivations are less than "pure." Of course, we will never be able to completely separate the two. Human motivation is always mixed, but we can never the less identify the extreme cases of where people join a collective movement for purely self-serving reasons. We call this group of participants the "mercenaries."

Noted psychologist Robert Jay Lifton studied the doctors who served in the Nazi concentration camps.[33] Among all the participants in the Holocaust, none evoke more outrage than these doctors. Having taken the lofty Hippocratic oath, physicians are expected to act as healers. Naturally, it astounds us to know that the same group of people would carry out the most inhumane experiments on innocent human beings—men, women, children, young and old. They are the ones who played god and chose which victims would be sent to the work camps and which would face immediate death. Perhaps expecting to see the Devil incarnate, Lifton only found some flawed human beings. Most of them joined the service or volunteered for concentration camp duties as a method of gaining quick promotion—hardly an extraordinary motivation.[34]

In a recent report, a Dutch research institute estimated that in 1995, fifty-eight countries all over the world, encompassing much of humanity, used torture on a regular basis.[35] Most, if not all, of these countries employ techniques of torture for social control as a part of deliberate government policy. The methods used target every part of the human body and mind capable of absorbing pain. Who are the perpetrators of this gruesome politics of pain? Miguel Angel Estrella, a renowned Argentine pianist who was tortured in Uruguay, described his experience as follows:

They were like sadists. . . . After two days of torture I hurt all over, and had no sensation whatsoever left in my hands. I touched things and didn't feel anything. They kept making like they were going to chop off my hands. The last time they even had an electric saw going. They'd pull on my finger and ask, "Which is the finger you use most in playing the piano? . . . Is it maybe the thumb?" They pulled on the finger and made like they were going to slice them off with the electric saw.[36]

However, despite the assertions of the victims, a careful evaluation suggests that the ranks of the most effective torturers are not filled from sadists or those who derive sexual gratification from inflicting pain on hapless victims, nor by driven ideologues.

In fact, the most effective torturers are professional law enforcement or military officers. They know exactly what kind and how much pain to administer to their victims for maximum result. In a similar situation, a sadist would get into the act of inflicting pain so much that the victim would soon be dead. Unless the aim of torture is to kill, a professional would employ cool and calculated methods to achieve his desired goals from torture.

For similar reasons, neither do the torturers usually come from the ranks of the true believers. Similar to the findings of Lifton, based on a careful study of personal interviews with torturers, Ronald Crelinsten discovered that the most successful torturers are what we call mercenaries. They are in this profession because they think that it may be the quickest way to career advancement and promotion.[37] In fact, a torturer named Massini told a Brazilian victim that he would be perfectly willing to work for the revolutionaries if they succeed in their enterprise. "I am a serious professional," Massini boasted with considerable pride. "After the revolution, I will be at your disposal to torture whom you like."[38]

Captive Participants

In a mass movement we are also likely to encounter those who take part in a collective action because members of their group have coerced them. These are the captive participants. Popkin, in his study of the peasants in Vietnam, found that many of them joined the Viet Cong, not for ideological reasons, but for fear of being punished for staying on the sidelines. The heiress Patty Hearst, who took part in a number of bank robberies after being abducted by the Symbionese Liberation Army, provides another well-known example of a captive participant.[39] The motivation for these kinds of people is not the glory of participation, nor do they join a collective action in anticipation of financial gains. For them, fear is the primary motivator. They join because the alterna-tive may be even worse. It is indeed interesting to note that after a successful revolution, most participants claim ideology as their prime motivation, while after a defeat, they claim that they were only captive participants.

THE NONPARTICIPANTS

To know the causes of collective actions of all sorts, including the ones we call collective madness, we not only need to know who is likely to participate and why, we must also seek reasons why many do not take part in collective ac-tion. Having identified three groups of participants, we can extend the same logic to see that there are three classes of people who are not likely to partici-pate in a collective action. We may call them the conscientious objectors, the easy riders, and the collaborators. Like their counterparts among the partici-pants, the conscientious objectors are motivated primarily by ideology, the easy riders by fear, and the collaborators by selfish interest.

The Conscientious Objectors

In a society gone insane, we always find those who refuse to be swept away by the frenzy. In the midst of madness, some people stand their ground and help the victims at tremendous risk to their own person, career, and families. Psychological analyses of those who participated in the Holocaust started soon after the war, but research on those who helped the victims did not start until nearly three decades later. The 1970 publication of Perry London's article, "The Rescuers: Motivational Hypotheses About Christians Who Saved Jews from the Nazis," opened up a new agenda for research.[40] Inspired by the call of Rabbi Harold Schulweis, an influential Jewish leader, to "balance the moral asymmetry which has distorted the image of man," a number of scholars fo-cused on the issue of those who refuse to be swept away by collective mad-ness.[41] London's pioneering work paved the way for a significant number of studies in the 1980s on altruistic behavior during World War II.[42]

Goldhagen's *Hitler's Willing Executioners,*[43] doling out blame to the entire German population, received instant recognition for its shock value. However, a more serious contemplation reveals that in reality there were many who tried to save the hapless Jews. Even in Stanley Milgram's famous psychological ex-periment, nearly 70% of the subjects were willing to inflict pain on others on command from authority figures, but about a third refused.[44] Who are these people who refuse to see every member of the rival group as part of a shared enemy? Why are they willing to serve as islands of individualism in the midst of the collective sea?[45] Unless we take into account the contributions of these brave individuals, we get a cynical and altogether unrealistic picture of human social interactions. As we concentrate on humans' capacity for brutality and their ability to inflict pain on those considered to be the "odious others," we must balance our views by studying the motivations of those who risk every-thing to help others—those who find individuals in the midst of "them."

A number of important works have explored this question through system-atic interviews of those Gentiles who saved Jews.[46] Since the researchers use different definitions, methodologies, and sample groups, their results provide us with varying measures of motivations. However, we may place the motiva-tions for rescue in two broad categories: ideology and empathy. Nechama Tec found that 51% of the Jews were saved by strangers.[47] These conscientious ob-jectors to the Nazi cause were motivated by ideology, either religious or hu-manitarian. Swedish businessman and diplomat Raoul Wallenberg saved nearly 100,000 Jews in Hungary from certain death. He issued Swedish pass-ports to the Jews so that they could claim protection of the neutral Swedish government. He sheltered Jews in many houses that he had purchased or rented for the purpose. Wallenberg's daring activities brought him in direct conflict with Adolf Eichmann. An angry Eichmann ordered Wallenberg's as-sassination, which eventually failed. In the end, the conscientious objector to collective madness was captured by the advancing Soviet army and died in their concentration camp.

The world that produces people who get easily swept away by the currents of collective madness also produces courageous conscientious objectors like the French naturalist writer Émile Zola. About 100 years ago, when France was awash with rabid anti-Semitism, Zola stood firm, like the Rock of Gibral-tar. In the war of 1870, Germany seized the Alsace and Lorraine provinces from France. Alfred Dreyfus was an obscure Jewish captain in the French army whose family had left its native Alsace for Paris when Germany annexed that province. In 1894 the French newspapers discovered in a wastebasket in the Office of a German military attaché that made it appear that a French military officer was providing secret information to the German government. Quickly, Dreyfus came under suspicion, perhaps because he was a Jew and, most impor-tantly, because he had access to the type of information that had been supplied to the German agent. The handwriting experts declared that Dreyfus' hand-writing was similar to the one found in the treasonous note.[48] Vitriolic con-demnation of the lowly officer came instantly from the entire nation, who cast Dreyfus in the role of scapegoat. The French Catholic newspaper *La Croix* screamed, "It is the Jewish enemy betraying France" and "Down with the Jews." In the midst of the madness, on January 13, 1898, Zola published an open letter, "J'accuse," defending the rights of Alfred Dreyfus.[49] For his act of bravery, Zola was convicted in a French court and sentenced to a year in prison. Zola had to flee the country. One hundred years later, on January 13, 1998, *La Croix* and Prime Minister Lionel Jospin apologized for the past sins of the nation.[50]

Wallenberg and Zola helped victims of collective madness from a sense of deep moral conviction. However, there are many, like Oskar Schindler, who rescued Jews out of empathy; having friendship with them, knowing them personally, and empathizing with their plight.[51]

Finally, simply having the intention of saving victims of genocide may not have been enough; the ability to rescue them was also needed. Therefore, those with the proper network connection to provide safe houses and arranging transportation out the war zones were more prone to help. For instance, Oskar Schindler developed empathy for his hapless workers. However, he was able to save as many Jews as he did was because he had the perfect hiding place, his factory.[52] Although having proper networking and the opportunity may be determining factors, after reflection it may seem that their importance in the revealed preference of the rescuers may be the result of a biased sample. That is, all of the studies on the rescuers were done well after the events took place. Therefore, it is entirely possible that the efforts of those Gentiles who attempted rescue but did not have the proper hiding place and network remained unreported, since the Jews they tried to save were eventually caught and therefore could not be included in the sample set. Further, it is also possible that many, like Schindler himself, fell into a situation that offered them the possibility of developing the proper network for saving the Jews.[53]

Therefore, I posit that the rescuers either take an ideological stance (based on religious conviction or secular humanism), or they act from empathy to save people they know.[54] In sum, these are the ones who can see individuals in the mass of the collective enemy; these are the ones who, due either to their upbringing or their taste for risk-taking—adventurous personalities—are somehow immune to the pandemic of collective madness.

The Easy Riders

In his seminal work, Mancur Olson demonstrated the logical fallacy of defining human rationality solely in terms of self-utility. He pointed out that the inveterate self-utility maximizing *Homo economicus* is an impediment toward understanding of our collective action. I argue that since this narrow assumption of human rationality inevitably would get bogged down in the free-rider problem, the only way out of his logical quagmire is to extend the domain of human rationality to include collective identity. Despite the theoretical confusion, in real life, we often solve free-rider problem. In real life, we find those who overcome the problem and join collective actions for the good of their defined community, while many others remain on the sideline. Since I am using a different definition of human rationality, I do not call the non-joiners free riders; I can them *easy riders*.

Thus, when an individual recognizes that it is in his collective interest to act but remains inactive considering all the other costs of participation, then we call him an easy rider. We all respond to external "push" and "pull" factors. When a situation arises, there are factors that push us to act, while others tend to pull us away. The final outcome of a binary choice (I did or did not) is the consequence of a tug-of-war between the two opposing motivations. An easy rider's inhibitions would soon disappear when the pull factors overwhelm the push factors beyond a certain threshold value.

Much of the 1980s were marked by rebellion by the turbaned Sikhs in India, known as the Khalistan (land of the pure) movement. The Sikh militants, dismayed by the manipulation of the central government in New Delhi, started an armed struggle to create a new independent state of Khalistan.[55] The extremists gained a good bit of notoriety by blowing up an Air India Boeing 747 in flight off the coast of Ireland, regularly bombing government buildings, buses, and trains in and around the state of Punjab (the home of the Sikhs in India), and even confronting the Indian armed forces. In 1984 group of Sikh ideologues among the bodyguards of Indira Gandhi assassinated the then prime minister. From the accounts of daily massacres and mayhem, Punjab appeared to be in the throes of a mass political movement to secede from India. That was the view from the outside.[56] However, when it comes to a complex phenomenon such as a mass movement, the picture can change radically when viewed up close. Noted Indian anthropologist Dipankar Gupta undertook field research in Punjab and failed to detect a mass movement.[57] The problem with the movement was that the Sikhs were always considered an integral part of India; Sikhism was never viewed as fundamentally different from the larger interpretation of Hinduism. In fact, the Sikhs are also known as "Sardar" or the leaders whose military tradition had always cast them as the defenders of the Hindu Indians against their fellow Muslims. The situation was further complicated by the fact that the Sikhs constitute one of the most prosperous communities in India, Punjab being one of the richest states.[58] They are also deeply involved in the Indian political system. Therefore, the majority of Sikhs felt much trepidation about joining a campaign of terror against India and Indians. Basically, for the majority of the Sikhs there was no overarching image of an enemy. The Sikh population was deeply hurt by the Indian army's invasion of the Golden Temple—the holiest shrine of Sikhism—and by the killings of Sikhs and the wanton destruction of their property in the aftermath of the assassination of Indira Gandhi. However, they had entirely too much to lose by taking part in the Khalistan movement. Therefore, the movement remained confined to a few militants and mercenaries who took advantage of the general condition of lawlessness. As Gupta points out:

In spite of the fact that the extremists were gaining ground . . . a mass movement did not emerge around the Khalistan programme. Majority opinion favoured the terrorists in a very limited and selective fashion. Many would concede that though the Khalistanis were misguided and often reckless, they were nevertheless uncompromising partisans.[59]

The easy riders reveled in stories of heroic sacrifices of true believers, whom they affectionately called "Mundas" or simply "boys." Driven solely by piety and patriotism, these boys were the romantic heroes who would avenge the wrongs of the larger society, and, if unsuccessful in defeating a much stronger enemy, would die the death of a martyr. Gupta points out; "Most Sikhs vicariously revel in the martyrdom complex and many hoped these terrorists would die honourable deaths." However, in reality, most of the revolutionaries did not fit the demands of "true believers."[60] The Punjab police and the Indian military put down the movement within a matter of months.

On the other side of the mountains, China experimented with a brand new kind of political system. Under the leadership of Deng Shao Ping and then Jiang Zemin, the Chinese Communist Party went ahead full steam toward economic liberalization. As the process of liberalization took place, along with it came the gradual recognition of property rights. However, in an interesting twist of policy, China has, so far, kept economic openness hermetically separated from the cries for political freedom. As the Tiananmen Square massacre demonstrated, the leadership showed little tolerance for political liberalization. This experiment stands in stark contrast with what has happened in Russia, where the rush to introduce democracy in a nation totally unaccustomed to the notion throughout its history created near anarchy on the political front, with the nation teetering precariously at the brink of bankruptcy. Therefore, having economic prosperity along with the stiffest possible punishment for political activity, China has created a nation of easy riders. Only history will tell how long this current condition of apparent political calm will prevail.

The Collaborators

History is particularly harsh to the *collaborators*. From Benedict Arnold to Vidhun Quisling, history is full of stories of those who betrayed their collective interest. Textbooks paint them in the most unflattering light. For these individuals, self-interest comes into direct confrontation with the interests of the collective, and wins. Of course, to be branded a collaborator, one must be viewed from the standpoint of those who espouse the collective goal. Thus, if the British or their loyalists had won in 1776, it is entirely possible that Arnold would have been accorded a much more sympathetic portrayal.

Many societies achieve their goals of stability through co-opting the leaders of the opposition. For instance, modern Mexico's ruling Institutional Revolutionary Party (PRI) has been particularly creative about co-opting its most vocal opponents. However, as a society becomes more complex, as followers become better informed, or as democratic institutions mature—as the PRI is discovering in Mexico—it becomes increasingly difficult to co-opt the opposition and achieve stability.

FROM IDENTIFICATION TO IMPLEMENTATION: THE PROCESS

Once the enemy is clearly identified, the path to violence is a matter of implementation. Human minds, however, are much too complex to be classified into a single category. Therefore, it would be a grave mistake to assume that everyone who responds to the call of a leader is inspired by him, or even that the leader himself is a complete believer in his own message. It is frequently the case that, like the butcher who turns vegetarian, the leaders make separate rules for themselves. Chairman Mao and his inner circle of friends used to revel in the evil pleasure of bourgeois capitalism, even at the height of the Cultural Revolution.[61] The leaders of theocratic nations, professing the strictest adherence to the religious laws, may break every commandment with unparalleled ardor. Like Machiavelli's prince, they perhaps assume that the laws that govern their conduct are different from those that apply to their followers.

In any case, when we look at the process through which a society descends to the depths of collective emotions, we find it to be strangely familiar. First, there are grievances: some are minor, others serious; some are longstanding, while others are of recent origin; some are of true concern (even to an outsider), while others are simply a magnification of cultural differences. Second comes a political entrepreneur with his (most are men) message of hate and suspicion. His message packages old historical events, recent examples of injustice, and pure mythology or paranoid pronouncements in one unified form.[62] Third, this message resonates with a segment of his client population. He attracts a group of ideologues. The faithful followers join in the nascent movement regardless of consequences. Having total faith, these adherents make the question of free-ridership entirely irrelevant. In their youthful exuberance (most of the followers in a mass movement are from the younger cohort) they take risks and often sacrifice personal goals for the "greater cause."

If a movement remains largely political, such as the civil rights movement in the United States, the followers, having few financial incentives to motivate their actions (such as protest demonstrations), fall in the category of "true believers." However, as the movement picks up momentum, and especially if an armed struggle is involved, it tends to attract different kinds of followers. Since maintaining an armed resistance often requires huge sums of money, unless supported by a foreign power, insurgent groups meet their financial needs by extralegal activities, such as bank robbery or trafficking in illegal drugs. As money starts flowing in, it is conceivable that the group's basic character will change. Money and arms attract more unsavory characters in the society. As a result, in many parts of the world, a nefarious nexus between political movements and criminal groups starts developing.

As the group gets stronger, it starts flexing its muscles through the application of coercion. In a civil society, the government reserves the sole right to prosecute and punish offenders. However, dissident groups, from Jim Jones' People's Temple to the hyper-nationalists in the former Yugoslavia, start increasing the costs of defection. These punishments can vary from ostracization to imprisonment, torture, and even death. In the beginning, the application of coercion, remains confined to the members of the group. However, as the power of the group increases, it extends its coercive capabilities beyond the

band of immediate followers. Within the strange dynamics among the true believers, the mercenaries, and the captive participants, a group or a society becomes collectively insane. Let us examine the process a bit more closely.

Mobilization

The power of a collective movement, whether insignificant or momentous,
depends on mobilization of ordinary citizens. From the classic study of
Charles Tilly to the more recent work of Ted Gurr, a vast scholarly literature
helps explain the significance of mobilization to a revolutionary movement.[63]
As more people get involved, the power of a movement increases. The power
of mass mobilization was amply demonstrated in the sudden demise of the
so-called Eastern bloc nations. As the size of the disaffected crowd increased in
size, the notorious regimes in Poland, Romania, and Czechoslovakia simply
crumbled away. Movements gain momentum; participation increases a snow-
ball effect takes place, drawing growing numbers of those who were reluctant
to join before.

The Media: Constructing Political Reality

Propaganda and political rhetoric have always played a vital role in mobilizing people. The constant barrage of biased information constructs a new reality for the people. It matters little to the listeners whether the message portrays
an accurate picture based on history or is a matter of pure fantasy. A prolonged
period of intense propaganda creates an unshakable reality for many listeners.

The art of propaganda is age-old. It is part and parcel of every mythology,
creating enemies and allies, good and evil, the eternal forces of light and darkness. The Roman generals used oratory to exhort their troops. In Hindu religion, even Lord Krishna had to reveal his divinity to inspire Arjuna, a mythical
hero beset with self-doubt about killing his own kin in war. However, back in
those days, the reach of oratory was limited to the range of the human voice.
With the advent of technology, from printing to voice and image transmission,
the importance of propaganda in shaping collective movements increased ex-
ponentially. Also, as the message becomes complicated, so does selling the job
to potential participants. In order to communicate, political entrepreneurs become increasingly savvy in their use of symbols to capture the most fundamental aspects of their incendiary message—the images of "us" and "them."

Sam Keen in his book and documentary film of the same title, *Faces of the
Enemy*, has shown the power of propaganda in forming the image of the enemy.[64] If we need to create the image of an enemy before we strike the first
blow, we need to come up with a symbolic representation of this evil incarnate.
Once this image is complete, we have created a coherent story of the vile enemy's mischievous past, which can be the focal point of all our projections of
anger and frustration.

For instance, Simon Schama, in his exhaustive study of the French Revolution, demonstrated how the assassination of the nobles and the royal family began long before the actual slaughter.[65] Pamphlets and tracts distributed throughout France established their culpability in creating the morass of a demoralized France. Queen Marie-Antoinette was portrayed in the most vicious manner with pornographic pictures as a flagrant debaucher and readily became the receptacle of communal wrath. A similar fate befell the czar and the czarina in Imperial Russia. A German princess in the public's mind, the czarina quickly became the embodiment of national humiliation in wars against the Kaiser's Germany and Imperial Japan.[66]

Propaganda played an unprecedented role in mobilizing the German people by the Nazis. In its effort to stoke the fire of patriotism toward the fatherland and hatred toward those who did not belong, the Nazi propaganda machine created a new standard for mass mobilization. In their quest to reach every German in the land, no medium of communication, from radio, to film, to art, to literature, to propaganda posters, was to remain unused. Hitler himself took great interest in every aspect of Nazi propaganda. Hitler fancied himself an artist and, in his early years during a series of failed careers, for a while drew posters extolling the virtues of hair tonic, soap powder, and an antiperspirant called Teddy.[67] Captivated by the power of symbolism, Hitler was directly involved in designing his party's symbols, including the swastika and the eagle.

Through meticulous planning the Nazis perfected the art of propaganda. Joseph Goebbels headed the organizational structure of the Nazi propaganda machine at the national level. Within the nation, each *Gau* or region had its own propaganda apparatus, as did all lower levels of the party's organizational hierarchy. The Nazi party hired trained orators and experts on specific topics who would literally overwhelm the region with propaganda activity, reaching every corner of its intended audience.

Syndicated columnist Georgie Anne Geyer provided a graphic account of the creation of mass hysteria by the clever use of the media in the Yugoslav civil war. Recollecting the events in 1989, Geyer reports that

the most terrifying indicator of what was to come was the television in my hotel room in the Inter-Continental [in Belgrade]. There, on that little screen—part of the new technology that so many thought would unite the world—one saw hours of Serb propaganda. Serb cemeteries from battles lost 800 years ago vied with Serbian women crying at the graves—the Serbs as eternal victims.[68]

It is no wonder that a frustrated Warren Zimmermann, the American ambassador to Yugoslavia during the war years, summarized the sordid situation thus: "It was TV that promoted the hatred, not ancient hatreds. It gave people myths and called them history."[69]

Naturally, given the power of the media, the promoters of collective ideology attempt to suppress information inconsistent with their own. Hence, it is hardly surprising that the first casualty in the war for the minds of the followers is the source of information that contradicts the official line. The hazards of being a reporter are amply demonstrated in Table 5.1.

Cultural Icons

Knowing our inherent penchant for adhering to authority figures, political groups all over the world recruit celebrities as their spokespersons. Similar to advertisements by well-known figures pitching beer or a particular brand of automobiles, cultural icons play a vital role in spreading the message. Therefore, the party propaganda machines enlist the help of cultural icons for mass mobilization. In almost every movement, cultural leaders are brought in to inspire the potential participants. Singers sing patriotic songs; poets write lugubrious poems dripping with sentimental images of the motherland or fatherland in mortal danger; motion picture directors create propaganda movies. Given our predisposition to obey authorities, it is not difficult to see how,

Table 5.1
Attacks on the Media, 1996

Killed	52
Missing	3
Arrested, still detained	82
Expelled or credentials refused	35
Assaulted	323
Material/equipment confiscated	71
Homes raided/destroyed	22
Threatened with death	44
Other threats	76
charged/brought to trial	163
sentences	79
given suspended sentences	7
Relatives/staff killed	10
Offices raided/occupied	38
Offices burned/bombed/destroyed	19
Censored (but continued to publish)	28
Licenses revoked/refused	6

Source: The North-South Institute, *Don't Shoot the Messenger: A Guide for Canadian Journalists on Promoting Press Freedom*. Posted on the Internet at *http://www.nsi-ins.ca*.

exhorted by the icons of culture, from Lord Tennyson to John Lennon, many would heed the call of the collective.[70]

Realizing the ability of cultural icons to mobilize the masses, Mussolini started honoring old Italian writers, scientists, and heroes, including economic philosopher Vilfredo Pareto. Again, true to their character, the Nazis set an example of co-opting cultural icons and directing their creativity to furthering the Nazi cause. Hitler and other Nazi elite emphatically stressed that in the "true culture" the arts had a symbiotic relationship with the *Volk*, the Aryan community. Any art form reflecting the inner expressions of an individual was considered anathema to the ideology of the National Socialist Party. To them, such acts would be considered seditious. Instead, through its all-encompassing ideology, the art and the artists would help bring about "a new artistic renaissance of the Aryan man."[71] Perhaps the most glaring (and almost amusing, had it not been for its implications for the lives of so many) example of directing arts to the purpose of a state ideology can be found in Hitler's July 19, 1937 speech dedicating the House of German Arts. Referring to the current trends of artistic renditions, Hitler asked:

But what do you manufacture? Deformed cripples and cretins, women who inspire only disgust, men who are more like beasts, children who, if they were alive, would be regarded as God's curse! . . . Let no one say that that is how these artists see things. From the pictures submitted for exhibition, I must assume that the eye of some men shows them things different from what they really are. There really are men who can see in the shapes of our people only decayed cretins: who feel that meadows are blue, the heavens green, clouds sulfur-yellow. They like to say that they experience these things in this way.

I do not want to argue about whether or not they really experience this. But in the name of the German people I want to prevent these pitiable unfortunates, who clearly suffer from defective vision, from attempting with their chatter to force on their contemporaries the results of their faulty observations, and indeed presenting them as "art." Here there are only two possibilities open: either these so-called artists really do see things this way and believe in that which they create—and if so, one has to investigate how this defective vision arose—if it is a mechanical problem or if it came about through heredity. The first case would be pitiable, while the second would be a matter for the Ministry of the Interior, which would deal with the problem of preventing the perpetuation of such horrid disorder. Or they themselves do not believe in the reality of such impressions, but are for different reasons attempting to annoy the nation with this humbug. If this is the case, then it is a matter for a criminal court.[72]

From this brief passage, the threats delivered to the artistic community should be abundantly clear. If art does not follow the dictates of the party, then the artist must be mentally incompetent or be acting against the collective interest of the people. Therefore such people should either be sent to mental asylums or to the extermination camps. Using almost identical words, the Soviet regime under Stalin and the Chinese Communists during the Cultural Revolution coerced artists into submission and molded the arts into their own image.

However, such efforts are certainly not confined within the totalitarian worlds of Hitler, Stalin, Mao, or Pol Pot. We may recall that much of the focus of the House Committee on Un-American Activities during the height of McCarthyism was directed toward the artistic community.

Ease of Participation and Costs of Defection

Finally, the cause of mobilization is greatly aided when the mobilizing group is able to punish its members for defection. In an organized society, only the legitimate government reserves the right to engage in coercion. Because they fear punishment, citizens adhere to the laws of the land, respond to conscription, and pay taxes. By imposing a high cost of defection, an organized society extracts participation from the naturally recalcitrant easy riders. However, when a dissident group becomes powerful enough, it creates its own structure for doling out sanctions for not abiding by its rules. Through their effort, along with the true believers and the mercenaries, they enlist the help of the captive participants. Mao Zedong's China, for instance, could enforce ideological purity by enlisting hundreds and thousands of old women, called the "granny patrol." These block leaders would freely roam around the neighborhood and would report any transgression, from heretical love of bourgeois culture to the desire to have a second child (the Chinese are allowed to have only one child per family).[73] Their report to the higher-ups in the party hierarchy would soon bring sanctions down on the offenders with a frightening force.

STRATEGIES OF PARTICIPATION

In the previous section, I argued that the process that leads a movement to a successful revolution or a war of independence from colonial rule is essentially the same as the one that draws a society to the very bottom of collective madness. Not all grievances that people feel as a group, however, lead to revolutions or genocides. In order to analyze which ones do, the movements need a strong enough collective identity to break the barriers of free-rider ambivalence. But, on top of collective identity and mobilization, a successful movement also needs proper leadership and organizational skills. Without organizational skills, many movements, from the Great Mutiny in India of 1857 to the turn-of-the-century Chinese Boxer Rebellion, quickly unraveled soon after they achieved some small measure of success. On the other hand, careful reading of history reveals the organizational skills of those like Lenin, Ayatollah Khomeini, Mao Zedong, and Adolf Hitler, successful leaders of collective movements all over the world. Therefore, using the three determining factors—strength of collective identity, mobilization, and leadership skills—we can draw a three-dimensional box diagram to chart the course of political movements.

In Figure 5.1, the vertical axis measures the strength of collective identity of group members from low to high. The horizontal axis measures the extent of mobilization, and the axis measuring depth indicates leadership skills. In this box, I have placed various outcomes of a collective movement. For instance, if all three factors are low, then regardless of the level of frustration, we are going to experience inactivity. In this case, low levels of collective identity, leadership skills, and lack of mobilization lead to little or no collective action. If we look at the American political landscape today, we will notice a remarkable weakness in organized political activity within the African American community. This relative inactivity is all the more remarkable in view of the fact that the community, on average, is no better off than it was thirty years ago during the height of the civil rights movement. Along with an extremely strong nonviolent movement headed by Dr. Martin Luther King, Jr., the nation also saw the rise of radicalism in the Black Panther movement. Yet, despite the fact that the income gap between blacks and whites has remained stubbornly wide, the current African American movements of Rev. Jesse Jackson's Rainbow Coalition or the Nation of Islam are but shadows of their strength three decades ago. In Chapter 6, I argue that despite widespread frustration, at least among the urban poor, the African American community has been unable to resist the corrosive effects of individualism. As a result, lack of collective identity, ineffectual leadership, and mobilization have resulted in the fizzling out of the black political movements—violent or nonviolent.

Figure 5.1
Classification of Collective Action

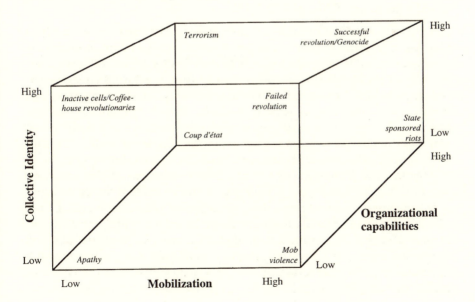

From the point of apathy in Figure 5.1, if we move along the horizontal line, there is low collective identity and low leadership but high mobilization. Such a mix produces urban riots, the kind the nation experienced in a number of U.S. cities in the last quarter of the twentieth century. These riots reflect the presence of deep-seated anger and frustration, but without the help of a strong enough collective identity or a coherent leadership, they manifest themselves as episodic explosions of aimless fury.

From inactivity, if we move up along the vertical axis, we reach a combination of factors that would produce typical coffeehouse revolutionaries. These inactive cells gather extremely small groups of ideologically inspired men and women. Although almost all the major collective movements start from this point, until these small bands of armchair revolutionaries are able to communicate to a larger society, their activities remain restricted within the group. Thus, a number of so-called patriot groups have sprung up in many parts of the United States. However, despite an increase in the number of their cells, they prevail as isolated bands of fanatics.

However, if these groups are able to muster enough organizational capabilities, where the leaders are able to provide a coherent plan of action, they can quickly transform themselves into terrorist organizations. At this point I should emphasize that although the term "terrorist" is highly value-loaded, since one group's terrorist is another group's freedom fighter, it is possible to offer a universal definition that can identify an act as "terrorism" regardless who commits it, or for however noble a cause. For example, Combs defines terrorism as "a synthesis of war and theater, a dramatization of the most proscribed kind of violence—that which is perpetrated on innocent victims—played before an audience in the hope of creating a mood of fear, for political purposes."[74]

It is possible for a small group of individuals to engage in a collective action out of its self-interest. These collective actions are not a public good which is going to be distributed to the general public, but rather are taken for private benefits for the group's members. These actions can vary from coups d'état to the activities of criminal gangs based on economic interest. Since they involve more than a single actor, these activities fall under the category of collective action.

The difference between a coup and a revolution is that while both may change the existing government, a revolution is fought in the name of the larger society, but a coup is primarily for the benefit of the leaders or the perpetrators. Similarly, there is a difference between mob violence and organized riots. Under the thin veil of a political purpose, state-organized riots are staged by mercenaries. For instance, in October 1984, Prime Minister Indira Gandhi of India was assassinated by her two Sikh bodyguards. At that time the country was in the throes of a rebellion by a segment of the Sikh population.[75] Shortly thereafter, while the nation was in a state of shock, New Delhi was awash with rumors that the Sikhs were distributing sweets in celebration. Rumors also started to flow that trainloads carrying hundreds of Hindu dead bodies had arrived at the Old Delhi railway station from Punjab. Taking advantage of this volatile situation, a number of Hindu members of the Congress Party (Indira Gandhi's ruling political party) deliberately started an organized riot against the prosperous Sikh community in New Delhi. For nearly ten days mercenary thugs, brought in by the busload, looted and burned Sikh-owned properties as police stood by watching, or, even in some instances, took an active part in the mayhem. When the smoke cleared, by some estimates, nearly a thousand Sikhs had lost their lives.[76] This riot was motivated less by any ideology of the collective than by an unrestricted opportunity to loot, rape, pillage, and kill people. This is an example of an organized riot caused through high levels of organizational skills and mobilizations with little collective identity.

If a high level of collective ideology and mobilization is combined with low organizational skills, we will see a failed revolution. I have mentioned the Boxer Rebellion in China. Chafing under the foreign influence which brought opium, Christianity, and foreign culture to the forbidden shores of China, a group of traditional Chinese of the White Lotus sect in northern China founded a secret society around 1880, called Yihquan (Righteous and Harmonious Fists). This sect was originally opposed to the Manchu dynasty. However, finding a common enemy, they united in their dislike of the foreigners and anything foreign. However, the inept and divided leadership was no match for the European colonists. Within a year, the rebellion was brought under control with a savagery far surpassing that of the perpetrators.[77]

In Figure 5.1, when intense collective identity is combined with high levels of organizational capabilities, but lacks mobilization, the combination spawns terrorism. In their often quoted study, Schmid and de Graaf point out that, in effect, terrorism is but a form of communication.[78] The aim of terrorism is to send a message either to the larger society or to the members of the terrorists' own group. To the society (and the dominant group) the message of terrorism is an appeal to take the demands of the perpetrators seriously; to the members of their own group, the message is a demonstration of self-importance and a call for greater mobilization.

Finally, when all three factors are present, a political movement is able to achieve its goals. The wars of independence are won, the old dictator or the Shah is overthrown, a genocide gets fully under way. In the following chapter, I discuss an example of a successful collective action, the Jonestown massacre. I attempt to explain how the Reverend Jim Jones was able make over 900 of his followers kill their own children, other relatives, and friends, and then commit suicide. In some ways, this is the story of one of the successful cases of collective action, the ultimate in submersion of individual identities into the collective.

THE DESCENT OF SOCIETY: PATH TO COLLECTIVE INSANITY

How does a society or a group that seems to have been functioning all of a sudden become dysfunctional? With regard to the descent of a nation into the abyss of collective madness, it is important to remember that a society does not slide into a genocidal frenzy overnight. Also, their torturous path shows some amazing similarities, demonstrating the constancy of human behavior. Since the state of collective madness lies at the extreme end of the spectrum of collective action, a society goes through a number of steps to reach it. My behavioral hypotheses posit that three behavioral factors, greed, ideology, and fear, explain why an individual would take part in a collective action. However, in order to explain the dynamics of collective action, we must consider the facilitating variables that shape the destiny of a social movement. We can classify them in the following order:

Greed (selfish interest)

1. Shrinking opportunity
2. Increased rewards for group membership

Ideology (collective motivation)

3. Collective culture
4. Rise of charismatic leadership
5. Ideology of paranoia and a clear identification of the "enemy"

Cost factor

6. Increasing social pressure for acceptance
7. High price for defection

Facilitating factors

8. Social acceptance of violence
9. Creation of militia/flow of arms
10. Creation of bureaucratic hierarchy
11. Lack of free flow of information/cultural or spatial isolation
12. International intervention

Shrinking Opportunity

Deprivation is the mother of rebellion. From the ancient Greeks to modern-day political scientists and sociologists, scholars have identified the presence of a feeling of deprivation as the starting point of a rebellion. In his book *Why Men Rebel*, Ted Gurr introduced the notion of "relative deprivation." That is, people rebel when their expectations of life fall short of their achievements.[79] Gurr argued that people do not rebel simply out of poverty, but from the frustration that is created from the expectation-achievement gap. That is, an average

Basque may be far more affluent in absolute measures than an average Bangladeshi, but that does not mean that the Basques will be less rebellious than the Bangladeshis. This is all a matter of perception. When a group of individuals feels deprived, it is likely to look for someone else to blame for its failure.

Further, when economic opportunity declines, so does the opportunity cost of participation in a collective movement. That is, with less to lose, people become more willing to devote their time, energy, and resources to the cause of the collective.

Increasing Rewards of Membership

We join groups because they offer many rewards, from purely emotional to financial. Therefore, when a young man joins the Brown Shirts, or any other group, he is deriving a number of important benefits reserved for the members only. At the psychological level, membership satisfies our inherent need to belong. That we are accepted and cherished as valuable associates produces an enormous amount of happiness and satisfaction. Most groups make specialized symbols to announce their allegiance to the collective and even to signify rank within the hierarchy. From time immemorial people have sought ways of differentiating themselves from others. Where skin color or other physical characteristics are not distinctive, attire, tattoos, the color of clothes or body colorings, or other symbols announce the collective identity of the individual members. Today in gang-infested inner cities of America or in a European soccer stadium, one can get into trouble by wearing the wrong color clothes. The color of a Jewish yarmulke declares the wearer's faith to the rest of the world. The type and style of turban separates a Sikh from his neighbors of a different cast or religious faith. In South India, the markings on the forehead differentiate the devotees of Lord Shiva and Lord Vishnu. Similarly, clothes and other symbols make obvious to the rest of the world the wearer's rank within an organizational structure, from a cardinal to a colonel.

These careful distinctions are made to mark separate privileges accorded to the members of the group. Therefore, a young man in India would join the Sikh Khalistani group for some of the same reasons German youths joined the Storm Troopers or young Jews joined the Stern Gang. Group membership offers special power, prestige, and, ultimately, financial benefits to the participants. As the society descends into madness, these special benefits available only to the participants become increasingly greater. The mixed motives of faith and greed in varied proportion attract people to the cause. If thes cause happens to be against a marked enemy, violence will surely erupt, and soon.

Collective Culture

Are some cultures more susceptible to bouts of collective madness than others? In the 1940s, Adorno et al., in their pathbreaking study, argued that there is indeed an authoritarian personality, one that is molded to accept the existing social hierarchy and to carry out orders from the authorities without question. They pointed out that perhaps the Teutonic culture of Germany produced a society of authoritarian personalities, which paved the way for the Holocaust.[80]

Social psychologist Erin Straub also argues that culture plays an important role in the conduct of the society. In his influential book, *The Roots of Evil,* he analyzed in detail four instances of genocide and mass killings: the Nazi Holocaust, the Turkish genocide of the Armenians, the politicide in Cambodia, and the disappearances in Argentina.[81] Straub points out that all of these cultures show a long history of "devaluation" of a group of people. For instance, in Germany, Russia, and a number of other East European countries there has been a long historic tradition of devaluing the Jews and Gypsies. Therefore, someone born in those cultures would be acculturated to holding the members of these groups in low esteem.

For Straub, another cultural precondition for genocide is the presence of what he calls a monolithic rather than a pluralistic society. To Straub, pluralism can be a matter of culture or a matter of political order. For instance, a pluralistic culture is open to many and varied ideas. In such a culture, one can separate issues from personalities. A direct criticism of the leaders does not constitute an attack on the entire nation. On the political level, a pluralistic society has a democratic structure. In contrast, many of these countries where genocide or other kinds of mass violence took place are more monolithic. For instance, among the fifty-eight countries identified by Schmid and Jongman as systematically using torture, only about half a dozen would qualify as being functionally democratic.[82] Even that number, in the estimation of most observers, would be generous.

In such monolithic cultures based on collective values, strong respect for authority is common. In such cultures, people seek answers from their leaders. In such a tradition, the role of a political leader often commingles with that of a religious guru, an ideological leader, and a moral authority. The unquestioned acceptance of the infallibility of those in authority sets these nations apart from those based on individual values.

In contrast, since the fundamental basis of liberal democracy is individualism, empirical research shows that democracies are less likely to have episodes of genocide, politicide, or the widespread use of torture.[83] Also, democracies seem more likely to settle their disputes through political means than through outright coercion.[84] Two democracies are much less likely to fight each other on the battlefield.[85] However, having a democracy is certainly no guarantee of a peaceful society. Democratic India ranks very high on the relative scales of systematic use of torture and other violations of human rights.[86] Democratic Sri Lanka is being torn apart in a continuing civil war. However, when we consider the entire spectrum of nations, we can safely claim that the democratic nations tend to offer a far more conducive climate for sectarian peace and harmony.

Ideology of Paranoia

The need to feel secure either as an individual or as a group is fundamental to all of us. If forced into a corner, most animals, however docile, attempt to strike back. Before descending to the depth of collective madness, the political entrepreneurs play on our primordial fear by painting a picture of widespread conspiracy by the rival group. There are stories floating around cyberspace about United Nations forces hiding in abandoned mines, ready to come out and subjugate true blue Americans at a moment's notice. In their paranoia, the faithful observe black UN helicopters swirl by taking pictures of the patriotic lot, computer chips embedded in street signs that direct the invading force to the points of strategic importance. Curiously, the name of the prime antagonist changes with time, but not the mode of operation. In the 1980s, Sam Keen's revealing documentary showed one General Mohr, a retired military officer turned right-wing preacher, telling his apprehensive flock how a fleet of Soviet ships unloaded thousands of soldiers in Mexico who were on their way to the north even as he was speaking.[87] Mouths agape, his audience trembled with the image of a bleak future under Soviet rule. Of course, the disaster could be averted only if the right-minded ones banded together and started a preemptive war against the invading army and their domestic collaborators.

Fanciful as the stories of General Mohr may sound, such tales flourish in abundance, causing what historian Richard Hofstader called the "paranoid style of American politics." Stories of such sinister intent by a marked enemy pave the path to collective paranoia. Hitler's description of the Jews in *Mein Kampf* or Habyarimana's characterization of the Tutsis and their baneful brethren within their own respective nations were designed to shake the listener's sense of security to its roots. And, given the right configuration of environmental conditions, communities all over the world have fallen into the trap of hatred and consequent violence.

The outcome of such paranoia is the clear identification of the enemy. Although social and other charitable movements are based on the notion of a community, no collective political movement for separation or independence can start without the clear marking of the enemy. No incident of collective madness can happen without a long campaign against a shared out-group.

The Rise of a Charismatic Leader

When we accept someone's directives, we accept the leader's legitimacy to give us orders. Max Weber points out that political legitimacy can arise from traditional leadership (such as the monarchy), the legal basis of the nation's constitution, or charismatic leadership. With few pockets of traditional leadership left in the world, the danger of collective madness comes mostly from the rise of charismatic leaders. Since the sole basis of the leader's legitimacy is charisma, the allegiance of the group rests with this person. Unquestioned authority supplies unlimited power to the group leader. Jim Jones, the Ayatollah Khomeini, Hitler, and Habyarimana have commanded such allegiance. By skillful use of their power of oratory, these leaders have bound many in their spell and created a ready supply of "true believers." By accepting the authority of their leaders, the believers suspend their own judgment. They do not have to think on their own. They can simply look at the world through the eyes of the leaders. They do not have to investigate, nor do they have to expend their intellectual energy trying to find out the facts. Being part of the leader's group, they find ready acceptance. They find that they are loved simply for what they were born with. Once such a condition prevails, people discover a larger meaning in life that transcends their personal lives. They live not for themselves but for the entire group; they find in the womb of the collective an incredible source of comfort and personal peace.

What is the source of charisma for the leaders of collective movements? How are they able to stir so many people? The answer to these questions is rooted in the unanswerable query whether leaders shape history or whether environmental conditions give birth to a leader. Would there be a Holocaust without Hitler and the Nazi party? Or, if Hitler were not there, would the prevailing social and political conditions have created another demagogue similar to him? No one will ever be able to answer these riddles. However, this much is certain: the mystery of their hold over their followers lies in their ability to weave a coherent story of good and evil which resonates well with long-standing hopes and fears, pride and prejudice, and myriad other preconceived notions and mythologies about a group's history. If we look at leaders throughout history, we will not find them to be exceptional in their physical characteristics or intellectual prowess. Charismatic leaders are rarely remarkable in appearance or intellectual brilliance. Their true distinguishing feature rests in their ability to articulate the basic predilection of their people, and in their apparently unshakable conviction in their belief.

What is the source of the leaders' all-consuming obsession to annihilate the collective enemy? Clinical psychiatrists who have studied the extremes of mental illness have often found a linkage between the construction of reality based on psychotic delusion and political process. For instance, James Glass observes, "It occurs to me after listening for several months to delusional utterances that some connection might exist between internal emotional structures and the construction of ethical and political systems of belief."[88] Psychiatry, of course, is not an exact science. It is not clear when individuals are delusional in their construction of reality. However, when we listen to some of the leaders who have taken their nations or their groups down the slippery slope of collective madness, we too may begin to wonder about the state of their mental health.

In October 1997, a Western reporter sat down with the dying seventy-two-year-old Pol Pot, the chief architect of the killing fields of Cambodia.[89] The revolutionary leader, even in the twilight of his life, imprisoned by his former comrades, was firm in his conviction and animosity toward Vietnam. "We had no choice. Naturally we had to defend ourselves. The Vietnamese." The feeble man, needing help even to get up from his chair, had little regret about deeds that horrified the entire world. In his mind, he was only reacting to the threats from the "evil" Vietnamese. The closest this man, whom many hold responsible for the murders of nearly 2 million of his countrymen, came to accepting his culpability was to say, "I do not reject responsibility—our movement made mistakes, like every other movement in the world. But there was another aspect that was outside our control—the enemy's activities against us."[90] If we want to call Pol Pot's obsession with the enemy, Vietnam, a delusion, we can perhaps do so. During his bloody reign, he put many of his close comrades to death. The deposed dictator was asked about the killing of Son Sen, one of his closest friends. In a raspy voice Pol Pot justified his action by insisting that Son Sen was conspiring with the Vietnamese. As evidence of Son Sen's treachery, Pol Pot pointed out, "The brother of Son Sen, Son Chhum . . . even let his daughter marry people who worked with Hun Sen [Cambodia's Prime Minister, originally installed in power by the Vietnamese forces]." The frail old man, despite the obvious reality of a failed revolution, took considerable pride in his past actions. "I want to tell you," he said, laboring to catch his breath, "I am quite satisfied with one thing: If we had not carried out our struggle, Cambodia would have become another Kampuchea Krom," referring to a Mekong Delta region seized by the Vietnamese in the seventeenth century.[91]

Social Pressure for Acceptance

Along with physical threats associated with opposing a collective movement comes social pressure. The Nazis fully understood the power of the arts and culture in bringing about a totalitarian system where one's individuality would be considered a threat to the entire community. They called this coordination of culture (*Gleichschaltung*). Hitler appointed Joseph Goebbels to the position of minister for public enlightenment and propaganda. In this capacity Goebbels was accorded complete control over the communications media as well as over the film industry, theater, and all forms of arts. German arts of all forms were to represent the Aryan ideals of the *Volk*. Any contrary representation would be considered a treasonous offense.

As a result of the sweeping powers granted to Goebbels, German arts took a sharp turn and became a tool of Nazi propaganda, the same way that state-sponsored arts became part and parcel of propaganda all over the communist world. By following developments in war-torn areas throughout time and space, we find similar manipulation of the arts to mobilize people. This cultural coercion increases peer pressure on the easy riders to join in and can transform many into true believers.

High Price for Defection

Finally, we should note that not all the members follow the dictates of the paranoid leadership into participating in acts of collective madness. Many try to resist. But the authorities in power apply severe coercion against any kind of defection. The stronger the force of the collective, the greater the punishment for deviation from the official line. Desertion from any collective body is considered a direct attack on the entire system. In fact, in order to stem the tide of defection, organizations based on collective principles often treat a defector more harshly than a captured enemy.

This process of increasing costs of defection creates captive participants, who find no alternative but to submit to the collective will. Others, who can somehow avoid direct involvement, become easy riders. As a result, without much opposition, the juggernaut of collective ideology moves on. From the outside, it may look as if the entire nation has become willing executioners, as Goldhagen characterized the German experience during the Nazi Holocaust, but closer scrutiny reveals differences in motivation which allow such abominations to take place.[92]

Social Acceptance of Violence

Scenes of violence and injustice should shock us. Where they don't, where a society gets desensitized to violence and brutality, especially against a certain group, it is ripe for descent into the darkness of shared insanity. In the Western world, we do not see corpses lying on the roadside while people go about their business without even casting a second glance. But in medieval times, severed heads would be stuck on London's bridges as a warning to future dissidents. In the South, the bodies of victims of lynching would sometimes dangle in the wind, with few protests from the people.

A cycle of violence, once started, is difficult to diffuse. As one group subjugates another by force, the memories of wrongdoing get relegated to the realms of collective grief, only to be passed on to the next generations for avenging the misdeeds of the past. For instance, currently Armenian terrorists are fighting the Turks for their participation in the Armenian genocide. However, the atrocities took place nearly a century ago. Alas, violence begets violence. In such cultures where violence becomes part of the folklore, with the enemy clearly identified, the scene is immediately set for a slide toward collective madness.

This brings us to the question, Can one culture be more conducive to violence than another? Ted Gurr points out, "Repression tends to be habitual: elites who have successfully used repression to secure and defend power against internal challengers are likely to use it again."[93] As we get desensitized to the sights of violence, it gets routinized. For instance, in Indian movies police stations are routinely shown as places of torture. These scenes are not necessarily shown to shock people, but to depict reality, just as in Hollywood movies gang-ridden inner city areas are shown filled with violence. Once we accept such violence as acceptable behavior, we get desensitized to its occurrence. Therefore, while incidents of unspeakable crime and violence occupy a few seconds in a local news broadcast, such events in the suburbs become a national preoccupation.

Creation of Militia/Flow of Arms

In my discussion of collective madness, I have defined it as an outcome of heightened collective identity, a state of hyper-identity. Collective madness can take many forms, varying from genocide, to mass murder-suicide, to widespread torture and other crimes of obedience. Frequently, it is the group in power that initiates a systematic program of genocide, politicide, or ethnic cleansing. Although in some instances the military may take part, it is most often paramilitary militias that carry out the atrocities.

For instance, in Nazi Germany, the party developed its own private army, the Brown Shirts or the Stormtroopers (Sturmabteilung—SA).[94] It was organized by the party leaders and played an important role in breaking up opposition rallies and intimidating the opponents of the Nazi party. However, when the party came to power in 1934, Goering formed the Gestapo, or the Secret State Police. Around the same time, by enlarging some aspects of the military intelligence-gathering units, Himmler formed the SS (Guard Squadron—Schutzstaffeln). The unholy alliance of the Gestapo and the SS was given the authority "to root out and fight all pernicious efforts throughout the country."[95] By German law and practice, the activities of these militia forces were not subject to court review.

We can see similar trends in the formation of the Hutu militias in Rwanda as well as other ethnic militias in Bosnia. In all of these cases, the militias were created outside the regular military and police organizations and were supplied with ample firearms. Having ideological indoctrination, a ready supply of arms, and complete immunity from legal oversight, the paramilitary forces constitute the primary engine for genocide and ethnic cleansing. Therefore, one of the most significant early warning signals for humanitarian crisis is the formation and arming of extralegal paramilitary forces.

Another interesting aspect of forming a militia is the possibility of organized crime entering into the fray. The distribution of arms creates opportunities for many, including members of organized crime. These people take advantage of the anarchy and license to terrorize ordinary people. In southern Italy, the Cosa Nostras were greatly aided by the Allied forces who sought their help in the invasion of Sicily. In India there were reports of Hindu thugs joining the

Khalistan movement in Punjab only to obtain AK-47 assault rifles, and then carrying on their unsavory activities.[96]

Creation of Organizational Hierarchy

The presence of an organizational hierarchy helps the cause of collective madness in two different ways. First, as I have argued above, it acts as a conduit for channeling the will of the leaders into concrete actions. The success of any movement depends upon the organizational capabilities of the group. In the organizational structure, the cohesion of the organization is maintained, its policies are implemented, rewards are given, and punishments are doled out. The organizational structure can be formal, coded in a national constitution, or informal. However, a movement that fails to establish a hierarchy has little chance of imposing its will on its opponents. The legendary organizational apparatus of Hitler's Germany, Stalin's Soviet Union, Mao's China, or Pol Pot's Kampuchea delivered its lethal message with efficiency. Max Weber was entirely correct in emphasizing the role of bureaucratic organizations—cast in the idealized form of the Prussian military establishment—in the development of a society.

Second, the presence of an organizational hierarchy helps individuals close their eyes to the growing discrepancy between their privately held values of compassion and humanity and their manifest actions. This is particularly true for those who commit what Kelman and Hamilton call *crimes of obedience*.[97] Members of organized groups carry out these acts, from genocide to the My Lai massacre. Within any organization, promotion is based on the degree of obedience to the laws set out by the leaders and the efficiency with which they are carried out. When a charismatic leader emerges, an organizational hierarchy is quickly set up where there was none; where there was already an established order, the power of the bureaucracy is further consolidated. A bureaucratic order works on a system of reward and punishment. The prospect of reward brings those motivated by the spoils of group membership—from moving up the organizational ladder to better living quarters and choice of mates in Jim Jones' People's Temple—to the fore. Those with moral trepidation succumb to the fear of punishment and become easy riders within the organization. Kelman and Hamilton show the social processes which allow individuals in the select organizational hierarchy to be willing participants in collective madness.

The motivation for participation, according to Kelman and Hamilton, lies in the interplay of what they call *authorization, routinization,* and *dehumanization*. Lowly prison guards or higher level apparatchiks participate in acts of unimaginable cruelty to fellow humans because they believe that their actions represent a *transcendent mission*. They either share the view of the authorities or, like those in military organizations all over the world, are trained to cast aside their individual doubts and obey authority. Organized society needs obedience, therefore in our evolutionary process we are acculturated to obey orders from authorities. Experiments by Stanley Milgram suggest that at least two-thirds of us are willing to go the distance to follow orders from authorities without question. Placed within an organized setup, one readily gets to know who is in a position to give orders, and most of us tend to follow them accordingly.

The process of routinization allows people to see their actions as a routine job, performed as part of their day-to-day work experience. Thus, if I don't actually kill or torture anybody, but only drive the truck that brings the victims to the location, I see my job as nothing more than routinely driving my vehicle. Even if I actively participate in crimes against humanity, I see my action as one of carrying out an order, part of my everyday duty. For instance, I can rationalize being the operator of a Nazi gas chamber as merely following an order to throw the switch.

Finally, we should note that while it is extremely difficult to kill another human being, it is relatively simple to exterminate an enemy. Through its process of indoctrination, an organization prepares its members to dehumanize its opponents. The opponents are not viewed as human beings worthy of life, but rather as subhuman. Kelman points out: "A central assumption in the contemporary practice of torture—just as in the early days, when it was used as a systematic part of legal criminal procedure—is that the victims are guilty. The question of whether or not they are guilty never arises."[98] To a torturer or a member of an extermination group, these people are simply labeled as "terrorists" "communists," "traitors," or simply the "enemy."

Stopped Flow of Information

Information costs. There are two types of costs, market and nonmarket. First, information carries a price tag because we may have to purchase its medium, either the newspaper, the magazine, a radio, or a television set. At a personal level, the cost also covers the time it takes to gather information. In standard economics, the time spent on an activity is known as the opportunity cost of time. We may call these the *market costs of information*. In a poor country like Rwanda, the market costs may become the dominant form of cost of information gathering. Since print media were in short supply and televisions were out of reach for most in the rural areas, radio acted as the primary source of information for most in Rwanda.

The other type of information costs, the *nonmarket* costs, are imposed by a group on its members for exposing themselves to information contrary to group ideology. One of the first things that victorious marauders did in the ancient world—from Sumeria to Alexandria—was to set the libraries on fire. Religious groups all over the world at some point in their history have banned certain books or have explicitly forbidden their followers to read books considered an affront to their faith. Most countries still ban books and other material contrary to their ideologies. The extent of group cohesion against a shared enemy depends greatly on the distribution of information. If we study the conditions leading to collective madness, we will almost always find strict imposition of extremely high nonmarket costs for information that does not carry the official line. As we have seen previously in the former Yugoslavia, members of one ethnic group would risk severe punishment if caught listening to the broadcasts of rival groups. Fundamentalist religious leaders from Jim Jones in Guyana to David Koresh in Waco, Texas, try to prevent their members from having free access to information. Right-wing groups in the United States are extremely suspicious of the mainstream press, just as theocratic nations try to avoid, at all costs, the contaminating influences of the secular press.

In some instances, information is distributed through the process of collective participation. In Nazi Germany, for instance, listening to radio broadcasts as a group activity was a typical feature of public life. Frequently work in offices, factories, and schools would be suspended for the occasion. People would gather around a radio set and would listen to the vitriolic propaganda engineered by Goebbels. In similar fashion, the world became familiar with Chinese youths waving Mao's *Little Red Book* and gathering for indoctrination lectures.

As the nonmarket cost of information gathering climbs, group members are forced to make their decision based solely upon fragmented information supplied by the leadership. Thus, being completely shut off from the "contaminating influences" of the outside world, Chinese people during the Cultural Revolution had little recourse but to adhere to the official line broadcast in endless repetition over the government-run radio and printed in the party newspapers. Similar cases of information deprivation can be found in just about every situation of genocide or other forms of collective madness.

International Intervention

International intervention can exacerbate an already deteriorating situation or may even help start a condition of collective madness.[99] This intervention can work in two different ways. A foreign country—a neighbor, a regional power, or a superpower—can supply arms and ammunition for a violent confrontation, or supply its client group with moral support through inflammatory speeches and other forms of political propaganda.

A coercive regime can also become emboldened when a foreign power threatens intervention and then repeatedly backs off. Inept actions of appeasement by the international community, such as Neville Chamberlain's acceptance of Hitler's acquisition of Czechosolovakia, have provided aid and comfort to the abusers of power throughout human history.

CASCADING TOWARD MADNESS

One important question remains: How does a society descend into collective madness, often with a rapidity that surprises even the most astute observers? In an important work, Kuran has offered a cogent analysis of this cascading process.[100] Kuran argues that people tend to hide their privately held preferences because of a host of potential costs that may be imposed on those who freely express their views. These costs can emanate from peer pressure or directly from those who hold power in the society. Thus, all over the world, people may hold prejudicial views toward another group of individuals—based on ethnicity, language, religion, national origin, gender, or sexual preference—yet espouse contrary (politically correct) views in public. Timur argues that when a large number of citizens hide their privately held preferences, it can undermine the stability of a society. These societies may appear to be perfectly stable, but a small change can suddenly bring about a major revolution.

Kuran supports his hypothesis on the cascading effect with a numerical example: Suppose a society consists of 10 individuals. Suppose, in a repressive society, people are concealing their private preferences. However, A and B would join the fray if 10% of the society's population joins. The threshold level for each of the members for joining the forces of rebellion can be presented as follows:

A	B	C	D	E	F	G	H	I	J
10	10	20	30	40	50	60	70	80	90

In this case, the society would look calm from outside. There is no indication of an opposition movement about to take place, since the two most receptive parties, A and B, are waiting for at least one other person to initiate the movement. Now, let us say, for some reason, A turns into a "true believer" and decides to start a rebellion. Now A's joining would satisfy B's requirement of 10% participation. As B joins, C's threshold point would be met, which will draw D into the movement. Soon, the rest of the members will join in causing a true revolution. Thus, a slight change in A's attitude would bring about such a catastrophic change, which would surprise every observer of the society. Kuran's exposition can be extended by developing several scenarios where a revolution will or will not take place. For instance, consider the following scenario:

A	B	C	D	E	F	G	H	I	J
0	10	20	30	50	50	60	70	80	90

In this case, the revolution will start with A's pioneering action. However, since E requires a 50% mobilization for his own participation, the movement will face a sudden roadblock.

Kuran expands his analysis by making a distinction between neutral activities and ethnic activities.[101] Neutral activities are regular economic activities that an individual gets involved with in the course of a day. Ethnic activities, in contrast, are those that promote ethnic identities, particularly those which are "divisive." For instance, parading through an African American neighborhood in a hooded Ku Klux Klan outfit or holding a Nazi parade in the Jewish section of town would be considered divisive. In a society, some people may have a private preference for taking part in such activities, but would refrain from doing so and present a false public façade. However, they may expose their privately held beliefs if they find that their open articulations are being matched by the rest of the society's publicly expressed preferences. Thus, if I express my bigoted views today and see that tomorrow many other voices are joining mine, I would increase my own divisive endeavors. Soon, as each one of the like-minded individuals sees their expectations being matched by the rest of the society, they will increase their activities and others will also join in. As a result, there will be a cascade of divisive activities where, only a short time ago, there were none.[102]

Kuran calls the gap between public pronouncements and private preferences "preference falsification" or the "preference gap." Although almost all societies hold the seeds of ethnic and sectarian divisions, they retain their political stability since such divisive views are often not articulated. Even when a small segment of the population does articulate its hostilities, the rest of the society does reciprocate according to its expectations. However, based on my analysis, I would argue that if the right political entrepreneur emerges, one who can frame the issues in a way that increases this preference gap, the society becomes a candidate for an explosion. And with the right antecedent events, such sublime antipathy can find its outward expression with a fury that confounds even the most astute observers.

NOTES

1. Quoted in "Notable & Quotable," *Wall Street Journal,* July 22, 1997, A14.
2. Quoted in Shahak (1994: 68).
3. Quoted in the *Washington Post,* April 7, 1994.
4. Keen (1986: 10). Emphasis in original.
5. Jung (1959: 4–5).
6. For many groups, the threat from another group is quite real. Ted Gurr (1993) demonstrates the extent of risk minority populations face all over the world.
7. See Volkan (1990: 82).
8. Ramet (1992).
9. See Mack (1984).
10. In India, Hindus and Muslims, in addition to having fought over beef (sinful to the Hindus) and pork (forbidden to the Muslims), disagree profoundly over how the animal should be killed. Devout Hindus may not eat an animal which has not been killed in one stroke, while Muslim law allows two and a half strokes ("halal").
11. See Kahneman and Tversky (1984).
12. An incomplete list, for instance, would include Sweetser and Fauconnier (1996) in cognitive science; Pan and Kosicki (1993), Lakoff (1996), and Cappella and Jamieson (1997) in communications studies; McCaffrey et al. (1995) in law; Tykocinsky et al. (1994) in psychology; Chong (1996) and Druckman (1999) in po-

litical science; Snow and Benford (1992) in mass movement; Gamson and Modigliani (1987) in sociology, etc.

13. See Keen (1986).

14. See Wasburn (1992).

15. See Poliakov (1974).

16. *The Turner Diaries* was written and published in 1978 by William Pierce, leader of the neo-Nazi National Alliance, under the pseudonym "Andrew Macdonald." It is a fictional account of the final war between the whites and the "System," symbolizing the power of the blacks, Jews and other non-whites. Since its publication, this novel has gained considerable circulation among the extreme right and neo-Nazi groups. Although its print version is difficult to obtain, the full text version of *The Turner Diaries* is available on many far-right Web sites.

17. It is indeed ironic to note that the Nazi swastika is the reverse image of the Hindu swastika, which, in Sanskrit, is the symbol of peace.

18. Sax and Kuntz (1992: 186).

19. A "mythology" is often defined in a tongue-in-cheek manner, as "other" people's religion.

20. See Tambiah (1991).

21. See Pfaffenberger (1990).

22. See Ghosh (1996).

23. For a fictional account that captures this primordial hatred, see Nasrin (1997).

24. See Harrison (1990).

25. See Melson (1992).

26. For the most comprehensive analysis of situation in Sudan, see Deng (1995).

27. See Ruane and Todd (1996).

28. See Nugent (1979: 84–87).

29. See O'Donnell (1978), especially 263–64.

30. My analysis of an ideologue is not based on individual personality traits. For an excellent discussion, see Haroun (1999) and Akhtar (1999).

31. For an excellent description of the training process of the U.S. Marine Corps, which turns an ordinary young man into a potential killer, see Ricks (1997).

32. See Lichbach (1995: 94).

33. See Lifton (1986).

34. However, along with their desire for fiduciary gains, this group of doctors had more of an authoritarian personality than those who did not (although no actual comparative study was made). And, most important, they had little regard for the lives of those who were sent to the death camps. Almost in every case, these doctors considered their wards as unworthy lives. In any case, other than a handful, few were fanatical ideologues.

35. These countries include: Afghanistan, Algeria, Angola, Bahrain, Bangladesh, Bhutan, Bosnia, Brazil, Burundi, Burkina Faso, Cambodia, Cameroon, Chad, Chechnya (Russia), People's Republic of China, Colombia, Congo, Djibouti, Egypt, Equatorial Guinea, Ethiopia, Gabon, Gambia, Guatemala, Guinea Bissau, India, Indonesia, Iran, Iraq, Kenya, Lebanon, Liberia, Libya, Mexico, Mozambique, Myanmar, Nigeria, North Korea, Pakistan, Paraguay, Peru, Philippines, Rwanda, Saudi Arabia, Senegal, Serbia, Sierra Leone, Somalia, Sri Lanka, Sudan, Syria,

Tajikistan, Thailand, Turkey, Venezuela, and Zaire (Schmid and Jongman 1997: 312).

36. Crelinsten and Schmid (1993: 65).

37. See Crelinsten (1993: 39–72).

38. See Langguth (1978: 201).

39. For a psychological profile of Patty Hearst in captivity, see Castiglia (1996). Also see Pearsall (1974).

40. See London (1970).

41. See Schulweis (1961). Quoted in Baron (1995: 139).

42. See Baron (1996).

43. See Goldhagen (1996).

44. See Chapter 2.

45. In fact, the actions of these isolated individuals were so out of the ordinary that we may even wonder about the "rationality" of their actions. For instance, we may wonder, along with Paldiel: "While rational explanations may be used to explain some behavioral facets, the decision to help Jews under such threatening circumstances defies rational explanation and, consequently, must ultimately have had its roots in an otherworldly dimension and in a transcendent intelligence" (1986: 90).

46. For an excellent overview of this burgeoning literature, see Baron (1995).

47. See Tec (1983; 1986).

48. For a detailed discussion, see Bredin (1986).

49. See Max Friedman (1966).

50. "French praise Zola's century-old defense" (1998: A10).

51. Oliner and Oliner (1988) reported 16% of people claimed "friendship" as the primary reason for saving the Jews, while Tec (1983) reported 15% and Fogelman (1994) 28% for similar motivation.

52. Wundheiler (1986: 333–56).

53. For other tales of heroism by "conscientious objectors," see Hellman (1980).

54. Huneke (1985).

55. For a detailed explanation of the intricate ebbs and flows of the movement, see Tully and Jacob (1985).

56. See, for instance, Gurr (1993).

57. See Dipankar Gupta (1996).

58. See Fox (1984). Also see Dhawan (1999). Consider, for instance, the following statistics:

Comparison of Socioeconomic Prosperity of Punjab to the Indian Average

	Punjab	India
Infant mortality per 1,000 births (1995)	54	74
Life expectancy (male) (1995)	66.6	60.6
Life expectancy (female) (1995)	66.9	61.7
Literacy (male) (1991 Census)	65.7%	64.1
Literacy (female) (1991 Census)	50.4%	39.3%
Per capita electric consumption (1994–95)	773 kwh	320 kwh

Sources: Statistical Abstract of Punjab (1996); *Indian Economic Survey* (1996–97).

59. Dipankar Gupta (1996: 83).

60. Ibid., 63.

61. See Bloodworth (1982).

62. See Glass (1985).

63. See Tilly (1978).

64. See Keen (1986). This was also made into a documentary film, distributed by Catticus Corporation in 1987.

65. See Schama (1989).

66. See Trotsky (1932).

67. See Sax and Kuntz (1992: 238).

68. See Geyer (1997: E3).

69. Ibid.

70. Many of the Beatles' (particularly John Lennon's) songs, such as "Give Peace a Chance," served as inspiration for anti-war protest marches.

71. See Sax and Kuntz (1992: 219).

72. Ibid., 230–31.

73. For a discussion of social control of political life in China, see Whyte and Parish (1984).

74. See Combs (2000: 7–8).

75. See Tully and Jacob (1985).

76. Evidence of this riot has been culled from a privately but widely circulated pamphlet by two noted Indian scholars, Mukhoty and Kothari (1984).

77. See Esherick (1987).

78. See Schmid and de Graaf (1982). Also, for an excellent discussion, see Hoffman (1999).

79. See Gurr (1970).

80. For a recent reevaluation of the authoritarian personality, see B. Smith (1997).

81. See Straub (1989).

82. See note 35, above.

83. See Gurr and Harff (1996).

84. See Gupta, Singh, and Sprague (1993).

85. The question whether democracies actually fight each other on the battlefield is an old question, one vigorously debated in an extraordinary exchange on the pages of the *Wall Street Journal*. Schwartz (1999) argued that the fact that the democracies don't fight each other is but a myth perpetuated in the hallowed halls of academia. They trace the origin of this "myth" to a 200-year-old essay, "Perpetual Peace," by Immanuel Kant. Wars have been unpopular mostly with the masses, since, in a war, they are the ones who suffer the most consequences. Therefore, Kant reasoned that where the masses govern, there would be fewer wars. Second, wars require instant decision making, often based on impulse. Hence, two democracies, hopelessly mired in bureaucratic inertia and red tape, would not be able to engage each other in a war. Further, in recent years, it has been popular to believe that since the democratic norm is that of peaceful conflict resolution, democracies will project their values on foreign policy. However, Schwartz and Skinner showed with historical examples that democracies have indeed fought each other. In response, diZerega (1999) argued that (1) There has never been a war between two democracies with universal suffrage and secure political liberties. (2) Democracies do not pursue a single set of goals with

single-minded devotion. Therefore, they are more apt to compromise than non-democratic countries. (3) It is the democratic nations that have created multinational bodies and have shared some of their sovereign power. Similarly, Owens (1999) pointed out that it is not an absolute truth that two democratic nations never go to war; rather, they are far less inclined to do so. Therefore, democratic pacifism is neither a myth nor an iron law, but a strong tendency.

86. See Gupta, Jongman, and Schmid (1994).

87. See Keen (1986).

88. See Glass (1985: 38).

89. See Thayer (1997: A13).

90. Ibid., A14.

91. Ibid., A13.

92. See Goldhagen (1996). For an excellent criticism of Goldhagen's thesis, see Stern (1996).

93. See Gurr and Harff (1996: 16).

94. The power of the SA declined in early 1934. The final blow to the old SA was dealt later in the year through the Blood Purge.

95. See Sax and Kuntz (1992: 367).

96. "Hindu boys join Khalistanis for guns" (1986: 2).

97. See Kelman and Hamilton (1989).

98. See Kelman (1993).

99. See Gurr and Harff (1996: 51).

100. See Kuran (1995b).

101. See, for example, Kuran (1998a: 35–60).

102. Kuran (ibid.) explains this with the help of a simple diagram (Figure A). In this figure, we plot "Actual Public Activity" on the vertical axis and "Expected Public Activity" in promoting divisive activities on the horizontal axis. The 45 degree line radiating from the origin measures parity between expectation and reality. The heavy line is the "diffusion function," showing which amount of actual public activity promoting divisive image would be undertaken for each level of expected public activity promoting divisive image.

In this diagram, the arrows show the direction in which the ethnic or sectarian behavior would progress. For instance, to the left of the point Epi_1, the small band of vociferous advocates of ethnic hostility would find the actual outbursts more than matching their expectations. This would lead to an upward adjustment of ethnic activities, culminating in finding a stable equilibrium at the point Epi_1. At this point, any greater advocacy of sectarian behavior would not be matched by the society at large.

However, if the society can reach the point Epi_2, it would prove to be an unstable equilibrium. That is, at this point, a resurgence of sectarian feelings would take the society to a much higher (and ominous) plateau of sectarian confrontations. In terms of Figure A, the society would quickly move toward the stable equilibrium point of Epi_4.

Figure A: Escalation and De-Escalation of Ethnic Hostilities

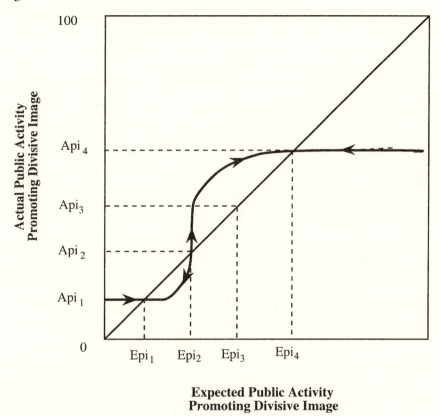

**Expected Public Activity
Promoting Divisive Image**

Note: Api = Actual Public Activity, Epi = Expected Public Activity

Kuran also points out that the situation can escalate (as shown in Figure B), where the diffusion registers a sudden jump. This, he argues, can happen because of the catalytic effects of international influences on domestic politics. Thus, if problems of the ethnic Albanians come to the fore in Yugoslavia, as a part of a super bandwagon effect, it can spread to neighboring Macedonia, which has a large Albanian population. Also, international events can lend credibility to a domestic leader, and events across the border can heighten people's expectations regarding the need for a greater level of ethnic activities. If these effects exert a strong enough influence, the diffusion function can jump, causing a sudden swell of ethnic activities from point Epi_1 to the point Epi_4.

Figure B: Shift in the Diffusion Function

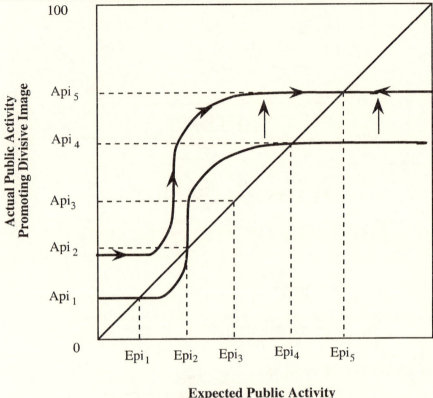

**Expected Public Activity
Promoting Divisive Image**

Kuran's powerful illustration explains the diffusion of ethnic dissimilation. In my present work, I am attempting to demonstrate the psychological forces that allow this process to take place. Further, for Kuran, forces outside of the nation play the role of a catalytic agent. In my analysis, it is the indigenous political entrepreneurs, through their skill in framing the issues and their ability to deliver through an efficient organizational hierarchy, who play the pivotal role in mobilizing people.

CHAPTER 6

MADNESS OR NOT:
THE ENDS OF THE SPECTRUM

[Pope John Paul II] is the anti-Christ, the man of sin in the church.
—Rev. Ian Paisley, Protestant leader of Northern Ireland[1]

FOR REASONS OF INSANITY

In the previous chapter, I explored the path through which a group descends into a state of shared madness. We saw that people choose to participate out of mixed motives, including ideology, greed, and fear of retribution from those initiating the movement. Similarly, those who remain on the sidelines, also do so for reasons of ideology, greed (too much to lose), or fear of negative sanctions from the authorities. Viewed at this level, most human actions stem from the same primal motivations. All collective movements have varying proportions of true believers, mercenaries, and captive participants. They sit on a pool of potential participants—the easy riders—who remain sympathetic to the cause but choose not to participate for fear of negative repercussions. To illustrate my hypotheses about the process through which extreme points of hyper-collectivism are reached, I will analyze two cases of shared insanity: the process through which the Rwandan genocide took place, and the path by which the mass murder-suicide of Jonestown came to pass. In both these banner cases of collective madness, we find all twelve factors mentioned in the previous chapter. On a solid foundation of mistrust, fear, and animosity, the isolated groups had little free information other than what they received from their leaders. With a strong hierarchical structure and an ample supply of arms, the price of defection from madness skyrocketed. In the end, the dynamics of the process drew many to engage in acts contrary to what we uphold as "normal."

In political science literature, political movements are seen separately from religious movements. Yet, even quick reflection will convince many that most social movements have religious roots; similarly, most religious movements quickly develop political implications. Therefore, this book being devoted to the study of collective actions, a fine distinction between the two movements is neither feasible nor desirable.

The third case study deals with the absence of collective madness. While violent racial/ethnic violence around the world dominates the current news, there is no national political movement in the African American community that truly threatens the nation. Yet, over three decades ago, during the height of the civil rights movement and violent confrontations with the Black Panthers, one could hardly have predicted today's containment. In fact, the report of the Kerner Commission, set up by President Lyndon Johnson to study the root causes of urban riots, placed blame for the unrest on racial inequity. The report warned that unless the economic gulf between blacks and whites was bridged, the nation might experience even more intense political violence from the African American community. Recent evidence indicates that the African American community, on the average, has lost economic ground since the 1970s. Yet we see little evidence of the kind of organized race-based political movements, that are wreaking havoc in many countries around the world. Under the circumstances, the traditional structural theories of social movements would have predicted an open political rebellion. However, I offer the hypothesis that despite widespread frustration, the African American community's collective identity, especially the notion of a "common enemy," has been diluted in the post–civil rights era. This accounts for the diffusion of contentious politics of race in the United States.

RWANDA: THE CHRONICLE OF MADNESS

> When I was younger, I thought that the only scientists who could cause evil were the chemists, physicists and biologists, but later I came to realize that the apparently innocuous social scientists held even more dangerous powers.
>
> —Eric Hobsbawm[2]

"The country we call Rwanda is not an 'ordinary' African country." So begins the authoritative chronicle of Rwandan genocide by Gérard Prunier. Nobody really knows if there is an "ordinary" African country, but if there is, don't look for it in Rwanda.[3] Rwanda does not fit the Hollywood image of a teeming jungle, sweltering in the combination of a merciless equatorial sun and the steaming moisture of a rainforest. Neither is it a land of pitiful bounty, swept by the shifting sands of sub-Saharan Africa. It is a small country—slightly larger than Vermont—characterized mostly by moderation in its physical setting. It is a land of gentle hills, except near the Ugandan border, where the Virunga volcanic range soars to an imposing height of 4,507 meters in the Kalisimbi peak. It is a land with a temperate albeit moderately humid climate. There are few of the wild animals that so pervade the image of Africa in the Western mind. In Rwanda, no lion prides bask in the sun in leisurely roll, no hordes of wildebeests thunder through the open fields in their paths of migration, no giraffes cast their elongated silhouettes against the setting sun; lumbering elephants do not compete for the dwindling watering holes with crocodiles and hippos. Except for a small area preserved as a wildlife sanctuary in Akagera National Park, which is the home of the mountain gorillas, this tiny nation of 26,338 square kilometers resembles many countries in Asia in its population density and abject poverty.

Early Rwanda: Restructuring Ethnicity

The first European explorers to reach Rwanda and its mirror image country of Burundi were struck by the fact that in this high plateau three distinct groups of people, of three "typical somatic types"—with most falling somewhere in between—resided side by side and spoke the same Bantu language. Among the inhabitants, the most numerous were the Hutus. Generally the Hutus physically resembled the Bantu found in neighboring Uganda or Tanganyika; most were farmers. Next to the Hutus lived the Tutsis. Typically extremely tall, thin, and with angular faces, they were cattle herders. Alongside the nomadic Tutsis and the sedentary Hutus lived the pygmoid Twa. Making a perfect contrast in physical appearance, one of the world's smallest people in stature, the Twa lived next to one of the tallest, the Tutsis, eking out an existence through hunting and gathering. Although there is no reliable way of measuring the relative demographic strength of the three groups, commonly cited figures estimate the current population of Rwanda to be 85% Hutu, 14% Tutsi, and 1% Twa. However, some observers believe that the Tutsi population is largely underreported and that the Hutu/Tutsi mix should be placed closer to 70% and 30%.[4]

The stereotyping of the division based upon appearance between the Hutus and Tutsis, which played such a crucial role in the life and death of the Rwandans, masks one important factor: Because of generations of intermarriage the two groups are often indistinguishable from one another. The vice president of the Rwandan National Assembly told a Western journalist, "You can't tell us apart, even *we* can't tell us apart."[5] However, the nineteenth-century Europeans, loaded with ideas of racial hierarchy, projected their own prejudices on the people of this central African nation. By the standards of their own perception of physical beauty, the early explorers started a myth that was to haunt the people of the land for generations to come. The famous Nile explorer John Hanning Speke started it all when he "deduced" that the racially

superior Tutsis could not have been natives of the untamed land. Speke concluded that the Tutsis were the "lost Christians," the descendants of the
biblical King David, and are related to the Gallas in southern Ethiopia.[6] As
new missionaries and explorers arrived, the myth of Tutsi origin became
more fanciful yet. According to Prunier, later nineteenth-century explorers
such as Sir Samuel Baker and Gaetano Casti, along with missionaries such as
Father van den Burgt, Father Gorju, and John Roscoe, promoted Speke's hypothesis about the Ethiopian origin of the tribe. While Father Pagés was certain that the Tutsis were descendants of the ancient Egyptians, De Lacger
placed their origins even further away, in Melanesia or Asia Minor. As more
and more anthropologists and ethnologists started arriving to the unfortunate upland, speculation about where the Tutsis came from turned increasingly bizarre. Some of the most respected academicians of the time suggested
that they had migrated from India. Others suggested Tibet, and yet others
the lost continent of Atlantis. Dominican Father Etienne Brosse proposed
the Garden of Eden.[7]

Before it spreads, cancer, starts small, perhaps in one tiny cell in an obscure
part of the body. Similarly, the beginning of cancer of the body politic of
Rwanda can, at least in part, be attributed to these fanciful utterings of the European settlers attempting to impose their own prejudices of racial superiority
on this foreign people. Following Nietzsche's distinction between "great" and
"servants of great" races, the Europeans imposed their view of racial hierarchy
on Rwanda by proclaiming that the tall and aquiline Tutsis were born to rule
the short and Negroid Hutus. This extreme view of the two people led to what
was known as the "ethnic division of labor"—the Tutsis were to rule over the
Hutus, and the Hutus were destined to serve them.

It is, of course, fashionable for many post-colonial writers to attribute much
of what ails a present-day society to the mischievous colonists. However, for
Rwanda such accusations, in retrospect, seem quite reasonable. Following my
hypothesis of collective identity, it is not difficult to see how such claims of class
division would poison a society. To be sure, the differences in physical attributes would be noticeable to anyone, even without their articulation by foreign
observers, but it is not certain that the presence of those "ideal" Semite types
would be enough to solidify the diverse tribes and clans into national groups.
The Italians or the Germans did not think of themselves as parts of a nation-state before Garibaldi and Bismarck hammered out a political unification.
It took nearly 200 years of colonial rule to forge India into one nation. Therefore, knowing how collective identities are formed, it is indeed doubtful that
without the illicit lumping by the foreign observers, the similarities of body
types would have overcome the more traditional allegiance to the smaller
grouping of tribes, clans, and families. However, the outcome of this
pseudo-science was to prove devastating for future generations of Rwandans.
Being favored by the colonial lords, the Tutsis dominated every aspect of
Rwandan life including the Catholic Church. Absurd claims of racial superior-

ity prompted the Tutsis to hold the Hutus, as a group, in contempt, while the Hutus began to view all Tutsis as oppressors and, most important, as outside invaders. Consequently, the Tutsis assumed that they had a divine mandate to rule, while the Hutus gradually started questioning not only the political legitimacy of Tutsi rule, but (having been repeatedly told of their foreign origin), also began to question the Tutsis' very right to live in Rwanda.

Although, as in any living society, the relationship between the two people remained dynamic and complex, the images of the "typical" Tutsi and Hutu deeply permeated every stratum of Rwandan society. In fact, analyzing the history of violence between the two groups, Prunier concludes that the Tutsi and Hutu have killed each other largely because of the mythical image they have held of each other rather than to gain any material advantage. Poignantly, he adds, "That is what makes the killings so relentless. Material interests can always be negotiated, ideas cannot and they often tend to be pursued to their logical conclusions, however terrible."[8]

The Fruits of Folly: Independence of Rwanda

The situation started to change in the central African uplands after the end of World War II. As colonial rule approached its inevitable end, the unquestioned domination by the Tutsis was also beginning to wane. With changing times, the Hutus began to develop their own collective identity. Also, a group of educated young Tutsis—breaking the age-old tradition of submitting to the king and the elders—began questioning the very basis of the Ubuhake system by which a Tutsi lord would allow a Hutu farmer to own cattle (a sign of economic prosperity and otherwise forbidden for the Hutus) in exchange for lifelong servitude. In 1957, as a step toward transfer of power from the Belgian colonialists to the native Rwandans, a UN trusteeship was proposed. Anticipating of a new political climate, a group of nine Hutu intellectuals published a tract that came to be known as the "Hutu Manifesto."[9] In this "Manifesto" the authors called for the end of Tutsi monopoly over all aspects of Rwandan social and political life. The reaction of the Tutsi elites to such developments was swift and brutal. In 1958—reminiscent of the Nazi "Racial Hygiene"[10]—the Royal Court, in a decree, forbade fraternization between the Tutsis and Hutus.[11] Such provocations could not go unanswered.

In response, a Hutu leader took aim at the most revered institution of the Tutsi-dominated Rwandan society, the king. In the traditional Rwandan society, the king not only was treated as a divine entity, he was the physical embodiment of all that was Rwanda. A story narrated by Prunier helps explain the king's position in Rwandan society: "When von Götzen [the first European explorer to reach Rwanda] shook hands with the king, all the courtiers were terrified: not only had the bizarre stranger actually *touched* the *mwami* (the king) without his authorisation, but shaking his arm might cause an earthquake since he was the personification of the hills of Rwanda."[12] Everything the king did or possessed was revered. His personal authority was symbolized by a sacred drum called the Kalinga. This drum could not be used by anyone but the king, and was decorated with the testicles of the king's slain enemies. This ritual symbolized the fact that it was more than an act of impudence to revolt against the king, it was an act of sacrilege. In response to the decree of the Tutsi court prohibiting fraternization between the Tutsi and the Hutu, a Hutu leader demanded the removal of the Kalinga. He claimed that its decorative testicles came from the vanquished Hutu princes, and therefore the Kalinga, the most sacred symbol of the Tutsi king, was offensive to the Hutus.

In 1959, the last ruler, King Mutara III, died without leaving any recognized heir to the throne. Soon the country descended into political chaos in which over 150,000 people lost their lives. However, the minority Tutsis suffered the heaviest casualties. A large number of Tutsis, estimated to be about 150,000, fled the country for Burundi and other neighboring countries. A largely joyless formal independence came on July 1, 1962, when the people of Rwanda opted for a democratic republic. Although Gregoire Kayibanda was elected president of the country, a segment of the exiled Tutsis decided to push for a military takeover. The Tutsi elite of neighboring Burundi, long united with Rwanda in common history, provided a base from which an estimated 50,000 Rwandan Tutsis continued to launch military forays against Rwandan positions.[13] In December 1963, the exiled Tutsis staged an ill-fated attack that was quickly beaten back by the Rwandan army. However, the Rwandan government, taking advantage of the situation, launched a ruthless campaign against the Tutsis in which most of their political leaders, along with about 10,000 other Tutsis, were killed. Such atrocities at successive stages created a huge migration of hapless people streaming into neighboring countries. By the time the genocide took place in 1994, the number of Tutsis in diaspora had reached a highly inaccurate but nevertheless telling figure of between 600,000 and 700,000 people.

At the time of independence, the nascent nation opted to be a democratic republic. Unfortunately, however noble the sentiments were for choosing democracy, it did not bode well for Rwanda. In deeply divided societies where extreme emotions run high, political expediency pushes politicians in democracies to extreme positions. If democracy simply means rule by the majority without any safeguard for the minorities, it quickly becomes as tyrannical as any other form of government. The democratic rule of President Kayibanda became a case in point. For the next ten years, his administration became hopelessly paralyzed in the quagmire of tribal politics. As any expedient politician would do in times of political and economic crisis, Kayibanda turned repeatedly to his Tutsi-baiting policies, making divisions within Rwandan society ever deeper.[14] As a result, the coup d'état of Lieutenant General Juvenal Habyarimana in 1973 was greeted with sighs of relief by educated, urbanized, moderate Hutus; those living far away from the power politics of Kigali in the villages, farming and cattle herding, hardly noticed the change. By this time, the Tutsi were totally marginalized in Rwandan politics. Facing strict quotas of only about 9%, imposed by the previous regime for school admission to civil service, the Tutsis had turned toward the private sector. The military was totally out of bounds for the Tutsis; men in uniform were even forbidden to marry Tutsi women.

The Best of Times and the Worst of Times: Setting the Stage

The first few years of Habyarimana's rule were the best of times in the tortured history of the tiny central African country. However, from those sunny days of relative peace and prosperity, the distant rumblings of the worst of times yet to come could be heard. The new president, despite the existing ethnic inequalities, presented a moderate face. Under his authoritarian regime, Rwanda achieved a level of economic growth that made it the envy of its neighbors. For instance, in 1962, Rwanda was the second poorest nation in the world. After three years of Habyarimana's rule, it rose to the seventh position from the bottom. By 1987, Rwanda had a per capita income of $300, which put it on a par with the People's Republic of China. In fact, between 1976 and 1990 Rwanda elevated its rank by twelve places (from seventh from the bottom to nineteenth). During the same time, all its neighbors either lost ground or experienced stagnation. For instance, in these fourteen years, Burundi's ranking remained unchanged, in eleventh place, while Zaire's slipped by fourth places (from sixteenth to twelveth), Uganda by twenty (from thirty-third to twelfth), and Tanzania's by a staggering twenty-three places (from twenty-fifth to second). All other qualitative signs of development were also looking up. The proportion of children at school went from 49.5% in 1978 to an impressive 61.8% in 1986, no mean achievement in the face of an extremely high 3.1% annual increase in population. Infant mortality came down; life expectancy at birth went up. Thanks to an international increase in coffee and tin prices, dependence on subsistence agriculture was reduced from 80% of the GNP in 1962 to 48% in 1986.

These hopeful signs—perhaps the best ever in the perennially impoverished nation—made President Habyarimana's rule look even more impressive. The achievements in Rwanda looked especially good in comparison with its neighbors. Next to the sheer inhumanity of Idi Amin Dada of Uganda, the murderous regime of Said Barre of Somalia, the repressive fundamentalism of Jaafar al-Nimeiri of Sudan, the faltering African socialism of Julius Nyerere in Tanzania, and the kleptocracy of Mobutu Sese Seko of Zaire, Rwanda shone like a star. Placed in the rogues' gallery of a continent adrift, the West was much impressed with Habyarimana. Foreign aid flowed in at an increasing rate along with foreign aid workers and NGOs of various kinds. Even some Tutsis—although pushed to the fringes of Rwandan society by now as an ethnic group—became prosperous in the private sector. Some even could claim personal friendship with the president.

Habyarimana, however, was not satisfied with rapid economic growth. He also wanted to develop a totalitarian regime in the worst tradition of communism. The entire nation was to have been built upon the new Habyarimana-ism: clean living, hard working, and a total focus toward economic growth. Despite the shiny façade of an island of peace, harmony, and economic prosperity through hard work, trouble was brewing in the underbelly of Rwandan politics. Unnoticed by the Western donors, either because of lack of knowledge or deliberate oversight, there were deaths with routine regularity; the deposed president, Kayibanda, was rumored to have been starved to death in jail,[15] scores of others, known and unknown, were disappearing, never to be seen again. Any faltering of the regime was conveniently attributed to the Tutsi extremists.

But, visible trouble soon visited Rwanda. In the international market, the price of coffee took a plunge around 1984–86. For a time, this slackening in export earnings was filled by an increased demand for tin. However, a worldwide economic recession quickly caused tin prices to head downward. This time, loss of export earnings hit the nation hard. With the largest money makers in ruins, the elite of one of poorest nations on earth had to turn to the only other source of hard currency: foreign aid. But in this area, unlike those based on the market system, resources were not allocated through the process of production and selling. Instead, money flowing from the donor nations had to be allocated through political influence peddling. The prospect of a rapid dwindling of resources intensified infighting within the ranks of the ruling Hutu elite. As a result, bodies from political killings in Rwanda started stacking up. No longer hidden from sight, political opponents were now being killed in the open.

Before long there were also problems from across the border. By now, according to most estimates, the number of Tutsi refugees living in Burundi and Uganda was crossing the half-million mark. Sensing the weakness of the Hutu regime, the expatriates, eager to reclaim their ancestral rights, began massing on the Rwandan border. Under the broad umbrella of the Rwandese Patriotic Front (RPF), the exiled Tutsis from Uganda started pouring across the border on October 1, 1990. The civil war had started. However, the rebels had underestimated the strength of the much better equipped and better supplied Rwandan military, aided greatly by a French government eager to retain its foothold in French Africa. Anxious to compete with the increasingly Anglophone, monopolar post-Soviet world dominated by the United States (and much less so by Great Britain), France, without trying to become an honest broker in the conflict between the Hutus and Tutsis, squarely placed itself on the side of Habyarimana's Hutu regime. Soon France, like many other countries who get directly involved in a civil war out of a false sense of national grandeur or hegemonic interest, found itself being drawn closer to the center

stage of one of the most embarrassing events of the twentieth century. France
aided and abetted a marauding regime in its genocidal frenzy. In an event
strangely similar to the Gulf of Tonkin raid, which drew the United States
knee-deep into the quagmire of the Vietnamese civil war, a staged "rebel attack" on Kigali on October 4 brought the French in as a full partner in the
Rwandan civil war.[16]

For decades, during times of internal conflict, Rwandan politicians had depended on evoking the images of the terrible Tutsis invading the country from
outside, ready to pounce on the hapless Hutus and decorate the Kalinga with
their obvious symbols of emasculation. In the 1960 mini civil war, the Tutsi
guerrillas were called the Inyenzi, the cockroaches. This epithet was given to
them partly out of spite and partly because of their ability to move freely at
night and strike at Hutu enclaves. Now, three decades later, the failed invasion
of the exiled Tutsis from Uganda provided the Hutu leadership with a perfect
opportunity to label all Tutsis as cockroaches. As we stomp on cockroaches,
this time-honored process of dehumanization would allow the Hutus to kill
the Tutsis with wanton abandon.

The Arusha Agreement: The Last Flicker of Light

By 1992, political turmoil had taken its toll on the already impoverished
Rwanda. Export earnings fell by nearly 40% in U.S. dollar terms, whereas im-
ports remained unchanged at nearly three times the value of exports. Foreign
debt approached the $1 billion mark, and with the hard currency reserve ap-
proaching zero, the country was at the brink of bankruptcy. Yielding to international pressure and a faltering economy rapidly spinning out of control,
Habyarimana agreed to a peace process with the RPF and his democratic opposition at a conference held in Paris on June 6. Soon after, actual negotiations
started in the city of Arusha in northeastern Tanzania. On July 14, a cease-fire
agreement was reached. There was for a moment a brief, last glimmer of hope
for peace in the tormented uplands of central Africa.

However, even before the ink on the agreement could dry, there was opposition to the cease-fire. The overtly ambitious plan aimed at ending unilateral
Hutu domination over Rwandan politics by establishing a broad-based transi-
tional government, returning the exiled Tutsis, and democratizing of the authoritarian political system. In the meantime, anticipating unacceptable
outcomes of the peace process, the most extreme groups of Hutus in the government administration and in the military had banded together under the
broad umbrella of the Committee for the Defense of the Revolution (CDR).[17]
Now the CDR wanted to be a full partner in the peace process. The exiled
Tutsis of the RPF, however, did not distinguish the CDR from Habyarimana's
party, and therefore vetoed their inclusion. Being outside the process, the
CDR, on the farthest fringe of the Hutu political spectrum, was to play a major
role in the ensuing acts of collective madness.

The murder of civilians had, in fact, already started. In small clusters or in isolated killings chosen deliberately by the Hutu radicals, many in Rwanda lost their lives. Some took part out of greed, some to settle personal grudges, and some for ideological reasons. For instance, in November 1993, journalist Calizte Kulisa, who played a major role in the making of the movie *Gorillas in the Mist,* was killed. His crime was that he had witnessed the murder of the famous naturalist Dian Fossey. One of Habyarimana's brothers-in-law was strongly suspected in the murders.[18]

The prospect of peace did not thrill Habyarimana and his cronies. Under a different political system they would have been certain losers. In fact, the most extremist section of the Hutu elite began portraying Habyarimana as a sell-out.[19] On the other hand, the United States and France continued to pressure the RPF to accept the murderous CDR as a party to the new coalition government. Instead, the RPF requested a UN peacekeeping force to neutralize the Hutu extremists.[20] Clearly unprepared—with its foremost member, the United States, still recovering from the shock of its misadventure in Somalia—the UN deployed an inadequate peacekeeping force in Rwanda in February 1994.

By 1994, it was common knowledge that a huge amount of weapons, from crude to sophisticated, had been freely distributed to the Hutu militia, organized outside the regular Rwandan armed forces by the extremists of the CDR.[21] Although the exiled Tutsis frequently denounced the increasingly dangerous situation being created by the distribution of weapons to the militia, the UN mediators were largely ineffective in stopping the flow. In fact, the UN representatives were totally lost in the chaotic history of Rwandan politics. Trying to take the middle of the road in dealing with the extremists, the mediators found themselves hopelessly confused. Frustrated, UN Secretary General Boutros Boutros-Ghali, in an April 4 report to the Security Council, threatened to "re-examine" the UN presence in Rwanda unless the provisions of the Arusha accord were not immediately implemented.

But the stage for starting genocide was set with a number of competing mythologies for each of the major actors. To the true believers of the Hutu supporters of Habyarimana, the Tutsis were marauding invaders bent on subjugating them to a position of virtual slavery or worse. By evoking the menacing images of an infestation of cockroaches, the political leadership quickly stripped the Tutsis of any semblance of humanity. To the Hutu extremists, the cockroaches had to be exterminated along with anyone sympathetic to their cause. For the Tutsi extremists of the diaspora, the Hutu regime of Habyarimana represented the rule of an inferior race of people over a superior one—to be rooted out at all costs. To the French, it was their archrivals, the British and their American allies, who were lurking behind the chaos in French Africa, ready to expand their political and cultural hegemony over the French backyard. Therefore, to France, the regime of Habyarimana had to be propped up at all costs. And to the world at large, it was a situation of poor Tutsis, victims of a ruthless regime, fighting for their right to return home. Each of these visions carried kernels of truth at the core but, carried to the extreme, they served as fuel in an already incendiary situation.

Message of Extreme Hate: The Media

The power of propaganda through radio, television, and newspapers has been evident in genocides all over the world.[22] Where literacy is severely restricted, radio plays an extremely important role. For instance, in 1994–95, only 35% of Cambodians above the age of fifteen could be considered functionally literate.[23] During the Khmer Rouge genocide, the figure was even lower. Similarly, in Rwanda, the corresponding literacy figure was about 50%.[24] On the other hand, by African standards, the Rwandan hate broadcasting originating from Radio-Télévision Libre des Mille Collines (RTLM) enjoyed a good share of the listening audience. The BBC estimates that radio ownership in Rwanda was about 25 per 100 persons, which is nearly double the figure for the sub-Saharan region.

The vitriolic tirade emanating from RTLM, founded by a wealthy Hutu businessman whose daughter was married to one of President Habyarimana's sons, saturated the Kigali area for four hours per day in French and in the Hutu language, Kinyarwanda. The broadcast was then transmitted to all corners of the country, via a network of government-owned and operated transmitters of Radio Rwanda. In 1938, a Halloween radio drama based on H. G. Wells' novel *War of the Worlds* created a near panic situation in several cities across the United States with comparatively much higher levels of literacy and access to varied sources of information. Convinced that the Martians had invaded New Jersey, many attempted to flee their homes. Order was restored when the true nature of the broadcast was revealed. Remembering that this famous radio drama could incite so many so quickly perhaps makes it easier to understand how the slaughter of the Tutsis could start in Rwanda. Most in Rwanda are poor, illiterate, and often isolated from the rest of the world. Therefore, it is not difficult to understand how a steady barrage of extremely hateful propaganda for a period of six or seven months from an authoritative—and to most the only—source of information, the government-run radio station, could whip many into a complete frenzy. In Hutu propaganda, the Tutsis were described as "Nilotic invaders, Hamitic minorities, arrogant, with a lust for power." Alternatively, they were called "rats," "cockroaches," "serpents," and "anti-Christ." Many publications openly called for the total extermination of the Tutsis.[25]

Based on the reports of NGOs such as Africa Watch, Frank Chalk, in an exhaustive study, compiled the following chronology of hate broadcasts.[26]

End of 1993	RTLM repeated broadcasts that identified Tutsi and Hutu individuals by name who opposed President Habyarimana. They were called the "enemies" of the people or "traitors" to the country, deserving death.
March 31, 1994	The Rwandan Patriotic Front (RPF), comprised mostly of Tutsis inside and outside of Rwanda along with the moderate Hutus, were locked in a power struggle with President Habyarimana's party in a political struggle. Although RPF played down ethnic rivalry, Radio Rwanda claimed that the RPF was planning an "ethnic purification" which would wipe out the Hutus. At the same time, it painted the Hutu extremist groups, such as Coalition for the Defense of the Republic (CDR) as the forces of moderation and pacifism. In their repeated radio broadcasts, the supporters of President Habyarimana "appealed to the RPF to give up their evil designs on the Hutus."
April 6	An airplane crash killed President Habyarimana along with Burundi's President Cyprien Ntaryamira. The crash was blamed on the Tutsis. The slaughter of the Tutsis in Rwanda starts.
April 7	The *Washington Post* quoted a Radio Rwanda broadcast warning the Tutsis in the country, "You cockroaches must know that you are made of flesh! We won't let you kill! We will kill you!"
April 12	An RTLM broadcast claimed that the International Committee of the Red Cross was treating only the Tutsis. This news report rekindled the deep-seated resentment of the Hutus toward the West for favoring the Tutsis.
April 19–25	The radio broadcasts continued to incite the Hutu militias to step up the killing of Tutsi and moderate Hutu civilians.
May 29	A radio broadcast falsely claimed that the RPF was killing Hutus. It specifically claimed without any basis of truth that the Tutsi cockroaches had butchered Hutus in the major Rwandan towns of Ruhengeri, Byumba, Kingungu, and Kigali.
June 23	Radio RTLM claimed that French soldiers were being dispatched to fight alongside the Hutu extremists to exterminate the Tutsis and that the French were also bringing with them a new supply of arms and ammunition.

The Bush Clearing: The Face of Madness

Ugly truth is hard to swallow. Therefore, acts of extreme revulsion are often swept under an euphemistic term. Like all mass killings in history, from the "final solution" and "ethnic cleansing" to the military use of "collateral damage," the Hutus used a euphemism for their genocidal activities, calling them "bush clearing." On April 6, 1994, with growing international pressure, especially from the UN, President Habyarimana agreed to install a coalition government in a meeting in Arusha with the regional mediators and representatives of the United States and France. On his way back, his plane was shot down, killing him and his companion, Cyprien Ntaryamira, president of Burundi.

The angry serpent, carrying its eggs in its womb, gave birth to a thousand snakes. Within hours of the plane crash, all the apparatus put in place for a fratricidal frenzy began functioning. The first victims of the slaughter were carefully chosen. Among the first to be killed was the moderate Prime Minister Agathe Uwilingiyimana. Her house was attacked by an angry mob spearheaded by the militiamen. A detachment of ten Belgian members of the UN peacekeeping force which was in charge of protecting the prime minister's home was lightly armed and had no clear mandate to fight. The Belgian soldiers were taken away to a nearby military camp and killed. The other victims of the early hours were the judges of the Constitutional Court, well-known journalists, civil rights activists and other community leaders, and prominent members of the Hutu opposition to the CDR.

The militias, all ready to go, immediately started erecting roadblocks and systematically killing Tutsis, moderate Hutus, and anyone else they wanted to rape or loot. Many priests and nuns were killed because they tried to stop the militiamen. Also killed were people who were well dressed or spoke French well, either because their social distinction separated them from the militia thugs or because they were better prospects for looting.

In the meantime, on the political front, after the death of Habyarimana a Hutu extremist named Theodore Sindikubwabo declared himself "president" of Rwanda. He systematically started replacing all the moderate staff or those unwilling to go along with the genocide, now in full swing. The hyper-nationalist Hutu leaders openly started to call for extermination of the Tutsis.[27]

The tradition of faith in authority, along with clear identification of the enemy, helped convince many to join the Hutu death squads. For instance, a twenty-nine–year-old peasant, Alfred Kiruhura, told a Western reporter that at first he did not want to kill his Tutsi neighbors. But the repeated radio broadcasts and exhortations from the political leadership convinced him that the Tutsis were coming to kill him. As a preemptive act, the young man joined the slaughter in fear of a Tutsi invasion.[28] As the process of "bush clearing" continued, the apathetic world was forced to look at the appalling pictures coming out of the heart of Africa. By that time, it was too late to stop the carnage.

Von Götzen's Curse: Why Rwanda?

There are many ironies in history. Many have written about the myth of the bearded god Quetzalcoatl, which played such an important role in the surrender of Montezuma to Hernando Cortez in Mexico. Similarly, in 1894 when von Götzen shook the hand of the *mwami* (the Rwandan king), his courtiers were simply horrified. Since the *mwami* was the personification of Rwanda, they feared their land would be destroyed by a devastating earthquake. Exactly

100 years later, devastation did come. Not in the form of a cataclysmic earthquake; the red earth of the tiny, isolated country of the highland of central Africa was soaked with the blood of its children. The world was horrified as the bodies, Tutsis and Hutus, important and lowly, men and women, young and old, bloated and disfigured, bobbing in the Rwandan rivers, washed into the great lake of Victoria.[29] Many stories of inspeakable violence were narrated. Some were written down for future generations to ponder about our capacity for cruelty and brutality. Many more were not. Estimates of those who lost their lives vary. Prunier estimates the figure to be around 800,000, but others put it well above 1 million.[30] Such large numbers have a numbing effect on our senses. Goebbels was known to have said that the killing of one is murder, but the killing of many is but a statistic. Indeed, what we cannot comprehend, we relegate to the sanitized anonymity of numbers. In our desperation, we often ask, why? In our utmost fear, when no one is around, we secretly ask ourselves, If placed in a similar situation, would we, like the woman who clubbed her neighbor's two small children to death, or the young peasant who had joined the death squad, do the same?

The Rwandan genocide offers a clear example of collective madness. Yet, we must not be too cynical. Not everybody got caught up in fratricidal frenzy. To an outside observer, looking only at the history of the last decade or so, it is difficult not to dole out blanket blame to every Hutu in Rwanda; but, as in Hitler's Germany, there were many who did not take part in the atrocities. There were many heroes. Prunier points out that many of those who saved victims from genocide were Christians, working out of their deeply held religious faith.[31] In a poignant last message, one lay church worker expressed his anticipation of reprisal from his own brethren. However, the strength of his conviction comes through loud and clear when we hear him say, "As for me, I walk in those hills to try to alleviate this misery with [my] limited means. . . . I use all my life energy for life and against death, for the Prince of Life against the princes of this world." Many others were similarly motivated by human decency, and their acts shine through the dark days with unparalleled brilliance. Unnamed and unsung, they heeded the call of a greater humanity. A Hutu schoolboy sheltered his Tutsi teacher, hiding him in the ceiling of one of the classrooms. Throughout the time when everyone around him went collectively mad, this brave boy fed his teacher and removed his excrement, and, in the end, they emerged together, alive.

However, a more important question is, How could a significant portion of Rwandan society be swept away by "collective madness"? By looking at the twelve steps of descent into the depth of communal insanity discussed in the previous chapter, we can see why Rwanda would be a poster child for our study:

Shrinking Opportunities. Perhaps the fate of Rwanda was sealed in the commodities markets of Chicago and London and on the coffee plantations in Brazil and other coffee-producing nations, far away from the central African highlands. Nature's fickle bounty created a glut in the international market. When world coffee prices tumbled in 1984, the tsunami of an economic catastrophe reached this tiny country highly dependent upon its export earnings. This was followed by a relatively mild economic recession in the industrial West, causing a sudden drop in the price of tin, the other major export product of Rwanda. This double punch proved decisive for the fragile economy and the nation.

Increasing Rewards for Group Membership and Costs for Non-Joiners. As the Rwandan economy started faltering, many lost their livelihood. Further, with market mechanisms disappearing due to the slump in the international markets for coffee and tin, the only way people could get resources was through the government. Therefore, in order to make a living in a nonmarket economy, where the Mouvement Révolutionnaire National pour le Développement (MRND) had the monopoly of allocating resources, the rational choice for the Hutus was to join the forces of extremism. Hence, membership in the party became increasingly attractive compared to the alternative.

The Hutu authorities played not only on the fears of the people, but also on their greed. Their incentive package was nearly complete, covering almost every group of Hutu society. "Authorities offered tangible incentives to participants. They delivered food, drink, and other intoxicants, parts of the military uniforms and small payments in cash to hungry, jobless young men. They encouraged cultivators to pillage farm animals, crops, and such building materials as doors, windows and roofs. Even more important in the land-hungry society, they promised cultivators the fields left vacant by Tutsi victims. To entrepreneurs and members of the local elite, they granted houses, vehicles, control of a small business, or such rare goods as television sets or computers."[32]

Collective Culture. The basis of a traditional society is tradition. And tradition exhorts people to submit to authority. Drawing from the works of cultural anthropologists, Prunier (1995) points out that the subjects of the old kings were supposed to adopt an attitude of absolute dependency, which extended to each and every facet of life. Therefore, when the ruler gave an order, he was to be obeyed, unquestioned and without any hesitation. A command from the authority figure had to be obeyed not because the order was morally right or wrong, beneficial or malevolent, but simply because it came from the *mwame.* The social hierarchy, from the king to the village chief, demanded the same kind of compliance. Prunier points out, "*This unquestioned obedience was to play a tragic and absolutely central role in the unfolding of the 1994 genocide.*"[33] This tradition of unquestioned obedience is the basic building material with which a collective mind-set is created. With time, the rule of the old kings came to an end, but the condition of environmental conduciveness remained with the vast majority of the illiterate, isolated, tradition-bound people of Rwanda. Therefore, when orders came down to exterminate the Tutsis, to many Hutus it might not have been a matter of choice.

Needless to say, there is no cross-national index of "collective culture." Therefore, we may sometimes have to draw upon anecdotal examples. With the help of a story in his revealing account of the Rwandan genocide, journalist Philip Gourevitch attempts to offer an explanation of the mind-set that allowed many Hutus to take part in one of the worst atrocities of the century.[34] Gourevitch was on a seventy-mile journey through the mountain roads from Kigali to Kibuye. When a sudden downpour sucked one of the vehicles into a ditch, the traveling party decided to wait out the night. All of a sudden the dank darkness was pierced by the "wild and terrible sound" of a woman's scream. Soon, her scream was joined by those of others. A few soldiers materialized from the side of the mountain and went down the trail toward the focal point of the many voices. Soon the valley fell quiet. Within an hour, the soldiers climbed back onto the road with a prisoner bearing obvious signs of having been roughed up. "This fellow was wanting to rape the woman who cried," Gourevitch was informed. "You hear it [the cry for help], you do it, too. And you come running." The interpreter said: "No choice. You must. If you ignored this crying, you would have questions to answer. This is how Rwandans live in the hills. . . . [T]here is responsibility. . . . This is normal. *This is community.*"[35]

Gourevitch is astute in his observation. This is the call of the community. Right or wrong, you must heed the call. To him, the genocide is the reflection of "communal obligation turned on its head."[36]

Ideology of paranoia and a clear identification of the "enemy." In my chronology of events, I have examined the development of the ideology of paranoia. Because their physical features pleased the Westerners, the Tutsis learned to look down upon the Hutus. It is, of course, true that every ethnic group in the world, with or without outside meddling, has its own hierarchy of the "other" ethnic groups. However, a systematic show of preference for the Tutsis during the century of colonial rule did much to consolidate perceptions of relative superiority. Therefore, in the natural course, the majority Hutus, in their deprivation, wrestled power away from the Tutsis after independence. And to avenge their past brutal exploitation, they started paying back the Tutsis by imposing their own system of exploitation. By the time Habyarimana assumed power, there was no political presence for the Tutsis. Their inclusion in all aspects of public institutions, from education to military service, was either severely curtailed or totally restricted. Through decades of pogroms, hundreds and thousands of Tutsis were sent fleeing across the border. It was, therefore, natural for the Tutsis in their diaspora to attempt to reclaim their rights to return to Rwanda by force. Their invasions, over the years, jarred the Hutus' sense of security. Hence, members of the two sides were acutely aware of their group identities and knew without a doubt who their enemies were. To the Hutu extremists, the humanity of the Tutsis was unmistakably diminished to the level of the cockroaches, while the Tutsi extremists were apt to view the

Hutus as subhumans, members of a genetically inferior race. The process of dehumanization was rampant and pervasive.

Rise of Charismatic Leadership. Every genocide and other act of collective madness, from an entire nation to a smaller cult group, needs the presence of a leader who draws political legitimacy from his charisma. The rise of Habyarimana from the political chaos and economic stagnation of the Kayibanda regime was propelled by promises of a better future for Rwanda. From the beginning of his rule, Habyarimana insisted on transforming Rwanda into a totalitarian society. Quickly, he outlawed every political party except his own MRND. Every Rwandan was required to be a member of the party. Every citizen had to carry an identity card showing his or her ethnic origin and place of residence. One could travel more or less freely but was not allowed to change residence without permission from the authorities. Without a proper reason, such as a new job or admission to a school, permission to move was denied. The MRND also took it upon itself to impose morality. From time to time (especially when times were rough), it would run campaigns against "loose women" (the prostitutes of Kigali or the Tutsi girlfriends of the Westerners) or, to placate the Catholic Church, against the sale of condoms.[37] The extent of his personality cult can perhaps be understood by the fact that in December 1983, Habyarimana declared himself the sole candidate for the presidency. The MRND's slogan was "One Hundred Percent," or to deliver every vote for the incumbent president. Much to their chagrin, however, the final tally showed Habyarimana with 99.98% of the vote.

High Price for Defection. In times of extreme polarization, the voices of moderation become the first victims. It is never easy to defect in the face of such coercion. It was not easy for the Tutsi moderates to oppose the repressive regime of their elders in the early 1950s. Similarly, it was not easy for the Hutu moderates to rise above the collective insanity and take a moderate view four decades later. The force of the Rwandan government, with its firepower and its network of informers, overwhelmed those who wanted a democratic change in the country. In fact, following time-honored traditions, as we have seen above, the Hutu moderates were among the very first victims of the genocide. For instance, Jean-Baptiste Habiyalimana, the prefect of Butare, who attempted to resist the pressure to slaughter Tutsis in his domain, was shocked by the government-controlled radio's announcement that he did not attend a meeting of the prefects. This accusation of negligence led to his arrest and summary execution. A handful of others also tried to stem the tide but were swiftly swept away by the waves of violence.[38]

Increasing Social Pressure for Acceptance. In the collective society of Rwanda, the influence of authority extended from the president to the burgomasters. Human Rights Watch, in its most comprehensive study, chronicles in great detail how every aspect of the Habyarimana administration was mobilized to incite people with greed and fear. After the genocide, many Hutus said that they killed because the authorities told them to kill.[39] To many, those in power had the "moral authority" to sanction such vile acts. This swayed them to commit crimes that would otherwise have been simply unthinkable.

Moreover, genocidal acts flourished in Rwanda with the explicit blessing of the churches. The Catholic Church of Rwanda was squarely in Habyarimana's corner. With 62% of Rwandans belonging to the Catholic Church, this became a formidable weapon of mass destruction. The archbishop of Kigali, Monsignor Vincent Nsengiyuma, used to wear Habyarimana's portrait pin on his cassock while saying mass and even served on the central committee of the MRND.[40] Although the several Protestant churches representing 18% of the population did not take any explicit stance, the Anglican hierarchy and the Baptist Church openly supported Habyarimana. The president of the Presbyterian Church was a member of the prefectural committee of the MRND in Kibuye.

Similarly, recruits were drawn from the elite groups of every walk of life in Rwanda. Most top journalists and television personalities as well as the university professors, took part in the mass mobilization effort. Also, apart from being part of the urban elite, these individuals had close ties to their rural communes of origin. They would frequently return to spread the message of fear and greed devised at the top in the capital city of Kigali.

Social Acceptance of Violence. With time, the constant cycle of violence desensitized the nation to violence and brutality. As cycles unfold, in their unchanging regularity, they create new sets of victims. And, in turn, the victims look for the opportunity to inflict the same kind of pain and suffering on their oppressors, or, failing that, on the children of their oppressors. The process of "routinization" makes everyone impervious to the pain of the others, robbing at an increasing rate its essential shock value. As the rest of the world looks on, the nation descends into the depth of insanity.

How does a society become desensitized to violence? Wondering aloud why he did not leave the country in the face of an impending catastrophe, one prominent Rwandan told Gourevitch: "[S]ince I was four or five years old, I have seen houses destroyed, I have seen people being killed, every few years, 'sixty four, 'sixty-six, 'sixty-seven, 'seventy-three. So probably I told myself it's not going to be serious."[41]

Creation of a Militia/Flow of Arms. Most incidents of genocide are carried out by members of armed militia, created outside the regular military. They are recruited from the young, the easily excitable, and the poor. Some of these men are "true believers" but many join for the prospect of promotion or loot. The members of the Hutu youth movement, the "Interahamwe" (meaning either "those who stand together" or "those who attack together")[42] militia, were no different. Its members were recruited from the poor. Many of them perhaps believed in the Hutu cause. However, as Prunier reports:

As soon as they [the Interahamwe] went into action, they drew around them a cloud of even poorer people, a *lumpenproletariat* of street boys, rag-pickers, car-washers and homeless unemployed. For those people the genocide was the best thing that could happen to them. They had the blessings of a form of authority to take revenge on socially powerful people as long as they were on the wrong side of the political fence. They could steal, they could kill with minimum justification, they could rape and they could get drunk for free. This was wonderful. The political aim pursued by the masters of this dark carnival was quite beyond their scope. They just went along, knowing it would not last.[43]

Arms, from crude machetes to sophisticated machine guns, started flowing freely to the militia by the beginning of 1994. Two years earlier, as the regular armed forces of Rwanda (FAR) progressively started to lose their professionalism, the French started to train Hutu militias, the Interahamwe and the Impuzamugambi. While the Mitterrand administration might have interpreted the events as an effort to bolster the legitimate government of Rwanda, to the Hutu extremists the signs were unmistakable: they had the blessing of France to go ahead with their savage plans for the Tutsis. These militias were formed by a small group of virulent Hutu nationalist members of the FAR, who were joined by others seeking a quick fortune. The new militia groups wanted absolute power through absolute terror.[44] Impatient with even marginally conciliatory gestures by Habyarimana, these groups started to prepare lists of the "traitors to the country." Within a year, the circle of the militia groups expanded, with the army slipping more and more arms, originally supplied by France and other nations, to the Interahamwe and the Impuzamugambi. Although sporadic killings had already started by the time the president's plane was shot down, an all-out war by the heavily armed militias began on cue.

Creation of Bureaucratic Hierarchy. Genocide, defined as "deliberate mass murder of a race, people, or minority group,"[45] cannot be accomplished without an administrative structure. As in Nazi Germany and other infamous examples of genocide, the Rwandan genocide was greatly aided by the administrative efficiency of the MRND. The party was everywhere in Rwanda. As in all totalitarian societies, the entire country was divided into small administrative units or "cells." Every hilltop, every valley floor, every community was included in cells.[46] Through these cells, the party could exert absolute control over its people. Within each cell everyone knew who the others were. The grip of the MRND in Rwanda was total and absolute. In fact, as Prunier points out, that administrative control of the party was perhaps the tightest among the noncommunist countries of the world.[47]

Lack of Free Flow of Information/Cultural or Spatial Isolation. In the case of Rwanda, as in Bosnia, propaganda played a major role. As we have seen, day after day an incessant barrage of vitriolic hate speech reached every corner of the isolated nation. For most, there was no other source of information. For the illiterate, the radio was the sole source of information. With the government and the party holding a monopoly over broadcasts, there was no other source of information. Also, given such tight control, many of those who might have held contrary viewpoints would have been content to take the safer path to avoid being branded a traitor or a Tutsi-lover.

Besides the radio, in Kigali, the most virulent voice of hate was spread by the newspaper *Kangura*. Although it was printed in the capital city, urban workers often went home to the remote hills carrying copies of this well-known newspaper. In community meetings, those who were literate would read the newspapers to those who could not. Frequently, the printed words were underscored by cartoons, most of them too graphic for the reader to miss the obvious message of hate and fear.[48]

International Intervention. International involvement came from three different sources. The first was Rwanda's neighbors. The governments of Uganda, Tanzania, and Burundi were either unable or unwilling to stop the Tutsi guerrillas from staging attacks across the border. The dissident Tutsis used their bases in neighboring Uganda to stage repeated raids against the Rwandan government. The governments of these countries, especially Uganda, were beholden to the Tutsis. After the overthrow of Idi Amin, Milton Obote was elected president in a largely staged election, after which the unfortunate nation sank once again into deep political chaos. Obote had viewed the Tutsi refugees in the diaspora in Uganda as outsiders and, in 1982, launched a series of attacks against the refugee camps. He started his own persecution of the Tutsis, many of whom had already become part of Ugandan society through birth, marriage, or long residency. The attacks galvanized the Tutsis; many of them joined the rebel forces of Yoweri Museveni, the National Resistance Army (NRA). In 1986, the 14,000-member NRA (3,000 of whom belonged to the Tutsi clan) took Kampala by storm. Quickly, the Tutsi military officers gained power and influence in the NRA, which had by now become the national army of Uganda. Their influence in the national army gave the RPF guerrillas opportunities to acquire arms and launch attacks deep into Rwanda. Although the Ugandan government consistently denied assisting the RPF—few countries ever acknowledge their support for dissident forces across the border—and even signed a formal agreement with the Habyarimana government in 1992 not to assist the RPF, it lacked the will or the ability to stop the Tutsis. Among its neighbors only Mobutu of Zaire was steadfast in his support of the Hutu government in Rwanda.

Second, the West contributed toward the genocide in Rwanda. At every step leading to the start of the genocide in 1994, the culpability of the West, especially France, has been well documented. The Germans, the Belgians, and the French had originally propped up the "regal" Tutsis, only to change sides to the Hutus when the times changed. This support for the ruling power of Rwanda reached the level of obsession after Habyarimana took the reins of power. At every turn, Habyarimana was given a nod and a wink bearing the clear message of French support for his actions.

Third, the UN contributed to the crisis through its ambivalence and hesitation. Facing the reluctance of its most influential members to commit their resources to corners of the earth deemed outside their interest, the UN had turned to the regional peacekeepers of the Organization of African Unity

(OAU). However, since nearly all its member nations face real or potential political instability, the OAU was slow to react to the Rwandan crisis.[49] And after
the Arusha Agreement, the rival parties in Rwanda sought the assistance of the
UN over that of the OAU. In November 1993, the UN Assistance Mission in
Rwanda (UNAMIR) was formed. However, its soldiers were ill-equipped and
totally outnumbered in densely populated Rwanda. As a result, the UNAMIR
soldiers watched helplessly as people were butchered in front of their eyes.
Sensing the UN's ineffectiveness and emboldened by French support, the
Rwandan extremists saw few barriers to the implementation of their own "final
solution." As we have seen elsewhere around the world, when the impotence
of the international community is revealed to an oppressive regime through
empty threats, it only strengthens the resolve of those in power to continue
with their mischievous course. Rwanda was no exception.

Incidents of collective madness are not inevitable. The right conditions can
create such catastrophes almost anywhere. Philip Gourevitch is correct when
he warns his readers that "the next time you hear a story like the one that ran
on the front page of *The New York Times* in October of 1997, reporting on 'the
age-old animosity between the Tutsi and Hutu ethnic groups,' remember that
until Mbonyumutwa's [a prominent Hutu chieftain] beating [by the Tutsi
radicals] lit the spark in 1959 there had never been systematic political violence
recorded between Hutus and Tutsis—anywhere."[50] The comprehensive report of Human Rights Watch correctly concludes that "this genocide was not
an uncontrollable outburst of rage by a people consumed by 'ancient tribal hatreds.' Nor was it the preordained result of the impersonal forces of poverty
and over-population. This genocide resulted from the deliberate choice of a
modern elite to foster hatred and fear to keep itself in power."[51]

JONESTOWN: THE TEMPLE OF DOOM

> It is a notorious fact that the Monarchs of Europe and the Pope of Rome
> are at this very moment plotting our destruction and threatening the exis-
> tence of our political, civil, and religious institutions. . . . The Pope has re-
> cently sent his ambassador of state to this country on a secret commission,
> the effects of which is [*sic*] an extraordinary boldness of the Catholic
> Church throughout the United States.
> —*Texas State Times*, September 15, 1855

The Massacre

The voice of the desperate woman could be clearly heard in the chilling re-
cordings of the last day's events left behind by the leaders of the mini-state
named Jonestown in the isolated jungles of Guyana. In November 1978, the
world woke up to the grisly sight of over 900 Americans lying dead in a heap,
most having taken their own lives.[52] The followers of the Reverend Jim Jones,

the charismatic founder of the People's Temple, had taken the lives of nearly his entire flock in a mass murder-suicide. But not everybody went quietly. The strong voice of Christine Miller, an elderly follower, left an imprint on the audiotapes of the final hours of the secluded society. There was one last glimmer of hope; Jim Jones had told his faithful followers that the Soviet Union was going to grant the group political asylum. As the hour drew closer, it was clear that the hope for political asylum had no basis in reality. Yet, Christine Miller, in a desperate bid to save her own life and those of the others, was heard pleading with Jones.

Jim Jones, a bisexual minister, had built the entire congregation on the basis of a strange concoction of charismatic Christian faith, the then popular mystical ideals of the New Left, Stalinist socialism, sexual hedonism, and even atheism, and had doused it liberally with paranoia. In order to save his People's Temple, he had moved its main mission from San Francisco to the remote jungles of Guyana in South America. He called his new settlement Jonestown.

Politics American Style: Paranoia

Paranoia has long been the hallmark of many of America's fringe religious and political beliefs. Noted historian Richard Hofstadter justified the use of the term "paranoia" in his famous essay, "The Paranoid Style in American Politics," thus:

I call it the paranoid style simply because no other word adequately evokes the qualities of heated aggression, suspiciousness, and conspiratorial fantasy that I have in mind. In using the expression "paranoid style," I have neither the competence nor the desire to classify any figures of past or present as certifiable lunatics. In fact, the idea of the paranoid style would have little contemporary relevance or historical value if it were applied only to people with profoundly disturbed minds. It is the use of paranoid modes of expression by more or less normal people that makes the phenomenon significant.[53]

I should be quick to point out, as I have shown, and as Hofstadter readily admits, that American politics has no monopoly on paranoia.[54] However, many important movements in the United States have depended upon the fear of the "others" to mobilize support for their causes. In American politics, the names of the villains have shifted from the Freemasons to the Catholic pope and his supporters among the European monarchs, to more recent days' menace from the communists, and lately, the United Nations and the government of the United States. In fact, one has to simply surf the Internet to get a taste of the power of paranoia.[55]

True to the tradition, Jim Jones' religion was heavily laden with paranoia. In the countercultural environment of the 1960s, Jones was one of many to preach mystical doctrines, which he sometimes described as "apostolic socialism."[56] However, compared to many newcomers, Jones had a relatively long track record. He began preaching in 1953 to a racially integrated congregation

in the "Crossroads of America," Indiana, long before integration was to become socially acceptable. Jones spoke the language of the poor and dispossessed, blacks and whites, and soon got himself involved in the integration
movement. The activities of this young preacher did not escape the notice of
the local press. In fact, a born publicist, Jones made sure of his media exposure.
The exposure quickly enlarged his flock and, in 1965, being ordained in a
mainstream Protestant denomination, the United Church of Christ, Jones
moved his mission to Ukiah, a small town in northern California, and in 1971
to San Francisco.

At a time when the integrity of every authority—political, social, and cultural—was being questioned, Jones delivered an attractive message of racial
justice and social equality. Yet, everything that Jones preached was counterbal-
anced by ideological contradiction, deception, and duplicity. Although his
message was one of racial justice, in a congregation made up of nearly 80%
poor blacks from inner cities, his inner circle was controlled by middle-class,
young, white suburbanites.[57] He promised equality, yet Jones, reminiscent of
Stalinist totalitarianism, dictated every aspect of life in the People's Temple.
He professed love, yet his rules were brutally administered at the slightest indication of defiance.[58] Jones preached virtue, yet his sermons were filled with
profanity. He demanded fidelity from his followers, yet he was openly bisexual.
He practiced bogus faith healing and even claimed to pull out cancerous cells
from the bodies of the patients, yet he was extremely paranoid about his own
health; the miracle healer was worried that "every mole in his body was cancerous."[59] Despite these contradictions and obvious personal failings, membership in the People's Temple grew at an explosive rate, doubling every two years
between 1965 and 1971.[60]

However, Jones mixed religion with political activism. Unlike most of religious cults before or after his, he was not only interested in the salvation of his
flock, but also, in keeping with the times, sought to change the world around
him. He would involve himself in local issues, delivering blocs of votes to the
politicians who, after their election to office, would remain beholden to Jones
and the People's Temple. On the other hand, if politicians, especially those
Jones had helped get elected, crossed him, Jones would start damaging rumors about them and write letters and make false innuendoes to the
news-hungry press. In his inner-city neighborhood, Jones would resort to the
accusation of racism time and again to discredit those who questioned his
methods and the goings-on in the People's Temple. Through seduction (a
number of newspaper editors and politicians were charmed by the apparent
tranquility and the "overflowing love" in the Temple) and intimidation, Jones
even managed to exercise considerable influence over the San Francisco
press.[61]

However, scrutiny from the outside world could not be held off for long. In
1973, eight members of the People's Temple defected. Jones had demanded
that there would be no sex between members, even if they were married, ex-

cept with the "Father"—himself. Jones claimed that these sexual encounters were not for his own pleasure; he was but a reluctant partner who agreed to have sex with his male and female disciples only to purify their bodies and souls. To Jones, defection by his followers was much more than simply leaving the fold; it was a personal affront. He called the defectors "Judas Iscariot," "traitors," or, more ominously, "fair game." The increased prominence of Jim Jones' operation, coupled with the defections, was drawing the attention of the larger community. This unwanted spotlight made Jones extremely uncomfortable and, when a *San Francisco Examiner* story critical of the People's Temple was published, Jones and his followers began looking for a place where they could continue their practices without any interference from the outside world.[62]

On August 1, 1977, the *New West,* a magazine freshly acquired by the Australian publishing tycoon Rupert Murdoch, went ahead with a scathing exposé of the People's Temple. Emboldened by their financial security, the magazine published "Inside Peoples' Temple," which described in great detail the faith healing scams, and the beatings and death threats to members who wanted to leave the group. To the naturally paranoid Jones, this was proof positive of an outside conspiracy to get him and his disciples. There would be no turning back. The entire congregation would move. Jim Jones would lead his flock in their exodus to their Promised Land from the corrupt, enslaving nation of the United States of America.

The secluded, steamy jungles of Guyana suited the group fine. In his sermons, Jones had often talked about how the "fascist" state (the United States government) would like to snuff out his fledlging apostolic socialism. He told his followers in great detail the unimaginably torturous fate that awaited them at the hands of their captors. After the defections in 1973, Jones suggested that in order to escape this horrible future they must all kill themselves. However, he let the group change his mind, but only if they could find an acceptable alternative location. Soon, Jones dispatched a team of three members, including an African American elder and a young white woman, to Georgetown, the capital city of Guyana.

The plan of granting asylum to a "persecuted" group of mostly black Americans appealed to the left-leaning political elite of Guyana—Chedi Jagan, the representative of the East Indian community, and Forbes Burnham, that of the black population.[63] At one of the most turbulent times in American history—with protests at home and war in faraway Vietnam—Jagan and Burnham put Guyana directly on a collision course with the United States. Fresh out of the colonial yoke, they had decided to oppose the "imperialist" war in Vietnam and open up a diplomatic relationship with the nearby archenemy of the United States, Fidel Castro. Finding a new propaganda tool, the government of Guyana decided to allow Jones' group to settle in their country.

The extreme physical isolation of Guyana was very much to the liking of Jim Jones. His newly founded mini-state, hours away from the capital city and the airport, without much of a paved road and surrounded by jungle, would be almost impossible to escape. Nearly 20% of the residents were elderly and about 30% were children below age sixteen. In addition, other residents were bound by emotional ties to their children, parents, elderly relatives, and friends.

In their isolated sanctuary, the micro-state based on the totalitarianism of Jim Jones survived and, by relative standards, even prospered. Jones depended on the monthly Social Security checks of his elderly members, who would hand them over to him. Donations also came from the members of the Temple living in San Francisco. However, threats to the People's Temple, once again, came from the outside. The concerned relatives and friends of the castaways started mounting political pressure in the United States. Stories of possible child abuse prompted California welfare officials to become suspicious of Jim Jones' operation in Guyana. The persistence of the concerned relatives paid off as Representative Leo Ryan (Dem., Calif.), a member of the House Foreign Affairs Committee, began an investigation into the matter of Jonestown and the People's Temple in the fall of 1978. In November 1978, Ryan, after being rebuffed a number of times, was granted permission to visit Jonestown by an extremely reluctant and highly suspicious Jim Jones.

During his visit, Ryan was presented with an idyllic picture of a reclusive agrarian community finding peace, harmony, and justice in an isolated sanctuary. Apparently Ryan was satisfied with what he saw. In the midst of thunderous applause during a reception on November 17, Ryan congratulated the people of Jonestown on finding the "best thing" that could happen to their lives. But the illusion of joy was broken when a small number of residents passed secret notes to the invited party; they wanted to leave. The next day, the five-member fact-finding team, along with ten defectors, including Larry Layton, a Jones secret agent, decided to fly to Georgetown on their way back to the United States.

As the small plane was being loaded outside the perimeter of Jonestown to take the congressional party back to Georgetown, Layton started firing inside the plane. In the meantime, a group of men had arrived from Jonestown on a flatbed cart attached to a tractor trailer. As firing began inside the plane, they brought out their guns and started shooting. Five people, including Representative Ryan, three reporters, and a defector, were instantly killed. The remaining ten were wounded.

As news of the assassinations came back to the camp, Jim Jones started preparing his flock for a "revolutionary suicide." The camp physician, Lawrence Schacht, with the help of two trained nurses, prepared a huge vat filled with a poisonous brew made of powdered strawberry flavored Kool-Aid, pain killers, lethal doses of tranquilizers, and a half-gallon of cyanide.[64] The orders were clear: everyone was to drink a lethal amount of the potion. The reluctant and the disabled would be assisted by the camp security guards. The nurses prepared syringes for small children. Those who had taken the poison were asked to lie down on their stomach in neat rows.

As the drama was unfolding, a tape recorder captured the conversations. Not everyone was compliant. Jones had given the residents of Jonestown the false hope that there might be a way out; the Soviets might be willing to accept his followers as political refugees. Christine Miller's insistent voice was recorded pleading with Jones to keep calling Moscow to see if they would let them go to Russia; she was refusing to accept death. As she engaged an increasingly exasperated Jones in debate, another man's voice was heard to scold her: "Christine, you're only standing here because he [Jones] was here in the first place." Others agreed. "So I don't know what you're talking about having an *individual life*. Your life has been extended to the day that you're standing there because of him."[65]

In a couple of hours, most of the nearly 1,000 residents were dead. In the midst of the dead and dying, Jones found himself almost all alone. Someone among his last surviving guards—we will never know exactly who it was—shot him in the head. Very soon, in the steaming heat of the equator, thousands of miles away from San Francisco, no more human voices were heard. As the elongated shadow of death enveloped the community, there was no one left to turn out the lights.

Why Jonestown?

Almost like a controlled experiment, the events of Jonestown offer us yet another picture of collective madness. In its frenzy, it defied the logic of all human relations. Parents killed their own children, children their parents, friends their friends. Neither age nor sex was a barrier. How could it happen? How does anyone compel nearly a thousand people to take their own lives? I argue that the answer to these questions lies in the necessary steps leading up to the outbreak of collective madness.

Shrinking Opportunities. Jim Jones went to Guyana out of increasing desperation. As the true nature of his group was being exposed to the outside world, he had real reasons for concern. The nosey reporters could no longer be held at bay in California. There were defections among his followers. Jim Jones correctly assessed the situation: he was running out of options. He could no longer count on his influential friends. His glory days of being considered a shining beacon of hope for the discards of American society were numbered. Jim Jones and his followers had to leave the United States.

Increasing Rewards for Membership in the Inner Circle. Entering the inner circle definitely had its privileges.[66] The ordinary residents of Jonestown received a meager ration of rice and gravy three times a day. On good days there might be scraps of meat in the gravy. The living conditions became so unbearable that many members often came down with severe diarrhea and high fever. Jones, however, liked to dine on steak with American catsup and drank imported coffee. And on extremely hot days, he had ham or tuna salad. The other members of the inner circle also received far better treatment than the rest.

They had access to the outside world; they could travel and indulge in other forbidden fruits denied as "venal" or "sinful" to the rest.

Collective Culture. The residents of the People's Temple accepted the total authority of Jim Jones over their lives. His followers came primarily from two groups. The vast majority were poor, relatively uneducated, elderly African Americans, some alone but others with their children and grandchildren. The second group was mostly middle-class, white, and young. These two groups were brought together at the confluence of two seemingly conflicting forces: old-time religion and the popular New Left philosophies of the time. Jones appropriately called it "apostolic socialism." The poor African Americans were attracted to Jones from his early days of preaching in Indianapolis. His faith healing, along with a strong message of racial integration, drew them to his mission. Indianapolis in the 1950s was a stronghold of the KKK and other racist groups. Segregation was the order of the day. The police and fire departments and public education were divided along racial lines. Even the textbooks used in the black school district taught young African Americans that they were mentally inferior to whites.[67] As the civil rights movement gathered steam in the South, it is not difficult to understand why some blacks would find Jones' message alluring. Jim Jones carried on his work in San Francisco, mixing his spoken words with political activism, which defined for his congregation the enemies of racial justice.

The sixties was a time for seeking. Disillusioned by an unpopular war that called young people to sacrifice their lives for something they either did not believe in or did not understand, many sought answers to the larger meaning of life in fringe religious beliefs. In the exciting days of experimentation in downtown San Francisco, Jim Jones found a group of young white men and women ready to embrace his version of the world.

The tradition of voodoo, magic, and faith healing, attractive to one segment of his flock, was not necessarily compatible with his message of essentially atheistic socialism. The only connection between the two messages was the allure of the collective. Each member had to evaluate his or her own actions in terms of seven deadly sins: elitism, intellectualism, and anarchism ("doing one's own thing"), lack of willingness to submit to authority, lack of commitment, self-pity, and dissatisfaction.[68]

As we can hear in the voice of the man admonishing Christine Miller, in the realm of the collective world of Jim Jones, she did not even have the right to claim her life as her own. This is the epitome of the collective mind-set. To those seeking order in the midst of chaos, insecure as lonely individuals, Jones offered the comfort of the collective, his version of a totalitarian mini-state in the faraway equatorial jungle of Guyana.

Paranoiac Vision and a Clear Identification of the Enemy. As Hofstadter tells us, in America there is a rich tradition of forming groups based on a dark worldview, where sinister forces conspire in the background. In their unseen yet at once recognizable forms they wait just around the corner to pounce on the innocent. The barely audible yet crystal clear sound of their hunger and lust can be detected if one is attuned to their dark designs. This is the ground zero of all conspiracy theories and, in this cultural milieu, Jones' world view resonated with a large number of his followers, united by the fear of the torturing forces of their own elected government.

In order to reinforce this fear, Jones continuously harangued the captive audience in Jonestown. They had to watch gory tapes from German concentration camps for hours. As the faces of the hapless victims—men, women, children, young and old, alone and with families—flickered by, Jones told his congregation that the fate that awaited them at the hands of the FBI and CIA was even worse than what they were seeing. Therefore, after years of indoctrination, to the isolated group, that became the constructed political reality.

The fundamental basis of Jim Jones' preaching was fear. The fear of American imperialism and the barbarity of its mercenaries were vividly depicted. The defectors were also marked as the enemy of the People's Temple and Jonestown. The media, especially when it cast its critical eyes at Jones and his followers, were seen as the tools of the evil empire determined to bring down a noble experiment in communal living. By the time Leo Ryan and the media representatives accompanying him arrived, they were clearly identified as the enemy.

However, the principal difference between the identification of the enemy in Jonestown and Rwanda was the fact that, in the case of the former, the group was under no illusions about the overwhelming force of the United States government. We can safely assume that if the group had perceived any chance of winning the fight, given the clear identification of its adversaries, like all other groups across time and space, they would have taken up arms. They had killed the investigating party; they had killed those reluctant to take they own lives voluntarily; if it had been feasible, they would have killed anyone they thought was their enemy.

Charismatic Leadership. Every group that engages in acts of collective madness does so at the behest of a charismatic leader. The doomed congregation of the People's Temple found it in Jim Jones. The rich mixture of religion, mythology, and the promise of a just world created a messiah-like aura around the paranoid preacher.

High Price of Defection. Hidden in the apparent Garden of Eden, there was a coercive system that would have put the Soviet gulag to shame. No one was spared from harsh punishment for the slightest infraction, real, imagined or made up. Neither age nor gender would protect an offender. Children were given electric shocks for bed wetting or made to wear soiled pants over their heads. For minor infractions they had their heads dunked in a bucket or were made to eat hot chili peppers.[69] For the lawbreakers of Jonestown, there was public "group shaming," designed to inculcate the collective values of the community.[70] Group shaming could consist of either physical or sexual violence. In incidences of physical violence, the offenders would be brutally beaten with a paddle on an elevated podium. When they were beaten, ostensibly to cure the sins forbidden by Jones' seven commandments, they were expected to say "thank you, Father" before they left the stage. The punishment could also involve pitting the offender against a much stronger opponent or even a group of opponents in a "boxing match."

Sexual violence took the form of having to commit public sexual acts. These acts could be homosexual or heterosexual and between the members of the offender's family. These bizarre acts were seen by every member of the community and wildly cheered. However, the harshest punishments were reserved for those who attempted to flee Jonestown. The potential deserters would be locked up in the isolation chamber, known as "the box," in unbearable heat for days. In keeping with the practice of the Soviet system, many were declared "mentally deranged." They were taken to the "extra care unit" of the hospital and given hallucinogenic drugs. These brutal coercive acts, along with a minimal chance of escape, go a long way toward explaining why there was no organized rebellion in the totalitarian society of Jonestown.

Acceptance of Violence. Violence was part and parcel of the life of the motley group, surrounded by miles of steaming, unfamiliar jungle terrain. It is not easy to prepare a large number of people, however devoted, for mass murder-suicide. The group must be psychologically ready to take such a catastrophic step. For this Jones had to make a ritual out of the performance of mass suicide. He called these drills "white nights." During white nights, the residents would be woken up from their beds in the middle of the night. The public address system would inform the congregation how hopeless it was for the group and what kinds of unimaginable torture were in store for them at the hands of the agents of the United States. The only way out of their ultimate misery was to commit mass suicide for the "glory of socialism."[71] Everyone, including the children, was lined up and given a cup of liquid to drink. They were told that all of them would be dead within forty-five minutes.

Life in Jonestown was hard. Everybody in the primitive agricultural colony, including the children, worked from sunrise to sunset under a fierce equatorial sun. After that they had to attend community meetings, where they were given Jones' version of reality, which often went until 3 A.M. Often there were public spectacles of punishments of the "guilty" ones. We can only imagine how disorienting it must have been for everyone to get up in the middle of the night and go through the ritual of mock suicide. It is well known that those who go through the experience of mock execution in a prison become depressed and disoriented. Therefore, the repeated drills of pretend suicide must have prepared Jim Jones' followers for their ultimate act of devotion to the man and his paranoid worldview.

Why did these otherwise sane people accept this bizarre lifestyle? Deborah Layton was one of the few lucky survivors of Jonestown. In a revealing statement to a newspaper, she said: "Nobody joins a cult. You join a self-help group, a religious movement, a political organization. They change, so gradually, by the time you realize you are entrapped—and almost everybody does—you can't find a safe way back out."[72]

Stopped Flow of Information. In many ways, Jonestown offers us a singular example of mass madness. Typical of the case of all other societies where such affliction took place, the free flow of information was among the first casualties. In the case of Rwanda, the poverty of the population deprived ordinary citizens of information from sources other than the Hutu extremist–run radio station. In the case of Jonestown, the information deprivation was deliberate. In the designed isolation of the jungle community in Guyana, the only information available was what the residents were told by Jim Jones and his inner circle. Outsiders were not allowed in the compound. Only the members of the inner circle were allowed to venture outside. Telephones were deliberately not installed. Once a week, Jones' version of the news was broadcast over the public address system. According to Nugent, a typical day's report would run something like this: "The Ku Klux Klan is marching in the streets of San Francisco, Los Angeles, and cities in the East. . . . There is fighting in the streets. . . . The drought in California is so bad that Los Angeles is being deserted."[73] Frequently, skits were arranged. In an often-staged play, a black man, with his eyes rolling and tongue lolling out, was lynched by a group of white men. These plays were written by skilled playwrights among Jones' followers, giving an extra dose of realism. In a clear asymmetry of information, however, the privileged ones had access to short-wave radios and information sent to them by their supporters in the United States. Only the members of the inner circle were allowed to go into the radio room, which was always kept locked.[74] But for the rank and file, the message was always clear: there is no alternative to or escape from Jonestown. Except one.

Organizational Hierarchy. Jim Jones' closest group of advisors consisted of ten people. Below them was a "planning commission" of about one hundred members.[75] Jones had quickly established an organizational hierarchy with himself undisputedly at the top. He had his own police force, fire department, education department, hospital, judicial system, and prisons.[76] This hierarchy and the delegation of roles allowed Jones to maintain a far-flung network which was able to deliver money and arms. It enabled him to establish his sanctuary in Guyana and to receive help from the political leadership in the United States. Without a strong organization, it would have been impossible for Jones to transport and provide for so many people in his jungle hideaway, and finally to commit perhaps the largest murder-suicide in the history of mankind.

Flow of Arms. No act of mass madness can be completed without a ready supply of weapons. In this respect, Jonestown was no exception. Jim Jones had an arsenal of forty weapons, including five M-16 semiautomatic rifles and an AK-47 automatic rifle.[77] These weapons were smuggled in as Jones' female devotees flirted with the Guyanese customs officers.[78] They were later used to kill Leo Ryan, his party, and those who attempted to escape the final episode of "white night."

International Meddling. If we consider Jonestown as a mini-state, then the impact of international meddling in its affairs becomes clear. Unfortunately for the victims of the mass murder-suicide, Jonestown became somewhat of a pawn in a much larger geopolitical game. The Guyanese government, for ideological reasons, welcomed the strange group to their country. The U.S. government also chose not to force the hand of Jim Jones much earlier in the life of the isolated colony for fear that his followers would seek asylum in the Soviet Union. At a time when President Jimmy Carter was promoting his human rights programs, it would have been embarrassing for the administration for a group of mostly black Americans to immigrate to the Soviet Union. However, at the same time, we must admit that international involvement did not play as critical a role in the development of collective madness in Jonestown as in Rwanda.

THE AFRICAN AMERICANS: WHERE IS THE REVOLUTION?

> The danger of a conflict between the white and the black inhabitants perpetually haunts the Americans, like a painful dream.
>
> —Alexis de Tocqueville

The title of Andrew Hacker's best-selling book, *Two Nations: Black and White, Separate, Hostile, Unequal* (1995), leaves no doubt about his main arguments. Published reports from diverse sources confirm that, using standard economic and social indicators, the average African American is worse off today than he or she was thirty years ago. In many areas African Americans lost economic ground from the mid-1960s, when the civil rights and Black Panther movements, along with widespread rioting in many urban centers were shaking up America. Yet, despite bluster by a handful of today's leaders, such as the Nation of Islam's Louis Farrakhan and the Reverend Al Sharpton, there is little organized black political radicalism. And despite the "Million Man March," sporadic riots, and the existence of radically different social views exposed by the O. J. Simpson trials, there is little indication of a well-organized national anti-systemic revolt in the mainstream African American community.[79] According to most theories on political movements, however, such a change of mood from the mid-1960s is a paradox. In contrast, while no national uprising by the African Americans is taking place, the puzzle of American politics is that some Anglo-Americans are increasingly confronting the established system through the so-called militia movement.

The Summer of Discontent

In the summer of 1967 the mood of the nation was somber. The continuing civil rights confrontations, the rise of radical youth movements, and destructive race riots had brutally vitiated the myth of a harmonious melting pot. Instead, it was being replaced by the pervasive perception of a cauldron about to burst open with the fury of gathering steam boiling over under extreme pressure. Reflecting the mood of the day, President Lyndon Johnson underscored the urgency of the situation by warning that the clock was ticking away and that the nation must take steps to mitigate the situation before it was too late. The Kerner Commission, which was appointed by President Johnson in 1967 to look into the causes of black revolt, released its report a year later.

The Kerner Commission placed responsibility for the great urban riots and discontent among the black citizens of the country squarely at the doorstep of the economically segregated society. Citing examples of disparities in earnings, health, housing, and education, the Commission warned that unless the nation took steps to bridge the gap of racial inequality, large-scale confrontation between the races was both highly probable and imminent:

Our Nation is moving toward two societies, one black, one white—separate and unequal.

Reaction to last summer's disorders has quickened the movement and deepened the division. Discrimination and segregation have long permeated much of American life; now they threaten the future of every American. . . .

To pursue our present course will involve the continuing polarization of the American community and, ultimately, the destruction of basic democratic values.[80]

In analyzing the root causes of race riots, the Commission isolated two broad categories. The first group of conditions relates to the causes of black economic misery, while the second relates to the changing mood of the black community toward socioeconomic injustice. In the first group, the Commission included the following three conditions, which it called the "results of long-standing white prejudice toward the blacks":

Pervasive discrimination and segregation in employment, education, and housing, which have resulted in the continuing exclusion of great numbers of Negroes from the benefits of economic progress.

Black in-migration and white exodus, which have produced the massive and growing concentrations of impoverished Negroes in our major cities, creating a growing crisis of deteriorating facilities and services and unmet human needs.

The black ghettos, where segregation and poverty converge on the young to destroy opportunity and enforce failure. Crime, drug addiction, dependency on welfare, and bitterness and resentment against society in general and whites in particular are the result.[81]

The Kerner Commission pointed out that the frustration felt within the black community was the result of these physical conditions of deprivation, which were being heightened by television and the other media. As a result:

Frustrated hopes are the residue of the unfulfilled expectations aroused by the great judicial and legislative victories of the civil rights movement and the dramatic struggle for equal rights in the South.

A climate that tends toward approval and encouragement of violence as a form of protest has been created by white terrorism directed against non-violent protest; by the open defiance of law and Federal authority by state and local officials resisting desegregation; and by some protest groups engaging in civil disobedience who turn their backs on nonviolence, go beyond the constitutionally protected rights of petition and free assembly, and resort to violence to attempt to compel alteration of laws and policies with which they disagree.

The frustration of powerlessness ha[s] led some Negroes to the conviction that there is no effective alternative to violence as a means of achieving redress of grievances, and of "moving the system." These frustrations are reflected in alienation and hostility toward the institutions of law and government and the white society, which controls them, and in the reach toward racial consciousness and solidarity reflected in the slogan "Black Power."

A new mood has sprung up among Negroes, particularly among the young, in which self-esteem and enhanced racial pride are replacing apathy and submission to "the system."

The police are not merely the "spark" factor. To some Negroes police have come to symbolize white power, white racism and white repression. And the fact is that many police do reflect and express these white attitudes. The atmosphere of hostility and cynicism is reinforced by a widespread belief among Negroes in the existence of police brutality and in [a] "double standard" of justice and protection—one for Negroes and one for whites.[82]

Since both popular wisdom and age-old scholarly hypotheses link collective violence to frustration caused by economic deprivation, there was no apparent reason to question the validity of the dire predictions of the Commission. With so many observers predicting open race-based confrontations, thirty years later we may legitimately ask, Where is the revolution?[83]

Indeed, this question takes on special significance when we compare race relations in this country with those in many other parts of the world. Few nations, regardless of economic development or political ideology, seem to be immune from the rising tide of sub-nationalism. Most of Africa is awash with fratricidal frenzy, and the newly democratic nations of Eastern Europe and Central Asia are experiencing group-based hostility. Even next door, Canada avoids being split apart by a razor-thin margin at the polls. Mexico suffers under a series of assassinations and open rebellion in the Chiapas region. Catholics and Protestants continue their bloody struggle in Northern Ireland, as do the Flemings and Walloons in Belgium. The Basques in Spain keep up their sub-nationalist struggle against the powerful majority.

Therefore, in this section, I seek some answers to the paradox why, in contrast to many countries around the world, the United States has so far been able to avert organized collective hostility even in the face of deteriorating economic conditions for the average member of the African American community.[84]

The Shape of the Paradox

If the assessment of the economic situation of African Americans was depressing in the sixties, the changes during the following three decades have left little joy for the community as a whole. Thus, a report by the National Research Council unequivocally concludes: "The greatest economic gains for blacks occurred in the 1940s and 1960s. Since the early 1970s, the economic status of blacks relative to whites has, on average, stagnated or deteriorated."[85] Statistical evidence suggests that although a distinct segment of the African American community, by taking advantage of the improved social and political environment, has benefited greatly during periods of steady economic expansion, the economic condition for a large segment of the community has deteriorated, often to a considerable extent.

Personal Income. In order to understand the economic plight of the African American community we may look at the relative earning potential of blacks and whites. In 1970 an average working African American male made about 61 cents to every dollar earned by an average white male. That figure declined to 57.6 cents in 1992, a drop of nearly 6% over a twenty-two-year span.[86] In the area of relative rates of unemployment, in 1960, the ratio of black to white unemployment was 2.08 (an African American was twice as likely to be unemployed as a white). In 1992, the ratio stood at 2.17, an increase of 4.3%.

Poverty. The plight of poor and uneducated blacks grew even more dire during the last couple of decades. In 1970, 14.2% of whites and 34.3% of blacks were under the official poverty line. In 1992, the corresponding figures were 12.3% and 38.2%. In other words, in 1970 the poverty ratio for blacks was 2.41, which by 1992 rose to 3.11. This means that the probability that an African American family will be poor increased by 29% over that of a white family.[87]

The situation does not improve appreciably for those with a bit more education. Thus, for black men with some college education but no degree, earnings in 1984 constant dollars fell to $315 a week in 1994 from $394 in 1969, a 20% drop. The corresponding loss of income for African American females was a whopping 32% (from $308 in 1969 to $242 in 1994).[88] However, according to one study, during this time period the earnings of well-educated black men rose relative to the earnings of similarly educated white males.[89] In 1984, a college-educated black male could expect to earn up to 74% of what his white counterpart earned. In 1993, it rose to a modest 76.4%, a mere 3% increase in nearly a decade.

Education. The gap in educational achievement between the two races has also been persistent, and in some important areas is becoming even wider. Although recent newspaper reports suggest that African Americans are staying in high school longer, their record of achievement in the area of higher education has remained disappointing. In 1960, 8.15% of whites had a four-year college education, while the corresponding figure for blacks was 3.15%. During the last three decades, higher education, the stepping stone to economic success, has spread throughout the society. However, educational achievement in the African American community continues to lag. For instance, in 1993, 21.9% of the white population had a college degree as opposed to 12.2% of the black community. Again, in the field of higher education the gap between blacks and whites has increased, from 5% in 1960 to 9.7% in 1993. For African American males, the gap is even wider. In 1993, only 11.9% of African American males had a college education in contrast to 25.7% of white males.

Health Care. The increase in the rate of black poverty since the 1960s has taken its expected toll on the most vulnerable of the community, the children, the sick, and the elderly. In 1986, 43% of African American children under age eighteen lived in households below the poverty level. Much of the plight of these children is caused by the prevalence of single mothers bringing up children in African American households. As a result, the National Research Council concludes that "[i]n the course of their childhood, 86 percent of black children . . . are likely to spend some time in a single-parent household."[90] However, I do not want to paint a uniformly bleak picture. The difference between white and black male life expectancy at birth—the composite measure of community health—was 8 years in 1970 (68 and 60 years, respectively). This gap narrowed slightly, to 7.5 years, in 1992 (73 and 65.5 years). White females were expected to live 7.3 years longer than their African American counterparts in 1970 (75.6 years and 68.3 years, respectively), but in 1992, this difference narrowed to 5.8 years.

Housing. Residential segregation facing the African American community has taken on a different character for the last two and a half decades. The passage of the civil rights laws and a general broadening of racial views have eased the problem of residential segregation at the upper end of the economic structure. Therefore, while the decennial census reports indicate a drop in residential segregation for the large metropolitan cities, this change has affected only middle- and upper-middle-class African American families. A detailed study finds evidence of what is called "hyper-segregation" based on economic class.[91] Therefore, it seems safe to conclude that, during the 1970s and 1980s, a portion of relatively affluent African Americans have been able to come out of segregated, impoverished neighborhoods and have become successfully assimilated into middle America. However, for the vast majority of African Americans, poverty and isolation have deepened.

Cold statistics often do not convey the entire picture. But what these numbers show in and of themselves is indeed frightening. Recent reports claim that the life expectancy of an African American male in Harlem is lower than that of a man in Bangladesh, one of the poorest nations on earth. Also, there are more

African American youths under the protection of the criminal justice system than are enrolled in college. In fact, the condition of African American males, in particular, was considered so dire that the U.S. Senate held hearings on the subject in the mid-nineties. These shameful statistics, however, pose a paradox: While disaffected minorities all over the world, from the Kwazulus to the Québécois, are engaged in confronting the established political system to further their group cause, here in the United States, where is the revolution? What happened to the apocalyptic predictions of the Kerner Commission and many sociologists? Instead, what we see today are episodic expressions of frustration which explode into aimless riots, heaping more self-inflicted pain on the community. Even the much-publicized Million Man March was a one-shot action, long on rhetoric and symbolism, but short on defining the potential movement's goals and the corresponding action plan.

Solving the Paradox: The Case for the Weakening of Collective Identity

In light of the above hypotheses, let us analyze the case of race relations in the United States from the perspective of the African American community. The change in the mood in race relations in the United States during the last quarter century is apparent even to a casual observer. Long gone are the angry black Olympic athletes with clenched fists at the victory stand. They have been replaced by those who would run through the Olympic stadium with the American flag in spontaneous demonstrations of patriotism. Even the most radical black leadership espousing war against the "white-dominated system" seems to deviate toward the center.[92] Yet, at the same time, frustration resulting from economic deprivation in the African American community is rampant. A significant 65% of the community does not believe that discrimination will end in their lifetime. A similar proportion of African Americans believe in a widespread conspiracy to shackle them through deliberate attempts such as introducing narcotics and the AIDS virus in black neighborhoods.[93]

In my behavioral model, I emphasize that, for a collective rebellion to take place, a strong collective identity must exist. Therefore, I argue that there are primarily two reasons why the African American community in this country has not exploded into open rebellion against the present political and economic system. First, it no longer has a strong enough collective (or political) identity, which requires a clear definition of "us" versus "them"—the "allies" and the "enemies."[94] Second, concerted government efforts at suppressing political radicalism, through such legislative initiatives as the Omnibus Crime Control Act of 1968 and later amendments, have raised the price of organizing radical groups to such an extent that it has not been feasible to form an effective organization. Therefore, despite abundant frustration within the black community, this frustration is not being channeled in a systematic fashion through political radicalism.

The "Us" Factors

A reader of black history is often struck by the brutality of the system and by the totality of subjugation of one race of people by another—physical, economic, political, and even psychological. Totality of dominance by whites over blacks can only be compared to the Hindu caste system, where the so-called untouchables were subjugated by the dominant caste Hindus for at least 2,000 years with unparalleled totality. And because of this totality of repression, until quite recently both groups failed to develop a cohesive sense of collective identity to confront the oppressive system. From the time of the early settlements in the New World, there was a systematic effort to destroy the collective identity of the slaves. They were not only scattered around the colonies to destroy their own tribal and linguistic groupings, but even their normal familial relationships were prevented from growing.[95] Also, unlike in the South American countries, where the plantations were large and the ratio of slaves to nonslaves was high, the plantations in the southern United States were not conducive to a mass-based open slave rebellion. Even in the post-bellum South, emancipated African Americans, due to a lack of economic power and the necessary political resources, failed to develop a sustained movement. Instead, during the Reconstruction period, the defeated whites felt most threatened by nascent black power. This led to the resurgence of white racial extremism, culminating in the enactment of Jim Crow legislation.

African American political identity entered a second stage from the last quarter of the nineteenth century to the end of the New Deal era.[96] During this period, the black and white conflict centered around white working-class retaliation against economic encroachment by blacks. Blacks were often brought in to replace striking whites; this and their large-scale migration out of the rural and repressive South intensified racial tension in many urban areas of the North.

The immediate postwar period was characterized by a growing sense of African American identity, which crystallized during the 1960s and 1970s.[97] This resulted in a change in the character of the conflict. The postwar black movement increasingly became political in nature. During both the great wars, and especially during World War II, the economic position of blacks really started to change, probably for the first time in American history. As more and more white males were called for active duty and, simultaneously, the industrial sector underwent a rapid enlargement, a great demand for skilled and unskilled labor was created. In relatively large numbers, African Americans took advantage of the changing socioeconomic conditions. Also, as African Americans started to join the U.S. military, their perception of the society in general, and of prevailing race relations in particular, started to change. Therefore, as a result of the war effort and the changing nature of the economy, African Americans started to abandon their traditional area of employment as unskilled agricultural laborers. The demographic shift from rural agriculture to urban manufacturing created a new cultural and political ethos for black communities across the nation, the most important upshot of which was the creation of a new middle class.

The middle class has always forced social changes in history. Aristotle was keenly aware of the power of the middle class; Marx predicted that, unless the middle class was moved, there was little chance for a revolutionary movement to succeed. The African American community proved no exception. The civil rights movement in the South drew its primary strength from the black middle class. Apart from the humiliation of being denied their fundamental rights, overt discrimination severely restricted economic opportunities for the African American middle class in the South. And it perceived these racial barriers to be much more onerous than did poor blacks living at the margins of urban society or those in rural areas. Therefore, the leadership in the southern political movement came from educated middle-class African Americans.

Even during the civil rights movement, the riots of the North were of a somewhat different nature. In the North, because of the lack of overt discriminatory practices the expressions of frustration took a different form than in the South. In the North, the expressions of frustration and anger took two different forms. Those with a stronger political orientation formed more radical youth organizations to engage the established white-dominated political system in a violent struggle. In contrast, the anger and frustration of the less educated, those with few or no political resources manifested themselves in the form of rioting.

If we look at the primary motivations of people who take part in peaceful demonstrations, they do so without much prospect of financial gain. Therefore, for them the primary motivation has to be ideological, especially when the prospect of the success of the movement is very much in doubt. Rioting, on the other hand, draws out a wide variety of participants. In a riot situation, we certainly find ideologues, who tend to attack the so-called symbols of oppression. Riots also attract people with other motivations, such as mercenaries or criminal elements, who take advantage of lawlessness. In a riot situation, we may also encounter those who take part largely for what Tullock and Banfield call the "fun factor."[98] Therefore, in the great riots of the sixties, some scholars have found the ideologically motivated "new ghetto man" or the "new urban black," and others, the seekers of "fun and profit."[99]

However, the strong awareness of racial identity, having reached its pinnacle, started to wane in the latter part of the 1970s and 1980s, almost immediately after the passage of civil rights legislation.[100] While Dr. King was eminently successful against the defined enemy of the segregated South, the last attempt of his life to mobilize the poor against the "system" was a dismal failure.

I argue that this diffusion of the movement was the result of the erosion of collective identity in the African American community after the passage of the civil rights legislation. Let me attempt to analyze some of the reasons for this change in black collective identity in the last three decades.

The psychological feeling of "us" is a reflection of group cohesion. Gurr[101] and Gurr and Moore[102] have demonstrated that group cohesion is extremely closely linked with minority groups' rebellious behavior. No group can feel a sense of cohesion when their economic resources are distributed in a highly skewed manner. Figures 6.1 and 6.2 depict the extreme economic fragmentation within the African American community. Figure 6.1 depicts the distribution of income in the black and white communities. Two important facts are evident. First, placed side by side, it is obvious that the two distributions are mirror images of one another. Income distribution in the white community is top-heavy, with 37.5% enjoying the top level of income. In contrast, distribution is bottom-heavy in the black community, with 38.2% earning less than $15,000.

Figure 6.2 traces the changes in distribution of income during the period 1970–92. While Figure 6.3 clearly shows that income in the African American community is distributed bimodally, the trend of the past two decades worsens the situation. During this time period, the relative size of only two income groups registered an increase: those who are at the extreme ends of the income spectrum. The fastest growing income group between 1970 and 1992 has been those who are earning more than $50,000, followed by those who are swelling the ranks of the poorest in society. If the current trend continues, the community will become even more bimodal in its income distribution. No community can be cohesive with such a distribution of income.[103]

This economic fragmentation of the community is manifested in the changing employment pattern and the resulting distribution of income within the racial group. Since the 1960s, African American males and females have seen a steady increase in their share of white-collar and professional jobs. However, this growth of higher-paying white-collar employment has been restricted to a relatively small minority of blacks, while the rest of the population continues to languish in low-paying jobs or with no employment at all. The effect of this disparity has been a chasm within the African American community much deeper than what exists in the rest of the nation.

I argue that this extreme fragmentation of class structure within the African American community has left it without a strong sense of shared identity. Coupled with "hyper-segregation," the level of isolation for the vast majority of the African American population from the rest of non-black society, as well as from their wealthier counterparts, has been enormous and unprecedented.[104] This fragmentation posed some unique problems of participation. For those who found their places in the middle of the "American dream," taking part in a political movement did not make much sense; the opportunity costs were entirely too high for them. Of those who were left out in the ghetto areas, many found easy money in the lucrative drug trade. The African American political movement was thereby denied its most natural ally—the backbone of any political movement, the youth. These youths had little ideological orientation.

Figure 6.1
Relative Distribution of Income, 1992

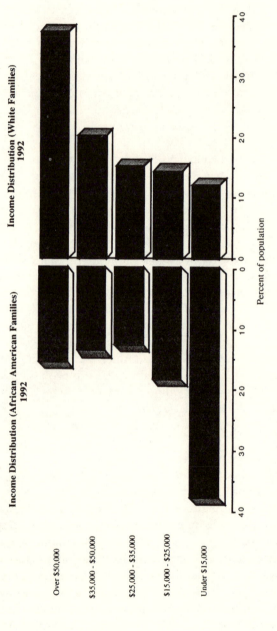

Source: Data from Hacker (1995: 104).

Figure 6.2
Changes in Income Distribution in African American Families, 1970–92

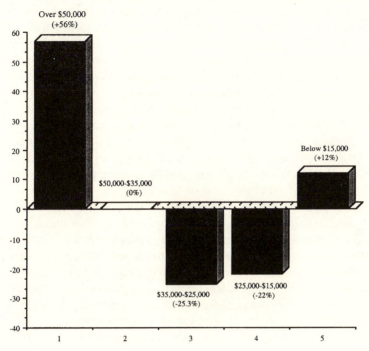

Source: Data from Hacker (1995: 104).

Therefore, for them, unlike their predecessors, it made little sense (economic or otherwise) to join any political movement.

The "Them" Factors

One of the greatest problems facing the black community has been the loss of a marked enemy.[105] In the past, oppression came in the form of overt discrimination, a nearly all-white police force, and the symbol of power, the all-white courthouses and city halls. The Kerner Commission was correct in its assessment:

The Crime Commission Police Task Force found that for police in the Negro community to be predominantly white can serve as a dangerous irritant; a feeling may develop that the community is not being policed to maintain the status quo. There is evidence that Negro officers . . . can be particularly effective in controlling any disorders that do break out. In studying the relative performance of Army and National Guard forces in the Detroit disorder, we concluded that the higher percentage of Negroes in the Army forces contributed substantially to their better performance.[106]

The Commission contacted a number of police departments, of which only twenty-eight responded with the composition of their police force. Within this group, which is likely to be biased in favor of overstating the average for the nation, the proportion of African American police officers ranged from 1 to 21% of the police force. This record was dismal when compared to the actual demographic mix of these cities. Out of these twenty-eight cities, sixteen (over 57%) had less than a 20% ratio of black police officers to black population. Only 2% of the police departments' ratio of black police officers exceeded half the demographic ratio of the black population in the city. As a result of the findings of the Kerner Commission, fears of racial disturbance, and the passage of the Equal Employment Opportunity Act, African Americans have made a remarkable improvement in their representation in the police forces across the nation. A later report studied forty-six cities in 1975 and seventy-two cities in 1985.[107] Lewis compared the percentage of blacks within each department to the equal employment opportunity (EEO) compliance ratio, which he then divided into four levels: an index of 0.75 or higher is considered "high compliance"; an index between 0.50 and 0.75 is considered "moderate compliance"; an index between 0.25 and 0.50 is considered "low compliance"; and an index of 0.25 or below is considered "non-compliance."[108] I reconstructed the percentage of cities that fell in the category "moderate compliance" or better by combining Lewis' data with those supplied by the Kerner Commission. By this measure, 5% of the cities had an EEO rating above 0.5. This ratio jumped to 47% in 1975, and to 65% in 1985. In the latest edition of his book, Hacker showed that, of the top twenty cities in the nation, only two (Kansas City, Missouri, and New York) had an EEO ratio less than five; ten (50%) had a high compliance ratio, including two having ratios at or above 1.0 (Washington, D.C., and Los Angeles).[109] Hacker's data also point to impressive gains for African Americans in other law enforcement areas. Thus, African Americans are overrepresented among correction officers by nearly 2.6 times their relative demographic strength, and among security guards by 2.3 times.

Unlike gains in employment made by blacks on police forces, African American representation in judicial services has not kept pace with their demographic ratio. However, their gains have been equally impressive considering the fact that, in the early 1960s, black representation within courthouses in the United States was largely confined to janitorial services.[110] Similarly, looking at the largest metropolitan aeas, we find that many of them have elected African American mayors and other officials, including one former governor. We argue that this large-scale inclusion of African Americans in the "system" has robbed the community of an easily identifiable enemy. Rapid nonwhite immigration from Asia and Latin America has also confused the strict duality of the black and white relationship of the past.

Although the hypothesis about the dilution of an "enemy" figure for the African American community cannot be directly proven, there are a few pieces of compelling evidence to suggest that the community no longer has a uniform image of the enemy as it did in the segregated South. Several surveys have consistently reported that a only small fraction of African Americans blame whites as the main cause for their social and economic deprivation. Instead, when asked, they point to lack of education, the breakdown of the family structure, and drugs as the primary reasons. For instance, the main message of the Million Man March of 1995 was not struggle against the dominant group, but rather taking personal responsibility.[111] The Inter-University Consortium for Political and Social Research (ICPSR) has compiled impressive time series data on numerous social attitudes.[112] ICPSR uses a "Feeling Thermometer" to measure the feelings of one group toward another. In this measure, on a scale of 0 (extreme negative feeling) to 100 (extreme positive feeling), the time series data of blacks toward whites from 1966 through 1992 show a positive slope (Figure 6.3).[113] Although the trend is not statistically significant, given the widening racial gap of average achievement, Figure 6.3 shows a remarkable pattern of American political life.

Even more startling evidence of change came in a recent CNN/Time national poll of 1,282 adults and 601 teens between the ages of twelve and seventeen.[114] The poll found that a significant number of youngsters, black and white, seem to have moved away from their parents' view of race relations in America. While 77% of the African American teenagers responded that they have never personally been discriminated against, only 45% of the adults felt that to be the case. When asked, "Are the problems that most blacks face today caused primarily by whites?," 74% of the African American teens disagreed. When these teens were further probed, 58% said that the major problem facing blacks today is that they do not take advantage of available opportunities, in contrast to only 26% who thought discrimination to be the major problem. When an abstract question of whether racism is a "big problem" or a "small problem" was raised, however, 62% of the teens agreed with the former characterization. However, perhaps the strongest clue as to why blacks do not identify whites as the enemy can be found in their optimistic outlook for the future. A majority (55%) of the African American teenagers agreed with the statement that "race relations in this country are getting better." Also, a full 95% of the black teens (as opposed to 93% of the white teens) thought that they were bound for college.

One of the facts of current American life is that myriad ethnic groups are socializing within their own groups. On college campuses all over the nation, it is obvious that students cluster around others of their own ethnic or national origin. Many consider this to be an ominous trend. However, I would strongly disagree. I would argue that socialization is a reflection of formation of communities. As long as the groups don't demonize one another and identify them as enemies, the nation, despite all its problems, will continue to avoid racial violence.

Figure 6.3
Racial Feelings of Blacks Toward Whites, 1966–92

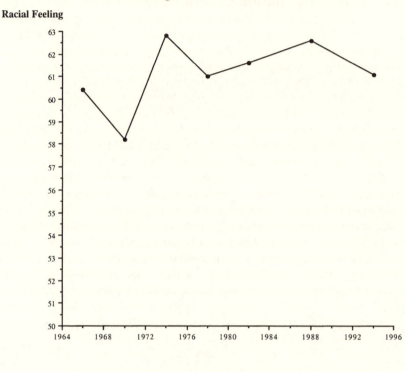

Racial Feeling Indicator of Blacks Toward Whites

Source: Data from ICPSR (1994: Variable 232).

Government Coercion: The Rising Cost Factor

A good deal of academic interest has been devoted to the question of the relationship between government coercion and dissident activities. Gurr (1970) suggested that the relationship between the two is quadratic. That is, overt coercion acts as a provocation for further action only up to a certain point. However, after a threshold level of high coercion and high anti-systemic violence, dissidents are brutally coerced into silence. Later empirical studies have corroborated Gurr's basic hypothesis, pointing out that no democratic regime has crossed the threshold to put down rebellion by force.[115] However, these studies deal with *overt* coercion. The high-handed tactics of Sheriff Bull Connor became the crystallizing force in the civil rights movement.[116] The relationship between dissident activities and coercion is different when we take into account covert acts of coercion.

Gary Marx has contributed a great deal to our understanding of the various counterinsurgency strategies adopted by police departments to successfully derail a political movement. Thus, he points out that through infiltration into the movement, a police department can make about a dozen strategic moves. It can (a) inhibit capacity for corporate action; (b) direct the energies of the movement to defensive maintenance needs and away from pursuit of broader social change goals; (c) create unfavorable public images to counteract a dissident ideology; (d) gather information on any movement for apprehension and prosecution of the participants; (e) inhibit the supply of money and facilities; (f) inhibit freedom of movement, expression, and action, create myths and facts of surveillance and repression, and apply legal sanctions; (g) damage the morale of the participants; (h) engage in de-recruitment; (i) destroy and displace leaders; (j) encourage internal conflict; (k) encourage external conflict with potential allies and opponents; and (l) inhibit and sabotage particular actions.[117]

Empirical evidence of covert action is almost impossible to obtain. Therefore, a number of studies have calculated a regime's "coercive potential" by measuring the amount of resources devoted to internal security.[118] Facing mounting political opposition, the nation adopted the Omnibus Crime Control and Safe Streets Act in 1968, which was subsequently amended during Richard Nixon's administration. As a result of this series of acts, the federal law enforcement effort was revitalized. Along with a soaring allocation of money for internal security (see Figure 6.4) came elaborate plans for suppression of political radicalism. New technologies allowed better surveillance and apprehension. Also, better knowledge in the area of political strategy, such as disinformation campaigns and other tactics used to spread confusion and weaken the ideological strength of the rank and file of the movement, gave the police force new weapons to stamp out organized dissident activities.

It is quite clear that, against such organized and well-financed efforts, the black radical organizations were no match. Therefore, these organizations received a fatal blow from which they have not been able to recover.

Where Is the Revolution?

The absence of overt sectarian hostility in the United States stands in stark contrast with the experience of most countries around the world. The Soviet Union, in spite of its supposedly equalizing, ideologically oriented regime of seventy years, discovered how enduring ethnic, cultural, and religious divisions can be. Almost the entire continent of Africa is awash with fratricidal frenzy. Like the Holocaust, Yugoslavia permanently contributed the term "ethnic cleansing" to the popular lexicon. Relatively progressive developing nations, such as Sri Lanka, after decades of political tranquillity and racial harmony, are caught in the deadly quagmire of full-blown civil war. Great Britain and Spain are no closer to solving their Irish and Basque problems than each was half a century ago. Both Canada and Belgium seem to be heading toward eventual dismemberment. Therefore, we can legitimately pose the question,

Figure 6.4
Total Criminal Justice Expenditure in 1955–96 (Constant $ 1982–84)

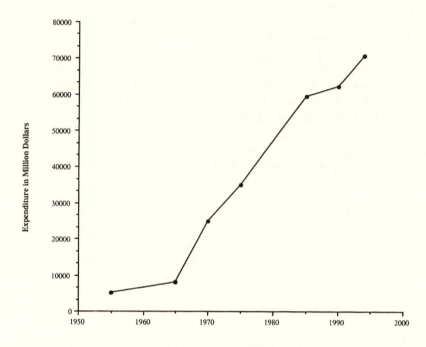

Source: Data from U.S. Department of Justice compiled from several years of publications.

does the United States has something important to teach these countries, or does it have something to fear from their unfortunate experiences? Once again, we can use our twelve steps to madness to illustrate the point. I would like to demonstrate that in this case, despite the presence of a large social and economic gap between white Americans and African Americans, most of the conditions for collective madness do not prevail in the United States. As a result, there are short-lived protests or even riots, but no sustained armed rebellion or a secessionist movement.

Shrinking Opportunities. In my discussion of the paradox of rebellion for the African American community, I attempted to show that the economic gap between it and the white society did not diminish and, in some cases, may have become worse during the last three decades. However, this persistent economic gap is measured in relative terms. In absolute terms, American society as a whole has benefited from continuing economic prosperity. With the rising tide, all boats have risen, but the divide has not been bridged. Further, as we have seen, the significant increase in the number of African Americans achieving the pinnacle of economic success—most visibly through sports and entertainment—may have riveted the attention of the youths of the community. Finally, the passage of the civil rights legislation and its consequent abolition of signs of overt discrimination have gone a long way toward paving the road for the emergence of a very small but vocal group of black conservatives.

Increasing Rewards for Membership in the Inner Circle. It paid to be a member of the inner circle in Jonestown or of the CDR in Rwanda, but being a member of the American Civil Liberties Union (ACLU) or even the Nation of Islam brings little other than intangible psychic rewards. Therefore, memberships in those organizations come mostly from those who are drawn to the cause for ideological reasons. Devoid of much of a prospect for pecuniary gains, the membership in many of those organizations has not shown explosive growth.

Collective Culture. Mass rebellion has not been an important part of African American heritage. In fact, unlike in many South American countries, the slaves were not concentrated large plantations. Second, from the earliest times in America, slaves from various tribes, with their completely different language structures, were deliberately mixed up, which reduced the level of communication among them. Even their family structure was deliberately broken up. Being deprived of communication within the community, most victims suffered the indignities alone or as part of small isolated groups. Therefore, from a historical standpoint, until the beginning of the civil rights movement there was little evidence of a tradition of collective movement within the African American community.

Further, being part of a larger culture that is the epitome of individualism, African Americans, like all others within it, remained individualistic at the core. This perception has been reinforced by the numerous examples of personal success of individual members of the community. With so many success stories in sports, entertainment, and politics, the plight of the average person has not been able to galvanize the community for a mass rebellion.

When we compare African Americans with Catholics in Northern Ireland, or Tamils in Sri Lanka, one difference stands out—lack of cohesiveness in the African American community. In Northern Ireland, Catholics are forced to stay within relatively well-defined geographical boundaries, have a similar socioeconomic standing, and have the same religion. U.S. blacks, in contrast, do not have a well-defined geographical boundary within the nation which they can claim as their "homeland."[119] They do not share a single religion. The question of a language differentiating them from the dominant group is, at best, a very complex matter that does not appear to provide a sustainable basis for the kind of intragroup differentiation that leads to social isolation.

Cultural ethos in promoting group cohesion is another largely unexplored territory. The permeation of individualism has been the hallmark of the American ethos since its colonial beginning. That is one reason why left-wing political radicalism has never been popular in this country, not even during the abyss of the Great Depression. Therefore, black children, unlike children in other parts of the world, grow up being inculcated with the notion of individual achievement. Hence, by our behavioral precepts, they would tend to have a lower preference for collective goods.

Paranoiac Vision and the Clear Identification of an Enemy. It is obvious that the most influential leaders of the community (with the possible exception of Malcolm X or the leadership of the present-day Nation of Islam) never espoused a paranoid view of the world. In fact, the main thrust of the black movement has been to get accepted in the mainstream. Facing overwhelming odds against guerrilla warfare and being comforted by the protection of a powerful constitution guaranteeing fundamental rights to all the citizens of the nation, the African American leadership eschewed the politics of extralegal confrontation and, instead, forcefully asked for their legitimate place in society.

Perhaps one of the most important reasons why the United States has been able to avert a blood-bath initiated by its deprived minority group is because, in a capitalistic society based firmly on the values of individualism, the African American community has not been able to find its clearly defined enemy. When it comes to the differences between groups, we can see that the identification of the enemy is easier in other countries besieged by ethnic violence. Thus, in Northern Ireland, the police force (Ulster Constabulary) is made up almost entirely of Protestants. It is the same with the British Army, which is viewed as nothing more than an occupying force. Unlike U.S blacks, Sikhs in India, Tamils and Sinhalese in Sri Lanka, and Basques in Spain and France, to give only a few examples, can identify their group enemy with much greater ease. The African American leadership, other than a handful of radicals, never identified white men and women as their enemy. Dr. King and his later followers always took the moral high ground of pointing to discriminatory practices as the real foe.

Since, in post–civil rights America, African Americans have been assimilated within the judiciary, law enforcement, and the wider political process, they have lost the ability to easily identify their common enemy. Therefore, despite widespread economic deprivation, especially among the underclass, the African American community has not been able to forge a strong identity in recent years.

Charismatic Leadership. The loss of Dr. Martin Luther King dealt a huge blow to the African American movement. No one has come close to the charisma of Dr. King. Although the tone of the charismatic leader Louis Farrakhan is often inflammatory, his main message is about taking responsibility and not about an armed uprising against a marked enemy.

Increasing Social Pressure for Acceptance. I would argue that the average African American child growing up in today's United States does not face strong pressure to belong to any anti-systemic groups with a broad political agenda. Many, of course, join street gangs, but they do not have any political ideology.

Further, for young African Americans, the images of their cultural icons belong to those who have made it in the outside world.

High Price of Defection. The price of defection in the United States has been high. The coercive force of the government is brought to bear on dissident groups not only through direct efforts at law enforcement, but, most important, through extensive surveillance and infiltration. Since there has been no accepted target of a shared enemy for the minority group, there is little broad-based support for such action. Hence, it has been relatively easy for the authorities to recruit volunteers for surveillance activities. Facing such an overwhelming adversary in the larger society, black political radicalism, despite all the grievances, could not take hold in the United States.

Social Acceptance of Violence. The nonviolent nature of the civil rights movement has left a permanent imprint on African American political activism. The more violent groups, such as the Black Panthers, despite their notoriety, remained essentially localized and at the fringes of black politics. As a result, violence against the white majority, as a political instrument, has not been found in the African American movement for social and political equality.

Flow of Arms. In an America awash with guns and other weapons, the spread of black political radicalism did not suffer for the lack of arms. It did not grow because there was no collective will to engage the United States government in an armed conflict.

Organizational Hierarchy. The civil rights movement and many other African American political coalitions have enjoyed a well-developed organizational hierarchy. As a result, many of the issues important to the community get aired, and some of them are addressed to the satisfaction of most. However, since there is no marked enemy, the organizational hierarchy of the NAACP and similar organizations do not espouse violence toward white society.

Stopped Flow of Information. As I have argued, for a community to sink to the depth of collective madness, it must be deprived of all other sources of information except for those which are permitted by the group leadership. Clearly, in an open society, such a stoppage cannot be maintained except for a small group of individuals, such as the followers of Jim Jones, David Koresh, or other small white racist groups. Being open to information from all different sources, like other vibrant, multidimensional communities all around the world, most African Americans remain immune to the ailment of collective madness.

International Meddling. The former Soviet Union and other communist and socialist nations around the globe attempted to provide moral support for many radicals such as Angela Davis in the 1960s and 1970s. However, being physically far away from and in fear of the most powerful nation on earth, there was no mass support for the dissidents of the kind we saw in other countries such as in Afghanistan. Without a safe haven, political extremists would have no hiding place.

THE LESSONS OF HISTORY

In answering this question let us look at some of the common elements of ethnic violence. First, as we have emphasized, in order to have a collective movement, one must have a collective identity. This feeling is likely to depend upon two aspects: *intragroup cohesiveness* and the degree of *intergroup differences*. In the first case, this collective identity will depend upon how close the individual members feel to their own ethnic group. Second, it will depend on how distinct the subgroup sees itself as being from the larger national group. Because many of the hypotheses are not measurable in quantitative terms, quite understandably, little empirical research has been directed toward discovering what contributes to the deepening of these two factors of ethnic feeling. However, we can conjecture that group cohesiveness is likely to be strong if the group in question is largely confined within a definable territorial boundary, is uniform in its socioeconomic structure, has a common language, cultural, religious, or ethnic heritage, and, last but certainly not least, has a cultural background promoting group cohesion. The intensity of the passion of intragroup difference will depend upon the ease with which a group can identify a common enemy to blame for its feeling of deprivation.

Does this point to a decline in the significance of race in American politics and economics? Yes and no. On the one hand, we believe the arguments developed here support the proposition that, at this point in U.S. history, race is less relevant as a rallying point for collective action. On the other hand, when we look at what determines economic well-being, unfortunately we find that race is just as important a determinant as it was three decades ago.

Therefore, to answer our question, we can with some surety point to the fact that the United States has indeed been fortunate in some areas of race relations compared to the rest of the world. Blacks, having been brought here as slaves in a young immigrant nation, were scattered, and therefore were denied a territorial identity, which is crucial to most ethnic struggles around the world.

Further, the promotion of individualism has always undermined collective ideology in this country. Affluent blacks who could leave the clutches of poverty did not feel any compelling need to promote and protect racial identity, finding it to be more advantageous to assimilate than to sustain their differences. With the disappearance of the signs of overt discrimination and the glaring examples of those who have "made it," less fortunate blacks, on the other hand, could not find a common enemy on which to place the blame for their economic and social woes.

Most important, the existence of a legal system with its strong adherence to the Bill of Rights has provided this nation with the most potent weapon in dealing with ethnic unrest. Furthermore, the change in administrative attitudes since the 1960s has been nothing less than remarkable. A great deal of effort has been devoted to integrating the police and the judiciary. Also, through the Law Enforcement Agency (LEA), a significant amount of effort has been made to educate law enforcement agencies on sensitive racial issues. In sum, this nation has effectively pursued procedural justice instead of distributive justice. In retrospect, it seems that the former has proved to be more potent in promoting the feeling of fairness than the latter.

The above conclusions are certainly not meant to promote the idea that this country has solved its racial problems. Far from it. Lack of open conflict is not peace; sullen calm is not harmony. So much concentration of economic misery in one ethnic group is bound to generate problems for generations to come, especially when, from all indications, the economic gap between the races seems to be widening. However, since the core of the African American problem has become or is becoming one of economics rather than race, we may not see a mass political uprising of the kind feared by the Kerner Commission. Instead, what we are seeing and will continue to see is the escalation of sociopathic or psychopathic violence born of individual frustration and hopelessness. One may indeed speculate whether the groups formed by blacks for the purpose of dealing drugs can incorporate political ideologies, which may then transform them into cells of terrorist organizations. Given the fact of hyper-segregation of the poor, this may turn out to be a persistent problem for the lower- and working-class neighborhoods, where low-level ethnic violence may fester for the foreseeable future.

Finally, before we address the question posed at the beginning of this chapter, whether the United States has something to teach to a world torn with ethnic violence, we should address the important issue posed by Kuran.[120] Is it possible that the current containment in race relations is the result of preference falsification by the African American community and that the nation is, in fact, sitting on a powder keg, ready to blow up in a quick-moving prairie fire of open rebellion? Since the extent of preference falsification is determined by the possibility of repression by the dominant group, we would argue that the presence of a constitutional democracy reduces such risks. Hence, the level of preference falsification is likely to be significantly lower in an open system based on individualistic values than in a collective society. It is true that the huge internal security mechanism in the United States poses a threat to the expression of violent anti-systemic feelings, especially when it comes to the African American community. However, there are many other societies with far greater internal security forces that have not been able to prevent violent uprisings by the disaffected group(s) within it.

In sum, the United States certainly has something important to teach to the rest of the world regarding the stabilizing effects of a political system based on the recognition of individual rights. But at the same time, unless the persistence of economic injustice is meaningfully addressed, the community will continue to writhe in accumulated frustration; without a collective outlet, anger will manifest itself in some of the most vulgar forms, as is commonly seen in urban America.

NOTES

1. Quoted in Mitchell (1999: 51).
2. Reconstructed from a passage in Prunier (1995: 37, footnote 90).
3. See ibid., 1.
4. See Stedman (1997: 344).
5. See Gourevitch (1998: 50).
6. See Speke (1969), especially Chapter 9.
7. Most scholars, however, agree that the Tutsis, a branch of the Masai tribe, invaded Rwanda about 600 years ago. See Lemarchand (1970: 70).
8. Prunier (1995: 40).
9. The "Manifesto" was, in fact, titled "Notes on the Social Aspect of the Racial Native Problem in Rwanda." For the entire text, see Nkundabagenzi (1961: 20–29).
10. See Sax and Kuntz (1992: 212).
11. See Lemarchand (1970: Chapter 5).
12. Prunier (1995: 9). Emphasis in original. This encounter of the Rwandan king with Count von Götzen took place in 1894, ironically exactly 100 years before the eventual genocide of the divine king's people.
13. Other neighboring countries, notably Tanzania, did not allow the exiled Tutsis to stage military attacks against Rwanda. Being treated well, the refugees gradually assimilated into Tanzanian society. See Prunier (1995: 55).
14. For the best description of the period see Lemarchand (1970).
15. Kayibanda was starved to death instead of being shot because of Habyarimana's superstitious fear of shedding the blood of his former boss. Because of his blood oath of loyalty, Habyarimana would be in harm's way (Prunier 1995: 82, footnote 72).
16. For a full account, see ibid., Chapter 3, 93–121.
17. See Adelman, Suhrke, and Jones (1996: 26).
18. See Gordon (1994).
19. See Prunier (1995: 161).
20. See Adelman (1996).
21. See Prunier (1995: 204–5).
22. For a comprehensive discussion, see Washburn (1992).
23. The definition of literacy carries little correlation with fluency in reading or comprehension. For data, see Central Intelligence Agency (1994: 67).
24. See ibid., 65
25. See Harff (1996: 56).
26. Chalk (1995: 12–13).
27. Many Hutu leaders had openly called for a Tutsi genocide for some time. For instance, Prunier (1995: 171–72) reports that Léon Mugesera, one of the influential members of Habyarimana's party, addressed party militants with the clear message of initiating a genocide against the Tutsis. Their vitriolic messages were delivered repeatedly in town meetings across Rwanda.
28. See Berkeley (1994: 18).
29. Eventually 40,000 bodies were pulled out of Lake Victoria in Uganda and quickly buried in mass graves (Prunier 1995: 255).
30. Adelman estimates the figure to be over 1 million. See Stedman (1997: 334).
31. Prunier (1995: 259–60).
32. Ibid., 11.

33. Ibid., 57.
34. Gourevitch (1998: 32–34).
35. Ibid., 34. Emphasis mine.
36. Ibid.
37. Such campaigns endeared Habyarimana's regime to some of the Christian NGOs, many of whom remained loyal to him until the very end, turning a blind eye to the obvious abuses of human rights.
38. Human Rights Watch (1999: 264–65).
39. Ibid., 12.
40. Ibid., 43–44.
41. Gourevitch (1998: 108).
42. Human Rights Watch (1999: 6).
43. Prunier (1995: 231–32).
44. Prunier (1995: 169).
45. *New Webster's Dictionary of the English Language* (1981: 405).
46. At the time of the genocide, Rwanda was divided into ten perfectures, each of which included subprefectures, administrative units. Below them were the communes, the essential building blocks of the Rwandan social and political structure. The head of each commune was the burgomaster, who exerted a tremendous amount of influence over the lives of his wards. See Human Rights Watch (1999: 41–44).
47. Prunier (1995: 77).
48. Human Rights Watch (1999: 66–72).
49. See Harff (1996: 55).
50. Gourevitch (1998: 59).
51. Human Rights Watch (1999: 1).
52. Although the exact number is somewhat difficult to ascertain, it is estimated to be around 970. See United States Congress (1979: 6).
53. Hofstadter (1965: 3–4).
54. Hofstadter admits: "I choose American history to illustrate the paranoid style only because I happen to be an Americanist. But the phenomenon is no more limited to American experience than it is to our contemporaries"; ibid., 6.
55. For an interesting angle on our discussion, see Cohn (1961).
56. Nugent (1979: 75).
57. See Kilduff and Javers (1978: 61).
58. See Fein (1991: 277).
59. See Nugent (1979: 16).
60. See R. Moore (1985: 12).
61. Nugent (1979: 43–44).
62. See Reiterman and Jacobs (1982).
63. Guyana is majority East Indian with about 30% of African origin.
64. Nugent (1979: 205).
65. Ibid., 213. Emphasis mine.
66. See Raston (1981).
67. Ibid., 10.
68. See Fein (1991: 279).
69. Nugent (1979: 143).
70. See S. Naipaul (1981).
71. Ibid., 281.

72. Quoted in Locke (2000: A6). For a detailed account of her personal ordeal, see Layton (1998).

73. Nugent (1979: 141).

74. Ibid., 89.

75. See Fein (1991: 277).

76. See Feinsod (1981).

77. Nugent (1979: 151).

78. United States Congress (1979: 25).

79. McAdam, Tarrow, and Tilly (1996: 17–34) coined a generic term, "contentious politics," to include all kinds of anti-systemic movements. Since the term "revolution" was used extensively in the protest literature of the sixties, I use it interchangeably here. In line with McAdam et al., I define "contentious politics" as "people collectively make claims on other people" (ibid., 17).

80. Kerner (1968, 1).

81. Ibid., 5.

82. Ibid.

83. In this context, it is interesting to note that while there is no coherent violent political movement within the African American community, a group of Anglos have started the so-called militia movement. I do not address the question why the militias are directly confronting the organized government in this book. However, one can use arguments similar to the ones developed here to explain their radicalism.

84. The Los Angeles riots in the aftermath of the Rodney King verdict were neither an exclusively African American affair nor the result of a coherent political movement.

85. National Research Council (1989: 6).

86. Median income of $30,903 for whites compared to $18,810 for blacks in 1970 as opposed to $32,368 and $18,660, respectively, in 1992 (in 1992 constant dollars); *United States Statistical Yearbook* (1994).

87. Data from ibid.

88. This drop in income was not restricted to blacks only. Whites also lost out in real income during this time period, even though the magnitude of their loss was considerably less than that of blacks.

89. See Smith and Welch (1986).

90. National Research Council (1989: 25).

91. See Massey and Denton (1989).

92. See Magida (1996).

93. See ibid., 180.

94. For a theoretical explanation, see Volkan (1988) and Tajfel (1970, 1978). For an empirical measurement of group ideology, see Gupta, Hofstetter, and Buss (1997).

95. Frederick Douglass, for example, says in his autobiography (1962: 27): "The reader must not expect me to say much of my family. My first experience of life, as I now remember it . . . began in the family of my grandmother and grandfather. . . . The practice of separating mothers from their children and hiring them out at distances too great to admit of their meeting, save at long intervals, was a marked feature of the cruelty and barbarity of the slave system. . . . It had no interest in recognizing or preserving any of the ties that bind families together or to their homes." In this context, also see Willie (1988).

96. See Wilson (1978).

97. See ibid.

98. See Tullock (1971); Banfield (1968).

99. Some of the earlier evaluations found ideologically oriented participants of the riots; see Caplan (1970); Feagin and Hahn (1973); Geshwender (1968); Lupsha (1969); and Sears and McConahey (1973). However, Hacker (1995: 22, emphasis added), in a later reflection, seems to side more with Banfield and Tullock, claiming that "the so-called riots in cities like Los Angeles and Newark and Detroit [were] marked by looting and burning within black neighborhoods. *In fact, these were not race riots,* if by that it meant actual confrontation of black and white citizens. The violence never reached downtown business districts or areas where whites lived."

100. See McAdam (1982).

101. Gurr (1993).

102. Gurr and Moore (1996).

103. Increased levels of economic cleavage lead to social fragmentation. For an analytical argument, see Kelman (1973); for an empirical corroboration, see Gupta, Singh, and Sprague (1993).

104. See Massey and Denton (1989).

105. For an extremely interesting discussion of the psychological dimension of the need for an identifiable "them" to foster the collective spirit of "us," see Volkan (1988). Volkan fuses individual psychoanalysis with national and international behavior.

106. Kerner (1968: 165).

107. See Lewis (1987).

108. The equal employment opportunity index is constructed on the basis of racial parity.

109. Hacker (1995: 246).

110. See Knowles and Prewitt (1972).

111. See Magida (1996).

112. ICPSR (1994). I am grateful to Professor Richard Hofstetter for the information.

113. Recalling that a score of 50 represents a neutral feeling, even in 1969 the average was in the positive range.

114. See Farley (1997).

115. See Gurr (1986); Lichbach (1987); Gupta, Singh, and Sprague (1993).

116. See Chong (1991).

117. See G. Marx (1982: 183).

118. See Bwy (1968); Hibbs (1973); M. N. Cooper (1974).

119. It is interesting to note that cultural geographers are becoming increasingly aware of the importance of geographic boundaries on the formation of identities. For instance, see Paasi (1996, 2000); Newman (1999, 2000).

120. See Kuran (1995b).

PART III

In Search of Policy

CHAPTER 7

WHERE THERE'S A WILL . . . : CAN ANYTHING BE DONE?

Is "Bosnia" the last dark page of the 20th century or the first page of the next? The truth, I think, is that the world of tomorrow resembles Bosnia. . . . Bosnia serves as the warning. We need mechanisms to stop Bosnias in the future.

—Haris Silajdzic, Bosnian prime minister[1]

It may seem strange to you here, especially the many of you who lost members of your family, but all over the world there were people like me sitting in offices, day after day after day, who did not fully appreciate the depth and the speed with which you were being engulfed by this unimaginable terror.

—President Bill Clinton, apologizing in Kigali, Rwanda, March 26, 1998

A MATTER OF WILL?

If the world seems shocked by what happened in Rwanda or Bosnia, it is only because the world was not paying attention. Our analysis demonstrates that episodes of collective madness, in whatever form, do not happen overnight. The path to collective madness is not only known but also eminently knowable. As a report from the Carnegie Commission on Preventing Deadly Conflicts bluntly points out, "It is implausible for modern governments to claim that they simply did not know."[2] Although we will never be able to forecast the precise point when genocide begins, there is absolutely no reason to believe that we cannot place nations in categories of relative risks of potential political and humanitarian crises. The situation is analogous to an avalanche. We can never know which snowflake will finally trigger an avalanche, but if we study the accumulation of snow and take preventive steps, we may be able to avert a catastrophe.[3] When a crisis develops, there is a universal cry to do something. People all over the world intuitively reject the idea that nothing can be done. As we have seen, when Iraq invaded oil-rich Kuwait, Western intervention was quick and decisive. In relatively less important Bosnia and isolated Rwanda, the world stood by and watched the carnage take place. Today, continuing low-level conflicts and total disregard for human rights go unnoticed in many parts of the world.

I argue that if there is a will, the world community, working together, can often put an immediate stop to the spread of insanity, at least in the short run. However, the results may not be predictable. Thanks to intense public pressure, the Western nations finally intervened in Bosnia and, when they did, the Dayton Agreement not only stopped the killings, it effectively prevented the epidemic of insanity from reaching Macedonia and other neighboring countries. In the same way, after nearly a million deaths in Rwanda, the international community did intervene. As a result, at the time of this writing, Rwanda's national twin Burundi has so far been effectively shielded from a similar fate of genocide. The record of Western intervention in Kosovo, on the other hand, is much more confusing. It is possible to argue that the NATO bombing of Yugoslavia exacerbated the difficulties faced by many ethnic Albanians in Kosovo and contributed to further intensification of ethnic cleansing by the Serb militias.

After analyzing the causes of collective madness, the next logical question that arises is, What can we do to prevent such future outrages? How the world community can help afflicted nations, or how such nations can help themselves, can be divided into long- and short-term solutions.

Long-term solutions require a mutually agreeable structural change that accommodates the aspirations of all the groups in the nation. However, the implementation of such changes rests mostly with the citizens of the country. In this effort, the rest of the world can provide some useful direction, but may not impose it by force. As for short-term solutions, the world can rely on advanced planning through an early warning system, preventive diplomacy, economic sanctions, direct military intervention, preventing the proliferation of small arms, and setting examples by vigorously and consistently prosecuting the perpetrators of crimes against humanity.

The unfortunate history of the last half century has taught us a lot about the causes, and precious little about the prevention, of deadly conflicts. This chapter addresses the question, What can and cannot be done?

STRUCTURAL CHANGE: PROCEDURAL JUSTICE

I have suggested that the true antidote to the widespread malady of collective madness is liberal democracy, based solidly on the foundation of individual rights. That is, in a society based on the values of individualism and holding out hopes for personal achievement based on merit, extreme submersion of individual identities into the collective will be less likely. The reason liberal democracies may offer an effective shield against collective madness is because they are based on the premise of *procedural justice*. This is a form of justice that relates to the process by which national resources are allocated. In a true liberal democracy, the authorities engender faith among their members that *even though the existing allocation of resources is not the most desirable or equitable, the process by which the resources are being allocated is more or less fair*. It is the guarantee of a level playing field where the factors of impenetrable *ascriptive* or birth characteristics of race, religion, language, or gender do not pose obstacles to individual achievement.

Philosophers and social scientists have spent inordinate amounts of scholarly energy pursuing the question of *distributive justice;* attempting to find ways to reach the optimal level of distribution of wealth. The Utilitarians, the Marxists, the Paretians, the Rawlsians, scholars of the right and left have lost their way in the quagmire of defining the fairness of distribution of wealth in a society.[4] Apart from the question of the measurement of distributive fairness,[5] in short, the problem for the leftists has been the fact that if we dissociate rewards from merit, then the resulting redistribution becomes confiscatory. In the end, forced redistribution of wealth creates more problems than it started out with. On the other hand, the rightists, proclaiming the supremacy of meritocracy, cannot escape the fact that much of what we regard as "merit" is inseparably linked with life's opportunities. Therefore, the prescription for a just distribution from the rightists appears to be one more way of maintaining the status quo of the existing power structure within a society. Studies in social psychology point to a close linkage between the conditions of liberal democracy and people's perception of procedural justice.[6]

I argue that procedural justice can be guaranteed for everyone in the society only in a liberal democratic setup. Looking at the world map, it is easy to be impressed by the steady increase in the number of countries calling themselves "democracies." Yet, political scientist Robert Dahl's notion of "liberal democracy" goes far beyond the outside appearance of a democratic nation.[7] It implies institutions with a civilian, constitutional, multiparty system with universal suffrage, free and fair elections, with free flow of information, extensive and guaranteed civil liberties and fundamental rights, with separation of powers and an independent judiciary.

Needless to say, Dahl's definition is an ideal type. No nation is completely free from institutional biases that keep a segment of its population perpetually outside its process of social justice. Nevertheless, through its many imperfections, the liberal democratic societies of today hold out the best hope of averting incidences of collective madness by providing the best promise for procedural justice.[8] Groups turn on one another only when the process of justice appears to be closed. It is, in some ways, analogous to a situation of market failure. When merit-based social mobility is impeded, collective frustration, with the help of a political entrepreneur, inevitably finds its ultimate expression in violent outbursts.

The concept of a nation-state, where each national group (defined by ethnicity, language, and/or religion) has its own independent state, is a matter of mythology. With the possible exception of Iceland, no country in the world can claim to have a truly homogenous populace.[9] Therefore, it is imperative that countries learn to live peacefully in multiethnic setups. A society deeply divided into ethno-linguistic and religious groups can find peace and stability in one of two ways: It can either try to share power through a set of agreed upon principles, or peace may be achieved through the coercive means of a benevolent dictatorship.

Power-Sharing

If there is one lesson to be learned from experiments with various forms of government in the twentieth century, it is that—for all its faults, hypocrisies, and misplaced expectations—in an otherwise imperfect world, liberal democracy is the best form of government. From the history of the last 100 years, we know that two democracies are much less apt to confront one another on a battlefield.[10] We know that democracies are much less apt to engage in incidences of mass hate.[11] And, in the long run, they hold out a better promise for economic prosperity.[12] Yet, democracy, by itself, is not enough to end the possibility of collective madness.

For instance, Arend Lijphart's life's work has been to promote power-sharing.[13] He distinguishes between what he calls *majoritarian* democracy and *consociational* democracy. A majoritarian democracy is based on the one person, one vote principle, and on the rights of the individual citizens alone. Although majoritarian forms are inextricably intertwined with the Anglo-American tradition, they are not the only forms of democratic government. The majoritarian form is very well suited for nations where the population is unimodal in its political views. That is, in such countries, popular opinion on most issues is distributed like a bell curve, with most opinions gravitating toward the moderate center. The United States provides a good example of a nation where, on most issues, the spread of public opinion resembles a bell curve. As a result, in U.S. presidential elections, most candidates jostle to be perceived as centrist. Barry Goldwater's famous line, "Extremism in the defense of liberty is no vice," may have won him a place in history, but it cost him dearly at the polls. In most United States elections, the candidates attempt to portray their opponents as too far to the left or to the right while staking their own claims to the center.

However, where popular opinion is not distributed along a bell curve and is characterized by a multimodal distribution, even in a democracy any attempt to be in the center will fail as a strategy for winning elections. Consider Northern Ireland, where on most critical issues public opinion shows a distinct cleavage along the lines of religious affiliation of the two competing sects of Christianity. Since most people lean in one direction or the other, it is extremely difficult to find support for a centrist position. Power-sharing forms of democracies are best suited to such deeply divided societies. A number of countries in Europe and Asia have found political stability by following the path of power-sharing democracy.

Power-sharing democracies, in contrast to majoritarian democracies, recognize the rights of groups along with those of individual citizens. For instance, distinctly multilingual countries like Belgium and Switzerland have formed governments based on power-sharing principles. In Switzerland each of the three major language groups—German, French, and Italian—has a share in the Federal Council, the seven-member governing body. The distribution of the seats approximately corresponds to the population share of the three language groups (about 70% German, 20% French, and 10% Italian). The fourth language group, Romansh, is spoken by less than 1% of the population and is not represented in the council.[14] Similarly, Belgium—divided into French-speaking Wallonia, Dutch-speaking Flanders, German-speaking eastern Belgium, and a cosmopolitan Brussels—has developed a complex process of power-sharing.[15] Divided along three major ethnic lines of Malays, Chinese, and Indians, power-sharing has been the hallmark of Malaysian politics.[16] India was long considered an aberration among the divided nations for not adhering to the concept of power-sharing and yet maintaining a stable political structure. However, Lijphart recently reexamined the case of India and found that it had all the ingredients of a power-sharing form of democracy.[17] Lijphart concluded that in India, as in all other power-sharing nations, the rights of groups are preserved by meticulous division of power and use of a quota system. Although an anathema in the Anglo-British tradition, the system of quotas and the acceptance of group rights may have preserved India's political unity over the last fifty years as an independent nation.

A majoritarian democracy, however, quickly becomes unworkable if the majority begins to exercise macho nationalism by trampling the rights of minority groups. War-torn Sri Lanka provides a perfect example of the failure of a majoritarian democracy in a nation where the distribution of public opinion was essentially bimodal along the ethno-linguistic lines of the Tamils and the Sinhalese.[18]

Unfortunately, power-sharing is not a panacea for all societies divided into subnational groups. In fact, doubts were raised from the beginning of the development of the concept of power-sharing regarding whether the system was too culture-bound to be exported to other countries.[19] What has worked well in Belgium and Switzerland, or even in Malaysia, may not work in Pakistan, Georgia, Ethiopia, or Bolivia. While that debate is still going on, it is generally accepted that while power-sharing may work in moderately divided societies, it is likely to be ineffectual in much more deeply divided nations.

However, I argue that power-sharing will fail to provide stability in societies where economic power is inextricably intertwined with political power. Compare, for instance, Switzerland with Yugoslavia. In Switzerland, power-sharing applies only to the political process. In a nation with a huge market-driven private sector, the sharing of political power has little impact on the economic lives of individual Swiss citizens. In contrast, in communist Yugoslavia, where the government sector overwhelmed its puny private counterpart, the allocation of political power went hand in hand with the allocation of private benefits. Therefore, in such societies, where each group pits its economic interest against the others in a zero-sum game, market failure in the allocation of resources leads to conflict. In such societies, power-sharing may not work; in fact, it is not very clear what would. In Rwanda, for instance, the prospect of sharing power with the Tutsis prompted the Hutus to engage in genocide. The paranoid leadership of Indonesia refused to share power with the minority in East Timor and ended up with a bloody war of repression. In the end, humanitarian disasters can be averted only when a liberal democracy is established. It is a tall order, no doubt. However, every effort should be made to stop the cycle of violence before deep fissures appear, tearing at the basic fabric of a society with savage fury.

Peace Through Coercion: Benevolent Dictatorship

A nation facing the threats of an insurrection can respond not only through offers of power-sharing; it can also attempt to quell rebellion by the use of brute force.[20] The idea is that if the authorities raise the cost of participation to an extreme height, prospective participants will simply join the ranks of the easy riders and not engage in anti-government activities. After all, Marshal Tito kept feuding groups under control through the use of force. Today, China is kept together not by lofty ideas of power-sharing, but by the threat of coercion from the Communist Party. Chile, South Korea, Taiwan, Singapore, and Hong Kong attained economic prosperity and political stability by controlling the aspirations of many groups within their political boundaries.

None of the above examples is from a democratic nation. Evidence suggests that such demonstrations of power work only in nondemocratic nations. This is because to respond to threats with counterthreats is part of the human psychobiological makeup. Hence, when we are told not to do something, our first inclination is often one of defiance. However, after a certain threshold level is crossed, dissidents become convinced of the resolve of the authorities and a rebellion is brought down by the use of brutal force. The democratic nations, working within the laws of their constitutions, are rarely able to cross the threshold of high coercion and high rebellion.[21] As a result, in such societies, the solution to a sectarian revolt cannot be found in military action alone and must be sought at the political level. Thus, after decades of efforts to put down violent rebellion in Northern Ireland, the British are inching toward a political solution. In contrast, in China, the brutal suppression of a student revolt in the Tiananmen Square massacre in 1989 quickly produced the desired results for the authorities.

Power-sharing forms of government face their biggest challenge from the rise of political entrepreneurs feeding on the insecurities of the members of their own group about the others by constructing the worst possible scenario which could befall the group if they did not take radical preemptive action. Thus, in Yugoslavia, as soon as the political climate changed with the constitutional reform of 1972, the various groups started playing on their mutual fears. Many observers of the Yugoslav crisis place the majority of the blame on the blatant political ambition of the Serbian chief, Slobodan Milosevic.[22] With Milosevic clamoring for increasing power, the other threatened ethnic groups fell into a classic situation of the "prisoner's dilemma," where a basic mistrust thrusts groups deeper down the path toward a solution where everyone loses.[23] Power-sharing, at least in the short run, may not work in deeply divided societies where political entrepreneurs create enemies out of the other groups. Such societies can quickly spin out of control and slide down the slippery slope to a state of collective madness.

Can Democracy Save the World?

Since the end of World War II, the Western democracies have been trying, with varied levels of enthusiasm and commitment, to spread democracy to the rest of the world. Political scientist Samuel Huntington calls such efforts since 1974 the "third wave."[24] During the last two decades the number of democracies has increased dramatically. If we define democracy by form alone, meaning rule by a civilian body, elected by constitutional means in a multiparty election, by the end of 1994 we can count up to 144 "democracies" in the world.[25] This number is nearly a 100% jump from a decade ago. Since there were 191 independent nations in the world in 1994, we must be thoroughly impressed by the fact that over 75% of them enjoyed democracy. However, our elation is tempered when we recognize that for many nations around the world, democracy has become a necessary buzz word.

Therefore, stripping away formal appearances, Freedom House has been conducting periodic surveys of freedom enjoyed by citizens for the last twenty-six years. The Freedom House survey put forty-two countries in the category of "free" in 1972, fifty-three in 1985, seventy-six in 1995, and eighty-eight in 1998. As the third millennium approached, about 40% of the world's population (approximately 2.354 billion people) lived in "free" countries.[26] In many countries, such as Pakistan, Turkey, and Guatemala, the ruling party was nothing but a front for the military or some other group. Freedom House defines these countries as "partially free." Therefore, as imperfect as it may sound, progress has been made in certain corners of the world. However, the flip side of the story is that in fifty countries (comprising 26% of the world's population) citizens are denied basic rights and civil liberties. Also, within the countries regarded as "free," there are deep pockets of human rights abuse and extreme poverty. In countries such as India, personal freedoms are often seriously compromised due to continuing internal conflicts. In fact, even within many countries we generally regard as "free," minority groups face threats from the organized state.

Progress in the planting of democratic roots in the Third World and the former Soviet bloc countries does not, however, eliminate the risk of collective madness. As a matter of fact, a growing number of critics are busy deconstructing democracy.[27] Since "democracy" is the rule of the "people," the true spirit of individualism must flourish before democracy can be successfully implemented. The overthrow of a functioning authoritarian system (such as in today's China) by a pro-democracy movement is no guarantee of peace. Oliver Cromwell and Maximilien de Robespierre brought about a tyranny far worse than what existed under the English and French kings. Rationalizing the actions of the Revolutionary Tribunal in Paris, citizen Georges Danton proclaimed, "Let us be terrible, so that the people will not have to be."[28] Fareed Zakaria, in a provocative article, contends that the helter-skelter imposition of democracy in an unprepared world leads to the establishment of "illiberal democracies"—where elected governments show complete disregard for the rights of the individual.[29] After all, Hitler and Mussolini came to power through the electoral process. Milosevic and Habyarimana also rose to power through election. Journalist Robert Kaplan points out that even in Great Britain, the development of a democracy based on universal suffrage was gradual. Therefore, without the prerequisites of democracy—"bourgeois traditions, exposure to Western Enlightenment, high literacy rates, low birth rates"—a forced implantation of democracy is likely to lead to disaster.[30] Kaplan correctly points out that the true stability of a political system comes from the rise of the middle class and not necessarily from the establishment of any particular political order.

Hence, there is no quick fix. The true solution lies with moderate policies that recognize ethnic divisions but build trust among various groups.[31] Outside interventions can only promote an environment where true liberal democratic institutions can flourish. Ultimately, the remedy for the malady of mass hate lies in the hands of the citizens of the country.

STRATEGIC MOVES: SHORT-TERM SOLUTIONS

Increasingly, the world community is realizing that it cannot overlook genocide, fratricide, and other incidents of collective madness. In a global village, every nation's vital interests are hopelessly intertwined. Today almost every major nation is worried about border security arising out of refugee flows. As the central state weakens from prolonged political crisis, the only other group with enough organizational capabilities often quickly fills the power vacuum: organized crime. These nefarious groups deal in drugs and arms, putting every nation's vital interests in jeopardy. Therefore, it helps to take preventive short-term actions to put a stop to the spread of collective madness. One of the ways the world bodies can devise a proper course of action is through an early detection system of political and humanitarian crises.

Early Warning

"Prevention is better than the cure," so goes the age-old adage. The best way to prevent an outbreak of humanitarian catastrophes may be found in our ability to forecast them and take the necessary preventive actions. But is it possible to develop early warning models for political and humanitarian disasters?

The Impetus for Predicting. In 1992, the UN Secretary General called the attention of the international community to security threats arising from ethnic, religious, social, cultural, or linguistic strife. In his *Agenda for Peace,* Boutros Boutros-Ghali emphasized the need for systematic efforts directed toward developing early warning systems. This new agenda paved the way for the UN Department of Humanitarian Affairs and the Centre for Documentation and Research of the UN High Commission for Refugees to carry out systematic research and data analysis for developing an early warning (EW) system. Today a number of prominent researchers in various universities, NGOs, and national and international governmental agencies all over the world are engaged in developing such a system for political crises, genocide, and refugee migrations. Although efforts at building EW models are fairly new in the field of political and humanitarian crises, early warning models cover a wide range of phenomena from natural disasters, such as earthquakes and floods, to outbreaks of epidemics and famines.

From the earliest recorded history people have tried to forecast the future; they have attempted to develop early warnings for disasters to come by interpreting omens, from animal entrails to tea leaves. In the book of Genesis, languishing in prison after being betrayed by his brothers, Joseph used his skills to gain the Pharaoh's favor by successfully interpreting his dreams. He warned the Pharaoh that there would be seven years of bountiful harvest followed by seven years of drought. So, he advised the Pharaoh to stock up his granaries during the fat years to prepare for the leaner ones. His early warning was proven right, and while Canaan and the surrounding areas were suffering, Egypt was able to avert the ravages of a disastrous drought. Throughout history people have feared the unknown future and have attempted to bring it within the realm of systematic analysis; frightened individuals as well as the political leaders of all ages have sought early warning of impending doom from shamans, oracles, astrologers, holy men, and, lately, the academics.

Within the social sciences, forecasting has largely been the domain of the economists. Emboldened by the policy implications of John Maynard Keynes' empirically testable hypotheses, the economic profession went full steam into the business of forecasting. Today we see established corporations, as well as many government agencies including the Office of Management and Budget and the Congressional Budget Office, routinely engaging in economic forecasting. Modern economies, all over the world, are heavily dependent upon forecasting for their economic stabilization policies. By using large econometric models, the effects of a tax increase or decrease are analyzed; monetary policies are guided by early warnings of leading economic indicators. Although economic forecasts, like the weather report, are often objects of much derision, evidence based on long-term data is fairly clear; we have been better able to avert extreme swings of business cycles in the postwar years compared to those prior to the world wars.

The virtual explosion in ethnic violence in the late 1980s and early 1990s, coupled with decades-long quantitative research into the causes of collective violence, has generated enthusiasm for forecasting political and humanitarian crises. However, forecasts, especially of catastrophic events, carry their own hazards. For instance, forecasts of cyclones, epidemics, and earthquakes can impose tremendous economic and political costs on the affected regions. Therefore, responsible forecasters must always be concerned about making false positive (predicting a crisis when nothing happened in reality) or false negative (predicting calm, yet the nation experiences an upheaval) predictions.[32]

In the meantime, a number of scholars have expressed deep skepticism regarding our ability to forecast political events.[33] For instance, in light of the failure of the intelligence community and political pundits to predict the sudden demise of communism in the Soviet Union and other parts of Eastern Europe, Timur Kuran points out our inability to forecast catastrophic events like war and revolution.[34] He bases his analysis on people's practice of falsifying their private preferences, fearing government oppression, reprisal by other powerful forces in the society, or peer pressure. If nobody expresses his or her true preference, observers have no way of measuring the pervasiveness of antipathy toward the established political system. However, when a small crack appears in the seemingly solid edifice, people join the bandwagon at an increasing rate, finding comfort in the anonymity of large numbers of protesters.

However, I argue that while it is impossible to predict the exact timing of a revolution or the start of a human rights catastrophe, it is eminently possible to develop EW models based on our knowledge of the causes of such events.[35] There are many ways of forecasting unique events such as these, and these techniques can provide satisfactory forecasts.[36]

Efforts at forecasting political and humanitarian crises are still in their infancy, and the possibility of disappointment with EW results prompted Gurr and Harff to warn that "if early warnings are too often inaccurate, early warning research may be discredited."[37]

Given the state of the debate, the problem boils down to measuring the relative effectiveness of the EW models. Although forecasting and developing EW models are commonplace in economics, they are new in the realm of political science. Yet, econometric literature is not particularly rich in explaining how to evaluate forecasting models, especially those used for policy analyses. Is accuracy in forecasting the only criterion for choosing a particular EW model or should we consider other factors as well?

Early Warning Models: What to Expect. Although economic forecasting has evolved over half a century, political forecasting is but of recent origin. Therefore, despite skepticism about our ability to develop early warning systems for political and humanitarian crises, we can safely state that although it is difficult to predict the exact nature of the future, it is not impossible to warn nations when they cross the threshold of a safety zone. However, there should be yet another caveat. Even under the best of circumstances, there is no necessary link between good forecasting and good policy. Hence, we should be extremely cautious about what we can expect from EW models.

In any case, there should be no doubt about the importance of the task. Gurr and Harff correctly point out that ethnic hostility remains the most vexing problem for the next century.[38] In Chapter 5, I identified twelve steps to collective madness. I would argue that successful models can be constructed by monitoring these and other variables and making periodic predictions for episodes of genocide. We should acknowledge that EW models offer one of the best tools for managing future humanitarian and political crises, but at the same time we need to be realistic and recognize their inability to provide fool-proof predictions.

FROM EARLY WARNING TO EARLY ACTION

The process of successfully preventing of deadly conflicts must be part of a continuing cycle. Figure 7.1 shows the process as a continuous loop linking detection, prescription, adoption, implementation, and evaluation. Once a troublesome scenario is detected, there should be a set of action plans. As the Carnegie Commission on Deadly Conflicts points out, these action plans can involve non-invasive measures such as economic sanctions, preventive diplomacy, and mediation.[39] As these measures are implemented, there should at the same time be a continuing process of evaluation of relative success in mitigating the probability of bloodshed.

It is one thing to forecast an incipient incident of mass insanity and another to develop an action plan. The gap between warning and action is complex and confusing. First, there is a detection gap. As we have seen above, scholars and members of the intelligence community worry about "false positives," where a predicted impending doom turns out to be barely a ripple. Many worry that too many cries of "wolf!" would create a condition of cynicism.

On the other hand, if people often hide their private preferences from public view, it can become difficult to predict social upheavals. As a result, we are frequently surprised by the speed of a cataclysmic tidal wave of social revolutionary change. When President Reagan delivered his famous "evil empire"

Figure 7.1
The Early Warning Loop

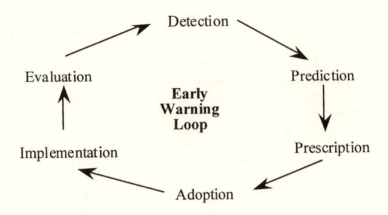

speech in the early 1980s, it would have been totally inconceivable to predict that in a matter of a few years the entire Soviet system would collapse, Yugoslavia would be submerged in ethnic genocide, and China would become a place of unbridled capitalism.

However, even if the forecasting gap is bridged and the warning alarms start ringing, without perfect clairvoyance there is likely to be little consensus regarding the correct course of action. The prescription for action should be divided into "structural" and "strategic." Action plans aiming at a structural change are long-term, where the root causes of social conflicts are addressed. These would include creating a situation where the fundamental rights of every citizen are protected and opportunities for economic development and growth are promoted. Short-term or "strategic" plans should aim at averting an immediate crisis from spreading throughout the society. Typically, in each of these cases, the motivational tools of "carrots" and "sticks" may be used with prudence and sensitivity, according to acceptable levels of commitment to the world community.

Preventive Diplomacy

The realm of preventive diplomacy covers a wide variety of actions taken by one or more foreign governments attempting to correct the conduct of the political leadership toward its citizens. Possible foreign policy options may include political sanctions, economic sanctions, and the use of military force.

Nonmilitary sanctions against a government can be either political or economic or a combination of the two. At the political level, sanctions can vary from adopting resolutions of disapproval by the United Nations to the cutting off of diplomatic relations by individual nations. Economic sanctions involve imposing a trade embargo against the offending nation, stopping the flow of all but the most essential items, such as food and medicine, into the country.

Sanctions. Common wisdom tells us that sanctions don't work. Nearly forty years of economic and political isolation by the United States has so far failed to topple Fidel Castro in Cuba. At the time of writing, sanctions don't seem to have had much impact on the longevity of Muammar Gaddafi in Libya, the Islamic regime of Iran, or Saddam Hussein of Iraq. On the other hand, the proponents of sanctions point to the possible success of international sanctions in bringing an end to the white exclusionary regime in South Africa. A recent report by the Carnegie Commission points out that there are at least four reasons why international sanctions may be effective in altering the behavior of a rogue regime.[40]

First, sanctions imposed by the international community demonstrate the community's disapproval and identify the culpable actors and their conduct. If imposed by an international body—such as the United Nations—they can deliver a strong message to those in power, especially when the message is unequivocal. Second, sanctions pave the way for more stringent actions, including military actions, against the offending regime. Strong foreign policy actions, particularly ones that require the use of force, are never easy. The imposition of tough sanctions serves as a warning to the adversary in addition to preparing others for possible military intervention as the next step. Third, sanctions limit the deviant state's options in the international arena. This is especially true in the post–Cold War era. During the Cold War, the offending countries, drawing the ire of one side, could automatically seek protection among those of the other side. However, such opportunities have become more limited in the post–Cold War era. Fourth, in a world moving at lightning speed in the global economy, sanctions impose significant costs in terms of lost opportunities in the long run. In the short run, as we see in the cases of Iraq and Yugoslavia, sanctions impose hardship among the populace. Necessities, from food to gasoline, start disappearing from open markets; the elite, used to traveling freely in the West, start feeling claustrophobic.[41]

Why Sanctions Fail or Succeed. One of the main reasons sanctions often fail to achieve their intended goals is because the goals are not sufficiently clear. Those who impose the sanctions must make clear their intended target. Do they want to punish the political leadership, the military establishment, or the entire population? However, the problem is that there are no defined rules regarding the imposition of sanctions. Neither is it clear how states can impose a blockade, which would successfully seal the country off from the rest of the world. For instance, should food and medicine be allowed to flow in? Although the humanitarian concerns prompted by a total embargo are obvious, if the legally traded items primarily benefit the ruling group and the military, it would defy the purpose of the sanctions.[42] Most countries with common international borders find it extremely difficult to completely stop trade across their political boundaries. Smugglers and gunrunners make extra profits from embargoes and in the process can develop a strong mercenary interest against any prospect of peace.

Hufbauer, Schott, and Elliott undertook one of the most comprehensive studies on the relative efficacy of economic sanctions.[43] They considered 108 cases of economic sanctions imposed by foreign nations since 1900. In order to determine the relative success of sanctions, they considered the desired outcomes of sanctions, such as destabilizing the existing government and/or significantly reducing the capabilities of the armed forces. By their measure, of the 108 episodes studied, 39 (about 36%) could be considered successful, and 69 (64%) failures. Hufbauer et al. conclude that the probability of success in imposing economic sanctions depends on four factors: (1) there has to be an asymmetry in size, that is, the nation imposing sanctions needs to be much larger than the target state; (2) the sanctions must impose a high cost on the target and a low cost on the imposing nation; (3) the target must be a former ally; and (4) the two nations must have had significant trade relations with each other before the conflict.

From the above list of factors, it is clear that, to be successful, economic sanctions must hurt the intended target. For instance, the white regime of South Africa capitulated to external pressure because the world body had more or less developed a consensus regarding the repugnance of the apartheid system. Since South Africa was clearly a close ally of the Western nations, with significant economic and cultural ties, it had little recourse but to give in to the will of the international community. In contrast, for nations which are much less industrialized and are enemies at the time sanctions are imposed, the impact of a trade sanction will be less than desirable. For example, we can contrast South Africa with Cuba. During the last forty years the United States has been steadily tightening its restrictions on contact with Cuba. Within a year of the Cuban Revolution in 1959, the United States banned all exports to Cuba. In 1963, all Cuban assets in the United States were frozen, thereby effectively stopping all flow of capital between the two nations. In 1982, all U.S. citizens were barred from traveling to Cuba. Then, finally, in 1996, the Cuban Liberty and Democratic Solidarity Act, popularly known as the Helms-Burton Act, was passed to prevent other countries from conducting business with Cuba. Yet Fidel Castro's hold on Cuba remains seemingly impervious to such overwhelming pressure. Looking at the four factors presented by Hufbauer et al., we can see that the U.S. trade embargo on Cuba has failed primarily because Cuba was not a U.S. ally at the time trade sanctions were imposed. Therefore, it could survive by developing trade relations with the Soviet bloc countries during the long Cold War era. Its ideological ties with the Soviet Union must also have given comfort to Cuba's national political psyche. The situation in Cuba turned serious briefly after the fall of the Soviet Union. However, during the 1990s, Cuba has effectively developed strong trade relations with many European and Latin American nations and with Canada. Therefore, with a leaking embargo, Castro never lost his grip on Cuban society.

Further, trade embargoes are blunt instruments. Most often, when they are successful in tightening the noose around the target nation, they hurt the innocent. In a revealing article Mueller and Mueller demonstrate that the devastating impact of trade sanctions is responsible for numerous deaths among the Iraqi people, particularly children.[44]

Stopping the Arms Trade. During the last decade of the twentieth century, about fifty regional conflicts have broken out. Of that number only two—the Gulf War and the NATO bombing of Yugoslavia—saw the use of heavy weapons as the primary arms of choice. Even then, only a small portion of the fatalities in Yugoslavia can be attributed to heavy arms. The vast majority of the casualties are from small arms. And most of the casualties of these conflicts have been civilians. Civilian casualties constituted only 5% of the total deaths in World War I; however, over 90% of those killed or wounded in recent conflicts have been innocent bystanders of war.[45] The UN Development Program estimates that since 1987, as a result of armed conflicts, 2 million children have been killed, 4.5 million disabled, 6 million orphaned, and 12 million made homeless.[46]

The United States and its Western allies are ever vigilant against the proliferation of nuclear arms and missile technologies, but they generally turn a blind eye to the problems created by the proliferation of small arms. Thus, another United Nations study concluded:

While there are some agreed global norms and standards against weapons of mass destruction, there are no such norms or standards that can be used in reducing the excessive and destabilizing accumulation of small arms and light weapons. These are the weapons increasingly used as primary instruments of violence in internal conflicts dealt with by the United Nations, they are responsible for large numbers of deaths and the displacement of citizens around the world, and they consume large amounts of United Nations resources.

The excessive and destabilizing accumulation and transfer of small arms and light weapons is closely related to the increased incidence of internal conflict and high levels of crime and violence.[47]

Estimates of the worldwide supply of small arms range from 500 million[48] to 1 billion.[49] Of this vast arsenal, the greatest concern is the spread of military-type automatic weapons, such as AK-47s and M-16 rifles. Every year hundreds of thousands more of these weapons of mass murder are manufactured.[50] These weapons have become the staples of militia groups and criminal thugs because of their relatively low price, easy availability, ease of use, and destructive capabilities. A handful of combatants with automatic weapons can wipe out an entire village in a matter of minutes.

Along with the flooding of the world with automatic and semiautomatic weapons, another ominous trend has been set. In increasing numbers, children, many of whom haven't yet attained puberty, are being used as foot soldiers in the ever more violent conflicts around the world. These boys (and sometimes girls) have caused tremendous damage in many countries and regions, particularly in Afghanistan, Algeria, Angola, Bosnia, Burundi, Cambodia, Chechnya, Colombia, Congo, Dagestan, Haiti, Kashmir, Mozambique, Rwanda, Sierra Leone, Somalia, Sri Lanka, Sudan, and Uganda. The boys, often plucked from their families, are used as foot soldiers, and the girls for sex.

Another often overlooked aspect of subnational conflicts is the nexus between so-called freedom fighters and criminal gangs. When we see pictures of ragtag armies with sophisticated arms on television, we often forget the costs associated with procuring such weapons. Anti-personnel mines can be relatively inexpensive, and it is estimated that hundreds of millions of them are planted all over the world. Other weapons can be much more expensive. For instance, a Carnegie Commission report states that an AK-47 costs between $40 and $200, and the ammunition costs money as well, usually many months' wages in a typical Third World country.[51] More sophisticated arms, from anti-tank weapons to shoulder-held Stinger missiles, cost in the hundreds of thousands of dollars. It is indeed mind boggling to consider where these men and boys in the most impoverished parts of the world find the money to accumulate such impressive arsenals.

The booming international trade in arms and armaments makes it possible for these people to acquire these weapons of destruction and sorrow. Many of these arms are, of course, produced in the industrialized nations of the world, with the United States taking the lead in production and worldwide distribution. If we want to slow down the fratricidal carnage, we must take decisive action against powerful economic interests in these countries.

Aside from the question of supply, another question must arise, Where do these groups, whether ragtag fighters or well-organized militias, get the money to purchase their lethal tools of trade? The money comes from one of three sources: (1) an international sponsor; (2) expatriates living in the industrialized nations; or (3) through illicit means such as the drug trade.

The international sponsor of arms can be a superpower. For instance, during the Cold War, under the pretext of a geopolitical jostling game, the superpowers routinely supplied arms to gain influence among the ruling elite of their client states, or to destabilize the client states of the opposite camp. The Soviets supported their client regimes in Afghanistan, Angola, Cambodia, Ethiopia and Cuba, to name a few. Similarly, the United States was liberal in supporting the Bay of Pigs invasion in Cuba, the Contra guerrillas in Nicaragua, the rebels in Afghanistan, and other guerrilla groups in many places in Asia and Africa. Outside the superpowers, France supplied arms to the governments of Rwanda, Chad, and other French African countries. Islamic revolutionary countries like Iran, Libya, Syria, and Iraq have supported many rebel groups all over the world.[52]

The expatriates of the war-torn nations who here now settled in the West have frequently supplied vital funds to carry on the military missions of the rebel forces. For instance, Irish immigrants in the United States have supported both sides in the Northern Irish conflict. Sikhs settled in the United States, Canada, and England have supported the Khalistan movement in Punjab.

The third source of large sums of money required for sustaining a war effort is the illicit drug trade. From the so-called narco-terrorists in Latin America to other rebel factions in many parts of the world, many groups have depended on drugs to satisfy their demands for arms and armaments. Although this noxious nexus between armed rebels and drug traders remains largely unexplored in the scholarly literature, there is increasing evidence to document this growing menace.

Direct Military Intervention. The use of military force is often seen as the last resort in preventing genocide and humanitarian disasters. However, force, when used as a last resort, produces the least desirable outcomes. For instance, the use of military force in Somalia was a disaster for the United States. Intervention in Liberia by the regional forces has only exacerbated an already deplorable situation. In Kosovo, the NATO intervention secured autonomy from Yugoslavia, but it failed miserably to prevent ethnic cleansing by the Serb militias. Even the NATO deployment in Bosnia has been ineffective in producing self-sustaining peace in the region. Therefore, evidence suggests that the early use of military forces can stabilize a situation before it reaches the point of no return.

In several cases early intervention by international forces has helped stabilize conditions in a country sliding fast toward collective madness. Macedonia is a case in point. Seeing up close the horrors of Bosnia, the member states of the United Nations organized a multinational peacekeeping operation. As a result, while blood has flowed freely in Serbia, and combatants remain just as belligerent as the day the NATO troops arrived in Bosnia, Macedonia remains free of extremes of emotion. Multinational forces, at least in one corner of former Yugoslavia, were able to stop the spread of collective madness in its tracks. I can similarly point to the success of the U.S.-led multinational forces in Haiti in stabilizing the island, at least in the short run. Likewise, despite occasional incidences of atrocities, Burundi has been spared the fate of its neighbor, Rwanda.

Why Conflicts Continue

In their bestselling book, *Getting to Yes,* Roger Fisher and William Uri of Harvard Negotiating Project chalk out the way to a negotiated settlement.[53] They argue that by changing the context of the dispute from "issue-oriented" to "need-based," many conflicts may be resolved. For instance, suppose there is a dispute between two groups: one group wants the other to leave a certain area, but the other group refuses to move. If we try to negotiate on the basis of the issue (to move or not to move), we may not get very far. But if we ask the first group why they want the second group to vacate that place, we may discover that the people in the first group are concerned about their personal security. Therefore, armed with that information regarding their security needs, we may attempt to work out a compromise where the second group does not move but somehow agrees to a mutually acceptable security arrangement. By following such strategies many of the world's long-standing disputes, from Northern Ireland to Kashmir, from North and South Korea to the Zulus and the followers of the ANC in South Africa, may be mitigated. Alas, despite innumerable attempts, such efforts bear fruit less frequently than we would like to see. An outsider concerned about the current escalation of a conflict may find the lack of willingness of the combatants puzzling. Yet, the answer to the intractable nature of many conflicts may lie in the complex motivations of the various individuals and groups involved in mutual hostility.

Peace creates winners and losers. While living in peace may be the most logical choice for those of us who are not involved in the dispute, for those who are, peace creates a new situation where much of the outcome may not be to their liking.

The Believers. The most dangerous time to visit Jerusalem or Belfast is when there is a real peace process afoot. As the involved parties move close to a solution to their long-standing conflict, someone from one group or another stages an act of violence against the other group. So wanton is its choice of targets, so egregious is its scope, that the incident shakes the peace process to its roots. Even the staunchest advocates of peace in the victimized group start questioning the value of peace itself. This change in attitude from accommodation to anger prompts its leaders to take actions at least of equal magnitude against the perpetrating group. As bodies line up, homes get destroyed, and hopes and aspirations get dashed, the prospect for peace retreats to the distant horizon; hatred compounds hatred, and animosity blossoms even in the middle of the most infertile desert land or in the bleakest urban sprawl.

To an outsider, the actions of the perpetrators seem puzzling for two reasons: First, presumably, the peace process would have brought their group closer to their ultimate goal. Second, by engaging in such activities, the perpetrators would strengthen the hand of those in the opposing group who are adamantly opposed to any compromise with them. Then what is the rationale for keeping the conflict alive? The answer to the first question is ideological, while the second is strategic.

To a true believer the world is painted in the starkest hues of black and white. Having no middle ground, no ambiguity about the desired outcome, and no room for compromise, to a true believer, a half-empty glass can be just as undesirable as an empty one. In fact, to a true believer, the seeking of a middle ground may be even more repugnant than a stalemate, as it may be as unacceptable as a pact with the devil himself. Therefore, from an ideological standpoint, the destruction of a compromise with the enemy is a holy cause, an end even worth dying for.

The destruction of a peace process can also be the outcome of a calculated strategy. The work of Nobel laureate Kenneth Arrow implies that a nation achieves political stability when the major groups are lined up along a bell curve of political ideology and public opinion, with some falling at the extreme ends, but most located comfortably in the middle.[54] In such a society with single-peaked preferences, the median voter (the one in the dead center of the ideological spectrum) represents the will of the majority. However, in contrast, in a society deeply divided by long festering historical wounds of mutual hostility and mistrust, public opinion tends to be bimodal (if there are two major groups, e.g., in Northern Ireland) or to have many peaks (e.g., in Lebanon). In such a society, any middle ground in compromise is regarded with utmost suspicion and is readily rejected. In such a society, until there is a sea change in public opinion, there can be no peace. Until then, these conflicts will not end.

However, even in a deeply divided society, if there is a move toward the middle, the extremists on both ends of the range may find it strategically beneficial to engage in acts which help the more militant adversaries rather than the peaceniks on the other side. Thus, viewed from this angle, the interests of those at the extreme ends of a conflict situation converge.

The Mercenaries. From outside a conflict zone, we believe that war and situations of sustained conflict offer an all around lose-lose proposition. Everyone loses when the entire society gets caught up in a civil war or other kinds of protracted low-intensity conflicts. Yet, reality can be far different from this presupposition. A large segment of the participants in collective actions comes from the ranks of the mercenaries, and mayhem offers them the best opportunity of making financial gains.[55] Once caught in the conflict, too often war becomes a permanent way of life for these boys and men. These untrained, uneducated, rootless young men become desensitized to violence and the sight of human sufferings. As Klare points out: "In societies where food and shelter are scarce, membership in an armed band that preys on the civilian population is a plausible route to survival. It is not surprising that many of these bands continue their violent activities long after the original, strategic rationale for their formation has ceased to have meaning."[56]

The identity of the mercenaries can vary from the Nazi era German industrial elite to petty black marketers and members of organized crime. In any case, peace can be a losing proposition for the mercenaries. Therefore, facing the prospect of peace, those who have a stake in the conflict often cloak their true feelings with the rhetoric of hyper-nationalists. Because they are indistinguishable from the true believers, it becomes nearly impossible to gauge their actual motivation without an intimate knowledge of their nefarious activities. As a result, this area remains one of the least explored in the academic literature.

WHERE THERE'S A WILL . . .

Is there a way? Can we prevent future incidents of collective madness? In this chapter, I have attempted to show that the problem is not that the world community doesn't know about or cannot take appropriate steps to stop incidents of fratricidal frenzy. The Carnegie Commission Report on the Prevention of Deadly Conflict boldly proclaims that "the problem is not that the states do not know, it is that they do not respond to warning, perhaps do not even want to know the danger."[57] However, the predominant problem for the states is the need for collective will. I argue in the following chapter that the future world of monopolar political ideology creates conditions for better management of such humanitarian crises. Yet, at the same time, the absence of a defined enemy along with the rampant progress of individualism makes it difficult to mobilize political support for such preventive measures.

NOTES

1. Quoted in Geyer (1997: E3).
2. Carnegie Corporation of New York (1997: 5).
3. In mathematics and theoretical physics, scholars have developed theories of "chaos" and "catastrophe" to account for a sudden change (for a popular explanation of an extremely complex methodology, see Gleick [1987]), but their application in the social sciences holds limited hope for success.
4. See Sen (1992).
5. See Sen (1973).
6. For a social psychological perspective, see Lind and Tyler (1988).
7. See Dahl (1971: 1–19).
8. Empirical evidence points to the fact that democratic nations experience significantly fewer incidents of political violence. See, for example, Dipak Gupta (1990: 200–204).
9. See Ra'anam (1990).
10. See Chapter 5, note 82.
11. See L. Diamond (1995: 6–7).
12. See Gupta, Madhavan, and Blee (1998).
13. See Lijphart (1984, 1990).
14. See Steiner (1990).
15. See Heisler (1990).
16. See Stubbs (1990).
17. See Lijphart (1996).
18. See Tambiah (1991).
19. See, McRae (1990).
20. In our empirical research, we found that governments can achieve political stability either through extreme coercion or through a liberal rule, particularly in a democracy. See Venieris and Gupta (1983).
21. See Gupta and Singh (1992).
22. See, for instance, Cohen (1993). Also see Woodward (1995).
23. See Dipak Gupta (1994: 399–403).
24. See Huntington (1991).
25. See Karatnycky (1995: 5).
26. See Karatnycky (1998). Also see Freedom House (1995: 3).
27. See Plattner (1998).
28. See Schama (1989: 707).

29. See Zakaria (1997).
30. See Kaplan (1997: 61).
31. See Horowitz (1990).
32. See Gurr and Harff (1996: 9).
33. See for example, Alker (1994).
34. See for example, Kuran (1995b).
35. See Dipak Gupta (1998a).
36. See Dipak Gupta (1999b).
37. See Gurr and Harff (1996: 9).
38. Ibid.
39. Carnegie Corporation of New York (1997: 10).
40. Ibid, 12.
41. Ibid.
42. For a critical account of the U.S. imposed sanctions on Iraq, see Mueller and Mueller (1999).
43. See Hufbauer et al. (1990).
44. See Mueller and Mueller (1999).
45. See Klare (1999: 18–22).
46. United Nations Development Program (1998: 35).
47. United Nations (1997: 9).
48. See J. Singh (1995: viii).
49. Klare (1999: 21).
50. See Renner (1997: 20).
51. Carnegie Corporation of New York (1996: 3).
52. See A. M. Smith (1997: 22).
53. See Fisher and Uri (1989).
54. See Arrow (1963).
55. On July 23, 1999, Michael Sheehan, at his confirmation hearing for the permanent position of Counter-terrorism Coordinator, testified before the Senate Foreign Relations Committee outlining the role of the mercenaries. Sheehan pointed to the growing threat from state-sponsored terrorists. Sheehan also stressed the ever increasing link between drug money and international terrorism. "Counter-terrorism expert tells of changing threat" (1999: A6).
56. See Klare (1999: 19).
57. Carnegie Corporation of New York (1997: 7).

CHAPTER 8

COLLECTIVE MADNESS: LOOKING INTO THE FUTURE

It is comforting, however, and a source of profound relief to think that man is only a recent invention, a wrinkle in our knowledge, and that he will disappear again as soon as that knowledge has discovered a new form.
—Michel Foucault[1]

People just do not maximize on a selfish basis every minute. In fact, the system would not work if they did. A consequence of that would be the end of organized society as we know it.
—Kenneth Arrow[2]

COLLECTIVE MADNESS

I have called the malady collective madness. In the beginning of this book I admitted the nonacademic nature of the term. Our social evolution can be analyzed as a part of many conflicting forces. In this book, I have presented a worldview based on the constant dialectical interactions between the forces of the individual and the collective. I have argued that all collective actions require the presence of a collective identity. I have also argued that the spectrum spanning the extremes of the two identities produces Hobbesian anarchy at one end and collective madness at the other. I define collective madness as a state of hyper-identity with the collective. It can afflict a small religious group or an entire nation. In traditional political discourse, what happened in Jonestown or in Waco is infrequently discussed in the same breath with what took place in Nazi Germany, Cambodia, or Rwanda.[3] In this book, I have explored this link by invoking the image of "madness." I argue that when there is a strong ideology of the collective, the boundaries between religion and politics disappear. Issues of religious fervor quickly become ones of politics. Similarly, matters of political ideology turn into religious faith, with all its symbolism, rituals, and zeal.

Until now, I have not addressed the term "madness" in depth. "Madness" is a popular term, perhaps never to be encountered in the scientific literature of medicine or psychology. Yet I choose it precisely because of its vagueness. Its ambiguity reflects the fine line that separates faith from reason, myth from reality, ideology from pragmatism, and rational thinking from insanity. I hope that in its obscure mirror, the term "collective madness" will offer a closer look at our own selves, both individual and collective.

In the 1960s, psychologist Thomas Szasz created a furor within the academic world with the publication of *The Myth of Mental Illness*.[4] In this controversial book, he argued that mental illness cannot be precisely diagnosed, which explains why the definition of mental illness has varied with time.[5] While at times talking to the invisible God or seeing apparitions would have qualified someone for sainthood, in today's world of psychiatric practice, such visions may identify one as needing treatment for biochemical imbalance. However, comparison between what an individual might feel in the throes of a sectarian conflict, during a deeply ideological rebellion, or in the midst of a cult movement can come strangely close to what many modern-day clinical psychiatrists would classify as "schizophrenia." To be sure, the question of the blurred line of distinction between hyper-nationalism and paranoid schizophrenia has been broached by many. For instance, renowned American historian Richard Hofstadter called his famous essay "The Paranoid Style of American Politics."[6] Recently, clinical psychiatrists have turned their attention to the similarities in the behavior patterns and the construction of reality between what they observe in their practice and what they see and hear in the behavior and speeches of ideological zealots. Psychiatrist James Glass, for example, notes: "It occurs to me after listening for several months to delusional utterances that some connection may exist between internal emotional structures and the construction of ethical and political systems of belief."[7] Glass further adds that in their delusion, his patients, similar to demagogues and their followers all over the world, develop a more or less coherent belief system. This belief system is characterized by inner images of sharp dichotomies between "good/bad, god/devil, American/communists, black/white," and so on.[8]

I should be quick to point out that in this book, I have not argued the case that the leaders and their faithful followers are necessarily delusional. However, they often construct a reality that is not shared by those observers who have little stake in the outcome. Does invoking the image of an illness imply that everyone associated with a collective movement gets infected with "madness"? Like an uncontrolled epidemic, can an abnormality of the brain that makes enemies out of one's neighbors spread from people to people? Unlike many works of psychobiography, this book does not attempt to explain the roots of the belief structure of a single political leader or an individual follower. Instead it explores the process by which the malevolent worldview of a political entrepreneur comes to be shared by a larger group of individuals.[9]

In fact, the line between sanity and insanity is indeed a thin one. Even psychiatrists cannot often draw a definite conclusion about the sanity of a historical figure. For instance, Fritz Redlich, a professor emeritus of psychiatry at Yale University and the University of California at Los Angeles, studied Hitler's life for ten years. His extensive study showed that Hitler had paranoiac visions about his own physical abnormalities. Hitler believed that his father was half Jewish and that he had inherited syphilis from his father. However, there is no reason to believe that Hitler would have been found "insane" or that he would have pleaded insanity in his defense. In fact, after an exhaustive analysis, Redlich ends his book by concurring with his wife's general observation, "He was an evil man."[10]

I should, however, also point out that while exploring the path to collective madness, I emphatically argue that not all the followers are necessarily "true believers." Many are, while perhaps many more are not. The dynamics of social evolution sweep people away into a common confluence from diverse sources. A collective movement is the outcome of an extremely complex process. If nothing else, my work argues against a simplistic explanation of the motives and the root causes of collective actions.

The trail of our biological evolution has led us to the social reality of group formation. Inveterate joiners, we constantly seek others in association. We form groups in an infinite number of complex overlapping circles, which may at points include or exclude everyone else on the planet. But not all group formations, even when pitted against one another in a zero-sum game, necessarily lead to bloodshed and violence. Why do some groups engage in violence for settling disputes, while many others don't? I present the view that violence is the outcome of the failure of voluntary exchange. Let me explain and then summarize my arguments.

The evolution of a collective movement is the dynamic outcome of interactions between individual members and the group. People join groups because they derive personal happiness, satisfaction, and utility as a result of their association. On the other hand, a group thrives when its members commit themselves to the collective goals of the group. History demonstrates that some groups have been able to maintain their special identity and have been able to survive through the ages. Others have become lost or been assimilated into different groups. It is no accident that some groups—ethnic, linguistic, religious, or national—have had a long history of survival, while countless others have merged into larger societies. The Jews have survived as a group for nearly 3,000 years, as have the British for at least a thousand years (counting from the time of William the Conqueror), while the Hittites, the Aztecs, and the Austro-Hungarians have lost their separate group identities.

The interaction between a group and its individual members is the outcome of what a group is able to give its individual members, and what the members, in turn, can commit to the cause of the group. A group may be considered efficient if it can provide its members with security, special benefits (quasi-public goods, meant only for the members), and the possibility of greater individual economic prosperity through nepotism (group members showing preference for each other in the marketplace). In situations where individuals believe that they will not be able to obtain what they need without the help of others, they form groups. In societies stressing the values of merit-based, free-market, liberal democracies, the need for forming groups becomes less pressing. In contrast, clans and religious groups dominate politics in traditional societies. In such societies, where national resources are not distributed by a merit-based market system, resources are allocated following tribal or some other non-market lines. Therefore, in these societies people rely less on the national government for allocation of resources and more on their tribal leadership.[11] As sectarian conflicts escalate, the need to belong to a group becomes even more pressing. During periods of ethnic hostility, it becomes logical for people to choose to belong to hyper-nationalistic groups for personal security and other aspects of personal welfare, thereby increasing polarization within a society.

Groups serve their members. In return, a member is obliged to contribute a portion of his or her personal endowment to preserve the group itself. This is the cost of membership. Members pay with their time, money, and, in many cases, unquestioned obedience to the leadership and its worldview. French cultural anthropologist Jean Jacques Rousseau Maquet best explains this traditional mind-set of obeying authority when he writes about pre-colonial Rwanda: "When the ruler gives an order, he must be obeyed, not because his order falls into the sphere over which he has authority, but simply because he is the ruler."[12]

I call groups based on birth characteristics—race, religion, language, and so on—*ascriptive* and those based on voluntary choice *adoptive*. Ascriptive group boundaries are almost impenetrable, with little chance of assimilation, at least in the short run. Of the various birth characteristics, race or ethnicity is most rigid, while language and religion are less so, since one can learn the language of the privileged group or in many cases can even convert to a different religion. However, most often in the larger society, religious and linguistic divisions follow the fault lines of the much more rigid ascriptive boundaries of race or ethnicity.

In contrast, adoptive groups are voluntarily formed by commonalities of interest, economic or social, and are comparatively easy to penetrate.[13] As long as they remain penetrable to those outside the group, the society remains stable. Following the dictates of the "invisible hand" of market adjustment, those groups offering a higher level of net benefits (advantages of group membership minus the costs of being associated with the group) to their members as compared to the other groups would enlarge in size. If a group's benefits exceed the members' contributions, the group will expand at a rapid rate as it will acquire new members. A point of equilibrium will be reached when a group's offering of protection, special benefits, and nepotism becomes equal to its members' contributions. If the benefits fall short of contributions, the group will experience a loss of membership. If it is based on relatively porous ascriptive grounds, such as language and religion, the prospering group's rank may swell as more people try to learn the dominant group's language or convert to its religious faith.

However, if the special group benefits are restricted strictly by impenetrable birth characteristics, such as race, ethnicity, or caste, because of the absence of easy entry and exit, disparities in net benefits of group membership will persist. In the animal world, this disparity would bring about an explosion in birth until the species reaches its optimum size relative to its environment. In fact, through dynamic interaction within an ecological sphere, groups of hunters and their prey have been observed to go through cyclical booms and busts. When the fox population is low relative to the rabbits', the foxes will propagate at a faster rate to the point that the rabbit population will get depleted. This will cause starvation among the foxes and, as they thin out in numbers, the rabbits will thrive. Then the cycle will start once again. In human society, however, an upset in the equilibrium may not be corrected through increase or decrease in population, but through revolution or other such nonmarket actions.

Driven at the base by biology and influenced by the needs of economics, culture, and the larger society, each of us chooses among the innumerable possibilities of group affiliation and determines our relative contribution to the group. Research in social psychology has shown the considerable strength of groups in determining individual behavior. From crimes of obedience, to genocide, to more mundane acts of individual decision making, the influence of groups on human behavior is undeniable.

COLLECTIVE IDENTITY AND SOCIAL SCIENCE RESEARCH

"I once heard a composer of folk music described as a man who could create songs that were so compelling that after one hearing it seems as if you must always have known them," writes economist Paul Krugman while describing advancements in his discipline. He states that most ideas in economics are not new.[14] Thus, Krugman points out, "There are economists who have the same talent: they manage to have ideas that are so basic, yet so simple, that once you've heard them it's hard to believe you didn't always understand them." When we come across some of the best ideas we are struck by the fact they seem so eminently commonsense. I hope that this book presents a hypothesis that will strike the reader as nothing terribly novel. As social animals we are born with two identities, individual and collective. When we take part in a collective action, we often do so on the basis of the latter. However, while individual identity is invariant, our group identities are transitory and interchange-able, and can be manufactured. As science advances, it allows us to recognize complex realities but proposes simple explanations. In this book I have bor-rowed from various disciplines to develop a complex foundation from which a set of simple premises can be derived.

Science, however, cannot be built upon premises that cannot be proven. Hence, metaphysical queries remain outside the realm of scientific inquiry. It may be thought that if we expand a fundamental behavioral assumption, it will render itself nonfalsifiable or tautological. However, since collective identity is changeable and we live in imagined communities of all sorts, we can develop testable hypotheses regarding an individual's choice and strength of collective identity. If these hypotheses are borne out by empirical evidence we can accept them; otherwise we proclaim them to be false.[15]

A new theory is considered to be an improvement over an existing one if (1) it widens the domain of behavior that counts as action, (2) is more powerful in that it brings actions of various kinds under one theory, and (3) provides a more accurate or precise set of predictions. I would like to evaluate my theoret-ical construct in light of these three criteria.

I would argue that, first, the generalized framework provided in this book offers a way of synthesizing the disciplines of economics and social psychology. This will allow us not to disregard a wide range of human behavior as arational or irrational.

Second, collective actions come in many forms. When we examine the mo-tivations of people who choose to participate in a collective action that gives them little or no individual benefit, we often feel puzzled. We fail to under-stand, for example, why rational individuals contribute to the Public Broad-casting System (PBS) when they can watch its programs without paying. We don't understand why we take the trouble to vote even when we realize that a single vote probably will not make a difference in the outcome of the election. We don't understand the genocidal activities of otherwise normal human be-ings in Bosnia or in Rwanda. As a result, we tend to push collective actions out-side the domain of explanation. By combining economics with social psychology we can begin to understand that the reason we tend to solve our social dilemma, often without even being conscious about it, is because an ac-tivity satisfies not just one but many needs of life. Therefore, if satisfying the need to serve a group becomes more critical, we participate in a collective ac-tion regardless of our personal costs.

Finally, I believe that my expanded methodology will provide us not only with a greater explanatory ability, but also with testable hypotheses for a more accurate forecast of much broader-ranging human behavior. The behavioral underpinnings can be understood through experimental designs as well as through econometric analyses of the actors' revealed preferences.

However, in the social sciences we never reach the terra firma of absolute truth. Karl Popper puts it best when he likens theory building in the sciences to constructing a structure above a swamp:

The empirical basis of objective science has thus nothing "absolute" about it. Science does not rest upon rock-bottom. The bold structure of its theories rise, as it were, above a swamp. It is like a building erected on piles. The piles are driven from above into the swamp, but not to any natural or "given" base; and when we cease our attempts to drive piles into a deeper layer, it is not because we have reached firm ground. We simply stop when we are satisfied that they are firm enough to carry the structure, at least for the time being.[16]

I hope I have been able to build a structure that can pass this minimal test of scientific salience. I believe that future research along this line will give us a deeper understanding of collective action in general, and of the phenomenon I call collective madness.

DESTINY INSANITY?

Knowing our biological bent, are we forever destined to form groups with some and view others as enemies? Will there always be groups that dominate others? James Sidanius and Felicia Pratto have attempted to answer this important question with the help of a series of experimental studies.[17] Their work has ushered in what is known as the "social dominance theory" of social psychology. Social dominance theory starts out with two fundamental assumptions about human social behavior: (1) all human societies are inherently hierarchical, and this hierarchy has had functional utility for the survival of the human species over evolutionary time; and (2) this group-based hierarchical structure is kept in place by our attitude toward most forms of social oppression. These attitudes take a wide variety of forms, such as racism, ethnocentrism, nationalism, sexism, classism (based on economic classes), and so on. In other words, in order to propagate our social existence, prodded by our very elemental needs of biology, we adhere to these social attitudes which maintain the hierarchy of social dominance. When the status quo of the existing hierarchy is challenged by a previously subordinate group or groups, ethnic conflicts and other kinds of mass violence erupt. However, if these previously oppressed groups take over the reins of the society, they create their own hierarchy, which they then attempt to maintain at all costs. The implications of the work of Sidanius, Pratto, and their associates are indeed profound. In George Orwell's *Animal Farm*—written as a parody of the Bolshevik Revolution in Russia—after the animals staged a successful revolution, they not only created their own hierarchy, but also, like their previous owner, Farmer Brown, the top animals became carnivorous and start feeding on the lesser animals!

Indeed, social dominance theory paints a rather pessimistic picture of the future of our social evolution. As Sidanius points out, his theory leads to the sad conclusion that "Martin Luther King's dream that all men be judged by the contents of their character rather [than] by the color of their skin is not only a noble dream but an unattainable fantasy."[18] It is by no means true that the African Americans will always be a socially oppressed group, but as this old hierarchy fades out, a new set of equally nefarious hierarchies will replace it.[19]

However, in my interpretation of history, I find somewhat fewer reasons for despair. It is true that as we evolve socially, we do constantly create new sets of hierarchies. However, these changes do not have to mean merely the replacement of old faces with new ones. While it is true that human society will perhaps never be completely non-hierarchical, a society will enjoy peace as long as these hierarchical groups are porous. As long there is social mobility and the hierarchy is not based on impermeable ascriptive characteristics, we will be saved from the fates of Rwanda, Bosnia, and Nazi Germany. But the question remains whether we will be able to create a world with interchangeable group identities.

In the following sections I argue that the conflict between the two identities is not over. On the one hand, we find a worldwide explosion of individualism that may prevent us from the worst ravages of collective madness. Yet, on the other hand, the forces of collectivism remain very much alive. Societies based on individual values leave large, gaping holes as some are left behind in the race for material accumulation. Such disparities create conditions for new political entrepreneurs to emerge with renewed calls of the collective based on values of race, religion, and language.

REIGN OF THE INDIVIDUAL: THE JUGGERNAUT

The history of human social evolution has been one of constant struggle between a collective "us" and the jostling amalgam of "me"s. However, when the comfort of the collective is pushed to an extreme, it quickly becomes confining to the individual soul. The very purpose of the Renaissance was to free the individual from the constriction of the ideologies of the collective. After the fall of the Soviet Union and a global trend toward democratization, Francis Fukuyama proclaimed in his popular book, *The End of History,* that individualism has won its dialectical battle with collectivism.[20] Let me examine why we cannot believe that an end of history of this dialectical evolution will come to an end any time soon.

The list of victories of individual values has simply been spectacular in the West. And, in the Western cultural tradition, the United States represents the epitome of individualism. Anyone visiting the United States is struck by the importance given to the individual, even in infancy. We may recall the seventeenth-century manual on child rearing prescribing the conquering of the "will of the child" with the most liberal use of the cane.[21] Compare it with the prevailing philosophies of early childhood development of today. For example, consider the following dialogue between a mother and a child shown with the help of cartoon characters in one popular book on parent-child relationships.[22] In the set of drawings, a child, who looks between six and eight years old, and his mother are having the following ideal conversation regarding the problem of the former not coming home on time from play in the evening:

Mother: I have been thinking that it probably isn't easy for you to leave your friends when you're having fun.

Child: Yeah!

Mother: On the other hand, I worry when you're late. Let's put our heads together and see if we can come up with some ideas that would be good for both of us.

Child: I'll come home at 6:30 and you won't worry.

The point of this blissful exchange is to present the authors' notion of an ideal method of conflict resolution within a family: First you present the current situation to the child, then make it clear to the child that you understand her or his desires. And, after you have articulated your own needs, you come to a mutually agreeable conclusion. A product of a different time and culture, this rather illuminating interaction between a mother and a child stands in stark contrast with my recollection of a much abbreviated motherly monologue: "Make sure you come back at 6:30—sharp." The liberal view of according equal status to every individual, even to a child, is endemic to the culture and creed of individualism. This has been a fundamental building block of American national identity and character. As Samuel Huntington points out:

Historically, American identity has had two primary components: culture and creed. The first has been the values and institutions of the original settlers, who were Northern European, primarily British, and Christian, primarily Protestant. The culture included most importantly the English language and traditions concerning relations between church and state and the place of an individual in the society. . . . The second component of American identity has been a set of universal ideas and principles articulated in the founding documents by American leaders: liberty, equality, democracy, constitutionalism, liberalism, limited government, private enterprise. These constitute what Gunnar Myrdal termed the American Creed.[23]

While no single individual or any society is completely free of the dualism between the individual and the collective, of late the world seems to be moving in the direction of the individual. Today, only China and insignificant Cuba and North Korea carry on their communist pasts. Even in these countries the ideals of communism are severely compromised. China embraces unbridled capitalism in the economic sector, while the Chinese Communist Party maintains the monopoly power on politics. Among Islamic fundamentalist nations like Iran, Saudi Arabia, and Kuwait, only Iran remains defiant of the West. Saudi Arabia had to open its soil, untouched until recently by nonbelievers, to U.S. troops during the Gulf War. Kuwait had to depend upon the Western alliance for its very existence. Even in Iran there are visible signs of cracks in its fundamentalist edifice. The election of a "moderate" cleric and his defiant appointment of women to his cabinet signals a shift from the rules of the previous enforcers of strict Koranic laws.

Karl Marx saw the onslaught of rampant capitalism bringing down a collective society nearly 150 years ago. In *The Manifesto of the Communist Party*, he colorfully described the process by which a primitive society, based on its tradition of collective values, is replaced by a capitalist one:

> The bourgeoisie, by the rapid improvement in all instruments of production, by the immediate facilitated means of communication, draws all, even the most barbarian, nations into civilization. The cheap prices of its commodities are the heavy artillery with which it batters down all Chinese walls. . . . In other words, it creates a world in its own image.[24]

Today, the world is connected from end to end with satellite communication links and cable connections. The preponderance of e-mail and the Internet is evident in just about every corner of the globe. Looking at the new world, it leaves little doubt as to who the current winner is in the age-old conflict between the two identities. As we travel around the world, we are struck by its assimilation into one broad cultural pulp. The buildings in downtowns all over the world are beginning to look similar. The supermarkets and the department stores display their wares in a strangely familiar way. Food, clothing, and cultural mores seem to converge toward the West. People in Bangladesh or Bolivia or Botswana, or at least the elite section of the populace, wear the latest Western fashions, listen to rap music, watch MTV and CNN, and worry about the ups and downs in the Dow Jones Industrial Average. This unprecedented assimilation may give the impression of a Western cultural juggernaut pulverizing collective identities of race, religion, and nationalism, steamrolling the entire world into one giant parking lot of individuals. As the forces of the collective retreat, we may have finally abandoned the path to collective madness. Or have we?

In a World Without Enemies: Giddy Globalization

It is indeed a strange new world. Standing at the beginning of the third millennium, we seem to find an unprecedented world of never-ending bliss. It is a world without a defined enemy. For the first time in history, the United States can look across the horizon and see nothing terribly menacing. Samuel B. Huntington explores this unknown land without enemies. With Rabbit Angstrom, a central character in some of John Updike's novels, Huntington asks: "Without the cold war, what's the point of being an American?"[25] In other words, what will it be like to be an American without the threatening "other"? What kind of a world will it be without an identifiable enemy? Extending Angstrom's question, we may also conjecture whether the world will continue to exist without the forces of the collective; can we expect to see an unopposed reign of individualism, pushed to its extreme end? Meta-theories of social evolution conclude with a description of the utopian end. It is indeed curious to note that the nineteenth-century constructs of neoclassical economics, as well as those of its ideological rival, Marxism, forecast a similar destiny where the individual reigns supreme, with the state governments withering away. Is that distant destiny, the Promised Land of the nineteenth-century political philosophers, in sight?

Before trying to answer this profound question, I would like to first ask if it is conceivable to have a society without a collective. Then, based on world political and economic trends, I would conjecture how likely is it that the ideology of the collective would rise like a phoenix from the ashes, somewhere, somehow.

The Incoherent Society

If the American creed and culture, in their extreme form, become universal, the first casualty is collectivism. Can a society of individuals survive without the collective? In our social and political existence we are in constant need of our collective selves. The most glaring example of this need is reflected in foreign policy. Although all collective actions require the presence of a collective identity, when it comes to an entire nation, perhaps no area of collective action requires the strong presence of a collective identity more than the formulation of foreign policy, particularly as it pertains to overseas military action. In the arena of foreign policy, we act as a single unit—a nation, a people, a unified political entity. In formulating foreign policy, a nation must speak with one voice to articulate its national interest. Therefore, the pluralism that we accept and even promote in our domestic policies is often abandoned at the shores of the nation. When a nation sends its troops abroad on a mission that may require the ultimate sacrifice, an unequivocal definition of national interest is in order. This articulation of national interest is greatly aided by the existence of a clear and present danger from an ominous enemy.

Thus, for a nation to feel united with a common purpose, it must have a shared enemy. Huntington argues that if there is no enemy in sight, it will be extremely difficult to conduct foreign policy. A president's foreign policy becomes widely accepted in times of war or when people are aware of an enemy. For instance, when Saddam Hussein occupied Kuwait and thereby threatened the world oil supply, President George Bush was able to forge an unprecedented coalition of disparate nations in opposition to Iraq. In contrast, without a clear enemy in sight, his policy to help war-torn Somalia proved to be absolutely disastrous. The death of each soldier was flashed on U.S. television screens and, predictably, opposition quickly grew against the U.S. effort. Saddam Hussein was correct in his assessment of a society based on individualism. The United States, based squarely on individual values, does not have the "staying power" to absorb the high costs of military intervention abroad where no immediate threat to the country is present. The days of Lord Tennyson are long gone. The Light Brigade charges no more for the glory of the nation. On the eve of the Gulf War, Saddam diagnosed the problem correctly, but failed to deliver the prescribed medication of a prolonged war to the United States and the allied forces by engaging them in a "mother of all wars."

DISTANT THUNDER: THE RISE OF COLLECTIVISM

Without the presence of a collective identity, an individual is often lost. We may be biologically destined to form groups, seek acceptance within a larger entity, and consciously or unconsciously attempt to continue our gene pool. Recent developments in biology as well as cognitive sciences are unraveling the mysteries of human perception and the process of decision making. Underneath our civilized exterior, we do not consciously recognize the call of the wild. It has been our experience that throughout history we have found comfort in the existence of an enemy. When there has been one, we have felt united, bathed in the warm glow of camaraderie and fellowship; when there has been none, we have sought an enemy within our own ranks.

Huntington points out that after the threat of the British dissipated, America descended into the depths of fratricide during the Civil War.[26] The end of the Cold War may revive what he calls "ethnic politics." We may revert to our narrower identity and form groups within our own kinds. In fact, recent studies warn us against a new harvest of rage coming, not from African Americans, but from increasingly marginalized groups of whites pushed out by the ever widening technology gap and its consequent problems.[27]

Today, the changing world offers many reasons to form groups based on ascriptive grounds. Trends in the relative distribution of income tell a story of growing disparity between rich and poor nations. Table 8.1, which presents data from a sample of nations around the world, puts the development effort of the lowest-income nations in perspective, showing their per capita GDP as a percentage of that of the United States. Each country's purchasing power parity (PPP) index was measured against the United States for 1987 through 1997. Table 8.1 shows the performance of the least developed countries in the catch-up game with the United States and indicates a growing income gap. I have defined a loss of 10% or more as "catastrophic decline," between 5 and 9.9% as "rapid decline," and between 2.1 and 4.9% as "moderate decline." Countries falling between −2% and +2% stagnation. By this measure, nearly 90% of the countries in the sample faced stagnation or worse. This table does not even include the worst of the war-torn nations, such as Afghanistan, Angola, Algeria, Mozambique, Somalia, Yugoslavia, and others. Because of the paucity of information, it also does not include nations such as Iran, Iraq, and North Korea. We should keep in mind that this gap between the rich and the poor nations is likely to widen much further in the years to come. In my previous work, I emphasized the relationship linking economic growth with politi-

Table 8.1
Purchasing Power Parity Estimates of Sample of Nations as a Percentage of
the U.S. GDP per Capita

Growth Performance	Rate (1987–97)	Number of Countries	Cumulative Percentage of Developing Countries
Catastrophic decline	> −10.0%	11	12.8
Rapid decline	−5.0% to −9.9%	7	20.9
Moderate decline	−2.1% to −4.9%	39	66.3
Stagnation	−2.0% to +2.0%	23	87.2
Moderate growth	+2.1% to 4.9%	2	93.0
Rapid growth	+5.0% to 9.9%	3	95.3
Spectacular growth	> +10.0%	4	100.0

*Includes rounding off errors
Source: World Bank, *World Development Report, 1998–99.*

cal instability.[28] As economic opportunities shrink, the resulting condition helps creates political instability. Political instability, in turn, sets a nation back on its developmental path. Also, there are other telltale signs of a brewing disaster. A recent UNICEF annual report finds a rapidly widening gap in literacy rates among children.[29] The survey indicates that as the the third millennium approached, nearly a billion people, a sixth of the world's population, were illiterate. The study predicts that the literacy gap will grow significantly in this century because only one in every four children in the poorest nations is now in school. The study also noted that widespread ethnic conflict has made refugees of millions of children and destroyed their schools at a time when international aid for education projects is decreasing.

As stark as the picture may appear from these renditions, they do not even tell the full story. The most glaring shortcoming of a free market system is that it fails to protect those who need protection the most. The gap between the rich and the poor is growing not only between nations but also within the most developed parts of the world. Although the British Empire, through its exploitative colonial rule, brought unimaginable riches to England, prosperity eluded most at the bottom. In the 1850s, when the entire nation was bristling with pride over its far-flung empire, an insightful Karl Marx saw in colonial expansion the exploitation of British commoners. In a series of articles, he pointed out that while a small group of individuals were benefiting from the fruits of colonialism, as far as the British public was concerned the cost of administrating India far exceeded the revenue.[30] Nearly a century and a half later, facing a brand new world gone giddy over globalization, we see similar patterns of income gap within the Western nations. As the industrialized West in general, and the United States in particular, becomes wealthier, the expanding economies are leaving significant sections of their populations behind in the race for economic prosperity. Global trade agreements such as the General Agreement on Tariffs and Trade (GATT) and the North American Free Trade Agreement (NAFTA) are creating a huge expansion in foreign trade, but working-class wages remain depressed in the lands of plenty.[31]

For instance, a recent study shows that in the United States, the income gap between rich and poor families with children has significantly widened during the last two decades.[32] The most significant finding of the study is that the income gap is not only increasing but also is pervasive in every state. Since the late 1970s the median household income of the lowest 20% of the population has taken a nosedive compared to that of the top 20%. For instance, in 1979, the bottom 20% of the U.S. population had 5.4% of the national income. In 1989, it went down to 4.6%, and in 1997 it registered a measly 4.2%. These ratios, however appalling they may appear, may significantly understate the actual differences. This is because these data include only earned income and do not consider income from capital gains as well as individual income earnings above $100,000. Without considering asset values, the income gap is certainly much worse than it looks.

Around 300 B.C., Aristotle professed that revolutions are spawned in a society divided into two groups, haves and have-nots. In contrast, a society finds political stability when the ranks of the middle class are strengthened. Evidence suggests that the prophecies of the old sage still hold water. New technology is fast creating societies with extreme distributions of income and wealth. Today's industrial economies are creating new jobs at a dazzling speed. At the same time, the character of the job market has also changed radically. In order to be nimble, few corporations are creating full-time positions. Instead, the vast majority of new jobs being created are part-time positions. Part-time status, unfortunately, creates a different set of social problems. An employer does not provide many benefits, such as pension plans or health insurance, for part-time workers. Neither do the wages of part-time workers keep pace with those of full-time employees. In order to survive, today many have to take more than one job, increasing commuting time and other associated costs, hidden and exposed. None of these developments is conducive to family stability. Since it is reasonable to assume that children's performance in school is directly related their family stability, we are witnessing a large number of children dropping out of school. Even a couple of decades ago, young people without a college education could reasonably expect to find their entry into the middle class through union-set, relatively high paying jobs in the manufacturing sector. However, as these jobs are being exported abroad, children born outside an increasingly narrowing privileged class will be condemned to a permanent state of economic deprivation. None of these developments portends good news for future social stability.

In fact, in 1998 an influential blue ribbon panel on international terrorism was assembled with bipartisan support from the president of the United States and House Republicans. After a year of work, the U.S. Commission on National Security, 21st Century, drew a somber conclusion: "America's military superiority will not protect it from hostile attacks on our homeland. Americans will likely die on American soil, possibly in large numbers."[33] Although many experts raise the specter of an apocalyptic attack by terrorist groups with nuclear, chemical, and biological weapons, it is clear that while such possibilities attract instant attention, a great deal of damage can be wrought by using simple, readily available conventional devices.[34] Also, as the handiwork of Timothy McVeigh and Terry Nichols has pointed out, threats to American lives do not need to come from abroad. Given the right opportunity, mass hate can find its expression next door to us.

THE GOLDILOCKS SOLUTION

As social animals we are born with a duality of identities: individual and collective. Western values and culture are based on individual freedom, while the forces of communism, religious fundamentalism, and ultra-nationalism promote collectivism. In the West, we recognize the inalienable rights of the individual. But rooted deep in our biology and psychology is our desire to form groups. We join groups for many reasons; groups serve our emotional needs to bond with fellow members of our species, our subliminal needs to preserve our gene pool, our need to feel secure, and our need to acquire goods of personal welfare through collective actions. However, in attaining these universal goals, groups can be benevolent or malevolent. Our entire social existence, with all its good and bad, blessings and curses, is the result of the dynamic interaction between the two identities.

It is easy to be concerned. In "The Coming Anarchy" Robert Kaplan draws a frightening picture of how the social fabric of our planet is being destroyed by scarcity, overpopulation, tribalism, and disease.[35] Indeed, those of us fortunate enough to be living in relative peace and prosperity may think of ourselves as riding a very long stretch limousine in the dead of night through the roughest part of town. We simply pray that our lifeboat in the turbulent water of unspeakable savagery does not spring a leak.

The unknown is always a cause of fear and anxiety. The enemy that we know, however powerful, often makes us believe that we will be able to handle it. But it is the one that is lurking behind the next dark corner of the future that worries us. We hear it breathing heavily, hiding just beyond the next turn, ready to pounce upon the unsuspecting. Judging from our past and based on current trends, it is highly probable that in the coming decades in many parts of the world, people will respond to the siren song of sociopaths like Jim Jones or demagogues like Radovan Karadzic, or Adolf Hitler. We can only hope that when it happens, the rest of us will have the will and the wisdom to deal with them properly.

We must recognize that we are born with a duality of identities. As the pendulum swings hard in one direction, a counterforce is sure to build up from within the social structure to push it back. When we recognize this and view the world with a broader perspective, we will see that these dialectics will continue to operate untill we are no more on this planet. The biblical account of paradise lost portrays human desire to seek knowledge of the self outside the bounds of the collective. The story is perhaps less one of paradise lost than of paradise outgrown. Once we left Eden, there was no going back. Yet, as we come out of the comfort of the collective and accept our own responsibility, we must realize that we also seek meaning beyond our narrow selves. We need to realize that our fulfillment comes not only through our personal achievements but also through what we make of our society, our entire planet. Like Goldilocks, in the jungle of life, we look for a bowl of porridge that is not too hot nor too cold; we are indeed destined to seek a balance between our dual identities, forever and inevitably.

NOTES

1. Foucault (1970: xxiii).
2. Arrow (1987: 233).
3. For one of the few examples of such a connection, see Bushnell et al. (1991).
4. See Szasz (1974).
5. With the discovery of the varied biochemistry of insanity, Szasz has somewhat modified his original claims. For one of the latest examples of his thinking, see his essays in Edwards (1997). Also see Szasz (1994).
6. See Hofstadter (1965).
7. See Glass (1985: 38).
8. Ibid., 61.
9. For a more psychodynamic perspective on this, see Post and Robins (1993, 1995, 1997).
10. Redlich (1998: 483).
11. See Migdal (1988).
12. Quoted in Prunier (1995: 57).
13. For a public choice explanation of benefit-based group formation, see Ostrom (1990).
14. Krugman (1994: 206).
15. For an excellent discussion, see Hedstrom and Swedberg (1998).
16. Popper (1968: 5).
17. See Sidanius (1993: 183–224). Also see, Sidanius and Pratto (1991); Sidanius, Devereux, and Pratto (1991).
18. See Sidanius (1993: 214).
19. See Sidanius and Pratto (1999).
20. See Fukuyama (1992).

21. See Chapter 2, note 17.
22. See Faber and Mazlish (1980: 47).
23. See Huntington (1997: 28–29).
24. See Marx and Engels (1848: Chapter 1, 64–65).
25. Huntington (1997: 29).
26. See ibid.
27. See Dyer (1997).
28. Dipak Gupta (1990).
29. UNICEF (1999).
30. See K. Marx (1859). Also see Avineri (1969: 18–24).
31. Jagdish Bhagwati has exposed this dangerous trend in a series of books and articles. For instance, see Bhagwati and Kosters (1994), Bhagwati and Krueger (1995), and Bhagwati and Hudec (1996).
32. Study by the Washington, D.C. based Center for Budget and Policy Priorities. See Phillips (1997: B2).
33. Kreisher (1999).
34. See Rapoport (1999, 1988); Sprinzak (1998).
35. See Kaplan (1994).

BIBLIOGRAPHY

Abel, Theodore. (1938). *Why Hitler Came to Power: An Answer Based on the Original Life Stories of Six Hundred of His Followers.* New York: Prentice-Hall.

———. (1965). *The Nazi Movement.* New York: Atherton.

Abrams, D., and M. Hogg (eds.). (1990). *Advances in Social Identity Theory.* New York: Harvester Wheatsheaf.

Adelman, Howard. (1996). "Preventing Post–Cold War Conflicts: What Have We Learned? The Case of Rwanda." Paper presented at the International Studies Association Annual Meeting, San Diego, California, April 17.

Adelman, Howard, Astri Suhrke, and Bruce Jones. (1996). *The International Response to Conflict and Genocide: Lessons from the Rwanda Experience. Study #2, Early Warning and Conflict Management.* Copenhagen: Joint Evaluation of Emergency Assistance to Rwanda.

Adorno, T. W., E. Frenkel-Brunswick, D. J. Levinson, and R. N. Sanford. (1950). *The Authoritarian Personality.* New York: Harper & Row.

Ajzen, Icek. (1991). "The Theory of Political Behavior." *Organizational Behavior and Human Decision Process, 50,* 179–211.

Ajzen, Icek, and Martin Fishbein. (1980). *Understanding Attitudes and Predicting Social Behavior.* Englewood Cliffs, NJ: Prentice-Hall.

Akerlof, George. (1976). "The Economics of Caste and of the Rat Race and Other Woeful Tales." *Quarterly Journal of Economics, 90,* 599–617.

Akerlof, George A., and Rachel E. Kranton. (2000). "Economics and Identity." *Quarterly Journal of Economics, 125*(3): 715–54.

Akhtar, Salman. (1999, June). "The Psychodynamic Dimensions of Terrorism." *Psychiatric Annals, 29* (6), 350–56.

Akhtar, Salman, and J. A. Thompson. (1982). "Overview: Narcissistic Personality Disorder." *American Journal of Psychiatry, 139*, 12–20.

Alchian, Armen A., and Harold Demsetz. (1972, December). "Production, Information Costs, and Economic Organization." *American Economic Review, 62*, 777–95.

Alcock, John. (1984) *Animal Behavior: An Evolutionary Approach.* Sunderland, MA: Sinauer Associates.

Alker, Hayward. (1994, July). "Early Warning Models and/or Preventive Information System." In T. Gurr and B. Harff (eds.), "Early Warning of Communal Conflicts and Humanitarian Crises: Proceedings of a Workshop." *Journal of Ethno-Development, 4*, 117–23.

Anderson, Benedict. (1983). *Imagined Communities: Reflections on the Origin and Spread of Nationalism.* London: Verso.

Andreoni, J. (1989). "Giving with Impure Altruism." *Journal of Political Economy, 97*, 1447–58.

———. (1990). "Impure Altruism and Donations to Public Goods: A Theory of Warm-Glow Giving." *Economic Journal, 100*: 464–77.

Arendt, H. (1963). *Eichmann in Jerusalem: A Report on the Banality of Evil.* New York: Viking Press.

Aristotle. (1984). *Politics.* Translated, and with an introduction, notes, and glossary by Carnes Lord. Chicago: University of Chicago Press.

Armstrong, J. S. (1978). "Forecasting with Econometric Methods: Folklore Versus Facts." *Journal of Business, 51*, 549–600.

Aronson, Elliot. (1984). *The Social Animal.* 4th ed. New York: W. H. Freeman.

Arrow, Kenneth. (1963). *Social Choice and Individual Values.* 2nd ed. New York: John Wiley. (Originally published in 1951.)

———. (1987). *Arrow and the Ascent of Modern Economic Theory.* Ed. G. Feiwel. London: Macmillan.

Asch, Solomon E. (1951). "Effects of Group Pressure upon the Modification and Distortion of Judgments." In H. Guetzkow (ed.), *Groups, Leadership and Men.* Pittsburgh: Carnegie Press.

Atkinson, Stella M. (1979). "Case Study on the Use of Intervention Analysis Applied to Traffic Accidents." *Journal of Operations Research Society, 30*(7), 651–59.

Avineri, Shlomo (ed.). (1969). *Karl Marx on Colonialism and Modernization: His Dispatches and Other Writings on China, India, Mexico, the Middle East and North Africa.* Garden City, NY: Anchor Books.

Axelrod, Robert. (1984). *The Evolution of Cooperation.* New York: Basic Books.

Ball, George. (1982). *The Past Has Another Pattern: Memoirs.* New York: W. W. Norton.

Banerjee, Sumanta. (1980). *In the Wake of Naxalbari: A History of the Naxalite Movement in India.* Calcutta: Subarnarekha.

Banfield, Edward (1968). *The Un-Heavenly City: The Nature and the Future of Our Urban Crisis.* Boston: Little, Brown.

Barber, Benjamin F. (1995). *Jihad vs. McWorld: How the Panet Is Both Falling Apart and Coming Together and What It Means for Democracy.* New York: Times Books, Random House.

Baron, Lawrence. (1995). "The Moral Minority: Psycho-Social Research on the Righteous Gentiles." In Franklin Littell, Alan Berger, and Hubert Locke (eds.),

What Have We Learned? Telling the Story and Teaching the Lessons of the Holocaust. Papers of the 20th Anniversary Scholars' Conference. Symposium Series, Volume 30. Lewiston: Edwin Mellen Press, 139–59.

———. (1996) "Religious and Secular Insights into 'Righteous Gentile.' " Review Essay. *Shofar*, 14 (Winter), 96–105

Batson, Daniel C. (1991). *The Altruism Question: Toward a Social-Psychological Answer.* Hillsdale, NJ: L. Erlbaum.

Becker, Gary. (1976a) "Altruism, Egoism, and Genetic Fitness: Economics and Sociobiology." *Journal of Economic Literature.* 14, 817–26.

———. (1976b). *Economic Approaches to Human Behavior.* Chicago: University of Chicago Press.

———. (1996). *Accounting for Taste.* Cambridge, MA: Harvard University Press.

Becker, Gary S., and William M. Landes (eds.). (1974). *Essays in the Economics of Crime and Punishment.* New York: National Bureau of Economic Research and Columbia University Press.

Belting, Hans. (1994). *Likeness and Presence: A History of the Images Before the Era of Art.* Translated by Edmund Jephcott. Chicago: University of Chicago Press.

Bentham, Jeremy. (1963). *An Introduction to the Principles of Morals and Legislation.* [Originally published in 1823.] New York: Hafner.

Berkeley, Bill. (1994, August 22). "Sounds of Violence." *The New Republic*, 18.

Bernanke, Ben. (1983, June). "Non-Monetary Effects of the Financial Collapse in the Propagation of the Great Depression." *American Economic Review*, 257–76.

Bhagwati, Jagdish N., and Robert E. Hudec (eds.). (1996). *Fair Trade and Harmonization: Prerequisites for Free Trade?* Cambridge, MA: MIT Press.

Bhagwati, Jagdish, and Marvin H. Kosters (eds.). (1994). *Trade and Wages: Leveling Wages Down?* Washington, DC: AEI Press.

Bhagwati, Jagdish, and Anne O. Krueger. (1995). *The Dangerous Drift to Preferential Trade Agreements.* Washington, DC: AEI Press.

Blaug, Mark. (1968). *Economic Theory in Retrospect.* Rev. ed. Homewood, IL: Richard D. Irwin.

———. (1980). *The Methodology of Economics: Or How Economists Explain.* Cambridge Surveys of Economic Literature. Cambridge: Cambridge University Press.

Bloodworth, Dennis. (1982). *The Messiah and the Mandarins: Mao Tsetung and the Ironies of Power.* New York: Atheneum.

Bloom, Allan. (1987). *The Closing of the American Mind: How Higher Education Has Failed Democracy and Impoverished the Souls of Today's Students.* New York: Simon and Schuster.

Bond, Doug. (1997). *FRED.* Weston, MA: Virtual Research Associates.

Bond, Doug, and Joe Bond. (1995). *PANDA Codebook.* Boston: Center for International Affairs. Harvard University.

Bond, Doug, Craig Jenkins, Charles Taylor, and Kurt Schock. (1996). *Contours of Political Conflict: Issues and Prospects for Automated Development of Events Data.* Boston: Center for International Affairs, Harvard University.

Boorstin, Daniel J. (1983). *The Discoverers.* New York: Random House.

Boutros-Ghali, Boutros. (1992, June 17). *Agenda for Peace.* New York: United Nations.

Box, G.E.P., and G. M. Jenkins. (1976). *Time Series Analysis Forecasting and Control*. Rev. ed. San Francisco: Holden-Day.

Braungart, Richard G. (1984). "Historical and Generational Patterns of Youth Movements: A Global Perspective." *Comparative Social Research*, 7, 231.

Bredin, Jean-Denis. (1986). *The Affair: The Case of Alfred Dreyfus*. Translated by Jeffrey Mehlman. New York: G. Braziller.

Brehm, John, and Scott Gates. (1997). *Working, Shirking, and Sabotage: Bureaucratic Response to a Democratic Public*. Ann Arbor: University of Michigan Press.

Brunswick, Egon. (1956). *Perception and the Representative Design of Experiments*. Berkeley: University of California Press.

Buchanan, James M. (1987). *Public Finance in Democratic Process: Fiscal Institutions and Individual Choice*. Chapel Hill, NC: University of North Carolina Press.

Bueno de Mesquita, Bruce. (1981). *The War Trap*. New Haven, CT: Yale University Press.

———. (1984). "Forecasting Policy Decisions: An Expected Utility Approach to Post-Khomeini Iran." *PS* (Spring), 226–36.

———. (1985, March). "The War Trap Revisited." *American Political Science Review*, 79, 156–77.

Bueno de Mesquita, Bruce, David Newman, and Alvin Rabushka. (1985). *Forecasting Political Events*. New Haven: Yale University Press.

Buford, Bill. (1992). *Among the Thugs*. New York: Norton.

Bull, Hedley. (1986). "International Theory: The Case for a Classical Approach." In John A. Vasquez (ed.), *Classics of International Relations*. Englewood Cliffs, NJ: Prentice-Hall.

Bushnell, P. Timothy, Vladimir Shlapenkokh, Christopher Vanderpool, and Jayaratnam Sundaram. (1991). *State Sponsored Terror: The Case of Violent Repression*. Boulder, CO: Westview Press.

Bwy, D. P. (1968). "Political Instability in Latin America: The Cross-Structural Test of a Causal Model." *Latin American Research Review*, 3, 17–66.

Campbell, Joseph. (1968). *The Hero with a Thousand Faces*. New York: Pantheon Books

Caplan, N. (1970). "The New Ghetto Man: A Review of Recent Empirical Findings." *Journal of Social Issues*, 26, 59–73.

Cappella, Joseph N., and Kathleen H. Jamieson. (1997). *Spiral of Cynicism: The Press and the Public Good*. New York: Oxford University Press.

Carnegie Corporation of New York. (1997). "Carnegie Commission Report on Prevention of Deadly Conflict: Second Progress Report." New York: Carnegie Corporation.

Castiglia, Christopher. (1996). *Bound and Determined: Captivity, Culture-Crossing, and White Womanhood from Mary Rowlandson to Patty Hearst*. Chicago: University of Chicago Press.

Central Intelligence Agency. (1994). *The World Factbook: 1994–95*. Washington, DC: Brassey's.

Chalk, Frank (1995). "Hate Radio Versus Democracy Radio: Lessons from United Nations and United States Experience in Cambodia, Mozambique, Rwanda, and Somalia." Unpublished monograph. Department of History, Concordia

University, and Montreal Institute for Genocide and Human Rights Studies, Montreal, Canada.

Chamberlin, William. (1987). *The Russian Revolution, 1917–1918*. Volume 1. Princeton, NJ: Princeton University Press. (Originally published in 1937.)

Chatterjee, Partha. (1993). *The Nation and Its Fragments: Colonial and Post-Colonial Histories*. Princeton, NJ: Princeton University Press.

Chong, Dennis. (1991). *Collective Action and the Civil Rights Movement*. Chicago: University of Chicago Press.

———. (1993). "How People Think, Reason, and Feel About Rights and Liberties." *American Journal of Political Science*, 37, 867–99.

———. (1996). "Creating Common Frames of Reference on Political Issues." In Diana C. Mutz, Paul M. Sniderman, and Richard A. Brody (eds.), *Political Persuasion and Attitude Change*. Ann Arbor: University of Michigan Press.

"Choosing a course: In setting Fed's policy, Chairman bets heavily on his own judgment. Greenspan loves statistics, but uses them in a way that puzzles even friends. Some forecasts go awry." (1997, January 27). *Wall Street Journal*, 1.

Christ, C. F. (1951). "A Test of Econometric Model of the United States, 1921–1974." Paper presented at the Conference on Business Cycles. New York: National Bureau of Economic Research.

Christie, Richard, and Marie Jahoda (eds.). (1954). *Studies in Scope and Method of "The Authoritarian Personality": Continuities in Social Research*. Glencoe, IL: The Free Press.

Clark, Lance. (1983). *Early Warning of Refugee Flows*. Washington, DC: Refugee Policy Group.

Cohen, Leonard. (1993). *Broken Bonds: The Disintegration of Yugoslavia*. Boulder, CO: Westview Press.

Cohn, Norman. (1961). *The Pursuit of the Millennium: Revolutionary Messianism in Medieval and Reformation Europe and Its Bearing on Modern Totalitarian Movements*. New York: Harper's.

Cole, Douglas (ed.). (1970). *Twentieth Century Interpretations of Romeo and Juliet*. Englewood Cliffs, NJ: Prentice-Hall.

Coleman, James. (1990). *Foundations of Social Theory*. Cambridge, MA: Belknap.

Combs, Cindy C. (2000). *Terrorism in the Twenty-First Century*. Upper Saddle River, NJ: Prentice-Hall.

Cooper, M. N. (1974). "A Reinterpretation of the Causes of Turmoil: The Effects of Culture and Modernity." *Comparative Political Studies*, 7, 267–91.

Cooper, R. L. (1972). "The Predictive Performance of Quarterly Econometric Models of the United States." In B. C. Hickman (ed.), *Econometric Models of Cyclical Behavior*. New York: National Bureau of Economic Research.

Cory, Gerald, Jr. (1999). "An Alternative Neurobehavioral Model for Theories of Socioeconomic Exchange and Rational Choice." Paper presented at the Annual Meeting of the Society for the Advancement of Behavioral Economics. San Diego, June 12–14.

"Counter-terrorism expert tells of changing threat." (1999, July 24). *San Diego Union Tribune*, A6.

Crelinsten, Ronald. (1993). "In Their Own Words: The World of the Torturer." In Ronald Crelinsten and Alex P. Schmid (eds.), *The Politics of Pain: Torturers and Their Masters*. Leiden: Leiden University, 39–72.

Crelinsten, Ronald, and Alex P. Schmid (eds.). (1993). *The Politics of Pain: Torturers and Their Masters*. Centrum voor Onderzoek van Maatschappelijike Tegenstellingen (COMT). Leiden: Leiden University.

Dahl, Robert. (1971). *Polyarchy: Participation and Opposition*. New Haven: Yale Universiy Press.

Davies, John, and Chad K. McDaniel. (1993). "The Global Events-Data System." In R. L. Merritt, R. G. Muncaster, and D. A. Zines (eds.), *International Events Data Developments*. Ann Arbor: University of Michigan Press.

———. (1996). "Dynamic Data for Early Warning and Ethnopolitical Conflict." Paper presented at the International Studies Association, San Diego. Center for Conflict Management and International Development.

Dawkins, Richard. (1976). *The Selfish Genes*. New York: Oxford University Press.

Deng, Francis. (1995). *War of Visions: Conflict of Identities in the Sudan*. Washington, DC: Brookings Institution.

Desmond, Adrian. (1979). *The Ape's Reflection*. New York: Dial Press.

Dhawan, Vinod. (1999, February 26). "People of Punjab Never Supported Militancy." *India Post*, 18.

Diamond, Jared. (1992). *The Third Chimpanzee: The Evolution and Future of the Human Animal*. New York: HarperCollins.

Diamond, Larry. (1995). *Promoting Democracy in the 1990s: Actors, Instruments, Issues and Imperatives*. A Report to the Carnegie Commission on Preventing Deadly Conflict. Washington, DC: Carnegie Corporation of New York.

Dixit, Avinash, and Barry Nalebuff. (1991). *Thinking Strategically*. New York: W. W. Norton.

DiZerega, Gus. (1999, January 20). "Democracies don't shoot each other." Letters to the Editor. *Wall Street Journal*.

Don't Shoot the Messenger. A Guide for Canadian Journalists on Promoting Press Freedom. North-South Institute. Posted on the internet at *http://www.nsi-ins.ca*

Douglas, Jack, Jr. (1997, August 15). "McVeigh gets death penalty for bombing. Breaks silence with quote from 1928 court opinion." *San Diego Union-Tribune*, A1.

Douglass, Frederick. (1962). *Life and Times of Frederick Douglass: His Early Life as a Slave, His Escape from Bondage, and His Complete History*. New York: Collier Books. (Originally published in 1892.)

Downs, Anthony. (1957). *An Economic Theory of Democracy*. New York: Harper.

Druckman, James N. (1999). "Do Party Cues Limit Framing Effects?" Paper presented at the Mental Models in Social Science Conference, University of California, San Diego, July 29–31.

Duffy, Gavan, Ted R. Gurr, Phillip A. Scrodt, Gottfriend Mayer-Kress, and Peter Brecke. (1996). "An Early Warning System for the United Nations: Internet or Not." *Mershon International Studies Review*, 39, 315–26.

Dunn, John. (1989). *Modern Revolutions: An Introduction to the Analysis of a Political Phenomenon*. Cambridge: Cambridge University Press.

Dunn, William N. (1998). *Public Policy Analysis: An Introduction*. 2nd ed. Englewood Cliffs, NJ: Prentice-Hall.

Dyer, Joel. (1997). *The Harvest of Rage*. Boulder, CO: Westview Press.

Edgeworth, F. Y. (1881). *Mathematical Physics: An Essay on the Application of Mathematics to the Moral Sciences.* London: C. K. Paul.

Edwards, Rem B. (1997). *Ethics of Psychiatry: Insanity, Rational Autonomy, and Mental Health Care.* Amherst, NY: Prometheus Books.

Ekeh, Peter P. (1974). *Social Exchange Theory: The Two Traditions.* Cambridge, MA: Harvard University Press.

Emerson, Richard. (1972). "Exchange Theory, Part I: A Psychological Basis for Social Exchange." In Joseph Berger, Morris Zelditch, and Bo Anderson (eds.), *Sociological Theories in Progress.* Vol. 2. Boston: Houghton Mifflin, 38–57.

Entman, Robert. (1993). "Framing: Toward Clarification of a Fractured Paradigm." *Journal of Communication, 43,* 51–58.

Erickson, Carolly. (1980). *Great Harry: The Extravagant Life of Henry VIII.* New York: Summit Books.

Erikson, Erik. (1968). *Identity, Youth and Crisis.* New York: W. W. Norton.

Esherick, Joseph. (1987). *The Origins of the Boxer Uprising.* Berkeley: University of California Press.

Etzioni, Amitai. (1988). *The Moral Dimension: Toward a New Economics.* New York: The Free Press.

———. (1993). *The Spirit of Community: Rights, Responsibilities, and the Communitarian Agenda.* New York: Crown.

———. (1995). *Rights and the Common Good: The Communitarian Perspective.* New York: St. Martin's Press.

Faber, Adele, and Elaine Mazlish. (1980). *How to Talk So Kids Will Listen: Group Workshop Kit.* New York: Negotiations Institute.

Farley, Christopher J. (1997, November 24). "Kids and Race: A New Poll Shows Teenagers, Black and White, Have Moved Beyond Parents' Views of Race." *Time,* 88–91.

Feagin, Joe R., and Harlan Hahn. (1973). *Ghetto Revolts: The Politics of Violence in American Cities.* New York: Macmillan.

Fein, Helen. (1991). "The Politics of Paranoia: Jonestown and Twentieth Century Totalitarianism." In P. T. Bushnell, V. Shlapentokh, C. Vanderpool, and J. Sundaram (eds.), *State Organized Terror: The Case of Violent Repression.* Boulder, CO: Westview Press.

Feinsod, Ethan. (1981). *Awake in a Nightmare: Jonestown, the Only Eye Witness Account.* New York: W.W. Norton.

Fernbach, D. (ed.). (1974). *Karl Marx: The Revolution of 1884.* New York: Vantage Books.

Fetsinger, Leon. (1957). *A Theory of Cognitive Dissonance.* Evanston, IL: Row, Peterson.

Fishbein, Martin, and Icek Ajzen. (1975). *Belief, Attitude, Intention, and Behavior: An Introduction to Theory and Research.* Reading, MA: Addison-Wesley.

Fisher, Roger, and Willian Ury. (1981). *Getting to Yes: Negotiating Agreement Without Giving In.* Boston: Houghton Mifflin.

Fogelman, Eva. (1994). *Conscience and Courage: Rescuers of Jews During the Holocaust.* New York: Anchor Books.

Fogelson, R. (1971). *Violence as Protest.* Garden City, NY: Doubleday.

Foucault, Michel. (1970). *The Order of Things: An Archaeology of the Human Sciences.* New York: Pantheon Books.

Fox, Richard. (1984). "Urban Class and Communal Consciousness in Colonial Punjab: The Genesis of India's Intermediate Regime." *Modern Asia Studies, 18*, 459–90.

Freedom House. (1995). *Freedom in the World: The Annual Survey of Political Rights and Civil Liberties, 1994–95.* New York: Freedom House.

"French praise Zola's century-old defense of accused spy Dreyfus." (1998, January 14). *San Diego Union Tribune*, A10.

Freud, Sigmund. (1930). *Civilization and Its Discontents.* Translated by J. Reviere. London: Hogarth Press.

Friedman, Max L. (1966). *Zola and the Dreyfus Case: His Defense of Liberty and Its Enduring Significance.* New York: Haskell House.

Friedman, Milton. (1953). *The Essays in Positive Economics.* Chicago: University of Chicago Press.

———. (1962). *Capitalism and Freedom.* Chicago: University of Chicago Press.

Friedman, Milton, and Ana Schwartz. (1963). *A Monetary History of the United States, 1867–1960.* Princeton, NJ: Princeton University Press.

Fritz, Mark. (1994, May 16). "Rwandan villagers defend motives for massacres." *San Diego Union Tribune.*

Frohlich, Norman, and Joe Oppenheimer. (1970, October). "We Get By with a Little Help from My Friends." *World Politics, 23*, 104–20.

Fromm, G., and L. R. Klein. (1973, May). "A Comparison of Eleven Econometric Models of the United States." *American Economic Review*, 385–401.

Fukuyama, Francis. (1992). *The End of History and the Last Man.* New York: The Free Press.

Funk, Wilfred. (1978). *Word Origins and Their Romantic Stories.* New York: Bell.

Gamson, William A., and Andre Modigliani. (1987). "The Changing Culture of Affirmative Action." In Richard D. Braungart (ed.), *Research in Political Sociology.* Vol. 3. Greenwich, CT: JAI Press.

Gardner, E. S., Jr., and D. G. Dannenbring. (1980). "Forecasting with Exponential Smoothing: Some Guidelines for Model Selection." *Decision Sciences, 11*, 370–83.

Gerner, Deborah, Philip Strodt, Ronald Fransisco, and Judith Weddle. (1994). "Machine Coding of Events Using Regional and International Sources." *International Studies Quarterly, 37*, 91–119.

Geshwender, J. A. (1968). "Civil Rights Protests and Riots: A Disappearing Distinction." *Social Science Quarterly, 49*, 479–93.

Geyer, Georgie Anne. (1997, November 24). "Control the media and win Bosnia." *San Diego Union Tribune*, E3.

Ghosh, Partha S. (1996). *The Rise of Political Hinduism in India: Genesis, Prognosis and Implications.* Stiftung Wissenschaft und Politik. Ebenhusen, Germany: Forschungsinstitut für Internationale Politik und Sicherheit.

Glass, James M. (1985). *Delusion: Internal Dimensions of Political Life.* Chicago: University of Chicago Press.

Gleick, J. (1987). *Chaos.* New York: Viking Books.

Goldhagen, Daniel J. (1996). *Hitler's Willing Executioners: Ordinary Germans and the Holocaust.* New York: Alfred A. Knopf.

Goldstein, J., B. Marshall, and J. Schwartz (eds.). (1976). *The My Lai Massacre and Its Cover-up: Beyond the Reach of Law?* New York: The Free Press.

Goodall, Jane. (1986). *The Chimpanzees of Gombe: Patterns of Behavior.* Cambridge, MA: Harvard University Press.

———. (1990). *Through a Window.* Boston: Houghton Mifflin.

———. (1991). "Unusual Violence in the Overthrow of an Alpha Male Chimpanzee in Gombe." In Toshisada Nishida et al. (eds.), *Topics of Primatology.* Vol. 1: *Human Origins.* Tokyo: Tokyo University Press.

Gordenker, Leon. (1986a). "Early Warning: Conceptual and Practical Issues." In K. Rupensinghe and Michiko Kuroda (eds.), *Early Warning and Conflict Resolution.* New York: St. Martin's Press, 1–15.

———. (1986b). "Early Warning of Disastrous Population Movement." *International Migration Review, 20*(2), 170–193.

Gordon, Nicholas. (1994). *Murders in the Mist: Who Killed Dian Fossey?* London: Hodder and Stoughton.

Goss, D., and J. L. Ray. (1965). "A General Purpose Forecasting Simulator." *Management Science, 11*(6), B119–B135.

Gourevitch, Philip. (1998). *We Wish to Inform You that Tomorrow We Will Be Killed with Our Families: Stories from Rwanda.* New York: Farrar, Straus and Giroux.

Granger, C.W.J. (1980). *Forecasting in Business and Economics.* New York: Academic Press.

Gupta, Dipak K. (1990). *The Economics of Political Violence: The Effects of Political Instability on Economic Growth.* New York: Praeger.

———. (1994). *Decisions by the Numbers.* Englewood Cliffs, NJ: Prentice-Hall.

———. (1997). "'Power in Movement' by Sidney Tarrow." Book Review. *Political Psychology, 18*, 181–184.

———. (1998a). "An Early Warning about Political Forecasting: Oracle to Academics." In Susanne Schmeidl and Howard Adelman (eds.), *Early Warning and Early Response.* New York: Columbia International Affairs Online, Columbia University Press. https://www.cc.columbia.edu/sec/dlc/ciao/bookfrm.ht

———. (1998b). *Clash of Identities: Albert W. Johnson Lecture.* San Diego, CA: San Diego State University Press.

———. (1999). *Forecasting of Unique Events: Subjective Assessment of Uncertain Events.* Working Paper, School of Public Administration and Urban Studies, San Diego State University.

———. (2001a). "Economics and Social Psychology: Explaning Collective Action." In Shoshana Gorssbard-Sechtman (ed.), *The Expansion of Economics and Other Disciplines: Toward an Inclusive Social Science.* Armonk, NY: M.E. Sharpe.

———. (2001b). *Analyzing Public Policy: Concepts, Tools and Techniques.* Washington, DC: Congressional Quarterly Press.

Gupta, Dipak K., Richard Hofstetter, and Terry Buss. (1997). "Group Utility in the Micro Motivation of Collective Action: The Case of Membership in the AARP." *Journal of Economic Behavior and Organization, 32*, 301–320.

Gupta, Dipak K., Albert J. Jongman, and Alex P. Schmid. (1994). "Creating a Composite Index for Assessing Country Performance in the Field of Human Rights: Proposal for a New Methodology." *Human Rights Quarterly, 16*, 131–62.

Gupta, Dipak K., M. C. Madhavan, and Andrew Blee (1998). "Democracy, Economic Growth and Political Instability: An Integrated Perspective." *Journal of Socio-Economics, 27*(5): 587–611.

Gupta, Dipak K., and Harinder Singh. (1992). "Collective Rebellious Behavior: An Expected Utility Approach of Behavioral Motivations." *Political Psychology*, *13*(3), 379–406.

Gupta, Dipak K., Harinder Singh, and Tom Sprague. (1993). "Government Coercion of Dissidents: Deterrence or Provocation?" *Journal of Conflict Resolution*, *37*(2), 301–340.

Gupta, Dipankar. (1996). *The Context of Ethnicity: Sikh Identity in a Comparative Perspective*. New Delhi: Oxford University Press.

Gurr, Ted R. (1970). *Why Men Rebel*. New Haven, CT: Yale University Press.

———. (1986). "Persistent Patterns of Repression and Rebellion: Foundations for a General Theory of Political Coercion." In M. P. Karns (ed.), *Persistent Patterns and Emergent Structures in a Waning Century*. New York: Praeger, 149–70.

———. (1993). *Minorities at Risk*. Washington, DC: U.S. Institute for Peace.

Gurr, Ted R., and Barbara Harff. (1996). *Early Warning of Communal Conflicts and Genocide: Linking Empirical Research to International Responses*. Tokyo: United Nations University.

Gurr, Ted R., and M. I. Lichbach. (1979). "Forecasting of Domestic Political Conflict." In J. David Singer and Michael D. Wallace (eds.), *To Augur Well: Forecasting in Social Sciences*. Beverly Hills: Sage.

———. (1986, April). "Forecasting Internal Conflict: A Comparative Evaluation of Empirical Theories." *Comparative Political Studies*, *19*, 3–38.

Gurr, Ted R., and Will Moore. (1996). "State Versus People: Ethnopolitical Conflict in 1980s with Early Warning Forecasts for the 1990s." Paper presented at the International Studies Association annual meeting, San Diego, April 16–20.

Gutteridge, Richard. (1976). *The German Evangelical Church and the Jews, 1879–1950*. New York: Harper & Row.

Hacker, Andrew. (1995). *Two Nations: Black and White, Separate, Hostile, Unequal*. New York: Ballantine Books.

Hardin, Garrett. (1968, December). "The Tragedy of the Commons." *Science*, *16*, 472–81.

Hardin, Russell. (1995). *One for All: The Logic of Group Conflict*. Princeton, NJ: Princeton University Press.

Harff, Barbara. (1984). *Genocide and Human Rights: International Legal and Political Issues*. Denver: Graduate School of International Studies, University of Denver.

———. (1987). "The Etiology of Genocide." In Michael Dobkowski and Isidor Wallimann (eds.), *The Age of Genocide*. Westport, CT: Greenwood Press, 41–59.

———. (1992). "Recognizing Genocides and Politicides." In Helen Fein (ed.), *Genocide Watch*. New Haven: Yale University Press.

———. (1996). "Early Warning of Potential Genocide: The Case of Rwanda, Burundi, Bosnia, and Abkhasia." In Ted Gurr and Barbara Harff, *Early Warning of Communal Conflicts and Genocide: Linking Empirical Research to International Responses*. Tokyo: United Nations University.

Harff, Barbara, and Ted R. Gurr. (1989). "Victims of the State: Genocides, Politicides and Group Repression." *International Review of Victimology*, *1*, 23–41.

Haroun, Ansar. (1999). "Psychiatric Aspects of Terrorism." *Psychiatric Annals,* 29(6), 335–36.

Harrison, Selig. (1990). "Ethnic Conflict in Pakistan: The Baluch, Pashtuns, and Sindhis." In Joe Montville (ed.). *Conflict and Peacemaking in Multiethnic Societies.* Boston: D. C. Heath, 301–326.

Haskin, K. (1980). *Northern Ireland: A Psychological Analysis.* Dublin: Gill and McMillan.

Hayek, Friedrich A. (1988). *The Fatal Conceit: The Errors of Socialism. The Collected Works of F. A. Hayek,* Vol. 1. Ed. W. W. Bartley III. London: Routledge.

Hedstrom, Peter, and Richard Swedberg (eds.) (1998). *Social Mechanisms: An Analytical Approach to Social Theory.* Cambridge: Cambridge University Press.

Heimer, Carol Anne. (1985). *Reactive Risk and Rational Action: Managing Moral Hazard in Insurance Contracts.* Berkeley: University of California Press.

Heisler, Martin O. (1990). "Hyphenating Belgium: Changing State and Regime to Cope with Cultural Division." In Joseph Montville (ed.), *Conflict and Peacemaking in Multiethnic Societies.* Lexington, MA: Lexington Books, 177–195.

Hellman, Peter. (1980). *Avenue of the Righteous.* New York: Atheneum.

Heng, Liang, and Judith Shapiro. (1986). *After the Nightmare.* New York: Alfred A. Knopf.

Hersh, Seymore. (1970). *My Lai 4: A Report on the Massacre and Its Afternmath.* New York: Vintage Books.

Hibbs, Douglas P., Jr. (1973). *Mass Political Violence: A Cross-National Causal Analysis.* New York: Wiley.

Hilberg, Raul. (1992). *Perpetrators, Victims, Bystanders: The Jewish Catastrophe.* New York: Aaron Asher Books.

"Hindu boys join Khalistanis for guns." (1986, October 17). *The Statesman,* Calcutta, 2.

Hinkle, S., and R. Brown. (1990). "Intergroup Comparisons and Social Identity: Some Links and Lacunae." In D. Abrams and M. Hogg (eds.), *Advances in Social Identity Theory.* New York: Harvester Wheatsheaf.

Hirschleifer, J. (1985). "Expanding the Domain of Economics." *American Economic Review,* 75.

Hirschman, Albert O. (1974, February). "Exit, Voice, and Loyalty: Further Reflections and a Survey of Recent Contributions." *Social Science Information, 13,* 7–26.

Ho Chi Minh. (1961). *The Selected Works of Ho Chi Minh.* Hanoi: Foreign Language Publishing House.

Hobsbawm, Erik J. (1981). *Bandits.* Rev. ed. New York: Pantheon Books.

———. (1990) *Nations and Nationalism Since 1780: Programme, Myth, Reality.* Cambridge: Cambridge University Press.

Hoffman, Bruce. (1999). "The Mind of the Terrorist: Perspective from Social Psychology." *Psychiatric Annals,* 29(6), 337–41.

Hofstadter, Richard. (1965). *The Paranoid Style of American Politics and Other Essays.* New York: Alfred A. Knopf.

Holstrom, Bengt. (1982). "Moral Hazard in Teams." *Bell Journal of Economics, 13,* 324–40.

Horowitz, Donald. (1975). "Ethnic Identity." In Nathan Glazer and Daniel Patrick Moynihan (eds.), *Ethnicity: Theory and Experience.* Cambridge, MA: Harvard University Press, 111–140.

———. (1985). *Ethnic Groups in Conflict.* Berkeley: University of California Press.

———. (1990). "Ethnic Conflict: Management for Policymakers." In Joe Montville (ed.), *Conflict and Peacemaking in Multiethnic Societies.* Lexington, MA: D. C. Heath, 115–30.

Hufbauer, Gary Clyde, Jeffrey J. Schott, and Kimberly Ann Elliott. (1990). *Economic Sanctions Reconsidered.* 2nd ed. Washington, DC: Institute for International Economics.

Huff, Darrell. (1954). *How to Lie with Statistics.* New York: W. W. Norton.

Hughes, Candice. (1998, November 1). "Pope calls for objective study of Inquisition: Historical context is sought from scholars." *San Diego Union Tribune,* A26.

Human Rights Watch. (1999). *Leave None to Tell the Story: Genocide in Rwanda.* New York: Human Rights Watch.

Humana, Charles. (1992). *World Human Rights Guide.* Oxford: Oxford University Press.

Huneke, Douglas K. (1985). *The Moses of Rovno.* New York: Dodd, Mead.

Huntington, Samuel P. (1991). *The Third Wave: Democratization in the Late Twentieth Century.* Norman: University of Oklahoma Press.

———. (1996). *The Clash of Civilizations and the Remaking of the World Order.* New York: Simon & Schuster.

———. (1997, September/October). "The Erosion of American National Interests." *Foreign Affairs, 76,* 28–49.

ICPSR. (1994, April). *American National Election Studies Cumulative Data File, 1952–1992.* No. 8475. Ann Arbor: University of Michigan Press.

Iyenger, Shanto. (1993). "An Overview of the Field of Political Psychology." In Shanto Iyenger and William J. McGuire (eds.), *Explorations in Political Psychology.* Durham: Duke University Press.

Iyenger, Shanto, and William J. McGuire (eds.). (1973). *Explorations in Political Psychology.* Durham: Duke University Press.

Janis, Irving. (1972). *Victims of Groupthink: A Psychological Study of Foreign-Policy Decisions and Fiascoes.* Boston: Houghton Mifflin.

Jenkins, Brian. (1982, September). "Statements About Terrorism." *Annals, 463,* 11–23.

Jenkins, Craig J. (1983). "Resource Mobilization Theory and the Study of Social Movements." *Annual Review of Sociology, 9,* 523–53.

Johnson, Chalmers. (1988). "The Democratization of South Korea: What Role Does Democracy Play?" Paper presented at the Second Ilhae-Carnegie Conference on Democracy and Political Institutions, Ilhae Institute, Seoul, South Korea.

Juergensmeyer, Mark. (1984). *Fighting with Gandhi.* San Francisco: Harper & Row.

Jung, Carl J. (1959). *The Archetypes and the Collective Unconscious.* Translated by R. F. C. Hull. Bollingen Series 20, Vol. 9, Part 1. New York: Pantheon Books.

Kahn, Si. (1982). *Organizing: A Guide for Grassroots Leaders.* New York: McGraw-Hill.

Kahneman, Daniel. (1973). *Attention and Effort.* Englewood Cliffs, NJ: Prentice-Hall.

Kahneman, Daniel, Paul Slovic, and Amos Tversky. (1982). *Judgment Under Uncertainty: Heuristics and Biases.* New York: Cambridge University Press.

Kahneman, Daniel, and Amos Tversky. (1984). "Choice, Values, and Frames." *American Psychologist, 39,* 341–50.

Kalt, J. P., and M. A. Zupan. (1984). "Capture and Ideology in the Economic Theory of Politics." *American Economic Review, 74,* 279–300.

Kaplan, Robert. (1994, February) "The Coming Anarchy." *Atlantic Monthly,* 44–76.

———. (1997, December). "Was Democracy a Moment?" *Atlantic Monthly,* 280.

Karatnycky, Adrian. (1995). "The Comparative Survey of Freedom, 1994: Democracies on the Rise, Democracies at Risk." *Freedom Review, 26*(1).

———. (1998, December 27). "Democracy and human rights, despite setbacks, score notable advances." *San Diego Union Tribune,* G-1.

Kauffman, Stuart A. (1995). *At Home in the Universe: The Search for Laws of Self-organization and Complexity.* New York: Oxford University Press.

Kawakami, K., and K. L. Dion. (1993). "The Impact of Salinet Social-Identities on Relative Deprivation and Action Intentions." *European Journal of Social Psychology, 23,* 525–40.

———. (1995). "Social Identity and Affect as Determinants of Collective Action: Toward an Integration of Relative Deprivation and Social Psychology Theories." *Theory and Psychology, 5,* 551–77.

Keeley, Lawrence. (1996). *War Before Civilization: The Myth of the Peaceful Savage.* Oxford: Oxford University Press.

Keen, Sam. (1986). *Faces of the Enemy: Reflections of the Hostile Imagination.* San Francisco: Harper & Row.

Kelly, C. (1993). "Group Identification, Intergroup Perceptions and Collective Action." In W. Stroebe and M. Hewstone (eds.), *European Review of Social Psychology.* Chichester, England: Wiley, 4: 59–83.

Kelly, C., and S. Breinlinger. (1996). *The Social Psychology of Collective Action: Identity, Injustice and Gender.* London: Taylor & Francis.

Kelman, Herbert. (1973). "Violence Without Moral Restraints." *Journal of Social Issues, 29,* 29–61.

———. (1993). "The Social Context of Torture: Policy Process and Authority Structure." In R. D. Crelinsten and A. P. Schmid (eds.), *The Politics of Pain: Torturers and Their Masters.* Leiden: Leiden University.

Kelman, Herbert C., and V. L. Hamilton. (1989). *Crimes of Obedience: Toward a Social Psychology of Authority and Responsibility.* New Haven, CT: Yale University Press.

Kerényi, C. (1976). *Dionysos: Archtypical Image of Indestructible Life.* Translated by Ralph Manheim. Bollingen Series 65-2. Princeton, NJ: Princeton University Press.

Kerner, O. (1968). *Report of the National Advisory Commission on Civil Disorders.* Washington, DC: U.S. Government Printing Office.

Kilduff, Marshall, and Ron Javers. (1978). *The Suicide Cult.* New York: Bantam Books.

Kirby, R. M. (1966). "A Comparison of Short and Medium Range Statistical Forecasting Methods." *Management Science, 4,* 202–10.

Kirscht, J. P., and R. C. Dillehay. (1967). *Dimensions of Authoritarianism.* Lexington, KY: University of Kentucky Press.

Klandermans, Bert. (1997). *The Social Psychology of Protest.* Oxford: Basil Blackwell.

Klandermans, Bert, and D. Oegema. (1987). "Potentials, Networks, Motivations, and Barriers." *American Sociological Review, 52,* 519–31.

Klare, Michael. (1999, January/February). "The Kalashnikov Age." *Bulletin of the Atomic Scientists*, 18–22.

Knowles, Louis L., and Kenneth Prewitt. (1972). "Racism in the Administration of Justice." In C. E. Rasons and J. L. Kuykendall (eds.), *Race, Crime, and Justice*. Pacific Palisades, CA: Goodyear, 13–27.

Kriesher, Otto. (1999, October 3). "Panel warns of turmoil, terrorism for U.S. Need for new national security structure seen." *San Diego Union Tribune*, A27.

Krugman, Paul. (1994). *Peddling Prosperity: Economic Sense and Nonsense in the Age of Diminished Expectations*. New York: W. W. Norton.

Kuper, L. (1984). *Genocide: Its Political Use in the Twentieth Century*. New Haven, CT: Yale University Press.

Kuran, Timur. (1991, June). "Cognitive Limitations and Preference Evaluation." *Journal of Institutional and Theoretical Economics*, 147, 241–73.

———. (1993). "Mitigating the Tyranny of Public Opinion: Anonymous Discourse and the Ethic of Sincerity." *Constitutional Political Economy*, 4(1).

———. (1995a). "The Inevitability of Future Revolutionary Surprises." *American Journal of Sociology*, 100(6), 1528–1551.

———. (1995b). *Private Truths, Public Lies: The Social Consequences of Preference Falsification*. Cambridge, MA: Harvard University Press.

———. (1998a). "Ethnic Dissimilation and Its International Diffusion" in David A. Lake and Donald Rothchild (eds.), *The International Spread of Ethnic Conflict: Fear, Diffusion, and Escalation*. Princeton, NJ: Princeton University Press.

———. (1998b). "Social Mechanisms and Dissonance Reduction." In Peter Hedstom and Richard Swedberg (eds.), *Social Mechanisms: An Analytical Approach to Social Theory*. Cambridge: Cambridge University Press, 147–71.

Lacouture, Jean. (1968). *Ho Chi Minh: A Political Biography*. New York: Vantage Books.

Lakoff, George. (1996). *Moral Politics: What Conservatives Know that Liberals Don't*. Chicago: University of Chicago Press.

Lane, Roger, and John J. Turner, Jr. (eds.). (1983). *Riot, Rout, and Tumult: Readings in American Social and Political Violence*. New York: University Press of America.

Langguth A. J. (1978). *Hidden Terrors: The Truth About U.S. Police Operations in Latin America*. New York: Pantheon Books.

Layton, Deborah. (1998). *Seductive Poison: A Jonestown Survivor's Story of Life and Death in the People's Temple*. New York: Anchor Books.

Le Bon, Gustav. (1960). *The Crowd: A Study of the Popular Mind*. New York: Viking Press, Compass Edition, 1960. (Originally published as *Psychologie des foules* in 1895.)

Lekachman, Robert. (1982). *Greed Is Not Enough: Reaganomics*. New York: Pantheon Books.

Lemarchand, René. (1970). *Rwanda and Burundi*. New York: Praeger.

Lenin, Vladimir I. (1969). *What Is to Be Done?* New York: International Publishers. (Originally published 1902.)

Levine, A. H. (1967, January). "Forecasting Technique." *Management Accounting*.

Lewis, William G. (1987). "Toward Representative Bureaucracy: An Assessment of Black Representation in Police Bureaucracies." Preliminary results of Ph.D. dissertation research. *Public Administration Review*, 49, 257–68.

Lewy, Guenter. (1964). *The Catholic Church and Nazi Germany*. New York: McGraw-Hill.

Lichbach, Mark I. (1985, September). "Protest in America: Univariate ARIMA Models in Post-war Era." *Western Political Quarterly, 38*, 581–608.

———. (1987). "Deterrence or Escalation? The Puzzle of Aggregate Studies of Repression and Dissent." *Journal of Conflict Resolution, 31*, 266–97.

———. (1995) *The Rebel's Dilemma*. Ann Arbor: University of Michigan Press.

———. (1997). "Contentious Maps of Contentious Politics." *Mobilization, 2*(1), 87–98.

Lifton, Robert Jay. (1986). *The Nazi Doctors: Medical Killings and the Psychology of Genocide*. New York: Basic Books.

Lijphart, Arend. (1984). *Democracies: Patterns of Majoritarian and Consensus Government in Twenty-One Countries*. New Haven, CT: Yale University Press.

———. (1990). "The Power-Sharing Approach." In Joseph Montville (ed.), *Conflict and Peacemaking in Multiethnic Societies*. Lexington, MA: Lexington Books, 491–510.

———. (1996, June). "The Puzzle of Indian Democracy: A Consociational Interpretation." *American Political Science Review, 90*, 258–268.

Lind, E. Allan, and Tom R. Tyler. (1988). *The Social Psychology of Procedural Justice*. New York: Plenum Press.

Lipset, Seymour (1960). *The Political Man*. Garden City, NY: Doubleday. Also see the 1981 edition, *Political Man: The Social Bases of Politics*. Baltimore: Johns Hopkins University Press.

———. (1990). *Continental Divide: The Values and Institutions of the United States and Canada*. New Yok: Routledge.

Locke, Michelle (2000, April 6). "Uganda cult deaths painful for survivors of Jonestown." *San Diego Union Tribune*, A3.

London, Perry. (1970). "The Rescuers: Motivational Hypotheses About Christians Who Saved Jews from the Nazis." In L. Berkowitz and J. Macaulay (eds.), Altruism and Helping Behavior: Social Psychological Studies of Some Antecedents and Consequences. New York: Academic Press, 241–50.

Loveman, Mara. (1998). "High-Risk Collective Action: Defending Human Rights in Chile, Uruguay, and Argentina." *American Journal of Sociology, 104*: 477–525.

Lucas, Robert, and Thomas Sargent. (1978). "After Keynesian Economics." In *After the Philips Curve: Persistence of High Inflation and High Unemployment*. Boston: Federal Reserve Bank.

Lupsha, P. (1969). "Explanation of Political Violence: Some Psychological Theories Versus Indignation." *Politics and Society, 2*, 80–104.

Lyons, H., and H. Harbinson. (1986). "Comparison of Political and Non-political Murderers in Northern Ireland, 1974–84." *Medicine, Science and Law, 26*(3), 193–98.

Mack, John E. (1984). "Cultural Amplifier." Paper presented to the Committee on International Affairs at the Fall Meeting of the Group for the Advancement of Psychiatry, White Plains, New York.

MacLean, Paul D. (1990). *The Triune Brain in Evolution: Role in Paleocerebral Functions*. New York: Plenum.

Magida, A. J. (1996). *The Prophet of Rage: A Life of Louis Farrakhan and His Nation*. New York: Basic Books.

Makridakis, S., and M. Hibon. (1982). "The Accuracy of Forecasting: An Empirical Investigation." *Journal of the Royal Statistical Society*, 97–145.

Makridakis, Spyros, Steven C. Wheelwright, and Victor E. McGee. (1983). *Forecasting: Methods and Applications*. New York: John Wiley.

Malcolm, Noel. (1998). *Kosovo: A Short History*. New York: New York University Press.

Mankiw, N. Gregory. (1997). *Macroeconomics*. 3rd ed. New York: Worth.

Mansbridge, Jane. (1990a). "The Rise and Fall of Self-Interest in the Explanation of Political Life." In Jane Mansbridge (ed.), *Beyond Self-Interest*. Chicago: University of Chicago Press.

———, (ed.). (1990b). *Beyond Self-Interest*. Chicago: University of Chicago Press.

Maquet, Jean-Jacques. (1954). *Le Systéme des relations sociales dans le Rwanda ancien*. Tervuren: MCRB.

Margolis, H. (1982). *Selfishness, Altruism and Rationality*. Cambridge: Cambridge University Press.

Marwell, Gerald, and Pamela Oliver. (1984, September). "Social Networks and Collective Action: A Theory of Critical Mass. III." *American Journal of Sociology*, *80*, 402–42.

Marx, Gary T. (1982). "External Efforts to Damage or Facilitate Social Movements: Some Patterns, Explanations, Outcomes, and Complications." In J. Wood and M. Jackson (eds.), *Social Movements: Development, Participation, and Dynamics*, Belmont, CA: Wadsworth, 181–200.

Marx, Karl. (1859, April 30). "Great trouble in Indian finances (I and II)." *New York Daily Tribune*.

Marx, Karl, and Friedrich Engels. (1848). *The Manifesto of the Communist Party*. New York: Modern Library.

Mashaw, Jerry L. (1997). *Greed, Chaos, and Governance: Using Public Choice to Improve Public Law*. New Haven, CT: Yale University Press.

Mason, T. David, and Dale A. Krane. (1989, June). "The Political Economy of Death Squads: Toward a Theory of the Impact of State-Sanctioned Terror." *International Studies Quarterly*, *33*, 175–98.

Massey, Douglas S., and Nancy A. Denton. (1989). "Hypersegregation in U.S. Metropolitan Areas: Black and Hispanic Segregation Along Five Dimensions." *Demography*, *26*, 373–91.

"Mastermind in N.Y. bombing gets life." (1998, January 9). *San Diego Union Tribune*, A2.

McAdam, Doug. (1982). *Political Process and the Development of Black Insurgency*. Chicago: University of Chicago Press.

McAdam, Doug, John McCarthy, and Meyer Zald (eds.). (1996). *Comparative Perspectives on Social Movement*. New York: Cambridge University Press.

McAdam, Doug, Sidney Tarrow, and Charles Tilly. (1996). "To Map Contentious Politics." *Mobilization*, *1*, 17–34.

McCaffrey, Edward J., Daniel Kahneman, and Matthew L. Spitzer. (1995). "Framing the Jury: Cognitive Perspectives on Pain and Suffering Awards." *Virginia Law Review*, *81*, 1341–1420.

McCarthy, John D., and Mayer N. Zald. (1977, May). "Resource Mobilization and Social Movements: A Partial Theory." *American Journal of Sociology*, *82*, 1212–41.

McClelland, J. S. (1989). *The Crowd and the Mob: From Plato to Canetti*. London: Unwin Hyman.

McCone, J. (1969, December 2). *Violence in the City: An End or a Beginning? A Report by the Governor's Commission on the Los Angeles Riots*. Sacramento: State of California.

McDowell, Patrick. (1995, September 28). "Rwanda's genocide included women as killers, say officials." *San Diego Union Tribune*, A12.

McFarland, A. S. (1969). *Power and Leadership in Pluralist Systems*. Stanford, CA: Stanford University Press.

McNees, S. K. (1982, January). "The Role of Macroeconometric Models in Forecasting and Policy Analysis in the United States." *Journal of Forecasting, 1*.

McRae, Kenneth D. (1990). "Theories of Power-Sharing and Conflict Management." In Joseph Montville (ed.), *Conflict and Peacemaking in Multiethnic Societies*. Lexington, MA: Lexington Books, 93–106.

Melson, Robert. (1992). *Revolution and Genocide: On the Origins of the Armenian Genocide and Holocaust*. Chicago: University of Chicago Press.

Melucci, Alberto. (1988). "Getting Involved: Identity and Mobilization in Social Movements." In B. Klandermans (ed.), *From Structure to Action: Comparing Social Movement Research Across Cultures. International Social Movement Research*. Greenwich, CT: JAI Press, 329–48.

———. (1989). *Nomads of the Present: Social Movements and Individual Needs in Contemporary Society*. Philadelphia: Temple University Press.

Merkl, Peter. (1975). *Political Violence Under the Swastika: 581 Early Nazis*. Princeton, NJ: Princeton University Press.

———. (1980). *The Making of a Stormtrooper*. Princeton, NJ: Princeton University Press.

Migdal, Joel. (1988). *Strong Societies and Weak States: State-Society Relations and State Capabilities in the Third World*. Princeton, NJ: Princeton University Press.

Milgram, Stanley. (1974). *Obedience to Authority: An Experimental View*. New York: Harper & Row.

Mill, John Stuart. (1861). *Considerations on Representative Government*. New York: Liberal Arts Press (reprinted 1958).

———. (1967). *Collected Works: Essays on Economy and Society*. Vol. 4. Ed. J. M. Robinson. Toronto: University of Toronto Press.

Mitchell, George J. (1999). *Making Peace*. New York: Alfred A. Knopf.

Moe, Terry. (1980, November). "A Calculus of Group Membership." *American Journal of Political Science, 24*, 593–632.

Montville, Joseph V. (ed.). (1990). *Conflict and Peacemaking in Multiethnic Societies*. Lexington, MA: D. C. Heath.

Moore, Barrington, Jr. (1966). *The Social Origins of Dictatorship and Democracy: Lord and Peasant in the Making of the Modern World*. Boston: Beacon Press.

Moore, Rebecca. (1985). *A Sympathetic History of Jonestown: The Moore Family Involvement in People's Temple*. Lewiston, NY: Edwin Mellen Press.

Moore, Will. (1998). "Repression and Dissent: Substitution, Context, and Timing." *American Journal of Political Science, 42*(3), 851–73.

Morris, Aldon D., and Carol McClurg Mueller (eds.). (1992). *Frontiers in Social Movement Theory*. New Haven, CT: Yale University Press.

Mueller, Dennis C. (1979). *Public Choice*. New York: Cambridge University Press.

Mueller, John, and Karl Mueller. (1999, May/June). "Sanctions of Mass Destruction." *Foreign Affairs, 79*, 43–53.

Mukhoty, Govinda, and Rajni Kothari. (1984). *Who Are the Guilty? Reports of a Joint Inquiry into the Causes and Impact of the Riots in Delhi from 31 October to 10 November*. New Delhi: People's Union for Democratic Rights and People's Union for Civil Liberties.

Muller, E. N., and K. Opp. (1986). "Rational Choice and Rebellious Collective Action." *American Political Science Review, 80*, 471–87.

Muller, J. (1996). *Adam Smith in His Time and Ours*. Princeton, NJ: Princeton University Press.

Musgrave, Richard A., and Peggy Musgrave. (1980). *Public Finance in Theory and Practice*. New York: McGraw-Hill.

Musgrove, Margaret. (1977). *Ashanti to Zulu: African Tradition*. New York: Dial Books for Young Readers.

Muth, John F. (1961). "Rational Expectations and Theory of Price Movements." *Econometrica*, 413–29.

Nagel, Jack H. (1987). *Participation*. Englewood Cliffs, NJ: Prentice-Hall.

Naipaul, Shiva. (1981). *Journey to Nowhere: A New World Tragedy*. New York: Simon and Schuster.

Naipaul, V. S. (1981). *Among the Believers: An Islamic Journey*. New York: Alfred A. Knopf.

———. (1997, May 26). "After the Revolution." *The New Yorker*, 46–69.

Nasrin, Taslima. (1997). *Shame: A Novel*. Translated by Kankabati Dutta. New York: Prometheus Press.

National Research Council. (1989). *A Common Destiny: Blacks and American Society*. Washington, DC: National Academy Press.

Navarro, Marysa. (1989). "The Personal Is Political: Las Madres de Plaza de Mayo." In Susan Eckstein (ed.), *Power and Popular Protest: Latin American Social Movements*. Berkeley: University of California Press.

Naylor, T. H., T. G. Seaks, and D. W. Wichern. (1972). "Box-Jenkins Methods: An Alternative to Econometric Forecasting." *International Statistical Review, 40*(2), 123–37.

Nelson, C. (1972). "The Prediction Performance of the FRB-MIT-PENN Model of the U.S. Economy." *American Economic Review, 62*(5), 902–17.

Newbold, Paul. (1973). "Bayesian Estimation of Box-Jenkins Transfer Function-Noise Models." *Journal of the Royal Statistical Society, 35*(2), 323–36.

Newbold, Paul, and C.W.J. Granger. (1974). "Experience with Forecasting Univariate Time Series and the Combination of Forecasts." *Journal of the Royal Statistical Society*, Series A, *137*, Part 2, 131–65.

Newman, David. (1999). "Real Spaces—Symbolic Spaces: Interrelated Notions of Territory in the Arab-Israel Conflict." In P. Diehl (ed.), *A Road Map to War: Territorial Dimensions of International Conflict*. Nashville, TN: Vanderbilt University Press.

———. (2000). "Boundaries, Territory and Post-Modernism: Toward Shared or Separate Scapes?" Paper presented at "Re-thinking Boundaries: Geopolitics, Identities and Sustainability," Panjab University, Chandigarh, India, February 21–24.

Nkundabagenzi, F. (1961). *Le Rwanda politique (1958–1960)*. Brussels: CRISP.

Nugent, John P. (1979). *White Night*. New York: Rawson, Wade.

Oberschall, Anthony. (1973). *Social Conflict and Social Movements.* Englewood Cliffs, NJ: Prentice-Hall.

Oberschall, Anthony, and H. Kim. (1996). "Identity and Action." *Mobilization, 1,* 63–84.

O'Donnell, James P. (1978). *The Bunker.* Boston: Houghton Mifflin.

Oliner, Pearl, and Samuel Oliner (eds.). (1988). *The Altruistic Personality: Rescuers of Jews in Nazi Europe.* New York: The Free Press.

Olson, Mancur. (1965). *The Logic of Collective Action: Public Goods and the Theory of Groups.* Cambridge, MA: Harvard University Press.

Oppenheimer, Martin, and George Lakey. (1964). *A Manual for Direct Action: Strategies and Tactics for Civil Rights and Other Non-violent Movements.* Chicago: Quadrangle Books.

Ostrom, Elinor. (1990). *Governing the Commons: The Evolution of Institutions for Collective Action.* New York: Cambridge University Press.

———. (1998). "A Behavioral Approach to the Rational Choice Theory of Collective Action: Presidential Address, American Political Science Association, 1997." *American Political Science Review, 92*(1), 1–22.

Owens, John M., IV. (1999, January 20). "Democracies don't shoot each other." Letters to the Editor. *Wall Street Journal.*

Paasi, Anssi. (1996). "Constructing Territories, Boundaries and Regional Identities." In T. Frosberg (ed.), *Contested Territory: Border Disputes at the Edge of the Former Soviet Empire.* Aldershot: Edward Elgar, 42–61.

———. (2000). "Space, Boundaries and the Social Construction of Territorial Identities." Paper presented at "Re-thinking Boundaries: Geopolitics, Identities and Sustainability." Panjab University, Chandigarh, India, February 21–24.

Paldiel, Mordecai. (1986). "Hesed and the Holocaust." *Journal of Ecumenical Studies, 23* (Winter).

Pan, Zhongdang, and Gerald M. Kosici. (1993). "Framing Analysis: An Approach to News Discourse." *Political Communication, 10*: 55–75.

Pearsall, Robert (ed.). (1974). *The Symbionese Liberation Army: Documents and Communications.* Amsterdam: Rodopi.

Pfaff, William. (1993). *The Wrath of Nations: Civilization and the Furies of Nationalism.* New York: Simon & Schuster.

Pfaffenberger, Bryan. (1990). "Ethnic Conflict and Youth Insurgency in Sri Lanka: The Social Origins of Tamil Separatism." In Joseph V. Montville (ed.), *Conflict and Peacemaking in Multiethnic Societies.* Lexington, MA: D. C. Heath, 241–58.

Phelps, Edmund S. (1975). *Altruism, Morality, and Economic Theory.* New York: Russell Sage Foundation.

Phillips, Michael. (1997, December 17). "Income gap between rich and poor grows nationwide." *Wall Street Journal,* B2.

Pizzorno, Allessandro, and Colin Crouch (eds.). (1978). *The Resurgence of Class Conflict in Western Europe Since 1968.* New York: Holmes and Meier.

Plato. (1963). *The Republic.* Edited by James Adam. 2nd ed. Cambridge: Cambridge University Press.

Plattner, Marc F. (1998). "Liberalism and Democracy: Can't Have One Without the Other." *Foreign Affairs, 77*(2), 171–80.

Poliakov, Leon. (1974). *The Aryan Myth: A History of Racist and Nationalist Ideas in Europe.* Translated by Edmund Howard. New York: Basic Books.

Popkin, Samuel. (1979). *The Rational Peasant*. Berkeley: University of California Press.

Popper, Karl R. (1968). *The Logic of Scientific Discovery*. New York: Harper & Row.

Post, Jerrold M., and Kenneth Dekleva. (1996, April). "Radovan Karadzic: The Poet of Death." *Psychiatric Times*, 47–48.

Post, Jerrold M., and Robert S. Robins. (1993). *When Illness Strikes the Leader: The Dilemma of the Captive King*. New Haven, CT: Yale University Press.

————. (1995) *Bosnia: What Happened*. Boston: Addison Wesley.

————. (1997). *Political Paranoia: The Psychopolitics of Hatred*. New Haven, CT: Yale University Press.

Prunier, Gérard. (1995). *The Rwanda Crisis: History of a Genocide*. New York: Columbia University Press.

Ra'anam, Uri. (1990). "The Nation-State Fallacy." In Joseph V. Montville (ed.), *Conflict and Peacemaking in Multiethnic Societies*. Lexington, MA: D. C. Heath, 5–20.

Raine, J. E. (1971, April). "Self-Adaptive Forecasting Considered," *Decision Sciences*, 11–21.

Ramet, Sabrina (1992) *Balkan Babel: Politics, Culture, and Religion in Yugoslavia*. Boulder: Westview Press, 1992.

Rapoport, Amnon, and Gary Borstein. (1989, September). "Solving Public Goods Problems in Competition Between Equal and Un-equal Size Groups." *Journal of Conflict Resolution, 33*, 460–79.

Rapoport, David. (1988). "Messianic Sanctions for Terror." *Comparative Politics, 20*(2), 195–211.

————. (1999). "Terrorists and Weapons of Apocalypse." Unpublished manuscript, Department of Political Science, UCLA.

Rashid, Abdur. (1997, March 15–18). "Averting Famine Through Linking Early Warning with Response Mechanism." Paper presented at the Synergy in Early Warning Research Conference, at York University, Toronto, Canada.

Rasler, Karen. (1996). "Concessions, Repressions, and Political Protest in Iranian Revolution." *American Sociological Review, 61*, 132–52.

Raston, James. (1981). *Our Father Who Art in Hell*. New York: New York Times Books.

Redlich, Fritz. (1998). *Hitler: Diagnosis of a Destructive Prophet*. New York: Oxford University Press.

Reif, Linda. (1986, January). "Women in Latin American Guerrilla Movements." *Comparative Politics, 18*, 147–69.

Reiterman, Tim, and John Jacobs. (1982). *Raven: The Untold Story of the Rev. Jim Jones and His People's Temple*. New York: E. P. Dutton.

Renner, Michael. (1997). *Small Arms, Big Impact*. Washington, DC: World Watch Institute.

Ricks, Thomas E. (1997). *Making the Corps*. New York: Scribner.

Ridely, Jasper. (1983). *Statesman and Saint: Cardinal Wolsey, Sir Thomas More and the Politics of Henry VIII*. New York: Viking Press.

Robins, Robert S., and Jerrold M. Post. (1997). *Political Paranoia: The Psychopolitics of Hatred*. New Haven, CT: Yale University Press.

Romer, Christina. (1986a, June). "Is the Stabilization of the Postwar Economy a Figment of the Data?" *American Economic Review, 76*, 314–34.

———. (1986b, February). "Spurious Volatility in Historical Unemployment Data," *Journal of Political Economy, 94,* 1–37.

Rosenthal, A. (1989). "Broad disparities in votes and polls raising questions." *New York Times,* A1, B14.

Ross, M. (1991). "The Role of Evolution in Ethnocentric Conflict and Its Management." *Journal of Social Issues, 47,* 167–85.

Rothstein, D. A. (1975). "On Presidential Assassinations: Academia and the Pseudo-Community." *Adolescent Psychiatry, 4,* 264–98.

Ruane, Joseph, and Jennifer Todd. (1996). *The Dynamics of Conflict in Northern Ireland: Power, Conflict and Emancipation.* New York: Cambridge University Press.

Rudé, George. (1964). *The Crowd in History.* London: Oxford University Press.

Rule, James B. (1988). *Theories of Civil Violence.* Berkeley: University of California Press.

Rummel, Rudolph. (1994). *Death by Government.* New Brunswick, NJ: Transactions.

Sabine, George H. (1969). *A History of Political Theory.* 3rd ed. New York: Holt, Rinehart and Winston.

Samuelson, Paul. (1954, November). "The Pure Theory of Public Expenditure." *Review of Economics and Statistics, 36,* 387–89.

Sartre, Jean-Paul. (1948). *Existentialism and Humanism.* Translated by Philip Mairet. London: Methuen.

Sax, Benjamin and Dieter Kuntz. (1992). *Inside Hitler's Germany: A Documentary History of Life in the Third Reich.* Lexington, MA: D. C. Heath.

Schama, Simon. (1989). *Citizens: A Chronicle of the French Revolution.* New York: Vantage Books.

Schmeidl, Susanne, and Howard Adelman (eds.). (1997, March 15–18). *Synergy in Early Warning.* Conference Proceedings, Prevention/Early Warning Unit, Centre for International and Security Studies, York University, Toronto, Canada.

Schmeidl, Susanne, and J. Craig Jenkins. (1997). "The Early Warning of Humanitarian Disasters: Problems in Building an Early Warning System." *International Migration Review, 13:* 89–115.

Schmid, Alex P. (1993). "Closing Address," Symposium on Ethnic Conflict and Human Rights Violations in Europe, Center for the Study of Social Conflicts, Leiden University, Leiden, the Netherlands, June 25.

Schmid, Alex P., and Janny de Graaf. (1982). *Violence as Communication: Insurgent Terrorism and the Western News Media.* Beverly Hills, CA: Sage Publications.

Schmid, Alex P., and Albert J. Jongman. (1997, March 15–18). "Mapping Violent Conflicts and Human Rights Violations in the Mid-1990s: Assessing Escalation and De-escalation, PIOOM's Approach." In Susanne Schmeidl and Howard Adelman (eds.), *Synergy in Early Warning.* Conference Proceedings, Prevention/Early Warning Unit, Centre for International and Security Studies, York University, Toronto, Canada.

Schrodt, Philip. (1995). *KEDS: Kansas Events Data System.* Lawrence: Department of Political Science, University of Kansas.

———. (1997). "Pattern Recognition of International Crises Using Hidden Markov Models." Paper presented at the annual meeting of the International Studies Association, at the Synergy in Early Warning Conference, Centre for Refugee Studies, York University, Toronto, Canada.

Schrodt, Philip, and Deborah Gerner. (1994). "Validity Assessment of Machine-Coded Events Data Set for the Middle East, 1982–1992." *American Journal of Political Science, 18,* 132–56.

Schulweis, Harold M. (1961, July/August). "After the Trial—What?" *National Jewish Monthly.*

Schumpeter, Joseph A. (1961). *The Theory of Economic Development: An Inquiry into Profit, Capital, Credit, Interest, and the Business Cycle.* Translated by Redvers Opie. New York: Oxford University Press. (Originally published in 1912.)

Schwartz, Thomas. (1999, January 7). "The myth of democratic pacifism." Editorial. *Wall Street Journal.*

Scott, James C. (1976). *The Moral Economy of the Peasant: Rebellion and Subsistence in Southeast Asia.* New Haven, CT: Yale University Press.

Sears, David O., and John B. McConahey. (1973), *The Politics of Violence: The New Urban Black and the Watts Riot.* Boston: Houghton Mifflin.

Sears, David O., Letitia A. Peplau, Jonathan L. Freedman and Shelley E. Taylor. (1988). *Social Psychology.* 6th ed. Englewood Cliffs, NJ: Prentice-Hall.

Sen, Amartya K. (1967). "Isolation, Assurance and Social Rate of Discount." *Quarterly Journal of Economics, 81,* 112–24.

———. (1973). *On Economic Inequality.* New York: W. W. Norton.

———. (1984). *Collective Choice and Social Welfare.* Amsterdam: North-Holland, Elsevier Science. (Originally published in 1979.)

———. (1990). "Rational Fools: A Critique of the Behavioral Foundations of Economic Theory." In Jane Mansbridge (ed.), *Beyond Self-Interest.* Chicago: University of Chicago Press.

———. (1992). *Inequality Reexamined.* New York: Russell Sage Foundation.

Shahak, Israel. (1994). "The Background and Consequences of the Massacre in Hebron." *Middle East Policy, 3* (Spring), 25–34.

Shaw, R., and Y. Wong. (1989). *The Genetic Seeds of Warfare: Evolution, Nationalism and Patriotism.* Boston: Unwin and Hyman.

Sherif, Muzafir. (1935). "An Experimental Study of Stereotypes." *Journal of Abnormal and Social Psychology, 29,* 371–75.

———. (1966). *Group Conflict and Cooperation: Their Social Psychology.* London: Routledge and Kegan Paul.

Sherif, Muzafir, and C. Hovland. (1961). *Social Judgment: Assimilation and Contrast Effects in Communication and Attitude Change.* New Haven, CT: Yale University Press.

Shils, Edward. (1981). *Tradition.* Chicago: University of Chicago Press.

Sidanius, James. (1993). "The Psychology of Group Conflict and the Dynamics of Oppression: A Social Dominance Perspective." In Shanto Iyenger and William J. McGuire (eds.), *Explorations in Political Psychology.* Durham: Duke University Press, 183–224.

Sidanius, James, J. Devereux, and Felicia Pratto. (1991). "A Comparison of Symbolic Racism Theory and Social Dominance Theory: Explanations for Racial Policy Attitudes." *Journal of Social Issues, 47,* 131–50.

Sidanius, James, and Felicia Pratto. (1991). "The Inevitability of Oppression and the Dynamics of Social Dominance." In P. Sniderman and P. Tetlock (eds.), *Prejudice and Politics in American Society.* Stanford, CA: Stanford University Press.

———. (1999). *Social Dominance: An Intergroup Theory of Social Hierarchy and Oppression.* New York: Cambridge University Press.

Simon, Brend, Stephan Stürmer, Michael Lowey et al. (1998). "Collective Identification and Social Movement Participation." *Journal of Personality and Social Psychology, 74*(3), 646–58.

Simon, Herbert. (1987). "Making Management Decisions: The Role of Intuition and Emotion." *Academy of Management Executives, 1*(1), 57–64.

Singer, J. David, and Michael D. Wallace (eds.). *To Augur Well: Early Warning Indicators in World Politics.* Beverly Hills: Sage.

Singh, Harinder. (1990). "Relative Evaluation of Subjective and Objective Measures of Expectations Formation." *Quarterly Review of Economics and Business, 30*(1), 64–74.

Singh, Jasjit (ed.). (1995). *Light Weapons and International Security.* New Delhi: Indian Pugwash Society and British-American Security Information Council.

Skocpol, Theda. (1979). *States and Social Revolutions: A Comparative Analysis of France, Russia, and China.* Cambridge: Cambridge University Press.

Smelser, Neil. (1963). *Theory of Collective Behavior.* New York: The Free Press.

Smith, Ann Marie. (1997). *Advances in Understanding International Peacemaking.* Washington, DC: United States Institute for Peace.

Smith, Brewster M. (1997). "The Authoritarian Personality: A Re-review 46 Years Later." *Political Psychology, 18*(1), 159–64.

Smith, James P., and Finis R. Welch. (1986). *Closing the Gap: Forty Years of Economic Progress for Blacks.* Santa Monica, CA: Rand Corporation.

Sniderman, P., and P. Tetlock (eds.). (1991). *Prejudice and Politics in American Society.* Stanford, CA: Stanford University Press.

Snow, David A., and Robert D. Benford. (1992). "Master Frames and Cycles of Protest." In Aldon Morris and Carol McClurg Mueller (eds.), *Frontiers in Social Movement Theory.* New Haven, CT: Yale University Press.

Soltan, Karol Edward, and L. Stephen (eds.). (1996). *The Constitution of Good Societies.* University Park: Pennsylvania State University Press.

Solzhenitsyn, Aleksandr I. (1973). *The Gulag Archipelago, 1918–1956: An Experiment in Literary Investigation, I–II.* Translated by Thomas P. Whitney. New York: Harper & Row Publishers.

Speke, John H. (1969). *Journal of the Discovery of the Source of the Nile.* London: J. M. Dent. (Originally published in 1863.)

Sprinzak, Ehud. (1998). "The Great Superterrorism Scare." *Foreign Policy,* (Fall), 131–50.

Stalin, Joseph. (1975). *Marxism and the National-Colonial Question: A Collection of Articles and Speeches.* San Francisco: Proletarian Publishers.

Steckler, H. O. (1968, July–October). "Forecasting with Econometric Models: An Evaluation." *Econometrica, 34,* 437–63.

Stedman, Stephen J. (1997, March 15–18). "Spoiler Problem in Peace Process." In Susanne Schmeidl and Howard Adelman (eds.), *Synergy in Early Warning.* Conference Proceedings. Centre for International and Security Studies, Toronto, Canada.

Steedman, Ian. (1977). *Marx After Sraffa.* London: Unwin Brothers.

Steiner, Jürg. (1990). "Power Sharing: Another Swiss Export." In Joseph Montville (ed.), *Conflict and Peacemaking in Multiethnic Societies.* Lexington, MA: Lexington Books, 107–14.

Stern, Fritz. (1996). "The Goldhagen Controversy: One Nation, One People, One Theory." *Foreign Affairs, 75*(6), 128–38.

Stewart, Charles, Craig Smith, and Robert E. Denton, Jr. (1984). *Persuasion and Social Movements.* Prospect Heights, IL: Waveland Press.

Stigler, G. J., and G. Becker. (1977). "De Gustibus Non Est Disputandum." *American Economic Review, 67*(1), 76–90.

Stiglitz, Joseph. (1988). *Economics of the Public Sector.* 2nd ed. New York: W. W. Norton.

Stohl, Michael, and George A. Lopez (eds.) (1986) *Government Violence and Repression: An Agenda for Research.* Westport, CT: Greenwood Press.

Stone, Lawrence. (1973). *The Family, Sex, and Marriage in England, 1500–1800.* New York: Harper & Row.

Straub, Erin. (1989). *The Roots of Evil: The Origins of Genocide and Other Group Violence.* New York: Cambridge University Press.

Stubbs, Richard. (1990). "Malaysia: Avoiding Ethnic Strife in Deeply Divided Society." In Joseph V. Montville (ed.), *Conflict and Peacemaking in Multiethnic Societies.* Lexington, MA: Lexington Books, 287–300.

Sugden, Robert. (1984). "Reciprocity: The Supply of Public Goods Through Voluntary Contributions." *Economic Journal, 94,* 772–87.

Sweetser, Eve, and Gilles Fauconnier. (1996). "Cognitive Links and Domains: Basic Aspects of Mental Space Theory." In Gilles Fauconnier and Eve Sweetser (eds.), *Spaces, Worlds, and Grammar.* Chicago: University of Chicago Press.

Szasz, Thomas S. (1974). *The Myth of Mental Illness: Foundations of a Theory of Personal Conduct.* Rev. ed. New York: Harper & Row (first published 1961).

———. (1994). *Cruel Compassion: Psychiatric Control of Society's Unwanted.* New York: Wiley.

Tajfel, Henri. (1970). "Aspects of Nationality and Ethnic Loyalty." *Social Science Information, 9,* 113–44.

———. (1978). *Differentiation Between Social Groups: Studies in Intergroup Relations.* London: Academic Press.

———. (1981). *Human Groups and Social Categories: Studies in Social Psychology.* Cambridge: Cambridge University Press.

———. (1982). *Social Identity and Intergroup Relations.* Cambridge: Cambridge University Press.

Tajfel, Henri, and James C. Turner. (1986). "The Social Identity Theory of Intergroup Behavior." In S. Worchel and W. G. Austin (eds.), *Psychology of Intergroup Relations.* Chicago: Nelson-Hall, 7–24.

Tambiah, S. J. (1991). *Sri Lanka: Ethnic Fratricide and the Dismantling of Democracy.* Chicago: University of Chicago Press.

Tarrow, Sidney (1989). *Democracy and Disorder: Protest and Politics in Italy, 1965–1975.* Oxford: Clarendon Press.

———. (1994). *Power in Movement: Social Movements, Collective Action and Politics.* New York: Cambridge University Press.

Taylor, M. (1988). *The Terrorist.* London: Brassey's.

Taylor, S. E. (1981). "The Interface of Cognitive and Social Psychology." In J. H. Harvey (ed.), *Cognition, Social Behavior, and the Environment.* Hillsdale, NJ: Erlbaum, 189–212.

Tec, Nechama. (1983) "Righteous Christians in Poland." *International Social Science Review, 18*, 12–19.

———. (1986). *When Light Pierced the Darkness: Christian Rescue of Jews in Nazi-Occupied Poland.* New York: Oxford University Press.

Thayer, Nate. (1997, October 23). "An interview with Pol Pot, master of the killing fields; Cambodia ex-leader denies Mass murder, tells his life story." *Wall Street Journal*, A13.

Theil, Henri. (1967). *Economics and Information Theory.* Amsterdam: North-Holland.

Thomas, P. (1990, October 14). "The persistent 'gnat' that Louisiana can't get out of its face." *Los Angeles Times*, M1.

Thoreau, Henry David. (1968). *Walden & The Essay on Civil Disobedience.* New York: Lancer Books, Inc.

Tiger, Lionel. (1984). *Men in Groups.* New York: M. Moyers.

Tilly, Charles. (1978). *From Mobilization to Revolution.* Reading, MA: Random House.

———. (1993). *European Revolutions, 1492–1992.* Oxford: Blackwell.

Trotsky, Leon. (1932). *The History of the Russian Revolution.* Garden City, NY: Doubleday.

Tullock, Gordon. (1971). "The Paradox of Revolution." *Public Choice, 11*, 89–99.

Tully, Mark, and Satish Jacob. (1985). *Amritsar: Mrs Gandhi's Last Battle.* London: Pan Books.

Turner, J. C., M. A. Hogg, P. J. Oakes, S. D. Reicher, and M. S. Wetherell. (1987). *Rediscovering the Social Group: A Self-Categorization Theory.* Oxford: Basil Blackwell.

Tykocinski, Orit, E. Tory Higgins, and Shelly Chaiken. (1994). "Message Framing, Self-Discrepancies, and Yielding to Persuasive Messages: The Motivational Significance of Psychological Situations." *Personality and Social Psychology Bulletin, 20*, 107–15.

UNICEF. (1999). *The State of the World's Children 1999.* New York: United Nations.

United Nations. (1997, August 27). *General and Complete Disarmament: Small Arms.* U.N. Document A/52/298. New York: United Nations.

United Nations Development Program. (1998). *Human Development Report 1998.* New York: Oxford University Press.

United Nations High Comissioner on Refugees. (1992). Geneva: United Nations.

United States Congress. House of Representatives Committee on Foreign Affairs (USHR). (1979). *The Assassination of Representative Leo J. Ryan and the Jonestown, Guyana Tragedy.* Washington, DC: U.S. Government Printing Office.

United States Statistical Yearbook, 1994. (1994). Washington, DC: U.S. Government Printing Office.

Van den Berghe, P. (1978a). *Man in Society: A Biosocial View.* New York: Elsevier North Holland.

———. (1978b). "Race and Ethnicity: A Sociobiological Perspective." *Ethnic and Racial Studies, 1*, 401–11.

Venieris, Yiannis P., and Dipak K. Gupta. (1983, July). "Sociopolitical and Economic Dimensions of Development: A Cross-Section Model." *Economic Development and Cultural Change, 31*, 725–56.

Volkan, V. D. (1988). *The Need to Have Enemies and Allies: From Clinical Practice to International Relations.* Dunmore, PA: Jason Aronson.

———. (1990). "Psychoanalytic Aspects of Ethnic Conflict." In Joseph V. Montville (ed.), *Conflict and Peacemaking in Multiethnic Societies*, 81–92. Boston: Lexington Books.

Waal, Frans de. (1982). *Chimpanzee Politics: Power and Sex Among the Apes*. New York: Harper & Row.

———. (1986). "The Brutal Elimination of a Rival Among Captive Male Chimpanzees." *Ethnology and Sociobiology*, 7, 237–51.

Wallimann, Isidore, and Michael N. Dobkowski. (1987). *Genocide and the Modern Age: Etiology and Case Studies of Mass Death*. Westport, CT: Greenwood Press.

Wasburn, Philo C. (1992). *Broadcasting Propaganda: International Radio Broadcasting and the Construction of Political Reality*. Westport, CT: Praeger.

White, James W. (1988, March). "Rational Rioters: Leaders, Followers, and Popular Protest in Early Modern Japan." *Politics and Society*, 16, 35–69.

Whyte, Martin K., and William L. Parish. (1984). *Urban Life in Contemporary China*. Chicago: University of Chicago Press.

Williams, John T., Brian Collins, and Mark I. Lichbach. (1997). "The Origins of Credible Commitment to the Market." Paper presented at the annual meeting of the American Political Science Association, Chicago, Illinois.

Williamson, Joel. (1984). *The Crucible of Race: Black-White Relations in the American South Since Emancipation*. New York: Oxford University Press.

Willie, Charles Vert. (1988). *A New Look at Black Families*. 3rd ed. New York: General Hall.

Wilson, William J. (1978). *The Declining Significance of Race: Blacks and Changing American Institutions*. Chicago: University of Chicago Press.

Wolfenstein, E. (1967). *The Revolutionary Personality: Lenin, Trotsky, and Gandhi*. Princeton, NJ: Princeton University Press.

Woodward, Susan. (1995). *Balkan Strategy: The Chaos and Dissolution After the Cold War*. Washington, DC: Brookings Institution.

Wrangham, Richard W., and Dale Peterson. (1996). *Demonic Males: Apes and the Origins of Human Violence*. Boston: Houghton Mifflin.

Wright, Stuart A. (ed.). (1995). *Armageddon in Waco: Critical Perspectives on the Branch Davidian Conflict*. Chicago: University of Chicago Press.

Wundheiler, Luitgard N. (1986). "Oskar Schindler's Moral Development During the Holocaust." *Humboldt Journal of Social Relations*, 13, 333–56.

Yamagushi, Toshio, and Karen S. Cook. (1993). "Generalized Exchange and Social Dilemmas." *Social Psychological Quarterly*, 56(4), 235–48.

Yotopoulos, P., and J. Nugent. (1976). *Economics of Development: Empirical Investigations*. York: Harper & Row.

Zakaria, Fareed. (1997). "The Rise of Illiberal Democracies." *Foreign Affairs*, 76(6), 22–43.

Zald, Mayer N., and John D. McCarthy. (1980). "Social Movement Industries: Competition and Cooperation Among Movement Organizations." *Research in Social Movements, Conflicts and Change*, 3, 1–20.

INDEX

Adelman, Howard, 200
Adorno, T. W., 96, 131
Afghanistan, 222
Africa Watch, 3, 159
African Americans, 179–199
AIDS virus, 184
Ajzen, Icek, 101
Akagera National Park, 151
Akerlof, George, 67, 101
Akhtar, Salman, 143
al-Nimeiri, Jaafar, 155
Alchian, Armen, A., 65
Algeria, 222
Alker, Hayward, 227
American Association of Retired People
    (AARP), 91–94
Amin, Idi, 155
Amish, 10
Angola, 222
Aquinas, St. Thomas, 25
Arendt, Hanna, 54, 65
Aristotle, 242
Arrow, Kenneth, 45, 224–225, 227,
    244
Athens, 22
Austro-Hungarians, 231

Authoritarian personality, 76–77
Aztecs, 231

Bagehot, Walter, 46
Balaklava, 10
Bandwagon effect, 54
Banfield, Edward, 186, 203
Barber, Benjamin, 12, 43, 47
Baron, Lawrence, 144
Barre, Said, 155
Basques, 57, 181, 193
Batson, Daniel C., 97
Becker, Gary S., 62, 66, 68
Beijing, 6
Belfast, 224
Belgium, 181, 193, 211
Believers, 86, 111–114, 224–215
Belting, Hans, 45
Bentham, Jeremy, 26
Berkeley, Bill, 200
Berlin Wall, 12
Bernanke, Ben, 67
Bjorn, Ake, 17
Blaug, Mark, 29, 45, 64
Blee, Andrew, 226
Bloodworth, Dennis, 145

Bloom, Alan, 45
Bolivia, 211
Boorstein, Daniel, 25, 45
Borstein, Gary, 65
Bosnia, 8, 167, 108, 208, 222, 234, 236; NATO deployment in, 223
Boutros-Ghali, Boutros, 158, 215
Boxer Rebellion, 126, 129
Bramhall, John, 46
Brandeis, Louis, 78
Bredin, Jean-Davis, 144
Brehm, John, 65
Breinlinger, S., 101
Brown, R., 96
Buchanan, James, 64
Burnham, Ford, 172
Burundi, 154, 168, 208, 222, 223
Bush, George, 239
Bushnell, P. Timothy, 244
Buss, T., 97, 101, 202
Bwy, D. P., 203

Calley, William L., Jr., 5, 76
Cambodia, 8, 222, 227
Cameroon, 37
Campbell, Joseph, 23, 44
Canada, 193, 220, 223
Caplan, N., 203
Cappella, Joseph N., 142
Captive participants, 86, 115–116
Carnegie Commission on Preventing Deadly Conflicts, 207, 217, 222, 226
Carter, Jimmy, 179
Carter, Tim, 7
Castiglia, Christopher, 144
Castro, Fidel, 172, 220
Catholic Church, 5, 28, 152, 166
Central Asia, 181
Central Intelligence Agency (CIA), 176, 200
Chad, 222
Chaiken, Shelly, 142
Chalk, Frank, 159, 200
Chamberlin, William, 66
Charles I of England, 21
Chatterjee, Partha, 97

Chechnya, 222
Chiapas, 181
Child soldiers, 221–222
Chile, 212
China, People's Republic of, 155, 213, 218, 237; Boxer Rebellion, 129; Cultural Revolution, 6, 43, 121, 125
Chong, Dennis, 66, 142, 203
Christie, Richard, 96
Clague, Christopher, 97
Clinton, William J.: apology for ignoring Rwandan crisis, 207; on the fall of the Berlin Wall, 13
Cognitive dissonance, 77–78
Cohn, Norman, 201
Cold War, 12
Collaborators, 86, 120
Collective culture, 131–133
Collective identity, 14, 80–83, 234
Collective insanity, twelve factors, 130
Collective madness (insanity), 8, 130, 229
Collectivism, 20
Collins, Brian, 65
Colombia, 222
Combs, Cindy C., 128
Communist Manifesto, 238
Comte, Auguste, 26
Congo, Republic of, 222
Conscientious objectors, 86, 116–118
Consociational (power-sharing) democracy, 210–212
Convergence, toward Western ways, 238
Cook, Karen S., 65
Cooper, M. N., 203
Cory, Jerry, 96
Crelinsten, Ronald, 115, 144
Crimean War, 10; Tennyson's "Light Brigade," 10, 11–12, 240
Cromwell, Oliver, 214
Cuba, 220, 222, 237; Bay of Pigs, invasion of, 222; Cuban Liberty and Democratic Solidarity Act (Helms-Burton), 220
Cultural icons, 124–126
Cultural Revolution, 6, 43, 121, 125

Dagestan, 222
Dahl, Robert, 209–210, 226
Danton, Georges, 214
Darwin, Charles, 26
Davies, Thomas, 18
Davis, Angela, 197
Dayton Agreement, 208
de Graaf, Janny, 67, 129
de Waal, Frans, 22, 44, 145
Deconstructing democracy, 214
Democracy, 132, 213, 214
Demsetz, Harold, 65
Deng, Francis, 143
Deng Shao Ping, 120
Denton, Nancy A., 202, 203
Descartes, Rene, 34
Dhawan, Vinod, 145
Diamond, Jared, 44
Diamond, Larry, 226
Dillehay, R. C., 96
Dion, K. L., 101
Distributive justice, 209
DiZerega, Gus, 145
Douglas, Jack, Jr., 97
Douglass, Frederick, 202
Dreyfus, Alfred, 117
Druckman, James N., 142
Duffy, Kevin, 3
Dunn, William, 66

Early warning, of political and humanitarian catastrophe, 215–217
Early Warning Loop, 218
East Timor, 212
Eastern Europe, 181
Easy-riders, 86–87, 118–120
Edwards, Rem B., 244
Eichmann, Adolf, 117
Ekeh, Peter P., 65
Elliott, Kimberly A., 220
Emerson, Richard, 65
England, 222
Esherick, Joseph, 145
Estrella, Miguel Angel, 115
Ethiopia, 211, 222
Ethnic cleansing, 193

Farley, Christopher J., 203

Farrakhan, Louis, 179
Feagin, Joe R., 203
Feinsod, Ethan, 202
Feldstein, Martin, 67
Fetsinger, Leon, 97
Fine, Helen, 201, 202
Fishbein, Martin, 101
Fisher, Roger, 223, 227
Flemings, 181
Fossey, Dian, 158
Foucault, Michel, 26, 45, 244
Fox, Richard, 145
Framing, 105–106
France, 156–157, 158, 167, 222;
    Jacques Chirac on Dreyfus case, 10
Freedman, Jonathan L., 96
Freedom House, 213
Freemasons, 170
Frenkel-Brunswick, E., 96
Freud, Sigmund, 28, 42, 45, 46, 104
Friedman, Max, 144
Friedman, Milton, 30, 45, 67
Fritz, Mark, 17
Fukuyama, Francis, 18, 34, 45, 236, 244
Funk, Wilfred, 17, 64

Gaddafi, Muammar, 219
Gandhi, Indira, 119, 128–129
Gandhi, M. K., 84
Gates, Scott, 65
Gay movement, 95
General Agreement of Tariffs and
    Trade (GATT), 242
Genesis, book of, 215
Georgia, 211
German Industrial Elite, in Nazi era, 225
Geshwender, J. A., 203
Gestapo, 5, 137
Getting to Yes (Fisher and Uri), 223
Geyer, Georgie Ann, 123, 145, 226
Ghosh, Partha S., 143
Glass, James, 134, 145, 146, 230, 244
Gleick, J., 226
Goebbels, Joseph, 123, 135–136, 162
Goldhagen, Daniel, 4–5, 10, 17, 137, 144, 146

"Goldilocks solution," 243–244
Goldwater, Barry, 210
Goodall, Jane, 21–22, 44,
Gordon, Nicholas, 200
Gourevitch, Philip, 96, 164, 166, 200, 201,
Gray Panther, 95
Great Britain, 36, 193
Great mutiny (India), 126
Gross Domestic Product (GDP), growing disparity in, 240–241
Group identity, adoptive and ascriptive, 83, 232
Guatemala, 213
Gulf War, 11, 221, 237
Gupta, Dipak K., 18, 65, 66, 68, 97, 101, 202, 203, 226, 227
Gupta, Dipankar, 119–120, 144, 145
Gurr, Ted R., 18, 65, 66, 86, 91, 100, 101, 122, 130, 136, 144, 145, 146, 147, 187, 203, 217, 227
Gutenberg, Johannes, 25, 26
Guyana, 7, 169, 172, 178, 201

Habiyalimana, Jean-Baptiste, 165
Habyarimana, Juvenal, 154, 155, 157, 158, 160, 164, 167, 200, 214
Hacker, Andrew, 179, 203
Hahn, Harlan, 203
Haiti, 222, 223
Hamilton, V. L., 17, 138, 147
Harbinson, H., 17
Hardin, Garrett, 65, 68
Hare Krishnas, 10
Harff, Barbara, 18, 145, 146, 147, 200, 217, 227
Haroun, Ansar, 143
Harrison, Selig, 143
Haskin, K., 18
Hayek, F. A., 44, 67
Hearst, Patty, 115
Heaven's Gate cult, 80, 112
Hedstrom, Peter, 244
Heimer, Carol A., 65
Heisler, Martin O. 226
Hellman, Peter, 144
Helms-Burton Act, 220
Heng, Liang, 17

Henry, O., 29
Hersh, Seymore, 17
Hibbs, Douglas P., 65, 203
Higgins, E. Tory, 142
Hilberg, Raul, 10, 18
Hindu caste system, 185
Hinkle, S., 96
Hirschleifer, Jack, 64
Hirshman, Albert O., 66
Hitler, Adolf, 33, 107–109, 123, 125, 134, 135, 214, 231, 244; *Gleichschaltung* (coordination of culture), 135
Hittites, 231
Hobbes, Thomas, 20–21, 35; Hobbesian anarchy, 229
Hobsbawm, Eric, 36, 46, 150,
Ho Chi Minh, 58, 66
Hoffman, Bruce, 145
Hofstadter, Richard, 133, 170, 175, 200, 230, 244
Hofstetter, Richard, 97, 101, 202
Hogg, M. A., 101
Holocaust, 5, 8 193
Holstrom, Bengt, 65
Homo collectivus, 72–73
Homo economicus, 52
Hong Kong, 212
Horowitz, Donald, 227
House of German Arts, 125
Hovland, C., 73, 96
Hueneke, Douglas K., 144
Hufbauer, Gary C., 220
Hughes, Candice, 18
Human Rights Watch, 169, 200
Humana, Charles, 13, 18
Huntington, Samuel, 44, 47, 213, 226, 237, 238, 239, 245
Hussein, Saddam, 219, 239
Hutus, 150–169; Hutu Manifesto, 153, 200
Huxley, Aldous, 44

India, 211; Hindu caste system, 185; Khalistan movement, 119, 223; Naxalites movement, 57
Individualism, 20, 26, 236
Information costs, 139–140

International intervention, collective madness and, 140
Inter-university Consortium for Political and Social Research (ICPSR), 191, 203
Intifada, 85
"Invisible hand," of market adjustment, 232
Iran, Islamic Republic of, 63, 219, 222, 237
Iraq, 208, 219, 222
Iyenger, Shanto, 101

Jackson, Jesse, 127
Jacob, Satish, 144
Jacobs, John, 201
Jagan, Chedi, 172
Jahoda, Marie, 96
Jamieson, Kathleen H., 142
Japan, 31
Javeres, Ron, 201
Jenkins, Brian 66
Jerusalem, 224
Jews in Nazi ideology, 109
John Paul II, 10, 18, 149
Johnson, Chalmers, 100
Johnson, Lyndon B., 150, 180
Jones, Bruce, 200
Jones, Jim, 7, 39, 112, 129, 134, 169, 179, 240; Apostolic Socialism, 175; Jonestown, 129, 169–179, 195; People's Temple, 112, 171–173, 176
Jonestown, 129, 169–179, 195
Jongman, Albert, 18, 144, 146
Jospin, Lionel, 117
Juergensmeyer, Mark, 66
Jung, Carl, 80, 97, 104, 142

Kahneman, Daniel, 96, 105, 142
Kalt, J. P., 18
Kant, Immanuel, 145
Kaplan, Robert, 214, 227, 243
Karadzic, Radovan, 113, 244
Karatnycky, Adrian, 226
Kashmir, 222, 224
Katsaris, Maria, 112
Kautski, Karl, 65

Kawakami, K., 101
Kayibanda, Gregoire, 154, 156, 200
Keen, Sam, 104, 107, 122, 142, 143, 145, 146
Kelly, C., 101
Kelman, Herbert, 17, 91, 138, 139, 147, 203
Kerner Commission, 150, 180, 181, 189–190, 199, 202, 203
Keynes, John M., 61, 101, 215
Khoa, Nguyuen, 6
Khomeini, Ayatollah, 43, 76
Kilduff, Marshall, 201
King, Martin Luther, Jr., 84, 127, 196, 236
Kirscht, J. P., 96
Kiruhura, Alfred, 161
Klandermans, Bert, 94, 101
Klare, Michael, 225, 227
Knowles, Louis J., 203
Koresh, David, 39
Kosici, Gerald M., 142
Kosovo, 208, 223
Kothari, Rajni, 145
Krane, Dale A., 66
Kranton, Rachel E., 101
Krugman, Paul, 233, 244
Kubrick, Stanley, 44
Kulisa, Calizte, 158
Kuntz, Dieter, 143, 145, 147, 200
Kuper, L., 18
Kuran, Timur, 100, 141–142, 147–146, 199, 203, 216, 227
Kuwait, 208, 237

Lacouture, Jean, 66
Lakoff, George, 142
Landes, William M., 66, 68
Lane, Roger, 7, 17,
Langguth, A. J., 144
Layton, Deborah, 177
Layton, Larry, 173
Le Bon, Gustav, 41, 46
Lebanon, 225
Lemarchand, René, 200
Lenin, V. I., 65
Levinson, D. J., 96
Lewis, William G., 203

Lewy, Guenter, 17
Liberal democracy, 208–210
Libya, 222
Lichbach, Mark I., 55, 59–60, 62, 65, 66, 68, 143, 203
Lifton, Robert J., 114, 143
Lijphart, Arend, 210–212, 226,
Lind, Allan, 226
Lipset, Seymour, 96
Livermore, Kentucky, 8
Livy (Roman historian), 39
Locke, Michelle, 202
London, Perry, 116, 144
Longfellow, Henry, 53
Lorenz, Konrad, 22
Loveman, Mara, 64
Lowey, Michael, 95, 101
Lucas, George, 47
Lucas, Robert, 67
Lupsha, P., 203
Lyons, H., 17

Macedonia, 208, 223
Machiavelli, Niccolo, 40
Mack, John E., 142
MacLaen, Paul D., 96
Madhavan, M., 226
Magida, A. J., 202, 203
Majoritarian democracy, 210–212
Malaysia, 2, 11
Mandela, Nelson, 12
Manifesto of the Communist Party, 238
Mansbridge, Jane, 44
Mao Zedong, 126
Maquet, Jean-Jacques, 232
Marie-Antoinette, 123
Marx, Gary, 193, 203
Marx, Karl, 27, 33, 36, 40, 42, 238, 241
Mashaw, Jerry L., 64
Mason, David, 66
Massey, Douglas, 202, 203
Mazzini, Giuseppe, 37
McAdam, Doug, 65, 202, 203
McCaffrey, Edward, 142
McCarthy, John D., 65
McConahey, J. B., 203

McDowell, Patrick, 17
McGuire, William J., 101
McRea, Kenneth D., 226
McVeigh, Timothy, 49–50, 71–72, 78, 243
Medieval Europe, 24
Melson, Robert, 143
Mercenaries, 86, 114–115, 225–226
Mexico, 181
Miedzyrzec, massacre of Jews at, 4
Milgram, Stanley, 75–76, 96, 116
Mill, John Stuart, 26, 29, 37, 40, 46, 64
Millenarians, 39
Miller, Christine, 170, 174, 175
Million Man March, 179, 184, 191
Milosevic, Slobodan, 213, 214
Mitchell, George J., 200
Mob, Western conception of, 38
Mobutu Sese Seko, 155
Moore, R., 201
Moore, Will, 68, 187, 203
"Moral hazard," 65
More, Sir Thomas, 39–40,
Morris, Aldon D., 65
Mother Teresa of Calcutta, 79, 80
Mozambique, 222
Mueller, Carol McClurg, 65
Mueller, Dennis, 65
Mueller, John, 221, 227
Mueller, Karl, 221, 227
Mukankwaya, Juliana, 3
Mukhoty, Govinda, 145
Murdoch, Rupert, 172
Museveni, Yoweri, 168
Musgrove, Margaret, 19, 44
Mussolini, Benito, 125, 214
My Lai, 5, 9, 138
Miedzyrzec, Poland, on Nazi police action, 4–5

Naipaul, V. S., 46, 63–64, 67, 201
Narcotics traffic, arms trade and, 223
Nasrin, Taslima, 143
Nation-state, 210
National Association for the Advancement of Colored People (NAACP), 197

National identity, American, 237
National Research Council, 182, 202
National Resistance Army (NRA), 168
Nationalist socialist ideology, 108–110
Navarro, Marysa, 66
Nazis (Nationalist Socialist Party), 5, 104, 108; propaganda, 123, 125, 135
New West magazine, 172
Newman, David, 203
Nguyen Thi Ngoc Tuyet, 5
Nicaragua, 222
Nichols, Terry, 243
Nietzsche, Friedrich, 32–33, 152
Nightingale, Florence, 79
Nixon, Richard, 193
Nkundabagenzi, F., 200
North American Free Trade Agreement (NAFTA), 242
North Atlantic Treaty Organization (NATO), 208, 221, 223
North Korea, 224, 237
Northern Ireland, Ulster, 195, 196, 211, 212, 222–223, 224, 225
Nsengiyuma, Vincent (Archbishop of Kigali), 166
Ntaryamira, Cyprien, 160, 161
Nugent, John P., 17, 143, 178, 201, 202, 203

Oakes, P. J., 101
O'Donnell, James P., 143
Oegema, D., 101
Oliner, Pearl, 144
Oliner, Samuel, 144
Olson, Mancur, 52, 64, 94, 96, 101, 114, 118; Olson's Paradox (Social Dilemma), 54–55, 59
O'Neil, Tip, 56
Organization of African Unity (OAU), 168–167
Organizational capability, collective identity and, 127–128
Organizational hierarchy, collective madness and, 138
Organized crime, 215
Orwell, George, 44, 235
Ostrom, Elinor, 60, 63, 68

Paasi, Ansi, 203
Pakistan, 211, 213
Palermo, Georgia, 8
Pan, Zhongdang, 142
Pareto, Vilfredo, 29, 30, 125
Parish, William L, 145
Park Chung Hee, 85
Pearsall, Robert, 144
People's Temple, 112, 171–173, 176. *See also* Jones, Jim
Peplau, Letitia, 96
Peterson, Dale, 22, 44
Pfaff, William, 46
Pfaffenberger, Bryan, 143
Phelps, Edmund S., 97
Pierce, William, 143
Pinochet, Augusto, 85
Plato, 39, 46
Plattner, Marc F., 226
Pol Pot, 135
Poliakov, Leon, 143
Political entrepreneur, 82–83, 105–111
Popkin, Samuel, 66, 100, 115
Popper, Karl, 34, 62, 67
Post–Cold War era, sanctions in, 219
Power-sharing, 210–212
Pratto, Felicia, 235, 244
Preventive diplomacy, 218
Prewitt, Kenneth, 203
Procedural justice, 209
Proletariat, 33–34
Propaganda and the arts, 125, 135
Prunier, Gerard, 150, 162, 163, 200, 201, 244
Public Broadcasting System (PBS), 234
Public Choice, 95
Public good (defined), 56, 65

Ra'anam, Uri, 46, 226
Radio-Télévision Libre des Mille Collines (RTLM), 159, 160
Rainbow Coalition, 127
Ramayana, 23, 110
Ramet, Sabrina, 104, 142
Raphael, 24
Rapoport, Amnon, 65
Rasler, Karen, 66
Ravana, 23

Reagan, Ronald, 217–218
Redlich, Fritz, 231
Reicher, S. D., 101
Reif, Linda, 66
Reiterman, Tim, 201
Renner, Michael, 227
Ricks, Thomas, 18, 87–90, 100, 143
Ridely, Jasper, 46
Robespierre, Maximilien, 214
Rothstein, D. A., 18
Rousseau, Jean Jacques, 21–22, 32, 37, 232
Ruane, Joseph, 143
Rudé, George, 66
Rummel, Rudolph, 18
Rwanda, 3, 8, 96, 150–169, 108, 208, 212, 222, 223, 229, 232, 234, 236; Arusha Agreement, 157, 167; Coffee producing nations and Rwandan genocide, 163; Committee for the Defense of the Revolution (CDR), 157–158, 161, 195; Ethnic groups in, 151–152; Impuzamugambi (Rwandan militia group), 167; Interahamwe (Rwandan youth militia), 166; Kalinga (the sacred drum), 154; Mouvement Révolutionnaire National pour le Développement (MRND), 163, 165, 167; Rwanda Patriotic Front (RPF), 156, 157, 168
Ryan, Leo, 173, 176

Sabine, George H., 45
Samuelson, Paul, 65
San Francisco, 171, 175
Sanctions, as a tool, 218
Sanford, R. N., 96
Sargent, Thomas, 67
Sartre, Jean-Paul, 31, 45
Saudi Arabia, 237
Sax, Benjamin, 143, 145, 147, 200
Schacht, Lawrence, 7, 173
Schama, Simon, 123, 145, 226
Schindler, Oskar, 118
Schmid, Alex P., 17, 18, 67, 129, 144, 145, 146
Schott, Jeffrey J., 220

Schulweis, Harold, 116, 144
Schumpeter, Joseph, 28, 45, 106
Schwartz, Anna, 67
Sears, David O., 96, 203
Sen, Amartya K., 45, 226
Shahak, Israel, 142
Shapiro, Judith, 17
Sharpton, Al, 179
Sherif, Muzafir, 73
Shils, Edward, 35, 46
Shining Path, 57
Shlapenkokh, Vladimir, 244
Shurke, Astri, 200
Sidanius, James, 235, 244
Sierra Leone, 222
Silajdzic, Haris, 207
Simon, Brend, 95, 101
Sinclair, Upton, 29
Sindikubwabo, Theodore, 161
Singapore, 212
Singh, Hari, 66, 68, 97, 145, 203, 226
Singh, J., 227
Sinhalese, 110, 211
Skocpol, Theda, 54, 65
Small arms trade and genocide, 221–223
Smelser, Neil, 54, 65
Smith, A. M., 227
Smith, Adam, 12, 26–27, 32, free market economics, 30
Smith, Brewster M., 145
Smith, James P., 202
Social dominance, theory of, 235
Social identity theory, 74
Soltan, Karol E., 64
Solzhenitsyn, Aleksandr, 6, 17
Somalia, 11, 87, 222; U.S. military action in, 11
South Africa, 12, 220; African National Congress (ANC), 224; economic sanctions, 220
South Korea, 85, 212, 224
Soviet Union, fall of, 216
Spain, 43, 193
Speke, John H., 151, 200
Spencer, Herbert, 27
Spinoza, Baruch, 34
Spitzer, Matthew L., 142

Sprague, Tom, 66, 68, 145, 203
Sri Lanka 110, 222
Stalin, Joseph, 36, 46; on definition of Nation, 36
Star Trek, 44
Stedman, Stephen J., 200
Steedman, Ian, 45
Steinbeck, John, 29
Steiner, Jürg, 226
Stephen, L., 64
Stewart, Potter, 36, 46
Stone, Lawrence, 25, 45
Straub, Erin, 132
Stubbs, Richard, 226
Stürmer, Stephan, 95, 101, 145
Sudan, 143, 222
Swedberg, Richard, 244
Swift, Jonathan, 24,
Switzerland, 211, 212
Syria, 222
Szasz, Thomas, 230, 244

Taiwan, 212
Tajfel, Henri, 73–75, 96, 101, 202
Tambiah, S. J., 143, 226
Tamilnadu, 110
Tamils, 110, 196, 211
Tanzania, 168
Tarrow, Sidney, 57, 66, 67, 202
Taylor, M., 17
Taylor, Shelley E., 96
Tec, Nechama, 117, 144
Tennyson, Alfred, Lord, 10, 11–12, 240
Terrorism, 128
Thayer, Nate, 146
Thoreau, Henry David, 14
Tilly, Charles, 65, 122, 145, 202
Tiananmen Square, massacre at, 213
Tito, Josip B., 79
Todd, Jennifer, 143
Torture and torturers, 115
Trotsky, Leon, 100, 105, 145
"True believers," 111–112, 224
Tullock, Gordon, 53, 65, 186, 203
Tully, Mark, 144
Tupak Amaru, 85
Turkey, 213

Turner Diaries, 108, 143
Turner, J. C., 101
Turner, John J., Jr., 7, 17
Tutsis, 3, 151–169
Tversky, Amos, 96, 142,
Twa (pygmies), 151
Tykocinsky, Orit, 142
Tyler, Tom, 226

Uganda, 155, 168, 222
Ukiah, California, 171
Ulster, Northern Ireland 9, 195, 196, 211, 212, 222–223, 224, 225
Ulster Constabulary, 196
UNICEF, 241
United Church of Christ, 171
United Nations, 133, 218–219, 221, 227; UN Assistance Mission in Rwanda (UNAMIR), 169; UN Development Program (UNDP), 221, 227; UN High Commissioner on Refugees (UNHCR), 13, 215; UNICEF, 241; UN Peacekeeping Force in Rwanda, 158
United States, 13, 36, 158, 170, 172, 178, 184, 199, 210, 219, 220, 221, 222, 236–237; Bill of Rights, 198; Black Panther movement, 150, 197; Commission of National Security, 243; Congressional Budget Office, 216; Constitution, 38; Equal Employment Opportunity Act, 190; Federal Bureau of Investigation (FBI), 176; income distribution, 242; Law Enforcement Agency (LEA), 198; Marine Corps, military indoctrination in, 87–90; national identity, 237; Office of Management and Budget (OMB), 216; Omnibus Crime Control Act (1968), 184, 193
Updike, John, 238
Uri, William, 223, 227
"Us" versus "them," 15
Uwilingiyimana, Agathe, 161

Vanderpool, Christopher, 244
Venieris, Yannis P., 65, 226

Viet Cong, 5
Vinci, Leonardo da, 24
Violence in primates, 22
Volkan, Vamik, 142, 202, 203
Volkgemeinschaft, 109
Von Götzen (first European explorer to reach Rwanda), 153–154

Waco, Texas, 104
Walloons, 181
Washburn, Philo C., 143, 200
Washington, George, 19, 38
Weber, Max, 27, 45, 84, 100
Welch, Finis R., 202
Wells, H. G., 159
Wesley, John, 24–25
Western cultural tradition, 236
Wetherell, M. S., 101
Whyte, Martin K., 145
Williams, John T., 65

Willie, Charles V., 202
Wilson, William J., 203
Wolfenstein, E., 47
Woodward, Susan, 226
Wrangham, Richard, 22, 44
Wright, Stuart A., 64
Wundheiler, Luitgrad N., 144

Xiao Hua, 7

Yamagushi, Toshio, 65
Yang Xiao Hua, 6
Yugoslavia, 8, 212, 213, 218, 219, 221; bombing of, 221

Zakaria, Fareed, 214, 227
Zald, Mayer N., 65
Zimmerman, Warren, 123
Zola, Émile, 117
Zulus, 224
Zupan, M. A., 18

About the Author

DIPAK K. GUPTA is the Fred J. Hansen Professor of Peace Studies, Professor in the School of Public Administration and Urban Studies, and the Co-Director, Institute for International Security and Conflict Resolution at San Diego State University. He has held numerous visiting fellowships, including at the UN Terrorism Prevention Branch, Office for Drug Control and Crime Prevention. Professor Gupta has published extensively on issues of violence and ethnicity, including *The Economics of Political Violence: The Effects of Political Instability on Economic Growth* (Praeger, 1990).

DATE DUE

GAYLORD   #3523PI   Printed in USA